Fifty Years of the

TEXAS
OBSERVER

Fifty Years of the

TEXAS
OBSERVER

Edited by CHAR MILLER
Foreword by MOLLY IVINS

TRINITY UNIVERSITY PRESS

San Antonio, Texas

PUBLISHED BY TRINITY UNIVERSITY PRESS
San Antonio, Texas 78212

Cover design by DJ Stout, Pentagram, Austin, Texas
Book design and composition by BookMatters

⊗ The paper used in this publication meets the minimum
requirements of the American National Standard for Information Sciences-Permanence of Paper for Printed Library
Materials, ANSI Z39.48-1992.

LIBRARY OF CONGRESS CATALOGING-IN-PUBLICATION DATA

Fifty years of the Texas Observer / edited by Char Miller;
foreword by Molly Ivins.
p. cm.
ISBN 1-59534-000-9 (hardcover : alk. paper)—
ISBN 1-59534-001-7 (pbk. : alk. paper)
1. Texas—Politics and government—1951– 2. Texas—
Intellectual life. 3. Texas—Social conditions. 4. Texas—
Environmental conditions. 5. Political culture—Texas.
6. Progressivism (United States politics). I. Miller, Char,
1951– II. Texas observer.
F391.2.F54 2004
976.4'063—dc22 2004008880

Printed in the United States of America
08 07 06 05 04 / 5 4 3 2 1

Contents

Acknowledgments

First, an apology. No single compilation of writings from the *Texas Observer* can do justice to this "journal of free voices." For fifty years, its staff and freelance contributors have covered an extraordinary range of issues in Texas (and far beyond), and have done so with insight, wit, and verve. There is no other magazine of its kind in the nation, a characterization made all the more unique by the sheer quantity and stunning quality of the articles that have appeared in its pages for five decades. The *Observer*'s enduring legacy of cutting-edge, investigative journalism has complicated my task of selecting which pieces would represent its arguments and perspectives. I can only hope that I have been able to capture the essence of its extraordinary recording of the people, the place, and the times.

I could not have produced this volume alone, of course, and am deeply grateful for the suggestions, aid, and commentary of current and former members of the *Observer* staff. Coeditor Barbara Belejack has been a tremendous help in thinking out the outlines of the project and its importance. David Denison offered detailed suggestions of potential articles to include and a framework by which they might best be understood. Conversations, by phone and email, with Lou Dubose, Ronnie Dugger, Molly Ivins (and her wondrous assistant Betsy Moon), Michael King, Kaye Northcott, and Geoff Rips were as essential as they have been supportive, yet another illustration of just how strong the *Observer*'s editorial staff has been since 1954. Another former staffer, Jeff Mandell, suggested a couple of key additions, and Steve Moore weighed in with some shrewd picks. Thanks, too, go to the many who kindly granted permission for their words to appear in this volume; their interest in the project has made it a pleasure to work on.

This collection would have been a lot more difficult to produce in an earlier era. But at the Coates Library at Trinity University, with its microfilm readers linked to digital scanners, I was able to read, copy, and then save articles on-line; a special thanks to University Librarian Diane Graves for securing this technology just in time for this project! Its implementation also facilitated the editing process, allowing me and my gifted research assistant, Laura Fries, to check and double-check the full run of the *Observer* with some dispatch. Alas, the scanned documents still had to be retyped, and I am greatly in the debt of Eunice Herrington, senior secretary of the History Department, who worked nonstop and at high speed to produce a working draft of the lengthy manuscript; Rosie de la Rosa contributed to this process as well. As they typed these documents, they also shared their reactions to them, which were invaluable as I made the final selections. The work that my staff, my research assistant, and I did on this project was in large part funded by the Joullian Endowment Fund of the History Department.

And, finally, I am doubly lucky to have been able to work with the staff at the Trinity University Press. Director Barbara Ras and Sarah Nawrocki are a dream team of skilled editors and writers who love to talk about books, and who help make them come to life. So do Dave Peattie of BookMatters and copyeditor Mike Mollett — their insights and comments were critical. But most of all, and again, I owe so much to Barbara Ras, who has been crucially involved in every aspect of this project, from its conception to its realization. Ever willing to talk about its fascinations and frustrations, she has been its best critic and greatest advocate.

Foreword

MOLLY IVINS

In journalism school, we were taught to avoid the word *unique* on the grounds it is highly unlikely there is anything totally unprecedented under the sun. But there is no other word for the *Texas Observer*. It is the only one of its kind, a publication in a class by itself. Fifty years of the *Observer* is a half-century of journalism so special and so remarkable it is actually awesome.

One can enumerate the excellence of the *Observer* in many ways. The roster of its editors is an extraordinary list of journalistic talent, starting with Ronnie Dugger, who did it all by himself for a long time, and including the late Willie Morris, Bob Sherrill, Larry Goodwyn, Kaye Northcott, Jim Hightower, Geoff Rips, Lou Dubose, Michael King, Nate Blakeslee, and many others. The *Observer*'s writers over the years have included pretty much everybody worth reading in the state, starting with the holy trinity of J. Frank Dobie, Roy Bedichek, and Walter Prescott Webb, and continuing with Bud Shrake, Gary Cartwright, Larry L. King, Larry McMurtry, Mad Dog Helmer, Billy Porterfield, Elroy Bode, Amado Muro, Katherine Anne Porter, and on and on.

Or you could list the scandals the *Observer* has unearthed, from the appropriations process of the 1950s to the drug busts in Tulia, or the politicians it has brought down over the years. You could count the number of squalid little deals it has exposed, the amount of money it has saved the taxpayers (including my memorable exposé of the great House Christmas card rip-off) or the number of Bad Bills the *Observer* has knocked off by exposing the idiocy of their content.

One could also bring back the years with the names of the politicians

and public figures we wrote about, from the heroic to the horrific—
Ralph Yarborough, Allan Shivers, John Connally, Lyndon Johnson,
Sam Rayburn, Martin Dies, Judge Woodrow Wilson Bean, Goodtime
Charlie Wilson, Ann Richards, George Bush (both father and son),
Tom DeLay, Mad Dog Mengden, the Unspeakable Bill Hollowell,
Barbara Jordan, Henry B. Gonzalez, Wright Patman. The names of the
places seem to roll out as well, from Alice to Dallas, from Ozona to
Odessa, from Dimebox to Del Rio. Dugger once observed, "To a
Texan, a car is like wings to a seagull. Our places are far apart and we
must dip into them driving. For an often-traveling man like myself, the
junctions in the highways and the towns are like turns in a city well-
known." I remember driving through the soft night air of the East
Texas piney woods with Willie Nelson playing softly on the radio and
blasting through the Panhandle under a blazing sun and pale blue sky
listening to Clarence Zugenbuler's stock report on WBAP, the Country
Giant. Generations of *Observer* editors have acquired some of their
best stories because their cars broke down in one unlikely place or
another. Our cars are always breaking down.

Texas, as has often been noted, is a peculiar place: it both deserves
and needs an independent magazine devoted solely to its politics and
other oddities. The extraordinary struggles for economic and political justice chronicled in the *Observer*'s pages go back to the days
when it was the only publication read by white people that addressed
the problems and concerns of black and brown Texans. This book is
an astonishing record of our state's clumsy, sporadic, painful, and
often comic efforts at progress.

It is not up to me to judge how far we've come: Texas still has a
nineteenth-century tax structure, and the *Observer*'s current coeditor, Jake Bernstein, recently wrote a brilliant article on this legislature's eerie parallel to the Texas legislature at the turn of the twenti-
eth century. Some of the things the *Observer* wrote about in the past
as a matter of course are now unthinkable: Dugger's dry, factual
account "The Consequences of a Dance" sounds today like unbelievable barbarism. But unbelievable barbarism continues, on Death Row
among other places in Texas. The colossal stupidities of yesteryear,
like the Texas Water Plan or the Itty-Bitty Bottle Bill, are easily rivaled

by the incumbent land commissioner's scheme to sell West Texas's water and by the current redistricting saga.

The first most striking thing about the *Texas Observer* is its level of journalistic excellence, and I think Dugger deserves the blame for that. Larry Goodwyn once described the *Observer* as the finest graduate school of journalism in the country; it has been that for all of us who have toiled there. The *Observer* gives journalists freedom—among other things, the freedom to make their own mistakes. But the standards set by Dugger in the beginning—the relentless insistence on accuracy and fairness—have never been eroded. We may not have always met them, but the standards were always there. Many of us have laughed over the years at Dugger's incurable high-mindedness—"We will hew hard to the truth as we find it and the right as we see it"—but I believe that is the soul of the *Observer*.

The second most striking thing about this small magazine is what a frayed shoestring it operates on. The *Observer* has just never had any money. It's the journalistic equivalent of the loaves and fishes. It doesn't pay worth squat; we can't afford to do half of what we do, yet we continue to do it. In my day at the *Observer* (1970–76), the business manager slept under the Addressograph, and the reporters stole pencils from the governor's office. Once Kaye Northcott and I had a great article about pollution in the Gulf of Mexico and we wanted to run a picture of seagull drowned in an oil slick to illustrate it. Everyone has seen those pictures of seagulls drowned in oil slicks, right? They're common as dirt. But the *Observer* didn't have one, couldn't find one, and so we ran a picture of chicken drowned in a flood instead. That's what putting out the *Observer* is like.

Living lean and on the run has its advantages. "Goodwyn observed that always being on the outs with the people in power bred in our reporters a certain coyote-like cunning." After my stint on the *Observer*, I reentered establishment journalism and was amazed to find that an acceptable excuse for not getting a story was "He wouldn't return my phone calls." It seems to me no one ever returned our phone calls. Our sources were rarely people with titles or elected officials—we talked to the people who worked for them. Not that all of us were young Izzy Stones. My own methods involved drinking truly impressive amounts of beer. I must also confess that no courage was required. I yearned for journalistic martyrdom, like the great William Brann of the *Iconoclast* in Waco, who was shot to death by an irate Baptist. I figured at least I could get horsewhipped. But all that ever happened—after I reported in the *Observer* that some pol sucked eggs, ran on all fours, and had the mind of an adolescent pissant—was I'd see him in the halls the next day and he'd spread his arms and holler, "Baby! Yew put mah name in yer paper!"

The *Observer* has attracted journalists of all kinds, old and young, successful and just starting, idealists and cynics, all drawn by the opportunity to write for a journal of free voices. Not only does the *Observer* not suffer from the limitations of corporate journalism, it is a place where no one even has to think about them. This is where you can tell the truth without the bark on it, laugh at anyone who is ridiculous, and go after the bad guys with all the energy you have, as long as you get the facts right. This is journalism practiced with a degree of freedom and at a level of excellence that I have never found anywhere else in forty years in journalism.

The *Observer* is more than the writers who work for it and the editors who put it out. Our first business manager was a wonderful woman named Sarah Payne, and perhaps her greatest contribution to the magazine was finding Cliff Olofson and training him to handle the business side of the *Observer*. Cliff was as close to a saint as anyone I ever knew. He came from a tough, working-class background, had spent many years in the Navy, and was deeply spiritual. He could fix anything, find anything for practically no money, and worked all the time. He simply dedicated his life to the *Observer* because he thought what we were doing was that important. He sometimes kept the magazine going with his own credit cards. He died of cancer in 1995. He left everything he had to the magazine. We shall not see his like again, but the *Observer* has been blessed with many dedicated volunteers, interns, and employees.

The *Observer* is also a community—sometimes even a rather contentious family—of readers. *Observer* editors are often broke, so they stay with our readers when on assignment: I slept on everything from mud floors in the Valley to dilapidated sofa beds to posh digs in Dallas. Our readers keep us honest, they point out our every error, and they raise hell when they disagree. I know how much the *Observer* means to them, especially to those who are among the very few liberals in small towns and cities across the state—I know because I first started reading the *Observer* when I was in high school, and I still remember the relief and comfort I took just from knowing there were other people out there who thought the same way as I did.

The secret to the *Observer*'s influence is that it is read by other journalists. The *Observer* does the kind of front-line reporting that gets picked up—sometimes we even get credit—by the establishment media and that ends up on the front page of the *New York Times* and on National Public Radio. As the rest of the media become more flaccid and timid, the *Observer*'s place in the media food chain becomes more critical. I think the extraordinary thing about our fiftieth anniversary is not that we get to stop and celebrate all our good works; it is rather that it reminds us how much Texas still needs the *Observer*.

Those of us who have put out this small magazine are suspender-bustin' proud of it, and of the *Observer*'s role in the history of Texas. That such an improbably quixotic venture should have outlasted so many of its imitators and competitors seems to me a great victory for Ronnie Dugger's high-minded idealism. Of all the business ventures with all the fancy spreadsheets and accounting tricks and marketing and advertising, we're still here, and so many of them are not. I think this speaks not only to the need for the *Observer*, but to the heart of all the Texans who have helped us, and some who have cussed us, over the years. Happy birthday, *Texas Observer*.

Fifty Years of the

TEXAS

OBSERVER

The one great rule of composition is to speak the truth. —*Thoreau*

The Texas Observer

An Independent Liberal Weekly Newspaper

We will serve no group or party but will hew hard to the truth as we find it and the right as we see it.

48th Year — Incorporating The State Observer — The East Texas Democrat — The State Week — Austin Forum-Advocate — Established 1906

DECEMBER 13, 1954 — AUSTIN, TEXAS — No. 35

Shepperd Urges Port Arthur Truce

FIGHT IN COURTS

Webb County Split By One-Party Rule

By RAMON GARCES
Laredo Correspondent
The Texas Observer

LAREDO, Dec. 13—An organization that claims to be non-political and looking only for efficiency in local government has brought the first opposition in nearly 30 years to a one-party Webb County political rule, which has often been likened to the turbulent brand now under state investigation in Duval County.

Webb County citizens for a long time have had the strong suspicion that their county was going broke because of bad administration indirectly brought on by the one-party rule, but nobody seemed to want to do anything about it.

Last December the Webb County Taxpayers and Citizens League was organized by some of the county's most prominent ranchers, bankers, businessmen and attorneys, headed by Radcliffe Gillam, a young and outspoken son of a Webb County oil millionaire.

The League, after some probing of county officials, charged that the County was using road bond issues to finance the whole county government operation, and that since 1945 Webb County had had fourteen bond elections totaling $6,138,000. Fifty percent of the county's tax money, the League charged, went to pay interest and principal on the bond debt.

The League quickly brought suit to stop a road bond issue coming up for election. The voters approved the bond issue by the usual huge majority of 7 to 1, but the bonds were held up by the court suit.

The League met a set-back in the courts. First the 111th District Court of Webb County sustained a plea in abatement filed by the County Judge and Commissioners. Appealing the decision to the Court of Civil Appeals, the League again met defeat as the Court upheld the District Court's ruling. Recently the Texas Supreme Court denied a writ of error sought by the League,

(Continued on Page 5)

Vets' Land Inquiry May Take 3 Months, Geppert Declares

AUSTIN, Dec. 13—The three-agency investigation of the veterans' land dispute may take another "three months or more," W. V. Geppert, head of the taxation division and director of the probe in the Attorney General's office, says here.

Asked if the situation looked serious, Mr. Geppert said "It looks that way at the present time." It is a very complex situation, he said.

A report will be ready for the press toward the end of this week, and it will take up the issue of legislative investigation, he said.

"No outside investigators have ben called in, nor will they be," Geppert said. "There has been some talk about it, but we decided against it."

"At least a dozen" investigators for the State are in the field, Geppert said, including five from the Attorney General's office. The investigation is being conducted by three agencies—the State Auditor's office, the Texas Department of Public Safety, and the Attorney General's Department.

The Veterans' Land Board Tuesday ordered strict measures to make certain that veterans know when they are buying land under the program.

TEXAS PROBERS MEET DEC. 27

SAN ANGELO, Dec. 12 — Sen. Dorsey B. Hardeman has called the State Senate Investigating Committee into session in Austin Dec. 27 to inquire into the veterans' land dispute. Hardeman, chairman of the committee, has asked the three state agencies working on the case to have reports ready for the session.

Shivers Says State Costs Outrun Income

AUSTIN, Dec. 13—A prospect of new taxes or reduced state activities is indicated by comments of Governor Shivers at his press conference last week.

While the State's general revenue fund will probably contain a slight balance at the end of the current fiscal biennium, Shivers said, automatic drains on state revenue are increasing. The Governor specifically mentioned expenditures on the foundation school program, welfare, and farm to market roads.

With school population increasing, he said, the State may reach a point in a few years when "general revenue will be nil." He did not say whether he will recommend new taxes to the Legislature in January.

Shivers also said he thought the Insurance Commission should be given roughly the same powers as those of the Banking Commission, which has more regulatory authority than the Insurance Commission.

Both Sides Spend Heavily In Test Case

By RONNIE DUGGER
Editor, The Texas Observer
(First of a series)
(Copyright, The Texas Observer)

PORT ARTHUR, Tex., Dec. 13—The tired but determined pickets are entering their second winter on the sidewalks of Port Arthur.

Christmas is near, the cold lake wind whistles through this embittered and divided town, there is no whisper of comboys, the bellhops, the waitresses, boys, the bellhops, the waitresses the dimestore countergirls keep up their vigil for union recognition and higher wages.

A few spokesmen of the business community here say the issue is communism. Some say that the strike began without recourse to established National Labor Relations Board procedures, and union leaders admit this was an error in the five stores over which NLRB has accepted jurisdiction. But most of the merchants seem to feel that the chief question is whether retail workers should organize.

So far as the local union leaders are concerned, the issue is the recognition of the local CIO union as the sole bargaining agent for the 400 retail workers who are on strike.

You ask a middle-aged woman picketing the Goodhue Hotel what she's striking for and she says:

"Well, we want recognition first, and then a little bit more pay, you know."

A 20-year-old Port Arthur girl, Nada Jean Rogers, pauses in her pacing to and fro in front of Woolworth's on the main Port Arthur stem to tell you that before the strike started nobody made over $30 a week, and "the average was about $23."

At first it seems a puzzle why a strike involving only 19 of the more than a thousand Port Arthur retail establishments, only one out of every hundred Port Arthur workers, and only one out of a thousand of the State's 450,000 retail workers has caused such statewide bitterness and emotion.

Continued on Page 5)

—*Staff Photo*

PICKETS MAYFAIR—Mrs. Bob Hughes, 20-year-old Port Arthur housewife, pauses in her picketing of the Mayfair shop in Port Arthur to pose for a picture. She worked at the Fair store down on Procter Street when the strike began 13 months ago.

Radar Road Signs 'Psychological'

Only 17 Speed Finders In Use, Garrison Says

AUSTIN, Dec. 13—Many thousands of motorists driving around the state have of late been startled—perhaps even startled into caution—by large signs on the sides of the roads reading:

SPEED LIMIT
RADAR ENFORCED

What do these signs mean? How are the limits being enforced by radar?

Colonel Homer Garrison, director of the Department of Public Safety, told The Texas Observer:

"Frankly, it's a psychological thing."

Only seventeen radar speed-measuring machines are now in use

(Continued on Page 4)

Red Charges Don't Apply Now He Says

AUSTIN, Dec. 13—Attorney General John Ben Shepperd has declared that the Port Arthur strike situation has "altered" since he said it appeared to be part of "a Communist plot to take over Gulf oil ports." Settlement of the strike would be "good for the state," he said.

"From all indications," he said, "it is now a straight labor-management dispute."

In a special interview with The Texas Observer, Shepperd said that "as far as I can ascertain, the withdrawal of the questionable international union has altered the picture."

Shepperd charged a year ago, on Nov. 25, that the strike-leading Distributive, Processing, and Office Workers Union, which had the full backing of the national CIO, was engaged in "what appears to be a Communist plot to take over the principal ports of the Texas Gulf Coast." Two days later, the Port Arthur strikers formed a local CIO union and DPO withdrew from the strike, but the next day, Nov. Shepperd declared:

"Any reorganization retaining the present leadership will not be acceptable to the people of Texas."

On Dec. 4, the local CIO union was recorded by the federal government as "in complete compliance with legal requirements." DPO was dissolved early in the year and its membership and officers entered the CIO retail workers' union.

In Austin, Shepperd told The Texas Observer that he thinks "CIO was sold a bill of goods by DPO-WA."

"I showed them that they (DPO) hadn't cleaned up, but they had their neck out so far they had to go on," Shepperd said.

"Settlement of any strike is good for the State," Shepperd said, "but that applies particularly to this one. It would be very helpful to the industrial peace and tranquility of the State, and it would be helpful to labor's standing with the people of Texas."

Asked if a representative of the Attorney General's Department would attend a management-labor conciliation session were one arranged in Port Arthur, Shepperd said that he would have to "cross that bridge when we come to it."

"It would have to be the bona fide leaders of both sides," he said.

The strike is not a "test case," Shepperd believes, but is merely a dispute in which the CIO erred by getting involved with what Shepperd regarded as a Communist-led union.

He declined to comment on whether he believes retail workers in Texas should organize. "That, of course, is up to the parties concerned," he said. "They themselves must pass on it, and no one in government should express an opinion about it."

Shepperd charged on Nov. 17, 1953, that leaders of DPO were "proven Communist sympathizers" who "have repeatedly refused to deny under oath that they are Communists" and who have "a long record for supporting subversive causes." On Nov. 25, eight days later, he said that one of the DPO

(Continued on Page 5)

WATCHES MOTIVES OF GROUPS

Texas Security Chief Warns of False Charges

AUSTIN, Dec. 13—Texas security investigators have to be "particularly sensitive to the presumed allegation or the false allegation," N. K. Dixon, chief of the Internal Security Division of the Texas Department of Public Safety, told The Texas Observer in a special interview.

"We have to be aware in this division that there are a lot of groups who exploit an issue for their own benefit and are prone to put the emphasis where it doesn't belong," said Dixon. "Our investigators have got to recognize the motive behind an allegation."

Dixon, who was promoted to his present position after a number of years as a Texas Ranger and has been with the Texas Department of Public Safety for 17 years, said that he selects investigators for the State's security checking work on the basis of their "judgment, diplomacy and tact, and flair for the academic." He said that since security work involves "philosophies, ideologies, and subtle meanings," investigators should be well-read and "alert for the dangers and pitfalls of this kind of work."

Asked if his division has turned up any disloyal personnel in the State Government, Dixon replied:

"As far as I know, we have no knowledge of anybody in State Government whose allegiance is not to the State of Texas and the United States."

Dixon's office is the agency charged with enforcing the 1951 Texas law requiring Communists to register with the State and the 1954 legislation outlawing the Communist Party. Colonel Homer Garrison, director of the Texas Department of Public Safety, told this newspaper that no cases have been filed against Communists, but he added:

"Keep in mind we are working with other agencies and not only filing cases against people. It's our job to get facts. I would rather protect the innocent than convict the guilty."

Dixon, granting that no Communists had registered with the State, added that they had not been expected to do so because of a Communist Party directive instructing them not to comply with "any restrictive laws."

"We have to work in close liaison with federal agencies," Dixon said. "We must accept the fact that the federal government has a national program, and any action on our part damaging that program would not be compatible with the national interest. "We presume the intent of the Legislature in these (anti-Communist) laws is to effectively smash organized subversive activi-

(Continued on page 5)

The first issue of the *Texas Observer* appeared on December 13, 1954, marking the emergence of a new, critical voice in the state's public life.

I. OPENING SALVO

IT WAS A GUTSY THING TO DO, and maybe a little daft: buying out the *State Observer* and *East Texas Democrat*, hiring a 24-year-old to edit the renamed *Texas Observer*, and expecting that the new Austin weekly—through its reporting on social tensions and labor strife, racial violence and political corruption—would radically alter the political landscape of the then largest state in the Union. But that's what Mrs. Frankie Randolph hoped to accomplish with an untested staff, led by editor Ronnie Dugger and his associate William Lee (Billy) Brammer. Heir to an east Texas lumber fortune and a committed liberal organizer—at a time when the number of liberals was as slim as their clout was insignificant—Randolph gathered together a like-minded board of crusading men and women and launched what has become an enduring testament to her philanthropic impulse, activist creed, and progressive instincts.

Then she did something truly astonishing, giving Dugger complete editorial control of the *Observer*, this despite her considerable financial investment in its production and distribution; from 1954 to 1967, when Dugger became the publisher, Randolph paid off deficits that ran upwards of $250,000, but apparently never used that leverage to influence coverage or shape interpretation. "Her sponsorship of the *Texas Observer* alone would have won Randolph a place in the annals of Texas politics," writes her biographer, Ann Fears Crawford. But "her allowing and encouraging the editors she hired to follow an independent course . . . was extraordinary. It won their lifelong respect and the respect of those who work toward an independent journalism."

As if in reflection of the newspaper's manifesto, "We will serve no group or party but will hew to the truth as we find it and the right as we see it" (later shortened to "a journal of free voices"), the *Observer* took in little advertising, a financial strain manifest in the minimal salaries its employees drew and the shoestring budget they worked within. That they managed to publish one issue after another was no mean feat given the pressures the tiny staff faced. "For two men each to write some 20,000 words of presumably literate journalism a week under deadline," remembered one-time editor Willie Morris in 1964, then "read all the copy and galley proofs, hobnob with politicians, and keep up correspondence means staying up two or three nights in succession, and eventually setting up a desk by the linotype operator and handing him the final editorial page by page. A final issue was never just an issue; it came out of the marrow of our bones."

The exhausting drill took its toll, and was the subject of an early 1960s conversation Morris had with another former editor, Lawrence Goodwyn, later recounted by Goodwyn in the *Observer*. As the two men downed pitchers of beer at Scholz's, a local beer garden, Morris confessed that he was resigning. When asked why, Morris answered, "I'm worn out," and Goodwyn acknowledged that he, too, had left for the same reason several years earlier. A shared sense of fatigue sparked some banter.

> Willie asked, "How old were you when you wore out?"
> "Thirty-one," I [Goodwyn] said.
> "I must have worked harder," said Willie. "I'm twenty-nine."
> On the steps in front of Scholz's, Willie said, with a touch of wonder, "I don't know how Dugger does it."
> I still don't.

Actually, they understood why and how their boss had persisted. Dugger's "devotion to Texas as a *place*, as a state distinctive from others," Morris observed, "was something that was vanishing from America," and he was committed to recounting its quirks and oddities as best he could. He also knew enough to get out of the office. "Once an issue was put to bed he would take out in his woebegone 1948 Chevrolet, crowded with camping equipment, six packs, notebooks, galley proofs, and old sardine cans," a home on wheels that he navigated, in Morris's words, "down a lonely stretch of highway between Austin and any-where." As he sped along, Dugger would compose "next week's editorial in a notebook propped on the steering wheel."

A risky business to be sure, but that was part of the motivating thrill. "The impulse to dissent in Texas scarcely existed," Brammer affirmed in a 1960 sketch of Dugger, "[before Dugger and] his newspaper erupted on the scene to shake us up a little in our hookworm belt complacencies. Soon there were hoots and wild cries and a crazy circus of exposures, denials, copped pleas, and even one or two indictments. All this devotion and energy help explain why the *Observer* has outstayed and out-shone other regional ventures in independent political journalism, right and left, recent and long-gone."

The journal's consistency in moral temper and reportorial tone was also bound up with the unique environment in which it was produced. "I don't think one can make much sense of *The Texas Observer*, or its writers, without pausing first to mark the defining impact on both of its founding editors," concluded Goodwyn in 1974. "The circumstances of those early years, when Dugger toiled away in isolation as editor, copy-editor, and layout man, shaped the *Observer* in fundamental ways and imparted the special independent character that has since defined it."

Still, it is hard to believe that Dugger had any clue what he was getting into when he accepted Frankie Randolph's offer to be the *Texas Observer*'s founding editor. Or fully understood the many costs that would come if he accepted, as he did, the challenge of Paul Holcombe, editor of the defunct *State Observer*, and Roy Bedichek, the cultural critic, in the inaugural issue to make controversy his full-time occupation. And how could he have anticipated that the two editorials he penned for the December 13, 1954, edition would be the first of so many, and would set the tone for those to come?

Char Miller

To Enlighten, and Not to Suppress

RONNIE DUGGER

DECEMBER 13, 1954—The editor and the backers are all of one mind on the principles of this enterprise.

The fact that the phrase has been terribly abused by hypocrites does not prevent us from saying proudly that we are dedicated to the people.

A fine condition of mutual trust and confidence exists among all of us.

The reader has a right to know, however, how this newspaper will resolve the classic problems of The Group which will surely arise as the months and years go by.

The editor runs the paper. Editorial policy is in his hands. Ultimate control of the newspaper is in the hands of the trustees, acting through their director.

If the editor ceases as an independent person, to represent the sentiments of the trustees; or if they decide he's not doing a good job, they fire him; if they instruct him to do something he cannot, he quits.

The trustees can of course fire the editor for any reason, but the agreement is that dismissal is the only mechanism of enforcement of the ultimate control. The editor speaks his mind freely on any subject at all times. The group conscience of the newspaper (that is, a majority of the trustees acting through their directors), exercises a continuing judgment as to whether the editor is following independently a course of fidelity to decent and intelligent policies.

This has been the means whereby the group believes we can successfully reconcile editorial freedom with the need for the continuing responsibility of the newspaper to the liberal tradition. The editor assumes the positive duty to enlighten, not to suppress; to be the advocate of principle, not the protector of doctrine; and to be dedicated to human values, not to arbitrary values of any special interest.

Trustees, who receive no stock earnings, vote all stock, so that the control of the paper may never be captured by stock purchases.

We have to survive as a business before we can survive as a morality; but we would rather perish as a business than survive as an immorality. Our business staff will seek advertising, but we will never sell anything but space. We will work hard to get subscriptions, but we will never shade a principle for fear of losing subscribers.

The paper is not to be a house organ of any group but is to be independent. Stock will be sold only to individuals.

These things needed to be worked out, but other things are more important. We must proceed in our single lives to serve the things we think are right. We in this venture together are doing only that. If there were any simple way for us to summarize our determination, it would be Paul Holcomb's rule of life: you can't always be right, but you can always be honest.

Keep Facts Straight, Stand By Convictions

PAUL HOLCOMB

DECEMBER 13, 1954 — Owning and operating a newspaper is the almost universal ambition of all news reporters. Austin is not only the Capital of Texas, it is also the political heart and the nerve center of State Government. Every Austin newsman knows that many matters of vital import are never adequately reported — for one reason or another — and that because of this lack of knowledge and understanding, the average citizen can read his daily paper religiously and still not know how his State government is being run, or even who is actually in control of it.

During the early "Depression Years," Vann M. Kennedy and Paul Bolton were in charge of the International News Service here in Austin. They talked and talked about "the great need of an independent newspaper," until they talked themselves into starting *The State Observer*. After the usual work and worry always experienced in starting a newspaper, *The State Observer* was entered at the Austin Post Office on April 26th, 1937, with Vann M. Kennedy as the owner and publisher.

In its beginnings, Vann Kennedy, as editor and publisher, did some of the writing, Paul Bolton did most of the writing, and Walter T. Fleet . . . did most of the manual labor in getting out the paper.

In its later development there were a number of "Bright Young Men" who wrote for *The State Observer*. Among them were D.B. Hardeman, Jack Guinn, and Alex Louis and others, whose names I do not recall. The "general tone" of *The State Observer* carried the implication that these writers were seriously concerned with never running afoul of the libel laws. The paper was informative and well written, but it carefully avoided controversial matters; it was my opinion at the time — and still is — that some of these writers "Would Rather Be Bright Than President."

When World War II broke out Vann Kennedy went into the service, leaving the *Observer* in the charge of his wife (Mary Kennedy) and Paul Bolton. The difficulties of running a newspaper in war time were terrific, and they finally started hunting a buyer. Being the only man in Texas (able to borrow the money) who was dumb enough to tackle the job, I (Paul B. Holcomb) bought *The State Observer* and took charge in January of 1944.

When I took over *The State Observer* I changed the policy of the paper — completely. In those days it was highly popular to "take pot-shots" at Franklin D. Roosevelt. Governors, Senators, and Congressmen, who had been riding "FDR's" coat-tails for 12 years in order to get themselves elected, asserted their "independence" and bragged about how many times they had "stood up to the President" and voted against his measures. I exposed the hypocrisy of these proclaimed "Heroes" in words that everybody could understand. It did not make *The State Observer* popular — but "look at the fun I had."

I have a few inviolable rules which I have adopted — for myself. I am fully determined to "KEEP THE FACTS STRAIGHT." I am also determined to tell the truth about both friend and foe. In dealing with men and measures I try to avoid showing personal enmity, and treat any man or measure as honestly and fairly as my nature will permit. But I make no pretense of being "an objective writer," simply because I do not believe that there is any such animal in existence — at least not among mortal men.

Sen. John J. Ingalls said, "Purity In Politics Is An Iridescent Dream." It is my firm conviction that "Objective Reporting and Editorial Writing" belongs in the same category. I know that I am biased in favor of the things that I believe to be right. I take some personal pride in my ability to discern my own "biased opinions," and also in my willingness to admit that I stand behind my honest convictions. This does not greatly inflate my ego, because I know that every intelligent reader would know the facts, regardless of any attempt to conceal them. The difference between me and other newspapermen is — I admit it.

It is obviously impossible for me to even touch the high spots of our eleven years' ownership of *The State Observer*. My wife (Mrs. Alice May

Holcomb) and I have done what was necessary to keep *The State Observer* alive. All along we have been harassed by financial worries, and time and again I was on the verge of "throwing in the sponge." But my wife always vetoed that — so we kept struggling on — and on — and on.

My real joy in this closing article about *The State Observer* is that we were able to keep it alive until it has grown into something better. *The Texas Observer* is the fulfillment of our dreams when we took over *The State Observer*. Hundreds of Democrats are behind this new paper who never did even subscribe to our paper. Ronnie Dugger, who will control *The Texas Observer*, has education and ability which the present editor never did possess. In addition he has youth and ambition which departed from the present editor — many years ago. As a Jay-hawker boy in Kansas, I used to lift up my voice and sing, "John Brown's body lies a-mouldering in the grave. His soul goes marching on." And while *The State Observer* is a thing of the past, I am constrained to hope that in *The Texas Observer* the soul of *The State Observer* will "go marching on."

Controversy Becomes "Treason" When Free Discussion Is Impaired

ROY BEDICHEK

DECEMBER 13, 1954 — The word "free" in the title may as well be dropped to begin with. If discussion is not free we have another name for it — propaganda. Propaganda indoctrinates; discussion educates. Propaganda is dominated by a given point of view. Education leads by mutual interchange of thoughts, opinion and information to some nearer ascertainment of truth.

Change has been called the only constant in human affairs. "New occasions teach new duties; time makes ancient good uncouth." Individually and in organizations, men must choose among changes — what change to make and when to make it. Nature herself abhors the status quo. Your life and mine are largely a series of choices, some of which are routine and reduced to habit. Others require thought, taking counsel with oneself, weighing the evidence, balancing opposing considerations, that is, carrying on a solitary debate or controversy within the mind. The act of thinking is itself a controversial form, generally recognized by psychologists. Hence, the proverb, as he thinketh in his heart, so is he. If he happens to be enough of a fool he censors his own thought. That is, he refuses to take cognizance of germane information or logical deductions. We say of such a person that he deceives himself.

Social units must also choose among changes and decide when a new course or action shall be taken. Thinking must be out loud if every member is to be free to make his contribution. This is group-thinking, or discussion; and any group of human beings, be it a local lodge, a state legislature, or the whole nation, for that matter, which suppresses germane information or relative argument, by just so much impairs its ability to make intelligent choices. It deceives itself.

Quite recently a sinister meaning has been attached to the innocent English word "controversial." A propaganda of enormous proportions and of diabolical skill has altered the meaning of this word in the popular mind from that of the standard dictionary definitions of it. Now we seem to believe that if a proposal is "controversial" in certain areas of public policy, it must not be discussed. You may think about it, but not out loud. If an individual is "controversial" in these same areas, he's not fit for responsible positions, public or private.

Presto! Note the magic of it! "Controversial" becomes "subversion," then "treason"—twenty years of it. This chain of linguistic perversions (disagreement is controversy is subversion is treason) is, with amazing audacity, used to justify censorship. . . .

The historian cannot name a single individual who has made any distinctive contribution to the education, art, science or religion of Western Civilization in the past two thousand years who was not at one time or another in his career "controversial," and the more "controversial" he was the more important his contribution. And, of course, the issues upon which the fame of these individuals rests were also "controversial." "Controversy" is an identification as well as a condition of progressive society.

I am impressed by *The Texas Observer*'s statement of principles, which seems to dedicate it to controversy, to discussion, to thinking out loud, to disputation with no holds barred and no essential information withheld, let the chips fall where they may. This is the method of Abelard, Europe's greatest liberator of thought. It is the method of all education worthy of the name, the method of our great liberating newspapers and magazines, and certainly the method for which the machinery of this, our democracy, was especially devised.

Ralph Yarborough flanked by Molly Ivins and Bob Eckhardt. Photo by Alan Pogue.

II. HEROES, HACKS, AND HUCKSTERS

TEXAS WAS NOT MINNESOTA, and for Molly Ivins that was a good thing. As she sped southward toward home in the summer of 1970 after spending three years as a reporter in Minneapolis and "whipped across the border doing 80," her exuberant patriotism — "I can't help it. I love Texas. It's a harmless perversion" — was tempered by worry and anxiety: had "I over-romanticized Texas? Again?"

Those concerns vanished when she pulled into Austin and took up her new job as coeditor of the *Observer*, sharing duties with Kaye Northcott; together they would re-energize the journal's political coverage. The state's riotous legislature alone lured Ivins back to the capital. "I rather relish the political situation here," she chuckled, "if only because there is no shortage of proper villains in Texas. The battles are so lifeless elsewhere, ever fought on tedious shades of gray. Down here the baddies wear black hats and one can loathe them with a cheerful conscience."

Ivins's predecessors and successors, whatever their temperaments, have shared her belief in investigative journalism as a full-contact sport, and have taken great delight in exposing the antics of the good, the bad, and the very ugly, of highlighting the larcenous and the noble (and those in between). Governor Allan Shivers belonged among the temporizers, Ronnie Dugger argued after listening to the governor's 1955 State of the State speech; Shivers talked a good game of expanding social services but would only fund them by regressive taxation, a sign of his cowardice. At least archconservative Martin Dies knew what he stood for, even if his principles and prejudices were anathema to Texas progressives. Then there was 1964 senatorial candidate George H. W. Bush, who touted his conservatism as "compassionate," yet demonstrated no sensitivity to the needy, a product, the *Observer* editorialized, of the "extremist-infected atmosphere of the Texas Republican Party." (Sound familiar?)

More intriguing were those shadowy figures who stayed behind the scenes, making deals, peddling influence, or stealing elections. Phil Fox, a public relations man, was a new breed of fixer who developed unique strategies to manipulate the electoral process. Ah, but no one knew how to finagle the system better than Billy Sol Estes; closely tied to Lyndon Johnson, his speculative ventures reaped untoward amounts of money, and also netted him more than twenty years in jail. By contrast, George Christian, another Johnson associate, was more circumspect, becoming Austin's master lobbyist in the 1970s by hooking up his high-end business clients with the legislature's power brokers. Making Christian look positively genteel is James Leininger, an evangelical with very deep pockets, who since the 1990s has flashed his cash to buy politicians, finance their campaigns, and push his right-wing social agenda.

This grim and corrupt world has had its share of saints, men and women who have struggled against very long odds (which is what makes them saintly, after all). Henry B. Gonzalez's filibuster against segregationist legislation in 1957 — and Dugger's account of his tireless energy — remains legendary. Maury Maverick Jr. was another indefatigable foe of oppression, whether in the state legislature or as a lawyer counseling conscientious objectors to the Vietnam War; Babe Schwartz, only the second Jew to serve in the Texas Senate, had a lengthy career in which he battled to extend governmental support to the destitute. Long before Barbara Jordan became a household word, the *Observer* had interviewed the sonorous state senator, and admired her pragmatic verve. As for State Senator Don Kennard, it wasn't clear how his liberalism added up, exactly, although Larry L. King manages to clarify its quirks. There were no doubts about Sissy Farenthold, however; her galvanizing, if unsuccessful, gubernatorial campaigns in the 1970s brought this rave endorsement: "GET UP OFF YOUR BUTTS AND MOVE. This woman is worth fighting for." Franklin Garcia received his much-deserved encomiums posthumously, and the gifted union organizer, who had done so much to empower agricultural laborers, would have wanted it that way. So would Senator Ralph Yarborough, yet he received plenty of public praise in the *Observer* as the white knight of Texas liberalism, the embodiment of what was possible, a politician who unwaveringly stood by, for, and with the people.

Like the other exemplars, Yarborough sustained Ivins's faith that there was a critical mass in Texas "to make this, at last, a place where people can grow up gentle."

Char Miller

The People's Hero at the People's Expense

RONNIE DUGGER

JANUARY 17, 1955 — If he is not careful, some of the wags in his own camp will start calling [Governor] Allan Shivers a liberal.

But Allan Shivers is careful.

In his State of the State speech, he laid before the people a good plan for expanded state welfare services. . . . But he would finance his program with reactionary sales taxes on gasoline, cigarettes, and education.

Who would pay his two-cent increase on every gallon of gas?

The people.

Who would pay his one-cent increase on every pack of cigarettes?

The people.

Who would pay his doubled college tuition rate?

The people.

Why did the Governor not have the courage to insist that the developers of our State's abundant natural resources start carrying their fair share of the load?

Why does he continue to retire behind his hypocritical defense mechanism: "I am opposed to a general sales tax," and then propose specific sales taxes on students and drivers and cigarette smokers?

Does he think the people are fools?

Allan Shivers . . . would tax those least able to pay, even as every good Democrat prefers to tax those best able to pay. . . .

Not content to insult consumers as a whole, the Governor once again baited organized labor. He seems determined to convince working people that he is their sworn enemy. In this, at least, he has been successful.

He repeated the false charge that Communists started the Port Arthur retail strike [in 1954]. The plain truth is that loyal Texas workers who were indignant about their $20 or $25 wages for 50 or 60 hours started it. Similar conditions prevail among 450,000 retail workers throughout Texas, and to the extent that the Port Arthur strike has been thwarted by Mr. Shivers . . . [he] is responsible for their continuance.

The Governor also proposed prohibiting picketing for recognition unless a majority of employees vote for the union, an idea that has been declared unconstitutional because picketing is grounded in the basic right of free speech.

Nevertheless all Texans concerned with the welfare of the people are glad that the Governor has at last admitted:

"There is no escaping that responsible government costs money."

We are glad that Adlai Stevenson's point that states' rights are meaningless without states' responsibilities seems to have taken hold of his mind.

We are glad that he has admitted that Texas boys and girls are living under "actually dangerous conditions" in corrective schools; that unemployment compensation payments to Texas workers are too low and are not authorized for enough workers; that Texas does not provide enough beds for tubercular patients, even for those under six years of age; that the mentally retarded are inadequately cared for in the state hospitals; that our loan shark laws need tightening . . . and on through a great number of reforms.

But Allan Shivers has been governor nigh onto six years. He was lieutenant governor before that, and a state senator before that. Never before in his public life did he stand before us all and protest his humanitarian concern for the people. What explains the change?

Perhaps the State of the State just got so bad he had to do something. Perhaps he wants to go to the U.S. Senate. Perhaps he wants a place in history as a generous Governor. Perhaps it is none of these, and he is sincere. We hope so.

But if he is, he will give up his taxes on the little man and admit that developers and out-of-state users of oil, gas, and sulphur are not accepting their fair share of our common duty to provide for the general good.

"Hit 'Em Where They Live"

BILL BRAMMER

MAY 9, 1955 — Phil Fox, the king of the political hucksters of Texas, doesn't play the No. 1 part very convincingly. He is quiet and retiring; he shuns personal publicity like the plague. The only way you can appraise his influence in politics — and some people say he's the most powerful man in the political netherworld of Texas — is by the results he gets. He wins.

. . . It was impossible to connect certain campaign issues and techniques directly with Fox, and he refused to grant an interview to this reporter. Much of the material here was collected from visits with his friends and enemies, many of whom think Phil Fox can elect just about anyone to public office in Texas. Fox has been connected with the campaigns mentioned below, and it is said that Fox never takes on a job unless he gives all the orders.

His offices are in the Great National Life Building in downtown Dallas. Most of his PR connections are non-political (such as the Dallas Symphony Orchestra, and the Metropolitan Opera) but he is most noted for his political PR prowess.

His political clients usually run to the conservative, but there are some who say this has no particular significance. Conservatives, the professional PR men like to point out, just happened to have most of the money in recent years — the kind of money Fox demands for the "right" kind of campaign.

There is talk that some prominent liberals have approached him on several occasions and that Fox turned them down. But, say the professional PR men, the reason was probably one of the economics and not ideology. Fox has also handled two campaigns for Lyndon Johnson.

Fox is a master of the glandular approach — and he doesn't overlook any media for reaching the ears of the people, and playing on their emotions. He has a genius for handling mass psychology, and he knows just when and where to hit the people where they live.

The glandular technique is not one of hard selling. You have your product repetition, your sloganeering, but the real message is concentrated in maneuvers against the competitor. It finds the PR man dancing across the nerve ends of the people, paralyzing them with fear of the opposition.

During the 1946 gubernatorial campaign this was worked to good effect against Homer Rainey, a distinguished just-discharged president of the University of Texas supported by Austin ministers, high scholars, the liberals and the old Roosevelt New Dealers.

Rainey was particularly vulnerable to the glandular pitch. He had defended several University professors who taught "controversial" things before the board of regents. He had spoken out on academic freedom. He indicated that labor unions weren't at all bad — that labor and capital could work together. There was also a book — or at least part of a book — on a required reading list at the University. It was a trilogy, *USA* by John Dos Passos, and there were some who said it was vile and unpatriotic.

In the middle of the campaign, a number of young men had a job to do. They boarded Greyhound buses and rode all over the state just talking to people. They were students at the University, they told their traveling companions, out for the summer vacation. When the talk got around to politics and the gubernatorial campaign, they rendered their little pitch. "I'm not so sure about Dr. Rainey," they would say. "He defended those Communist professors, you know, and that book he likes so much is pretty vile."

There were also groups who went around the state reading passages from books of the *USA* trilogy which were not on the UT reading list. Women were barred.

Other campaigns have featured persons touring the state, stopping at country stores, and saying, "I like this fellow but I don't hold with his idea of putting colored children in the same classrooms with white kids."

Then last summer there were the Port Arthur "truth teams," which went over the state and on radio warning citizens against the CIO and left-wing unions. Once on the radio, a truth team member talked about the "lust in the eyes" of one Negro picket ogling the little girls at a Port Arthur school.

(It has never been clear if Phil Fox or Syers, Pickle and Wynn, an Austin PR firm, spawned the "Port Arthur Story.")

Another technique is the wet-dry gimmick. In wet areas, such as German settlements, citizens are told this or that opponent is going hard for prohibition. In dry areas, the same opponent is pictured as a man on the verge of alcoholism.

This technique is also considered unbeatable for circulating rumors in bars and taverns for local option elections.

None of these tactics has ever been connected directly to Fox. But he worked in the campaigns — he was in charge of many of them — and it is a fair inference that he knew what was going on.

Fox is an ex-newspaperman; he was something of a crackerjack reporter for the *Dallas Times Herald* back in the early twenties. He soon found that longer, greener pastures lay just outside newspaper work in public relations.

He handled publicity for the Ku Klux Klan in Dallas for a while, and he was so good at it that he soon was sent to Georgia on a bigger assignment. About seven years later he was back in Dallas and in business with "Watson Associates."

The name still sticks, although Watson is no longer living. Hardly a major campaign is run if Fox is involved without the name "Watson Associates" coming out in some burst of oratory about the opposition's methods.

In 1946 the Rainey people, after taking as much of the whispering campaign as they could, decided to do something about it. A "newspaper" was put out, seven pages in length dealing with Fox, his methods, his Klan background and a prison term he once served in Georgia.

Beauford Jester [Rainey's gubernatorial opponent] grabbed the paper at a rally one night, waved it in his fist and fumed in effect: "Here's a man who once made a mistake. He paid for it and lived to become an honored and respected citizen. Now they're going back into the past, trying to defame him, while the whole philosophy of Christianity is based on one major proposition — a second chance."

Jester's impromptu defense was effectual, and the Rainey people were demoralized. Fox had known exactly where to draw the line on his propaganda, and just where and when to hit the people with it. The fine line of acceptability wasn't evident in the scandal sheet put out on Fox.

There are some who say Fox created W. Lee [Pappy] O'Daniel: Others say he was simply hired by O'Daniel after Pappy got the bug for governor. The former theory holds that Fox handled the O'Daniel radio program — with all the pass-the-biscuits homily and good Christian sayings — invented by Watson Associates. It's certainly the most intriguing theory, although Fox neither confirms nor denies it.

He worked for O'Daniel in several campaigns, dropped him once to work for Lyndon Johnson in a senatorial race against Pappy. He also handled Johnson's campaign against Coke Stevenson [in 1948]. The story goes that in the middle of that campaign, Johnson was in trouble and trailing. One of Johnson's wealthy advisors called him, "I'm hiring Phil Fox for you: I'm getting the best. Is that okay?" Johnson said it was, and he gained all the way from the time Fox was hired.

This reporter has never heard a bad word against Fox personally. His friends and enemies say that he is a fine fellow and his PR compatriots rarely argue about his professional prowess. They say he's the best in the business.

One outstanding PR man who has been associated with more liberal causes than conservative does object. "Give me as much money as he (Fox) gets for a campaign, and I'll win every time, too." In addition, he said he could win with "clean publicity."

The same man also is a bit miffed about Fox's pet campaign issues — CIO [Congress of Industrial Organizations] and segregation. "Every time they campaign against the CIO. They talk and talk and talk about this horrible cancer, but they never cut it out after the election. They need it for the next campaign."

Another PR man puts it this way: "Phil gets the people to the point where they can't think — they just feel. He goes directly to their emotions."

Fox has had losses, however, and some say he is in eclipse. Some point to a younger man, Paul Cain, of the Cain Organization, Inc., of Dallas, who has also perfected the glandular approach and whose star is in ascendancy.

Fox lost last year in his campaign to elect Wallace Savage to Congress from Dallas. He did a good job against Lester Hackler, Savage's opponent for the Democratic nomination, but Savage lost to a Republican, Bruce Alger, in the November election. Either Fox misjudged the strength of Alger, or he just couldn't figure out how to discredit an old-line Republican.

He also lost in a campaign against Barefoot Sanders. Some people went so far as calling Barefoot a Communist sympathizer. Critics say this was going a little too far, that citizens couldn't quite believe that a fine looking red-headed fellow with "Barefoot" for a name and a beautiful wife with him on television could possibly be a subversive.

Sanders, the young Dallas legislator, had something to do with it though.

At a public rally, someone from the audience yelled out a hint that Barefoot was a Red. Enraged, Sanders challenged the fellow — not to a debate but a good old-fashioned fistfight. When citizens saw the young man ready to get down and brawl with anyone who would call him a communist, they loved it.

Said a Dallas PR man who was not involved in the fight: "It was perfect; it was right out of the Phil Fox book, and Phil would have loved it. Barefoot hit 'em right where they lived."

"Name It!" Says Dies

RONNIE DUGGER

JANUARY 2, 1957 — In every major Texas election the conservative wealth of the state picks a man early and sees him through. For the Senate race the man is Martin Dies.

His good friends think of him as the prophet of the thirties who alerted the people against communism in the United States and an able defender of free enterprise against socialistic enterprises. His foes think he would be "another McCarthy from Texas" and class him — to use his own words — as "a bigot, a reactionary, an old Southern boy just coming outa the woods." Be that as it may or may not, his name is magic at the Texas ballot box, and he knows it. He pulled 900,000 votes last summer without leaving Washington.

He signed the Southern Manifesto against integration, and he opposes public housing and federal aid, yet he believes he has a "progressive record." Wary of the passionate concourse of state politics, he says no one can tie him to Allan Shivers or Price Daniel, says he's never failed to support the Democratic nominees when he, himself, was also a nominee.

In manner, he's a trial lawyer in the Darrow tradition, different as he is from Clarence Darrow in most other ways. His hair is stringy and falls over the heavy waves of flesh across his forehead; his nose is broad, flaring with deep grooves and enclosing his soft lips. He is young physically and moves about with easy grace.

He has been making several speeches a day, yet he never makes the papers. The reason is he is talking to churches, lodges, legions, farm groups, P.T.A.'s on God, Mother, and America. "Now tomorrow night," he said, sprawled over a bed in a Houston hotel room, "I'm going over to Bridge City, they expect a thousand students and the P.T.A. Well, I'll talk about youth, the future of America as far as our youth is concerned, and what they can expect. . . . I'm an extemporaneous speaker, so it doesn't bother me. If I'm half-way rested I can do pretty good."

He has made three score such speeches in the state since he announced for senator — says he gets three invitations a day. With practically no statewide publicity he was able to pull 33 percent of the straw vote in the Beiden poll on the Senate candidates, so he must be making time.

. . . "I'm positive Shivers won't run," he says, "and the odds are against even [Ralph] Yarborough being a candidate. [James P.] Hart has been in it, of course. He and Yarborough draw from the same group. If they ran it's gonna be a pretty good split among some people."

On the Dies side of the fence, Senator Searcy Bracewell and Republican Thad Hutcheson have announced. (Wright Morrow of Houston is also a possible candidate.) Dies says Bracewell is a very nice fellow but won't get many votes. He believes Hutcheson would have pulled "probably 200,000 votes in the November election but doesn't have a chance now."

"As long as I am the nominee of the party I'm gonna support the nominees," Dies insists. For those who judge a man by his party loyalty, this will serve to distinguish him from Bracewell who was for Eisenhower in 1952 and 1956 but considers himself a Democrat. But Dies too has left the national ticket. In 1944 he opposed Roosevelt for a fourth term.

"I couldn't support him because I thought he was nearly dead," Dies told the *Observer*. "So I quit Congress. As long as I'm a nominee of the Democratic Party, I'm gonna support the nominees. . . . I told the people in my campaign that Roosevelt wouldn't live. That wasn't the only reason. There were others; they were crowding me pretty hard."

Dies likes to remember his crusades of the late thirties and early forties as unpopular wars against U.S. reds. "Between 1938 and 1943 I investigated and exposed around 500 from organizations of the Nazis, fascists, and communists," he says. "Most of them went out of business by the time I quit in '43." He feels hostility to this work forced him out of politics.

"Everything I said has been proved," he says. "It was unpopular work. A politician doesn't do an unpopular thing unless he does it out of conviction, does he? Now does he? In 1954 my bill outlawing the Communist Party and its subsidiaries won hands down — all the liberals supported it and everybody voted for it. 'He's been right,' they said."

Dies carefully avoids direct statements against school desegregation but his position is clear enough in its effect.

"I believe that the operation and control of the public schools belongs to the state and the local community. . . . If they of the Supreme Court can take away that right, then what is there to keep them from taking away every other right? They can't come along 100 years later and say that ain't what the Constitution is, after all. I'm not getting into the social question or anything else. But I am thinking seriously about joining with a strong committee of 100 congressmen with some legislation to provide the only way to change the interpretation of the Constitution is by constitutional amendment.

"I voted against public housing — I'm against it," he said. "I don't think it's right to subsidize some realtors at the expense of others. One fellow paying $100 rent and taxes subsidizes another guy who is paying $50. It tends to make people wards of the state and it develops political machines in the cities."

What, then, should be done about the slums?

"That's a serious problem," Dies says. "We should enable people to buy homes with very long term, very low-interest finance — make it possible for anybody to own a home. The FHA plan should be more liberalized for people in low-income groups."

Federal aid to school construction foundered in Congress in good part because of Dies' work. "I opposed it as it was, with the Powell Amendment," to bar aid from segregated schools, he said. Would he have favored it without the amendment? "I would have voted against it either way," he said. "Texas has ample resources and revenues for its schools. That bill (federal aid to education) was designed to set up in Washington a bureau to let them go out and build schools. It would have set up a number of conditions and requirements, not only in methods, but in curriculum."

Dies is for 90 percent of parity for all basic crops with strict crop controls.

He says he will work next session "for a resolution calling on our (federal) reclamation system to submit to Congress a comprehensive program for the drought-stricken states." He would favor a 50-50 cost split between the states and the U.S. "without any further delay." He favors the construction of reservoirs throughout the affected states.

He opposed the $20-a-dependent tax cut the Democrats espoused and also voted against the Eisenhower Administration's tax bill, which the Democrats said helped the richer taxpayers. Dies says he is opposed to "any tax cuts."

He is opposed to any plan of national health insurance which he would view as "socialized medicine." He is a member of a House group on health and science; however, he feels proud of his work on health resources and mental health legislation, especially legislation helping finance medical research with federal grants-in-aid.

On the current crisis in the Suez, he tends to justify the invasion of Egypt. "It may turn out to be one of the most far reaching things that ever happened," he says. "If Russia took over Eastern oil, the very life blood of the democracies, where would any of us be? So I think it's not wise to be quick to condemn them (Britain, France and Israel) for moving in quickly."

This is Dies readying for the heavy campaigning of the next few months. He thinks Ralph Yarborough will be his chief opponent if he announces and he is anxious to get the fight into the open. "What can he say about me?" he asked. He thinks his position on party loyalty secure and unexceptionable: he has kept out of state politics. "Will he call me a reactionary? If he says I voted against federal aid to education, why every Texas member voted against! Is he against Lyndon Johnson and Sam Rayburn? What vote have I cast against the best interest of the people? Name it!"

The Segregation Filibuster of 1957

RONNIE DUGGER

MAY 7, 1957 — A tall Latin man in a light blue suit and white shoes and yellow tie and yellow handkerchief was pacing around his desk on the Senate floor. It was 8 o'clock in the morning. An old Negro was brushing off the soft senatorial carpet in front of the president's rostrum. Up in the gallery a white man stood with his back to the chamber, studying a panel of pictures of an earlier Senate. The Latin man was orating and gesturing in a full flood of energy, not like a man who had been talking to almost nobody for three hours and had another day and night to go.

Why did they name Gonzales, Gonzales if the name wasn't honored in Texas at the time? he asked. Why did they honor Garza along with Burnet? My own forebears in Mexico bore arms against Santa Anna. There were three revolutions against Santa Anna — Texas was only one of its manifestations! Did you know that Negroes helped settle Texas? That a Negro died at the Alamo?

The angry crystal-voiced man stopped his pacing and raised his arms to plead. "I seek to register the plaintive cry, the hurt feelings, the silent, the dumb protest of the inarticulate."

No one in the Capitol this week will deny that Henry Gonzalez registered it — that through him and Sen. Abraham (Chick) Kazen of Laredo and four other senators who spelled the two talkers-in-chief during their 36-hour marathon on the Senate floor, the minorities were heard with eloquence and impact as never before in Texas.

In a larger way the filibuster was the splitting up of the Texas culture into some of its varied ways of life. On one side of the Senate chamber stood South and far West Texans with more than a million Latin-Americans behind them — Latin-Americans they think are threatened by general segregation bills which do not say they aim at Negroes. On the other side of the chamber were white East Texans with a million Negroes behind them, some of them restive for what the Supreme Court says are their rights. In the middle stood senators of moderate persuasion, some of whom voted with the minorities, some of whom voted with the East Texans — then switched at the last minute to vote their personal convictions.

Spelling Gonzalez and Kazen with long questions, readings from novels and essays, repeatings of the text of the bill, spellings-out of the words of the sections were four other senators — Charles Herring of Austin, Bruce Reagan of Corpus Christi, Hubert Hudson of Brownsville, and Frank Owen III of El Paso. Voting with these six senators against final passage of HB 231, by Rep. Virginia Duff of Ferris, were Carlos Ashley, Llano; Preston Smith, Lubbock; and Dorsey Hardeman, San Angelo. Smith and Hardeman voted to bring the bill up and cut off the filibuster when Gonzalez gave out.

Early on the first day, Sen. William Fly, Victoria, explained that 10 of his 12 counties have started integration and said he was worried that the bill would reverse that. "We want to do this thing. It's generally community-wide acceptance," he said. Sen. R.A. Weinert, Seguin, asked Kazen if it were not so that the bills would "only foment litigation." But when the vote came, another day and two nights later, at 2:25 A.M., Fly, Weinert and five other senators were not present.

The talkers won their point for the week: Sen. Wardlow Lane, Center, who originally wanted to pass out all five bills before the Senate, except the one barring NAACP members from public employment, gave in when Gonzalez refused all blandishments and importunations and talked on into early Friday morning. Only HB 231 was passed. . . . Monday, Senate State Affairs passed out two more bills but (by a 9-7 vote) referred to Atty. Gen. Will Wilson one requiring some advocates of integration and segregation to register with the secretary of state.

"I intend to fight every one of 'em to the last ditch — every one of 'em.

It's the least I can do," said Gonzalez after 22 hours and 2 minutes of continuous argument. Replied Kazen, who held the floor 15 hours without a break, slept two and a half hours, and returned to rest Gonzalez with long questions: "As long as you want to stay on your feet, I want to help you."

Sen. Wardlow Lane of Center, the Senate leader of the East Texans, explained very briefly that HB 231 permits school boards to use 17 factors (not including race) in assigning students to schools. It ought to be passed "if you trust your trustees or the local authority," he said. "This places it on entirely the local level," he said.

As passed by the House, HB 231 also permits parents who object to integration to withdraw their children from the public schools, all other laws to the contrary notwithstanding, and says they will then get educational grants as provided by law.

Kazen, the son of Lebanese immigrants and a member of the powerful Kazen family of Laredo, was dressed in a dark blue suit, red tie with a gold clasp, and black shoes as he started the fight Wednesday morning at 11:16 with a pre-lunch statement of 44 minutes. He said the bill was meant to deter integration and circumvent the U.S. Constitution. Sen. Dorsey Hardeman of San Angelo, who presided over the filibuster, passed its early hours reading the Magna Carta. . . .

Gonzalez and Kazen started talking Spanish to each other. Discussing the "psychological qualifications" to be used by the school boards as a test for pupil assignments, Kazen said: "El leon juzga a todos de su condicion" (The lion judges everybody by his own condition, or, all looks yellow to the jaundiced eye).

Sen. Jimmy Phillips, Angleton, objected to using "that kind of language" on the floor, and Hardeman ruled Senate debate has to be in English. At that point, Gonzalez turned to Macauley's *Essays* (an 1878 edition presented to Frederick S. Healy in 1881 by Cardinal Manning as a prize for mathematics in a grammar school examination). "It is all in the best of the Queen's English," Gonzalez assured the Senate. It is written in "those choice words that only the English can preserve in their imagination. . . ."

At ten of eight [P.M.] Kazen for the first time drew from his book-littered desk *The Voice at the Back Door* by Elizabeth Spencer. Opening it up, he told the Senate, "This'll read like a novel, because it is a novel."

The passages he chose dealt with the woes and wiles of Negro laborers. For a while Gonzalez spelled him with a passage from a personal sketch by W. E. B. DuBois in *An Anthology of Negro Literature*. . . .

At 9:50 Gov. and Mrs. [Price] Daniel came in. Daniel talked with everybody, chewed on his cigar, listened to the filibuster. Hardeman, by this time, was reading the *American Bastille*, a book on the Lincoln era's civil rights abuses. Gonzalez said of Daniel, "He's wavering a little bit; if he just stays with us long enough we might convert him."

. . . Owen launched a search for *Et Al*, "co-author of the bill." "If *Al* were here tonight I'm sure he would disclaim any connection with this bill. *Al* is a good friend of mine," said Owen. "But perhaps here is a man gone astray." A couple of newspapermen played poker in a committee room for half an hour. One gentleman of the fourth estate fell down as he left the chamber and was helped home.

"You know what rain does to cantaloupe?" Kazen asked.

"*Sine die*? That any kin to *Et Al*?" asked Herring.

And so it went until Henry Gonzalez was wakened and came to the chamber at 5 A.M. Lane grumbled about Gonzalez's big words. "Maybe he'll strangle on one of them," he said hopefully. Kazen gave Gonzalez his lemons, his Hershey bars, and his *Schools in Transition*. Herring gave him the American Bar Association *Journal*. Then Kazen sat down after 15 hours straight.

The argument was advanced, Gonzalez said, that the bills had to be passed of necessity. "Necessity is the creed of slaves and the argument of tyrants. They have sown to the wind and reaped a whirlwind!" he shouted. A voice from the third floor behind the chamber shouted out to him to be quiet. It was Kazen, trying to sleep in his office. . . .

Gonzalez told of times he had been discriminated against because of his ancestry. "The Irish have a saying, 'It's easy to sleep on another man's wounds,'" he said. "Well, what's the difference? Mexican, Negro, what have you. The assault on the inward dignity of man, which our society protects, has been made. . . . We all know in our hearts and our minds that it is wrong."

At 9 o'clock [A.M.] Kazen returned from his rest, and at 9:07 Gonzalez got his first relief with a long question. All day, as citizens and representatives flowed in and out, he held forth, now repeating himself more. . . . In mid-afternoon he read from the *Columbia Encyclopedia* on anthropology. He chewed on a lemon rind and ate from two boxes of raisins.

About 3:30 [P.M.] negotiations started for a compromise. At 5:07 Lane asked him if he had yielded the floor, because he was sitting against his desk. At 5:13 his friends came to him and asked him to quit. They had received a firm offer from the majority to pass the annual sessions-annual pay resolution; Gonzalez's slum clearance bill, which is still pending, had been mentioned to him. Lane wanted one bill passed then and one more Monday — with no promises on the others. Otherwise, they threatened, they would pass three or four when he quit.

"Henry," said [Bruce] Reagan to Gonzalez, "I think we ought to go." Willis told him they were going to move the previous question. Reagan said something to him about getting "urban renewal up." Hudson said, "We've done all we can, Henry." Owen said to him, "It's how far we're gonna push the chair."

Gonzalez replied to them: "I think compromise on one, you're sunk on all. They're fanatical!" He told a reporter, "Everybody agreed to a compromise, but I'm not. They're gonna have to shut me up. Hell, they don't compromise, they're fanatic on these bills. I think I'm going on all night and half the morning — I mean till noon."

At 5:31 Lane moved the previous question. The vote was 12-12; [Lt. Gov. Ben] Ramsey broke the tie in favor of the motion. When Gonzalez sat down, debate would be over. He started talking again. Even in the thirteenth hour, he was gesturing with enormous energy, and his voice was strong. . . .

Governor Daniel came in again. He heard Kazen and Gonzalez discussing whether an item of punctuation was "two dots or a dot and a comma." Kazen: "Curricula, curricula . . ." Gonzalez: "Not lum?" Kazen: "Senator, please don't interrupt me." . . .

At 1:30 [A.M.] Gonzalez took off his shoes and walked around in his yellow socks, answering questions. He was very tired, lurching about, moving his arms and legs disjointedly, and leaning on the desks often; but he said he was fresh and ready for more.

About 1:45 Lane came in unhappily. They would pass only HB 231. The call for a quorum went out and the senators started dragging in sleepily. The voting was finished, the Senate adjourned. People gathered around Gonzalez's desk. "I could have gone on to 8:30," he said. But it would have been no different then, he said. "The next time," he said, "we'll make it more extensive."

He had held the floor 22 hours and two minutes. He and Mrs. Gonzalez, and Senator and Mrs. Kazen, went on home to bed.

A Smart Man Won't Get Bloody

WILLIE MORRIS

APRIL 21, 1962 — "He was the original wheeler and dealer, the biggest wheeler and dealer there ever was," one citizen of Pecos, that dry and forsaken township in far West Texas, says of another and more troubled one.

Curious that he, and others like him, use the past tense. When Billie Sol Estes had just been freed on $100,000 bond, his vast empire crumbling under multiple charges of fraud, he told a reporter: "We're making an awful fight of it. We're going to pull out, you bet. We've got friends rallied to our aid all over the nation — friends we didn't know we had."

What drives work on a man who will define his professional ethic: "A smart man is one who can win the battle and not get blood all over him"? What strange sources shape his contradictions: fundamentalist Christian and liberal Democrat; idle dreamer and architect of a thousand pyramid schemes?

He preaches occasionally for the Church of Christ, and once he gave a pink church to the Negroes. Ten years ago the Jaycees named him one of America's "ten outstanding young men." He threw a barbecue one night that cost $35,000. During the 1952 election, he was about to corner the market on parakeets, and he was going to set several thousand of them (which he had caged away in some little town) loose over big Northern cities — after they had been taught to say, "I like Adlai."

West Texas folklore has it that he was given a lamb at the age of 13 and five years later he had built up $28,000 in capital. Others in Pecos remember him coming to town with one battered suitcase when he was

25. By the time he was 37, he was said to own or control something in the vicinity of $150 million.

Estes brought in a daily newspaper last year to oppose the highly conservative semi-weekly *Pecos Independent*. When the *Daily News*, the Estes paper, tried to drive the *Independent* out of town by sharply undercutting on advertising rates, 28-year-old Oscar Griffin and 38-year-old Alan Propp of the *Independent* decided to do a little undercutting on their own.

For years there had been talk around town about Estes' financial dealings. Griffin overhead some talk in a barber shop about ammonia tanks. The two of them began to investigate.

In the eleven-county area there were supposed to be some 33,500 tanks, which Estes had used to obtain mortgages. About $34 million in such securities had been passed along to finance companies, but 33,500 tanks were enough to stock an average-sized nation. Where were the tanks? The newspaper, without mentioning names, decided that most of them didn't exist except perhaps on paper. It cited one man who listed only $60,000 in personal property and yet who theoretically owned $1.2 million in ammonia tanks.

A few weeks later representatives of 12 big finance companies met in Dallas. What followed continues to make headlines. Estes and three associates, Harold Orr and Rual Alexander of Amarillo and Coleman McSpadden of Lubbock, were later indicted by a federal grand jury in El Paso on charges of committing 57 overt acts of fraud. The indictment charged that the four men schemed to defraud nine of America's largest finance and investment companies. Estes' bail was set at a whopping $500,000, the largest in a civil suit in Texas history. It was later reduced to $100,000. The others are out on $25,000 each. Estes' financial empire has gone into federal receivership.

. . . In earlier courts of inquiry, witnesses [who were fertilizer dealers] testified that Estes sold fertilizer to farmers for $60 a ton, when it was costing at least $90 a ton, in an effort to undercut them and run them out of business; that he stored almost three million bushels of grain for the federal government in 1959, rising to 5.6 million in 1961; that Commercial Solvents of New York manufactured fertilizer for Estes at about $30 a ton and sold it to him for $90 and over; and that Estes owed Commercial Solvents $5 million, having turned over to that company some $6 million in three years which he had received as government fees for grain storage.

[Texas Attorney General] Will Wilson called Estes a "Washington operator," and said "much of his rapid expansion was based on the fact that he could get grain for storage," under the federal crop storage program. "From that he pyramided it into the sale of anhydrous ammonia fertilizer and the financing of ammonia equipment. It is already apparent that this promotion results from loose money."

. . . A witness in Plainview quoted Estes as having said: "I am Commercial Solvents." A fertilizer dealer, complaining that Estes undercut him and drove him out of business, said the young financier bought him out for $25,000. The witness said Estes commented: "We'll just temper the rod with a little mercy." . . .

This Man George Bush

EDITORIAL

OCTOBER 30, 1964 — Let us look steadily upon this man George Bush, outwardly so graceful and amiable, who is asking to be our senator.

He is opposed to hospital care for the aged under the social security principle, and he argues against it with the sophistry that it requires working men to pay for rich men's medical care, although this is obviously a minor imperfection having nothing to do with the main thrust of the program.

He is opposed to federal aid to build college classrooms.

He is opposed to the area redevelopment act that gives assistance to fledging industries and to communities in trouble. His theory is that it is not proper to assist "failing industries" and "dying towns," because their failing and dying is simply competition at work.

He is opposed to the entire idea of a war on poverty by government action. He dismisses it with a reference to the "suntan project" of the thirties, the Civilian Conservation Corps, which he says failed, although in fact it built many of our parks and kept many youths from roaming the streets jobless.

Not only a dedicated Republican, he is also a dedicated right-winger in his party. He was a key figure in the Goldwater movement in Houston and helped lead Texas Republicans gung-ho into San Francisco, there to unleash on the country the campaign of fear, hate, and character assassination that has now sickened this land. He introduced Goldwater in Fort Worth saying he was "honored to be on the ticket with Goldwater." He said last week in Forth Worth that he "enthusiastically supports" Goldwater. He is part and parcel of this Goldwater disaster.

Presenting himself as "responsible," he says his conservatism is "compassionate," yet he has so little sensitivity for the feelings of the needy aged; he wittily compares medical care for the aged with a federal program to air-condition ship holds for apes and baboons, a program which he has dubbed "medical air for the caged."

He represents himself as in favor of equal rights for all, and he opposed, before and after passage, the 1964 civil rights law.

He says he is above a "personal" attack on [Ralph] Yarborough, yet he calls Yarborough a turncoat and the teller of a filthy lie; far from apologizing, as he should, for his oft-repeated unfair arguments about Yarborough and Estes, he has ventured himself into character assassination by asking, as late as last week, in the Estes context, "What is the price of a United States senator?"

In foreign policy, also, this young man confirms his identification with the far right wing of his party.

He says that the United Nations is "deficient" and has not preserved the peace. He would prejudge a pending controversy in the UN, requiring that all nations pay their dues or get out, at the risk of wrecking the UN completely. Yet Gallup found that nine out of ten Americans approve of the UN.

He proposes that the United States arm a new invasion of Cuba. Specifically, he says we should recognize a Cuban government-in-exile, give it economic and military assistance and then, "When this government goes to liberate its own homeland, let's not be lacking in courage." This is the vacant posturing of Goldwaterism, the adventurism heedless of nuclear risks that we cannot tolerate any longer.

However nice a guy Bush is, however much he sends young matrons who are not well informed on issues, this is no responsible politician: this is a product and creation of the extremist-infected atmosphere of the Texas Republican Party.

We endorse Ralph Webster Yarborough for re-election.

A Conversation with Miss Jordan

INTERVIEW

MAY 27, 1966 — Unless circumstances take a sudden and unexpected turn, Miss Barbara Jordan, a Negro, will take her seat in the Texas Senate next January, representing the eleventh district in Harris County. This month, some 25,000 voters in that district selected her by a margin of two to one over State Rep. W.C. (Charlie Whit) Whitfield, who had served four terms in the Legislature before trying to step up.

. . . A child of the Houston ghetto, Miss Jordan practices law from a walk-up office on Lyons Avenue, in the steamy middle of that city's Fifth Ward. Her offices are a cool, elegant oasis.

She works in a small room with a huge desk and a high-backed leather chair much like the one she will occupy in the Senate. On the desk are scattered briefs, newspapers, law books, campaign material, and letters to be signed, and there is a small brass version of the scales of justice.

Miss Jordan is a large woman who wears dark, severely tailored clothing. She has an infectious campaigner's grin, which alternates with a stern set of jaw, when she is concentrating on something, which molds her features into a bold likeness from some dark Roman coin.

She uses her hands when she talks, and the way she talks is unusual — a striking compound of Houston and Boston, clipped sentences delivered in a measured tempo, a rather deep voice which converts anecdotes to pronouncements with a querulous twist at the end.

In her words, this is her story:

"I was born in what is now the eleventh senatorial district in the Fifth Ward, is what it's called, and went to elementary school out here, high school and after graduation, went to Texas Southern, and got a bachelor's degree in political science and history. After graduating there, I went to Boston University Law School and got a law degree, and got admitted to the Massachusetts Bar and the Texas Bar, and started practicing law. (I did not practice in Massachusetts. It was just after graduation, and I took the bar exam because I was up there.) I had always intended to practice in Texas.

"Nobody in my family is a lawyer, although I understand I have a great-grandfather, at least I *had* one, who was a lawyer, but no one in my family is a lawyer or interested in law, particularly. I did not come from a middle-class family. My mother was simply a housewife and my father was a Baptist preacher, who supplemented his income by working as a checker in a warehouse. He was just very wise in managing the little money that he had. He put it into my education and the education of my two sisters.

"When I was in high school, everybody was trying to decide what they wanted to do and what they wanted to be, and I was among them. I was in the 10th grade. One day we had a high school assembly program and Edith Sampson, who is a Negro woman lawyer in Chicago — she's a judge now there — she was guest speaker at this program, and at that time she was an alternate delegate to the United Nations. Well, I sat there in that auditorium, and I listened to her talk, and by the time she got through, I just knew that I was going to be a lawyer, that was just it. I saw her about four or five months ago, when I was in Chicago, and we got together and had lunch. I told her then, and she was quite pleased — in fact, she was quite emotional about it — that this was the thing that made me go into law.

"There were very few women students in my freshman class at Boston U. There were 300 freshmen law students, and of that 300, about six were women, and two of the six were Negro women, and I was one of the two. Of that, 125 made it out, and only two women survived, and that was the two Negro women. We survived it, and it's really fantastic; we laugh about it now.

"My family thought I was just out of my mind. Literally. They said, 'Why don't you just do something safe and sound and practical like teach school?' I just determined that I wouldn't.

"When I got out of law school in 1959, I needed some money to open a law office, so I took a job teaching political science at Tuskegee

Institute in Alabama, for one summer, and saved every nickel that they paid me, and got that money and came back here and opened a law office.

"Tuskegee disturbed me, and I think it was the most frustrating summer I've ever spent. I got the job because they had just fired the political science professor for activities that they considered to be against the best interest of Tuskegee. Teaching political science, I understand he had the students reading things like Karl Marx and they were quoting him, and that kind of disturbed folks at Tuskegee. I stepped into that situation and stood it as long as I could, which was one summer. I could not have been in the permanent employ of that school.

"I think that when I first got involved in politics was when I first got involved in law.

"At the time, the Kennedy-Johnson campaign was just getting underway, and, of course, I was just a lawyer with no business and I was interested in the campaign, so I called around to find out where I could go to do something, and I ended up at the Harris County Democrats' office. Of course, nobody there knew me, but I just offered to do what I could do, so I addressed envelopes, and I licked stamps.

"One night, somebody who was to make a talk at the Rev. L.H. Simpson's church here in the Fifth Ward didn't show up and they asked me if I would do the reading of whatever had to be read. I said I'd be happy to — anything that needed to be done, and I did that, and ever since then, it looks like I've been shot into political orbit.

"I ran twice for the Legislature — 1962 and 1964. I had about 46,000 votes in '62 and about 62,000 in '64; these are county-wide races. Now I think we have the best district in the state from which a Negro might be elected.

"There is a commission studying the city charter at this time, and one of the things that they're going to talk about will be carving the city up into districts so that city councilmen can run from a given district. Now, they run at large. As long as it remains as it is, with a city-wide or a county-wide race, the chances are going to be very, very slim for a Negro. It takes too much money, and the votes of those who would be interested in seeing a Negro get elected would be diluted by the votes of those who are not interested in seeing one elected. The only solution to this is going to be to carve the city up into districts and get the commissioners' precincts districted on a proportionate population basis. I suppose a lawsuit similar to the one that gave us redistricting on the state level is a possibility. The prediction can safely be that eventually, this one-man vote kind of representation is going to be translated in terms of local politics.

"My organization is a combination. I'm on the ticket of the Liberal Democratic Coalition and, insofar as a cooperative effort on my part, working with them wherever possible, we're using that existing structure on the Coalition. There are people who are personally committed to my campaign, and I do hope to hold them intact after the election is over so that we won't have to start from the beginning every time a Negro decides he wants to run for something. I think that we do have the makings of an organization with some degree of permanence."

. . . Soon after the campaign started, [Charlie] Whitfield and Miss Jordan sought the endorsement of the liberals who call themselves the Harris County Democrats. Miss Jordan won the endorsement handily, and Whitfield led his followers out of the meeting to stage a rump meeting of their own. The *Observer* asked Miss Jordan about what happened that night.

"I wouldn't call that a rump group. The press — the [Houston] *Chronicle*, at least — carried the story with a headline: 'Liberal Democrats Split.' Well, there were more than 900 people at that meeting, and about 50 walked out. I don't think that's very much of a split. And the ones who walked out were people who had not worked with the Harris County Democrats anyway, and were not a part of the structure of it, and didn't really go along with the program, but simply were people who had been brought in. Whitfield had made every effort to get them there, too. He had run an ad in the paper asking all of his friends to come out, and he sent letters telling them to come out and 'let's make our stand tonight.' He made every effort that he could to get his friends to the meeting. And I guess all 50 of them showed up.

". . . Let's say organized civil rights work has been tangential with me. I have always been active with the NAACP here. I have always served on the board of directors of the Houston branch, and now since we have broken down into several branches, I'm on the board of the branch which is in this area, and I have given it financial support and have helped in its programs in any way that I could. This has been a major part of what I've done in the civil rights movement.

"When I got back here to start practicing law and establishing myself, most of the demonstrations in Houston were over, and the situation was going into a kind of a lull with the accomplishments that have been made under the Progressive Youth Association.

"I think the civil rights situation here is in kind of a lull. I think that there is unrest among those Negroes who have never been involved in the middle-class civil rights organizations like the NAACP. Unless somehow we break through the crust and get down to those people who really have not received any benefits whatsoever from the gains that we consider we've made in Houston, then we will be in trouble. The city administration has to understand this, as well as everyone else that has anything to do with it.

"We can go into the cafeterias, the movies and the hotels. And, of course, these are status gains, as far as I'm concerned. Until we get the welfare gains, we are not going to see any progress over here on the North Side. The reason why the people live in these shanties over here is because they can't earn any more money to improve their houses. Until we can really break wide open this problem of training and employment, there will not be significant gains made over here in the North Side. I could care less about eating at the counter at Woolworth's. I guess some people think this is the height of their ambition. This is all fine, and it removes the visible traces of discrimination, but the underlying cause — the eating cancer of the whole business — has really never been attacked over here. I'm just still looking forward for the day when it will be.

"I realize the point where we have to start is education, and I don't mean that we have to delay everything until we make everybody Ph.D's.

"There are proposals and programs that the liberals of this state have always been interested in. Bob Eckhardt has done a very excellent job in trying to push them, and I'm just going to step up and follow suit on industrial safety, effective air and water pollution, and minimum wage — all of the traditional programs we've always been concerned about. I think we need a sound and resolute voice pushing these things. I also expressed great concern, in the campaign, over Charlie Whitfield's support of the city sales tax in the last session of the Legislature. A source of funds for this state is always an issue, and I understand that there's going to be a necessity to find new sources of revenue, and I want to try to protect the working man's pocketbook when we start this kind of a discussion.

"[Negroes] needed a victory. . . . A victory in a body like the state-house will do more to help the Negro recognize his voting strength than anything I can think of.

"I don't feel the effect of any militant attitude on the part of Negroes here. . . . I have heard anxieties expressed that we're really sitting on a powder keg, that it might blow up overnight, any minute. I don't think we are that close, but . . . I think that there's still time to avoid this kind of explosion. I would say less than a year. I would say that we ought to start working now. I've heard people say that it will be this summer or this fall, at the latest, that something could happen.

"You see, the problem in Houston is the age-old problem of communication. Nobody is working on it — not the Houston Council on Human Relations, not the NAACP, or anything else. This is something that we've got to break through somehow, and bridge the gap.

"I guess you have read the statements that the mayor has made: 'This couldn't happen in Houston. This community has such a high employment that it's just not ripe for this kind of situation.' So long as this is the attitude expressed by the administration, I suppose we can expect that nothing will happen from this level.

"If the people see that there is an opportunity to break through the crust of the structure without being an Uncle Tom, without selling your soul, or without being militant — just to present yourself as a candidate of quality asking the opportunity to represent the people of a district — if they can see that this approach does have the chance of succeeding, I think we will have more Negroes seeking political office."

Governor Kennard Has a Day

LARRY L. KING

MAY 9, 1969 — From my vantage point near the punch bowl, it appeared that State Sen. Don Kennard served Texas as its governor-for-a-day by doing it minimal damage — a claim not easily made in behalf of his predecessors nor in the names of the more spirited camp-followers gracing the Austin festivities. Some may insist that Governor Kennard did little to raise the cultural flags of Texas in offering greasy barbecue accompanied by Ernest Tubb and the Texas Troubadors on the Capitol grounds at noon, but these are a pretentious few who shall not be heeded by the enlightened, foot-stompin' majority.

It could be that several million Texans slept or bumbled their way through the entire Kennard administration abysmally ignorant of the Fort Worther's rule, for no public mandates attended his ascension nor was the throne seized in fire and blood. No, Senator Kennard as president pro-tem of the Texas Senate was merely accepting the ceremonial due of that office in his proper turn; consequently, he refrained from dangerous experiments with democracy.

Gov. Preston Smith and Lt. Gov. Ben Barnes honored protocol in departing the state so that Kennard might enjoy a one-day gubernatorial reign, and though this was doubtlessly sporting of those fine gentlemen one hasn't the gall to claim that thousands missed them or that any strangleholds of power were broken. There was, however, enough drinking and (some say) adequate wenching coinciding with the Kennard administration so that no hasty gubernatorial breaks were made with a past of many years standing. We traditionalists found this comforting.

Governor Kennard did break with the past, however, in refusing to use his day on the throne as an excuse for an off-season Christmas. So many expensive gifts (cars, money, color TV sets, diamond-studded do-dads) from sources suspected of special axe-grindings have visited governor-for-a-day ceremonies in the past that pharaohs, potentates, and possibly the Aga and the Ali Khans may have stared in awe and envy. Governor Kennard (who managed publicly, if humbly, to compare himself with the Kennedys and Andy Jackson within the first 15 minutes of his rule) opted against material tributes in favor of throwing open the governor's quarters to The Folks. Some twenty-seven busloads of Kennard's Tarrant County constituents invaded Austin, along with favored old cronies from other Texas points, plus a few outlanders from Oregon and the District of Columbia. More than 2,000 of The Folks were made of such stern stuff as to run the culinary gauntlet of the Odessa Chuck Wagon Gang, many of the survivors going on to sip punchless punch in the rose garden behind the Mansion while being serenaded by any number of cowboy Paderewskis. Puritans will be happy to know that motel reunions among many old friends involved less sex than reminiscences.

During a rare lull at the punch bowl, your correspondent claimed the podium to deliver a rose garden oration on Texas governors past, present, and future. Praise of a sort was bestowed upon Governor Kennard, and other of our native heroes, customs, and institutions. This oration was received with less thoughtful appreciation and thunderous ovations than one might have hoped; I particularly resented the balding fat cat who remarked, at its conclusion, that to call me a son-of-a-bitch would defame dogs more than mothers. But then he was probably in the oil business.

Near the shank of the rose garden ceremonies Governor Kennard received a Hoss Cartwright hat from Sheridan Taylor, a Fort Worth attorney, and took it like a man. After reciting his proper thank-yous he made the most sensible suggestion any Texas governor has ever uttered within my hearing: "Now let's all go drank us some whiskey." This unexpected burst of leadership was convincingly cheered by the masses.

Billy Kugle, himself a former Texas legislator and thus no stranger to the whiskey-drank, tossed an artful example of same at the Villa Capri on Saturday night. Along about midnight, as the clock ticked doom for Governor Kennard's brief brush with glory, His Excellency walked to the edge of the swimming pool diving board while Doug Crouch of Fort Worth led the assembled patriots in a bellowed rendition of "The Eyes of Texas *Were* Upon You." Adventurers assumed that Governor Kennard would hurl himself into the pool, fully clothed, as the last thrilling notes and his gubernatorial commission faded away. The old pro-pol proved he had mastered the art of compromise by hurling nothing more weighty into the water than his drinking tumbler.

On the Sabbath morn, Kennard's minions and vassals awoke to contemplate sadly a fallen hero. State Sen. Charles Wilson, of Lufkin, saved the day by hosting high atop the Westgate roof a champagne brunch. Though blonde Jerry Wilson had matchbook favors on hand proclaiming no message other than the painful one, "Ex-Governor Kennard," many of the assembled continued to treat the Forth Worth senator as courteously as if he actually amounted to something.

This group allegedly was made up of what Texans considered to be "Liberals," though Rep. Ben Atwell of Dallas was on hand in an admiral's summer whites with short pants, proclaiming that as a freshman legislator many years ago he had charted a course of wisdom religiously calling for him "To vote with the conservatives and socialize with the liberals." Admiral Atwell was not the only Texan to choose peculiar dress, there being a high percentage of mod turtlenecks, blazers, ascots, baremidriffs, bell-bottoms, mini-skirts and other sartorial delights. An old snuff-and-overalls relic like Land Commissioner Jerry Sadler, who had just ordered his employees to shave their sideburns and lower their skirts before Hell caught up with them, might have suffered apoplexy. It's a damned shame the commissioner missed the party.

Perhaps helped along by the Wilson bubbly, "Governor" Kennard announced his "cabinet," made up of many old cronies from among the political, academic, and literary worlds of Texas, and which, as his enemies spread the word, contained three pot smokers and two prominent thieves. During this ceremony there ensued the following exchange.

Senator Wilson (After conferring with a black waiter): "Governor, I got a man here says you forgot to appoint a Soul Brother to your cabinet."

Governor Kennard (After a 23-count hesitation and with an uncertain grin): "Well, Barbara Jordan couldn't make it."

Senator Wilson: "Well, you gotta name *one* Soul Brother."

Governor Kennard: "Well, send that fella there up here."

Senator Wilson: "Naw, he's got to serve drinks."

Governor Kennard (Pointing): "Well, how about *him*?"

Senator Wilson: "Naw, he's got to mix drinks."

At this point there approached my present wife, who though sweet and precious beyond any standard measurement is handicapped by not being a native Texan. "Didn't you tell me," she demanded, "that this group constitutes the Texas liberals?"

I admitted this was so.

"Then will you explain that little scene about the Soul Brothers?"

I said I was afraid I could not.

"Did you not explain to me about the oil business and the Alamo? Didn't you explain dust-storms and rattlesnakes' habits and dirt-daubers and Billie Sol Estes and the politics of HemisFair?"

"Yes," I said, "but some things just can't be explained. Not even in Texas."

This Man Yarborough

EDITORIAL

FEBRUARY 20, 1970 — With Ralph Yarborough facing two rich candidates of the special interests this year, we shall not lack for set campaign career summations about the senior senator. Let me offer, rather, samplers from my idiosyncratic Yarborough Reader.

As chairman of the Senate's Labor and Public Welfare Committee Yarborough has had a great deal to do with the improvement of ordinary people's lives, and he will play a central part in future reforms in medical care. "In America," he said in the *New York Times* May 9, 1969, "we have the concept of health industry, not health care. There hasn't really been any move from medicine for money to a full-fledged concept of health care for all our people."

In San Antonio last month he added, "Our medical science is unquestionably superior. But we haven't brought it to the mass of the people." His committee will give immediate attention, he said, to medical costs and insurance against them. "That will bring us face to face with the hard question of the organization and delivery of health care."

He says that of about 40 million Americans living below the poverty level, only 7.5 million are receiving Medicaid benefits. "We're squandering our national resources in Vietnam at the rate of $3 billion a month. The average Mexican-American lives ten years less than the average Anglo-American. And that's not genetic. It's the lack of food. One doctor testified before our committee that more money was spent conserving migratory birds than is spent on health care of migratory workers."

The allocation of $2 billion, the cost of 20 days of war in Vietnam, could end the hunger problem in the United States within a year, Yarborough says.

There has been an attempt by the two men running against Yarborough to classify themselves as dewy-eyed youths and him as an aging rooster. Compared to the 66-year-old Yarborough, those two guys think like Rip Van Winkle before he woke up. And when Lloyd Bentsen, Jr., announced, Yarborough said that if Bentsen could campaign more hours than he could, he'd get out of the race, adding, "My father lived to be over 100. We Yarboroughs don't get really efficient until we are 70 or 75."

Among the many causes Yarborough has championed and brought to fruition, bilingualism shows how young he is in his mind and his values. For generations Texas schoolmarms punished Mexican-American children for speaking, even whispering, in their native tongue when they arrived in school often not knowing as much as a word of English. Yarborough almost single-handedly has turned that around, making the cherishment of one's mother tongue, whether Spanish or English, one of the fundamental values of the public schools in the bicultural Southwest.

Speaking at the American Association for the Advancement of Science in Dallas in 1968, he said, "There is no doubt that the language barrier faced by youngsters of the ghetto is in every sense as real and as impenetrable as that faced by the child who speaks no English at all; he is penalized by the educational system, chastised as being ignorant when that may not be the case, and turned down when he seeks any kind of employment that involves communication.

"It is through language and through language alone that understanding can be achieved. In many ways we are prisoners of our tongues; faced with beauty or faced with terror, words escape us."

Yarborough is a scholarly, brilliant, widely-read man. He has a large library, loves books, and collects and proudly shows off rare ones that he has picked up rummaging around used book stores. Accordingly, he respects, although not foolishly, men of arts, letters, and ideas. . . . The consensus now is that Bentsen, with all his money, the old Shivers machine, and the natural reactionaries behind him, will mount a solid challenge, but that Yarborough should take him with votes to spare. Bentsen, after all, is special interest personified, and Yarborough is the people's interest personified.

One close observer of Yarborough, who has watched him in Texas courtrooms many times and regards him as one of the shrewdest, ablest rough-and-tumble lawyers in the state, hopes that the senator's proven sixth sense in politics and his mastery of public affairs will not lull him into that characteristic failing of successful, high-up politicians, excessive confidence in their ability to extemporize pointedly. Yarborough, says this friend, should give time, before each major appearance, to finishing his speech in his mind before he makes it.

Yarborough is expected to face his most serious challenge this year in November rather than in May. For that very reason, however, it is important that he finish as far ahead in May as possible.

This man Yarborough is the substance and the soul of progressive politics in Texas. He licked Shivers. He took on the bedsheet brigade [the KKK]. He beat the states' righters, the federal-haters. He called down the Texas Rangers. He fights for workers in a non-union state. He was for Adlai Stevenson when Lloyd Bentsen was running for cover on the tidelands issue, he was for John Kennedy while Lloyd Bentsen was busy piling up dough in Houston, he was for Eugene McCarthy while the wizen-worded men running against him were having their drinks at their country clubs, he is for the poor people, whatever their color, and the ordinary middle-class people, and the farmers and small businessmen, and he wants this damnable war over and the killing and maiming stopped. He has earned everything we've got.

In short, in the matter of Ralph Yarborough's re-election don't trust anybody under 60.

An Interview with Maury Maverick Jr.

MICHAEL VANNOY ADAMS

AUGUST 7, 1970 —

> During the 1960 Presidential campaign, Maury Maverick, Jr., was
> in charge of the arrangements for Sen. John Kennedy's visit. Ken-
> nedy gave a speech before 10,000 people in front of the Alamo;
> when he had finished, Maverick and the other local Democratic
> leaders took him and his party on a tour inside. One of Kennedy's
> men said, "Maury, let's get Jack out the back door to avoid the
> crowd." Maury replied, "Hell, there's not a back door to the Al-
> amo. That's why we had so many dead heroes." Unfortunately
> a reporter from a San Antonio newspaper overheard this remark,
> and the next day the headline read: "Maverick Says No Back
> Door." This kind of wit can be expensive, especially with a re-
> porter around, and Maury wrote an abashed apology to the
> Daughters of the Republic of Texas.
>
> —Willie Morris, *North Toward Home*

A decade has passed since Maury Maverick, Jr. appeased the little-old-
lady guardians of Lone Star history. So far, the ghosts of Travis,
Crockett, and Bonham have spared the San Antonio lawyer. Unlike
those frontier Texans, Maverick survived. He knew the wisdom of
retreat.

The irony to Maverick's off-hand humor is not that his joke was
taken too seriously but that it was not taken seriously enough. He really
meant it when he suggested that live heroes are better than dead heroes,
that live humans are better than dead ones. The past four years he has
been trying to open backdoors, frontdoors, sidedoors — any kind of
exit — for young men who rebel against America's present-day version of

the Last Stand: the Vietnam war. He says he is motivated by pure hatred for the Southeast Asian conflict. And on those few occasions when this negative enthusiasm flags, a quick visit to San Antonio's Brook Army Medical Center renews his determination: "Just walk through those orthopedic wards once. And look at those kids who got their arms and legs blown off in Vietnam. All that some can do now is rock back and forth to keep their circulation going."

As one of the few Texas attorneys who cares or dares to take draft cases, Maverick has helped dozens of resisters at the administrative level. This stage of the work entails preparing conscientious objector briefs for presentation to local draft boards. He is prohibited, as are all other lawyers, from representing his clients in person before the boards. He has choice words for the restriction: "As Senator [Ralph] Yarborough pointed out on the floor of Congress, this is the only United States court in which a man is denied legal representation and in which he can receive the death penalty. Suppose a man really is a conscientious objector, and yet he gets killed in Vietnam just because he couldn't have a lawyer stand up for his rights? I go down to the draft board with every client and beg to be let into the hearing, but they say no every time."

Even so, his clients have had better luck at the administrative level and at the federal appeals court in New Orleans than they have had in district court, where cases go once a board turns down a C.O. applicant. "I had a client who was a Methodist preacher's son. He went to court and proceeded to invoke the name of Jesus Christ 18 times, the name of God 20 times and the names of various saints about six or seven times. The district judge turned him down anyway. But he won the appeal in New Orleans," Maverick says.

"I can't understand the difference, unless the district judges just don't understand the subtlety of the federal law as well as those on the higher bench. Of course, some Democratic judges are still afraid they'll be called communist if they rule in favor of somebody opposed to war. You'd think the damned Nixon Republicans would be tougher. But usually they're OK. We Democrats just go crazy on communism and crazy on war, I guess."

Maverick says the really big obstacles to obtaining conscientious objector classification are two: The substantial evidence rule and proving a client's sincerity. According to him, the former "stipulates that if the government has any worthwhile evidence at all, the court must rule in its favor. In other words, a kid can have 90% of the evidence on his side, and the government can have only 10% on its side. And yet the government wins every time. That's sure as hell not 'proving guilt beyond a reasonable doubt,' if you ask me," he says.

The latter obstacle — convincing a board or judge of a client's sincerity — has been eased only negligibly by recent Supreme Court decisions (*Seeger* and *Welch*), according to Maverick. The average man probably believes the official removal of religious qualifications has made conscientious objection easier to prove; Maverick says not so. "Religion never was that big a problem. We could get by with mostly philosophical objections if we had any religion at all mixed in. I'd usually just ask my client if he believed in anything greater than man himself. Judges haven't ordinarily insisted on a three-decker God like military courts do. The army still thinks God's a seven-star general sitting in an easy chair, with colonels flying loop-de-loops around his head and saluting him."

Like many men who try to maintain some semblance of day-to-day sanity in the face of depressing circumstances, Maverick occasionally indulges in fantastic, yet half-serious, nonsense to explain the inexplicable. One hypothesis of his might be called the "Theory of Dissidence." By it he explains the origins of San Antonio's and Texas's anti-war sentiment. "This class of liberals and radicals emerging from the Vietnam war is unique," he says. "They don't come from the traditional sources. Over half of them are Roman Catholic, and most of the rest are Methodists or Baptists. The Episcopalians are all in the National Guard, the Jews all have spastic colons, and the Unitarians are all in Canada." As if by stimulus-response, Maverick's mustache always twitches into a smile when he hits "spastic."

Although he can joke about Unitarians emigrating to Canada and although he is working to keep draft resisters out of the military, he opposes the northward trek. It isn't that he has lost the wisdom of retreat in this instance, he says. It's just that he does not regard a stretch in the penitentiary as too awful a burden to bear for the good it might do in dramatizing the draft and war. He even says he believes yielding to induction is better than fleeing across the border.

"First of all, these young men should realize that in all probability they'll never be able to come back. But more important, they ought to realize that if they really want to end war, the way to do it is to stay here and resist. The only good I can see in going to Canada would be if the 75,000 American boys already up there would cross en masse back into the U.S. about two weeks before the next Republican and Democratic national conventions. They could just smile and ask, 'What are you going to do with us?' You see, the problem is not just Vietnam but a hundred more Vietnams on the way. If we don't stop the military now, we'll end up murdering the whole world.

"Daddy Warbucks capitalism is over with. And we've got to realize that. The best thing we can hope for in these developing nations is democratic socialism — and we've got to help that come about. If we keep killing instead, we're going to push them into a Stalinist-type communism — and it'll be the Democratic Party that does it."

By the same logic, Maverick also opposes a volunteer military. According to him, it would "mean that instead of becoming the incipient new Nazis of the world, we would become just plain out and out Nazis. A conservative friend who is a professor recently told me 'we want a volunteer army just like you liberals do.' He said that in the future we'll have to go into more places like Cambodia and the Dominican Republic, and that a draft army just wouldn't be gung-ho enough to win. He said it'll be a matter of survival. Well, hell, if he's right, I don't know how important it is to survive.

"I take considerable solace in the knowledge that in a draft army you have loud-mouth, bellyaching Private Ronnie Duggers raising hell, writing their congressmen, going to court, and telling the army to go screw itself. There may not be a lot of hope with them, but there would be none without them."

Maverick says the way "to get the Duggers into the army" is to do away with the II-S student deferment. As he sees it, abolishing the four-year educational reprieve is the key to stopping the war. He reasons that putting an end to the university haven would bring Vietnam's horror home to America's middle and upper classes, which so far have been able to buy their sons' safety with college tuition. According to Maverick, extending the draft equitably across all social strata would jolt the silent majority into exercising its collective vocal cords. Spiro's [Vice President Spiro Agnew's] fan club would start yelling for peace too, he says.

"If at midnight, when the dead soldiers' bodies roll into San Antonio from the West Coast — if those coffins started rolling into the well-to-do sections of the city, that's when you'd see the war end. You see, all the protest up to now has come from the middle class. Although the average white isn't affected nearly as drastically the poor, the black or the chicano, he has the education to know when he's getting screwed and how to fight back," Maverick theorizes. Consequently, he says the way to hike the protest volume is to spread a fair share of the war burden over more of those whites who have a suburban home with two cars in the garage.

Trying to involve poor Mexican-Americans and blacks in war resistance by convincing them of draft discrimination is largely ineffective, he says. To both minority groups, the problem of Vietnam is remote and unreal . . . : "Blacks and Chicanos are having too much trouble just surviving to worry about peace. Besides, they say the army gives them a better standard of living and more democracy than they get in civilian society. That's a damned sad commentary, isn't it?"

Old-fashioned ideas about proving one's manhood also confuse the issue, Maverick says. He calls the Chicanos "the biggest dopes in Texas because they don't understand the patriotism hoax the establishment is playing on them." According to him, the Mexican-Americans on San Antonio's West Side are taken advantage of by military propagandists who play on the Chicanos' traditional concept of family honor.

Lest the false impression be created that Maverick feels draft-age Chicanos should be neglected while war dissent is fomented among middle class whites, it is necessary to mention his close cooperation with San Antonio's draft counselors. Three young resisters, all about half Maverick's 50 years, run a store-front operation two blocks from the attorney's office. Maverick has defended two of them in court — one on a C.O. application and the other against a charge of trespassing on a military base. The playful verbal jibing that goes on among them is evidence of the affection and respect they hold for each other. The liberal Maverick speaks of former VISTA volunteer John Dauer as a "truly non-violent, peaceful person." The radical Dauer praises the help "Mr. Maverick" has been to him and others. On Maverick's office wall hangs a framed thank-you letter from Dauer — testimony to the successful two-year struggle to keep Dauer out of the American eagle's claws.

Dauer and his cohorts concentrate their counseling effort among San Antonio's poor, Chicanos and blacks. When a white comes to them for answers to his draft problems, they respond. But they do not spend their time hunting middle class draft-eligibles to advise. They believe that most whites have more than adequate access to lawyers and counselors.

Their reasoning is a simple sort of economics — allocating one's resources where the need is greatest. Immediate profit is not their motivation. If it were, they might be too discouraged to continue. Despite repeated efforts to awaken an anti-draft consciousness among San Antonio's Mexican-Americans, Dauer and friends have met little success. Last spring they mailed out 800 letters to graduating Chicano high school students: included was an interview with a Mexican-American ex-Marine who said he would not volunteer again unless he was "starving to death." According to Dauer, only about 25 Chicanos responded to the offer of free draft advice. Still, the number was no surprise, he says. He explains it in terms straight from Maverick's vocabulary: "The poor just don't have the free time to sit around and intellectualize abstract peace-war ideas. Chicanos have to deal with the gutty issues of life in their daily struggle to survive. What political effort they put forth is channeled through the Mexican-American Youth Organization [MAYO], and MAYO doesn't regard Vietnam as one of their most pressing concerns.

"What we have to do at this stage is not draft counseling, but draft education," he says. "For example, we have to show MAYO how ROTC in the West Side high schools not only makes army recruitment easier, but also how it ruins the educational atmosphere. We have to convince the individual Chicano that he's being discriminated against in the draft. We have to fight the fatalism that accompanies the idea of 'serving one's country.' We have to show these people that you don't have to go kill and be killed — that there are other alternatives."

Dauer unfurls rolled-up maps of San Antonio to illustrate his contention that Chicanos are discriminated against in the draft. The ink representation of the city is divided into draft board sections, and Dauer immediately points to an incriminating statistic — only one Mexican-American serves as a board member. That man was appointed as a result of his and the other resisters' political agitation. Then Dauer's index finger traces a line around the West Side and hesitates momentarily on a few of the red crosses that make the map look like a Florence Nightin-gale memorial.

"These are the Chicano dead," he says solemnly. "One of the San Antonio newspapers printed statistics that showed the percentages of Mexican-American war casualties were in line with the percentage of the city's Chicano population. The comparison was supposed to prove that Mexican-Americans aren't discriminated against in the war. What it neglected to mention was the old idea of 'defending one's country.' Chicano America is different from defending a three-bedroom home in Alamo Heights or Terrell Hills. Why should a Chicano be obligated to risk his life for a country that really isn't his at all?"

Last spring, Dauer and company ran a counseling station on the West Side. They rented an office next door to the area army recruiter, taped a peace sign on the window and tried to counteract the military's presence. They left after a month, at the landlord's insistence. But they say they will be back somewhere on the West Side this fall, if not in a permanent location then perhaps with an arrangement with high school officials.

"We would just like an equal opportunity to explain the draft. The army recruiter has his day, so why can't we? A lot of Chicanos run into trouble because they don't understand selective service technicalities. How to appeal a 1-A classification, for example. One 20-year-old who was having trouble graduating lost his deferment this spring. If he had known the appeal process, he could have delayed final action until the fall, when he could already have been enrolled for another year. That way he could have finished his education before going into the army. Now he'll be a permanent drop-out — just because he didn't know the loop-holes."

One reason Dauer feels such an intense commitment to keeping Chicanos out of Vietnam is his pessimism. Unlike Maverick, he empha-sizes the immediate situation. That is, he believes Chicanos and other minorities will continue to be the main victims of the war. He has no real hope that the government will ever reform the draft so that whites will be threatened. He does not see a time when middle class Americans will rise up and force an end to the war.

"I know Nixon has said he'll end college deferments this fall," he says. "But I doubt it. It's an election year, and it would be suicide for Congress to alienate all those voters whose sons are safe in school. So our main job still is going to be helping those who can't take refuge in college, buy a psychiatric deferment or otherwise get out of the draft."

Dauer points to the protest button on Maverick's coat lapel. Despite the orange surface, its message comes across appropriately in Spanish slang: "*Chale con el draft*." Or, as Maverick translates, "Screw the draft."

No "Remember the Alamo" psychology there. One wonders what the Daughters of the Republic of Texas would think.

Texas Needs Farenthold

KAYE NORTHCOTT AND MOLLY IVINS

MARCH 3, 1972 — Until quite recently, the *Observer* tried to avoid considering this year's governor's race because the trio of announced candidates left us in a deep funk. And then a rare and lucky thing happened. A politician we believe in entered that race. We are struck by the singularity of that event. One who works closely with politicians is not apt to have many heroes among them. . . . And in Texas, it is possible to go through a political lifetime with no opportunity to be grateful only for lesser evils.

We have read back through the *Observer*'s endorsements over the years and are saddened by their consistent pain and tepidity. With the exception of endorsements for Ralph Yarborough and Don Gladden, these old typewriters have not had much enthusiasm tapped out on them. It feels good to be doing this for someone as fine as Frances Farenthold.

Farenthold is not a bleeding heart liberal, and we do not use that term pejoratively. If a few more hearts bled a little more, we might all be better off. But while Farenthold is not without compassion for the maimed of this society, we doubt that compassion is the primary motivation of her public life. We have found that she acts out of an implacable sense of justice.

Her passion for justice seems to have been both inherited and trained into her. Her grandfather was a well-known judge and law professor and her father, a strong influence in her life, was a prominent lawyer in Corpus Christi. Her own legal career has been heavily weighted on the side of those who are fashionably called "the oppressed." Before she came to the Legislature in 1968, she was the director of Legal Aid in Nueces County.

Her approach to problem solving is almost invariably legalistic. One of her constituents once came to her office to recite a horrible tale of human suffering caused by bureaucratic sloth. All the others in the office muttered, "How awful. That poor child." Farenthold's only apparent emotion was an edge in her voice as she said, "That was unconstitutional on three grounds," and then proceeded to cite them.

Her lawyer's mind was reflected in both her major battles in the House — the Sadler resolution and the effort to get the Legislature's role in the Sharp banking bills investigated. She is no demagogue to stand and make emotional denunciations: she simply worked and worked and worked through the system, through the rules, through the law. . . .

For the *Observer's* money, marbles and chalk, Sissy Farenthold has got more guts, brains and integrity than the other three candidates in the gubernatorial race added together and multiplied.

. . . O.K., so white liberals are a bad joke. O.K., so Texas liberals are a national laughingstock — petty, disorganized and more prone to fight one another than the perverted priorities of the people who call themselves conservatives in this state. We don't give a damn. GET UP OFF YOUR BUTTS AND MOVE. This woman is worth fighting for.

George Christian: The Lobby's Mr. Big

JO CLIFTON

FEBRUARY 2, 1979 — George Christian, 52, former newsman, press secretary to President Lyndon Johnson and to Govs. Price Daniel and John Connally, now calls himself a public affairs consultant. He counts among his clients the Texas Association of Taxpayers (which is made up not of common taxpayers but of about 2,000 corporate members such as Exxon, Dr. Pepper and Rockwell International), the Texas Association of Bank Holding Companies, the Texas Savings and Loan League, and the Texas Ophthalmological Association, as well as the Motion Picture Association of America and the Associated General Contractors of America.

Christian's office, 18 floors above Austin in the garish-gold American Bank Tower, is that of a journalist turned rich — it's not ostentatious, but conspicuously expensive. Seven enormous windowpanes form two walls of his office; mementos from various clients and from his years with LBJ accent the room. An old manual Royal typewriter sits in an honored position close to his constantly ringing telephone. During an hour-and-a-half interview, Christian took calls from Mark White, Robert Strauss, Austin pollster George Shipley, and Tom Hagen, a former Christian employee now on the staff of U.S. Sen. Lloyd Bentsen. This consultant is as well connected to the Democratic establishment as anyone in Austin, and such connections are his primary stock in trade. Indeed, no member of the Texas House or Senate is as well connected as George Christian, and when he calls one of them, it's almost flattering and plenty effective.

Christian, who quarterbacked the successful fight for coal-slurry pipeline legislation during the last session of the Texas Legislature [in

1977], doesn't like to think of himself as anything so crude as a lobby-ist. "I do so little lobbying," he says, and he is surprised the *Observer* considers him as such. But we do. Not the old breed, to be sure, but the epitome of the new breed — the sophisticated, low-key "Austin repre-sentative." In fact, Christian is at the head of his class. He tells other lob-byists what to do, gathers them in his office and advises them, coordi-nates the efforts of various business groups trying for the same goal, as he did in the coal-slurry fight.

Although he refuses to say how much his clients pay, he smilingly con-cedes that he is making money. Mostly, he says, he charges his corporate clients by the hour, just as lawyers do. But also his fee depends on what he has to do to persuade the media and the Legislature that his client's position is the one they should embrace. The cost depends on "how many points I use up," he says. "Most of what I do involves news-papers," and he clearly cannot run down to the *Austin American States-man* every day on every account without losing the attentive ear of its editorial writers. So Christian gauges how much of his political capital he must expend and charges accordingly. And if he must actually contact a member of the Legislature, then the price goes up. In 1977 Christian's point man for direct lobbying was Hagen, now press secretary to Senator Bentsen. Companies like Eli Lilly, a pharmaceutical firm that opposes passage of legislation allowing pharmacists to substitute generic drugs for brand-name remedies, have their own individual lobbyists, Christian says, but bills like the one proposed last session by then-Rep. Mickey Leland "bring out a team effort," so there are many lobbyists united either for or against such measures.

It's hard to understand how anyone, except a drug company, could oppose a bill allowing substitution of less expensive drugs for more ex-pensive brands when all companies must meet the same federal mini-mum standards for quality. Christian admits that at first "it looks like a rip-off. That would be my reaction if I didn't know anything about it." However, he says that once he has analyzed all the pros and cons, it's generally "not all that difficult to accept the client's position." So this year, he probably will be involved again in an effort to prevent drug sub-stitution bills from being approved by the Texas Legislature.

Christian's personal feelings? "I personally feel the way my client feels," he states matter-of-factly. He says he doesn't represent clients if he disagrees with their philosophy or what they're trying to accomplish. He also refuses to engage in losing battles and won't represent clients whose interests might be in conflict with the goals of his number-one account, the Texas Association of Taxpayers.

Why does he represent only conservative kinds of groups, mostly corporations? For one thing, they were the ones who gave him business when he returned to Austin ten years ago. And as the years went on, more and more businesses were added to the list. Now Christian can pretty much choose his clients — and he chooses "not to mix apples and oranges." So he will not do anything "contrary to the business viewpoint." For example, Texas Woman's University asked him for help in gaining a new medical school, but he had to refuse, because "most of the people I represent think we have enough" medical schools.

"I've got a philosophy of government that fits my clients," says Christian. He broadly describes that philosophy as one of "fiscal responsibility." What that means to his clients is that Christian will fight whatever will cost them money, and he will promote whatever will help them make money, either in the area of taxation or in state spending. . . .

Even though he was registered as a lobbyist for the big consumer finance companies in 1977, when they were seeking rate increases, Christian says he never actually did any person-to-person lobbying for their bill. He subcontracted that job to long-time Austin lobbyist Randy Pendleton. Christian's work for the Texas Consumer Finance Association involved advising the group on its public image, which was no small task, since nobody loves a loan shark. Says Christian, "They had a good case, but it was hard to sell. [Sen.] Bill Patman cut it to pieces" in his successful fight against raising rates on small loans.

Christian says he is not involved with the loan company battle this year but he has signed on to help the Texas Savings and Loan League in its efforts to raise interest rates on home mortgages above the "usury" level of 10 percent. His work on this issue, mostly already done, involves selling Texas newspaper reporters and editorial writers on the line that there will be no home loans in Texas if the usury ceiling isn't lifted. Christian says that all he'll do is tell them that California, which has no limit on mortgage loan rates, will get all the Texas loan money and home-seekers here will be left with none. Christian tells the story well, and a number of Texas editorialists and business writers have swallowed it whole. He speaks in well-modulated tones and presents facts to buttress his every assertion. And Christian's preaching on behalf of the savings and loan industry is echoed by the realtors and home-builders all across Texas, who have had lobbyists touching base with local papers and legislators. No one is doing any comparable PR on behalf of borrowers so it looks as though there's only one side to the story.

What about the other side? Does it bother him that small business, farm, and consumer borrowers aren't represented? Christian's answer, stated without tongue in cheek, is that the argument against raising the ceiling is "so weak and ill-formed" that no one will listen. He predicts that the battle will be fought early in the session and his side will win.

One reason for the early battle is that legislators have already been inundated with information on the mortgage-interest-rate issue in their hometowns. Christian and his long-time friend, Austin ad-man Jerry Hall, joined forces in 1978 to make their case with local news editors and legislators, and they favor an early run at passage before any opposition has a chance to form.

Christian explains that this kind of "grassroots lobbying" was used two years ago to convince the Legislature to approve Dolph Briscoe's $528 million highway bill, which was passed in the opening days of the session. "Before the legislators got to Austin in 1977, they were made familiar with the problems in 1976 by groups like local chambers of commerce, highway people, tourist organizations, auto and truck people — everybody who has anything to do with highways and streets. That is the most effective type of lobbying." Add to that "media awareness," and you have a form of persuasion that far transcends the old formula of booze, broads, and bags of money traditionally associated with lobbying. It's expensive, but pays off for the clients who can afford it.

Christian's expense reports filed with the secretary of state's office certainly reflect the low priority he puts on the care and feeding of legislators. For example, he reported spending only $46.05 for entertainment on behalf of Houston Natural Gas, his coal-slurry client during April of 1977. He concedes that some members of the Legislature spend a lot of time being wined and dined at the Headlines Club, a few doors away, but he adds that those members are few. "The entertainment factor is pretty far down the ladder in lobbying these days," says Christian.

So, if freebies are not the answer, perhaps it's really in campaign contributions? Well, the legislator "does remember if he got help from some organization," Christian agrees. "But I don't know how the poor senator or representative sorts out how to reward one group and punish another, when so many groups contribute to the same candidate."

The real key to persuading most legislators is "appealing to reason," says the eminently reasonable Christian. Give them information and give information to their staff members — who have become very important in recent years. Once a member or his aide gets to know a lobbyist, knows he can trust the lobbyist not to mislead him, then the lobbyist is doing his job, according to Christian. A lot of lobbyists are "very good at maintaining relationships," he says, adding, "a legislator expects you to be partisan," so any lobbyist who doesn't put forth the strongest possible argument for his client's position is "picking the client's pocket."

Well, what about the public? Isn't the average Texan, who can't afford to hire a Christian, left out by this influence peddling? Christian asserts that as a plain citizen, he feels he is "not represented in a lot of things up here either," but he says with a straight face that the little folks can rely on "our representative government" to serve them fairly.

"I think it works. We've got a good Legislature. The public is well represented by the Legislature. Now the influence imposed by all the business and labor and teacher and consumer groups — that's important," Christian says. The idea that business has more power than other groups or exercises undue influence is just flat wrong in his opinion: "If the Legislature were in the pocket of business, it wouldn't be necessary for business to spend so much money lobbying. . . . Ultimately things work out and ultimately the public is represented by the people they elect. By and large, from my vantage point, I like the way it works."

The Second Best Little Whorehouse in Texas

A. R. "BABE" SCHWARTZ

AUGUST 14, 1981 — This is not really a story about a house of ill repute "for working girls." It's more of a tale about 25 years in a place where everybody hustles in different ways. One does not always get to know all the others in the Biblical sense, but one certainly learns about them in every other way.

The Texas Capitol, built for habitation by giants, has always been occupied by some giants and some pygmies. The giants who roam those grand chambers and halls are stars on stage. Like all stars, they are surrounded by groupies, and as is true for all groupies, the wish of the star is instantly met by individual groupies or by the whole group. There are the young groupies, and then there are the old ones, lobbyists of one brand name or another.

I was a young groupie and later a star, and now I'm an old groupie. It was and is all good. In our "Lege" (Molly Ivins' tag), humor was the music that soothed the savage beast during the day, and at night it was country music. The members loved every minute of it. We could even work and "grade the silk" at the same time. (Secretaries used to be permitted at members' desks during the session.) Through it all the Legislative Wives (that is, the wives of the House members) and the Senate Ladies are reassured by the oldest adage for political wives: "Never fear dear, they may roam, but they always come home."

Well, almost always. Some go to hell in a basket, damned by new habits of excess in all things — the classic blondes, bourbon, and beefsteak syndrome. Some go to the Congress. Worse excesses. Some just go a hundred yards from the House to the Senate. It is often said that that raises the average IQ of both bodies. Some of us lucky ones, for our eternal reward, even die and become lobbyists.

Dick Slack, when asked why in the world he ever stayed in the House 25 years, allegedly answered, "Have you ever lived in Pecos?" For my 20 years in the Senate I have no answer that anyone could understand. Galveston has been Heaven for 55 years, and I know there is evenly divided sentiment from friends and enemies alike that I should have stayed there.

It started for me in 1955 as a freshmen House member when almost everybody was a bigot, a racist, and a good old boy. The Texas rule for getting elected since Reconstruction days was simple. It was a nice, safe place to be a Democratic WASP. Some Catholics, an occasional Valley "Meskin," an accidental Jew every 50 years (I was #2), and absolutely "no niggers." Only a few of us liberals steadfastly refused to refer to Mexican-Americans and blacks in the common parlance of the day — damn few folks were even nice about it. In Fort Bend County they still had a "Jaybird primary" for white folks before the regular Democratic primary. Republicans in Texas snuck into the legislature by special election contests where runoffs were not required — and then were more promptly defeated in the next regular election.

The result of all this was a great sterile cubicle of rural conservatism cast in concrete, being chipped away at by the D. B. Hardemans and Maury Mavericks, the Barefoot Sanderses and Bob Eckhardts, and defended by the old-line combinations such as Swindell, Cheatham, and Fly. (Bill Swindell, Tom Cheatham and Bill Fly were three conservative members of the time. I liked to combine their names into a symbol for the joint venture that the majority seems to me to be.)

The memories of the great two-act play of my four House years came together in a sweet and sour rush. The taste of blood from a few victories paled by comparison with defeat after defeat on issues of simple social change in a state owned and operated by big oil, big business, and big agriculture.

My life-long affair with politics, which had started when I tried and failed while still in law school to get elected to the House, was a constant tug-of-war between love and hate. Day in and day out, some giants rose to the challenge of battle against the old conservative line with no hope of victory but with the certain inner confidence that change would come sooner or later.

Old Conservatives are defined well by Mort Sahl as those who say, "No, we ain't gonna never change nothin', never." We had plenty of them. New Conservatives are those who say, "Sure we'll change that, and it needs changing, but not now!" We believe some of them, but I lived long enough to see the New Conservatives grow into Old Conservatives.

I witnessed great men trying to accomplish a few small things and failing because everybody does whore. (I did, too.) The fix is in, or the vote trade is made, or the Speaker says not this year, or the Governor will appoint my cousin to the egg-grading board. We all knew the game; it's only the price that changes from time to time.

I remember great moments when we minority dissidents (everybody who dissented in those days was sooner or later called a communist) stood at the front mike in the well of the House telling the world confidently that it would be all different in ten or 25 years when Texans learned that the Establishment's evil ways had depleted our precious natural resources, used up our irreplaceable water in the west, polluted our pristine environment with toxic chemical wastes, and generally fouled our nest while paying minimal or no state taxes. Yes sir, you just wait 'til the folks look back and see what you old conservatives have done to them while they were bent over the plow, or the kitchen sink, or looking for the soap in the shower.

Well, we waited! What a change! Big oil, business, and agriculture have screwed, blued and tattooed Texas for 25 years and the folks are still eating out of the hands of their oppressors. . . .

In retrospect it's easier to see who screwed who, but even at the time we didn't need a crystal ball to see that if the legislative and executive branches were whoring, it was the folks who were getting screwed.

Damn. I remember D. B. Hardeman and Maury Maverick losing a battle in 1955 to raise the food allowance in mental institutions from, say, 54 to 97 cents a day and the *Dallas Morning News* captioning the next day's story, "Liberals run amuck in the House." Great bleeding hearts! In '57, when I proposed an amendment on an appropriation bill to spend a million dollars to open a completed, but long-vacant section of a building at John Sealy Hospital in Galveston as a Children's Hospital, I succeeded only because Col. Ed Winfree of Houston stomped down the center aisle to speak after me and jabbed the House air full of holes with his gold-headed cane telling 'em how it is to be crippled.

During the segregation battles of the same years we all got cards in the mail making us honorary members of the Ku Klux Klan, and I got up in the House and renounced the membership because one couldn't be an honorary member of a dishonorable organization. The threats came by the score, but the best news came in the next mail advising me that I couldn't be a member anyhow because I was ineligible as a Jew. Thank God for little favors.

Barefoot Sanders let me co-author the Mental Health Code, and we bled all over the House floor for a modicum of justice and rights for the mentally ill. Twenty years later, I heard a newer liberal member of the Senate refer to our noble work as a cruel hoax perpetrated upon the mentally ill under the guise of rights. I told him about the good ole days when as a boy prosecutor every Friday afternoon I sent hundreds of mentally ill, and some folks who were just senile, to Rusk State Mental Hospital on the decisions of juries from the park across the street from the courthouse (no wine bottles in the jury box, please). Our bill was a milestone then, but happily it was not the end of progress.

Blood was going to run in the streets if the schools were integrated. Whites and blacks would NEVER mix. A bill passed the House declaring that a person who belonged to the National Association for the Advancement of Colored People would be ineligible to work for any public entity in Texas. I publicly said this was an outrage and unconstitutional and an unconstitutional outrage. They all laughed and snickered and without apology, shame, understanding, or conscience, voted for that and eight more of the worst racist bills ever passed in the United States. It was my introduction to how much some folks lust to keep a piddling little old elected job in the legislature.

I never even felt sorry for the ones who thought it was right. Ignorance is easy to forgive even in a bigot. Joe Chapman, an author of one of the worst bills, became an East Texas district judge. With a bigot on the bench, who says justice is blindfolded? I hurt deeply for the ones who voted wrong and knew better, but it was a wasted emotion. They all survived just fine and in later years several went on to higher office with solid minority support.

I guess I fared as well as any "aginner." A fellow told me after I made the first speech against the bills in committee and on the floor that he was going to miss me, since I was a dead duck politically. I agreed, since 87% of my constituency had voted for all the proposals in a state-wide referendum earlier that year. (Not many blacks voted in those days. The good old poll tax.) To stay in politics by giving up one's basic principles was like being invited to join an exclusive club that you knew was vile. One can live without the honor better than with it. I just told the fellow in good humor that I wasn't sure I wanted to stay in a club whose standards were low enough to have me.

As it turned out, though, I stayed around 25 years on principle. I think he got beat when he changed the squirrel season in his home county. . . .

"The good ole days" weren't so good. The business lobby dictated the terms of workmen's compensation laws, and injured workmen were denied decent compensation and cheated out of adequate medical care. Unemployment compensation was called "Pennies" by the unemployed and appropriately. Labor and the Texas State Teachers' Assn. were the only people's lobby in Austin. They still are alone for all practical purposes except for the consumer lobby and various environmental groups. Sometimes the Texas trial lawyers do the people's work. In Texas, where it is needed the most, Common Cause is a failure for reasons still vague to all of us.

It would all get better when we won the redistricting cases. Then the minorities would integrate the legislature, even for Republicans, and we would storm the walls of the King's castle. They did and we did but we are the same. The longest journey does indeed begin with one step — in my life, with my one step to the Senate. For 20 years some of us worked to persuade the Speakers, Lieutenant Governors, and Government to let Texas make a little progress. I tilted at all the windmills and at least for a time my enemies were equally divided — 15 on each side of every issue. I was happy when Oscar Mauzy came to the Senate, because then we each had one friend.

History reflects that our gains were far exceeded by our losses. As our hospitals got better, our prisons got worse. Our schools got better, but parents say Johnny can't read, or add, or subtract. Federal Judge Wayne Justice had to first impose a federal court order upon the state to achieve the humane treatment of juveniles in our state facilities, and then in 1981 he had to require change and supervision of our prisons, where 3,000 prisoners slept on the floor each night.

. . . Only in Texas can all God's children sustain such wonderful, logical conclusions. . . .

Franklin Garcia: A Union Man

RUPERTO GARCIA AND FRANCES BARTON

FEBRUARY 10, 1984 — There weren't a lot of people at Franklin Garcia's funeral. It wasn't because he was not well-known; he was that. He was common ground for a lot of people involved in issues and movements across the state, and sometimes, when two activists met for the first time and weren't sure what each other had been involved with, Franklin's name would pop up and there they were: common ground, you see. No, it wasn't because of that.

It was, probably, because he didn't want his death advertised so much. And so, each of us, his family and friends, had called each other quietly and ended up there, some 80 people huddled together against a sunny chill—45 degrees at 3:58 P.M. after the service, according to a local bank off IH-410 East in the north side of the city, San Antonio. The graveside service was held around one of those small, green tents one usually sees in a cemetery only from a distance, put up for family and close friends. Around it, in what was once an open field, small, white, table-like gravestones stood quietly in formation in Ft. Sam Houston. Since the end of WW II, when Franklin left the navy, it was probably the only time he'd been in a formation of any sort.

Above the tent, a bluejay sitting in a leafless tree watched the ceremony draw quietly to a close: a priest said a few general words about dying and friends, about eternal life and the hereafter, then sprinkled a little holy water here and there, said a final prayer, and began to dismiss us.

The service shouldn't end so quickly, I thought. It wasn't the way Franklin would have wanted it. He liked to draw things out: relationships extended over years through surprise phone calls out of nowhere, slowly sipped beers, and long conversations.

But just as the priest began to dismiss us, Franklin's son stopped him and turned the service over to Tom Walker, who made his way to the front, said something quietly to Franklin's wife and daughter, and began to tell stories about Franklin's life. And as Tom talked, looking at a notepad in his hand to recall dates and places where they had worked together and known each other, others began to add their own stories from where they stood — about how they'd met Franklin, and how they knew him, and about how his death had affected them even more. And by the end of the funeral, after we'd had our say about Franklin Garcia — and how he'd lived a good and full life — I felt a peaceful sense of closure for a man who'd been such an important part of us.

"Franklin Garcia," the San Antonio papers had said that morning, "was a union man."

Franklin worked as an organizer for the Meat Cutters from 1961 until he retired for health reasons in 1978. He had first become involved in the labor movement after the war, when he went to work as a machinist at the Temco plant (now LTV) outside Dallas. Franklin joined the union in that plant, local 390 of the Auto Workers, and after some time decided to run for chairman of the grievance committee. As his old friend and Meat Cutter co-staffer Paulia Weaver tells it, the UAW folks hadn't planned for Franklin to be involved in that election. But, she says, it was just typical of Franklin to foul up anything that was assumed foregone.

During the campaign, Franklin's organizing talent came to the attention of the Meat Cutters' Sam Twidell, who asked Franklin to go to work on a new project in the Rio Grande valley that came to be known as the South Texas Project. Franklin said, not yet, he had some unfinished business to attend to. So he continued to campaign for the grievance chair, won the election, and on the day he was to be installed in office turned around and quit the plant, saying he was on his way to South Texas.

He arrived there in 1961, talking up the industrial brand of unionism that had never before taken root in the Valley. But Franklin managed to organize plants there — some of the names come to me like a litany, Elsa Plastics, Booth Fisheries, Texsun — and as he organized plants, he organized minds, too, so that many of the people who joined the Meat Cutters locals in the Valley also became social and political activists. When the United Farm Workers Organizing Committee called a strike against La Casita Farms in 1966, Franklin was there to give support and to serve as a liaison between the Farm Workers and other unions, student activists, church people involved in social causes, Young Democrats, Democratic party regulars. The farm worker organizing effort grew into something of a movement, and Franklin's hand could be seen there in the background for those who knew how to find it — always in the background, for he was an organizer, not a front man.

Franklin moved his organizing base to San Antonio in the mid '70s, where he worked on the Handy Andy and Piggly Wiggly campaigns, among others. Tom Walker often visited with Franklin during this time, and Tom told us at the funeral how he remembers Franklin using a couple of rooms in the old Corral Motel in the San Antonio stockyards district as his office suite. Tom said that those rooms became sort of a nucleus that drew together people from South Texas. "I first met Jose Angel Gutierrez there," Ron said. "And I first met Willie Velasquez there; also Carlos Truan. Then when Franklin moved his headquarters into an old house on SW Military Drive, that's where I first met Cesar Chavez." But this was Franklin's way, his life and his work were the same; the people he worked with were his friends, and Franklin's friends had a way of getting to know each other and then going on to work together.

The cold weather didn't seem to matter as we stood there at the cemetery together and said these things. After Tom had had his say, and Maury Maverick, Jr., Roy Evans, and Franklin's brother Bobby Garcia had theirs, I had my own things to say about Franklin. I told about the time, just a few months ago when Franklin's health was taking a bad turn, that he called me, out of nowhere, and asked me if I wanted to buy his car. I asked him why he wanted to sell it, and he said he could no longer drive because he had lost his leg. And that's the way he let me know how sick he was getting to be. Not directly, but by asking if I wanted to buy his car. For this was his way, too. . . .

At the end of the service, when people had had their say, Frances Barton began to sing:

I dreamed I saw Joe Hill last night
Alive as you and me.
But Joe, says I, you're ten years dead.
I never died, says he,

I never died, says he.
Joe Hill ain't dead, he says to me.
Joe Hill ain't never died.
Where working men are out on strike,
Joe Hill is at their side,
Joe Hill is at their side.

Franklin Garcia was a union man. And while I stood there it occurred to me that of the people who care for the poor, and of those who work to amend social ills and fight for causes and against injustice, one had been removed. . . . He was young, only 58, and as much good as he did while he was around, one can never get enough of that, and we will miss him.

The Pols He Bought

ROBERT BRYCE

FEBRUARY 5, 1999 — John Sharp didn't lose to Rick Perry. Nor did Paul Hobby lose to Carole Keeton Rylander. Instead, the two Democrats lost their races [in 1998] to James Leininger's money. Leininger helped guarantee two loans — a $1.1 million loan to Perry on October 25 and a $950,000 loan to Rylander on October 1 — that likely made the difference in the races for lieutenant governor and comptroller, the closest races on the statewide ballot. Perry beat Sharp by 68,700 votes. Rylander beat Hobby by 20,223 votes, in one of the closest statewide races in Texas history. In each race, about 3.7 million votes were cast. Sharp lost by 1.8 percent of the vote, Hobby by 0.55 percent. Handicapping political races is an inexact science, and there is no way to prove that Leininger's loans were the decisive factor in the two races. "It's almost impossible to narrow down the result to a single thing," says Bruce Buchanan, a professor of government at U.T.-Austin. "But when the races are as close as those two races, it's reasonable to suggest that money like that may have made the difference."

Leininger's money certainly provided critical ammunition to both Perry and Rylander:

- More than 10 percent of the $10.3 million that Perry raised before the election came from the loan guaranteed by Leininger and two other businessmen.

- Nearly 25 percent of the $3.85 million that Rylander raised in the year prior to the election came from the loan guaranteed by Leininger and four others.

- On the same day Leininger's loan to Rylander was approved, her campaign wrote a check for $850,000 to National Media in Alexandria, Virginia, for media buys.

- Within five days of getting the money from Leininger, the Perry campaign spent slightly more than $1 million on media, with the bulk of that money ($966,000) going to David Weeks, Perry's Austin-based media consultant.

- Leininger's money came at critical times for both campaigns. When Rylander got the money from Leininger, she was trailing Hobby in the polls and was being outspent more than two to one. From July through September, Hobby had spent $3.7 million. Rylander had spent almost $1.7 million. In late October, when Perry got his loan, he was in a dead heat with Sharp, with polls showing both candidates with 37 percent of the vote. And Perry was being outspent by a margin of almost three to one. From July to September, Perry spent $2.3 million. Sharp spent $6.8 million.

Weeks, who made the media buys for the Perry campaign, discounts the notion that Leininger's money catapulted Perry to victory. "We stayed competitive all the way through," said Weeks. "Even without the loan, we would have been competitive."

But would Perry have won without Leininger's money? "Yeah, he would have won," said Weeks, who added that buying TV at the end of a campaign is difficult. "We did increase [TV] buys at the end of the campaign but not significantly. It was not a huge amount. We were already pretty maxed out. It's hard to plan for because you assume it's going to be sold out." Weeks conceded, however, that "every dollar helps. But it's an assumption to say [Perry and Rylander] would have lost without" Leininger's money.

Reggie Bashur, a political consultant to Rylander (and a paid lobbyist for the city of Austin) refused to comment, saying he is not authorized to speak for the Rylander campaign. Messages left for Scott McClellan, Rylander's campaign manager, were not returned.

Kathy Miller, deputy director of the Texas Freedom Network, has no doubt that Leininger's loan made the difference. "When you have a race as close as the Sharp-Perry race, one or two million dollars can make one, two, or three percentage points difference," she said. And Miller argues that Leininger's activities "undermine the power of the electorate to see what they want done. It weakens Texas' democracy."

Miller's group is one of several working to counter Leininger's influence. Recently, much has been written about the reclusive San Antonio hospital bed magnate, whose net worth has been estimated at $340 million. And to be fair, he did not provide the loans to Perry and Rylander by himself. The Perry loan was co-signed by chemical company executive William McMinn of Houston and telecommunications executive James Mansour of Austin, who chairs Putting Children First, the pro-school-voucher group that Leininger funds. Leininger and McMinn also co-signed the note for Rylander, along with Harlan Crow of Dallas, Kenneth Banks of Schulenberg, and J. Virgil Waggoner of Houston. (Waggoner and McMinn have also worked with Leininger in a successful tort reform campaign that involved funding elections and hiring lobbyists.)

Although the other co-signers have deep pockets, none have the network of influence that Leininger has. And none have dumped as much money into political campaigns as has Leininger. In 1996, according to figures compiled by the *Houston Chronicle*, Leininger's political contributions topped $550,000. His political donations and loans in 1998 may well exceed that amount. One member of the Sharp campaign estimated that Leininger, along with other advocates of school vouchers, contributed some $700,000 to Perry's campaign. As an individual, Leininger gave Perry $56,908. In addition, three of Leininger's brothers and his mother all gave money to Perry, with contributions ranging from $1,000 to $25,000.

Perry's connections to Leininger also include stock and airplane deals. Perry made $38,000 trading stock in Leininger's hospital bed company, San Antonio-based Kinetic Concepts. In 1996, Perry's campaign bought a 10 percent interest in a 1980 Piper Cheyenne I turbo prop airplane; Leininger and his brother Peter bought the other 90 percent of the plane. In 1997, the *Houston Chronicle* quoted Leininger as saying that Perry convinced him to buy the plane. "Rick's the guy who talked me into getting an airplane," Leininger said. In July of 1997, the Perry campaign bought the Leiningers' 90 percent interest in the plane for $346,000 — a price that Sharp loyalists claim was far below the plane's market value. Perry's campaign manager, Jim Arnold, defended the price to the

Houston Chronicle, saying the plane was worth less than planes of similar vintage because of the high number of hours on the engines.

The Leiningers also financed Perry's purchase of the plane. According to Perry's latest expense report, on December 1 the campaign paid Covenant Aircraft Investment Inc., a company run by Daniel Leininger, $3,040 for "airplane expenses." Perry's spokesman Ray Sullivan said the Perry campaign has "approximately $300,000 outstanding on the airplane loan" that was made to the campaign by Covenant. Sullivan said the Perry campaign makes regular payments to the Leiningers' company to pay off the debt on the airplane. Despite Leininger's close ties to Perry, Sullivan said that Perry "owes one group of people in Texas, and that's the citizens who put him in office and entrusted him with that office. He owes nothing to any of our donors and contributors. He owes everything to the citizens of the state."

The citizens may find reason to doubt Perry's reassurances, as Perry and Rylander are already working to stay in the good graces of the Texas Public Policy Foundation, a conservative, pro-school-voucher think tank that gets most of its financial backing from Leininger. On January 26, all the statewide elected officials including Governor Bush attended the T.P.P.F.'s tenth anniversary dinner at the Four Seasons Hotel in Austin. And on February 3, perhaps as a payback to Leininger, Rylander will deliver the keynote speech at the foundation's "1999 Legislative Conference," also at the Four Seasons. Topics for discussion at the conference include "government downsizing" and "school choice."

T.P.P.F. is working hard to shape this year's legislative agenda. It is also hoping to get conservative operatives into state jobs. The foundation recently formed a "job bank placement service." Its agenda, according to its web site, is "to help place conservatives with public policy oriented employers." Toward that end, T.P.P.F. has posted a long questionnaire on its web site (www.tppf.org), asking applicants, among other things, to indicate how much they agree or disagree with a list of statements including: "Communism has been sent to the trash can of history. There is no chance it will resurface as a serious threat to world peace." And, "Busing of school children to achieve racial balance is wrong." The application also asks applicants to rank their feelings toward individuals from a wide political spectrum, including Austin Democratic Congressman Lloyd Doggett, former Democratic Governor Ann Richards, and Nobel Prize winner

Alexander Solzhenitsyn. Others listed — presumably those more appealing to T.P.P.F. — include Governor George W. Bush, Senator Jesse Helms, Rush Limbaugh — and surprise! — Rick Perry and Carole Keeton Rylander.

In a January 8 column in the *San Antonio Express-News*, political columnist Rick Casey quoted T.P.P.F. president Jeff Judson saying that Rylander had given the group "strong encouragement" for its job-bank effort. Speaking of the comptroller's office, Judson told Casey: "That is the one institution that will probably use this more than anybody. Over time, there will be a shift of the focus of that agency. They'll need the people who are consistent with that policy."

Two weeks after Casey's column appeared, Rylander's spokesman, Keith Elkins, wrote a letter to the paper, saying that Rylander was "informed in passing of the job bank, but at no time did she support, endorse, or make any commitments about the service."

For his part, Perry made certain that he repaid Leininger's loan. Records show that his campaign paid off the $1.1 million loan on December 17, an amazingly quick turnaround. How did he do it? In part, by pressuring lobbyists. After the election, several lobbyists who had supported Sharp were contacted by Perry's campaign and told that they were expected to help retire Perry's campaign debt. In some cases, they were given specific amounts of money to raise and/or contribute, with amounts ranging up to $50,000. Said one lobbyist who asked not to be identified, "There was no direct mention of the Leininger loan, but you don't have to do any high math to put two and two together. Most of the people who were contacted understood where that debt came from." Republican Party political director Royal Masset even circulated a memo, advising Republican statewide elected officials to tell lobbyists who supported Democratic candidates that it was now going to cost them a premium to get on the "late train" with the Republican winners.

Sullivan insists no fundraising quotas were given and dismisses the complaints as "sour grapes from lobbyists whose guy lost the election." Perhaps so. But questions about Leininger's influence over Perry and Rylander will undoubtedly continue, particularly as the issue of school vouchers becomes more prominent. Sharp, an opponent of vouchers, says he has no choice but to admire Leininger's effectiveness. "I congratulate Leininger," he said. "He wanted to buy the reins of state government. And by God, he got them."

Cover, April 13, 1987. The English-Only Movement of the 1980s was a backlash against the growing power of poor African Americans, Hispanics, and immigrants in Texas politics—a coded form of racism that the *Texas Observer* marked in Jeff Danziger's cover illustration.

III. LOCAL ANGLES

WHEN THE FIRST ISSUE of the *Observer* rolled off the press in December 1954, Texans were only beginning to cotton to the enormous changes then shaking up the largely rural, agricultural state. The paired forces of industrialization and urbanization were given a multibillion-dollar boost from federal wartime spending, courtesy of Texas's long-in-the-tooth congressional delegation. This funneling of money only intensified during the cold war gold rush, and threw the Lone Star state's economy into high gear. Cities were the direct beneficiaries of the steady inflow of investment capital, and of the new work and cultural amenities it produced, leading migrants to pour into the booming metropolitan centers; Dallas and Houston especially grew at rapid rates.

What the new urbanites left behind were the occupations that had once tied them to the land, and the shrinking communities of the Panhandle, Hill Country, and Piney Woods that had depended on these former farmers, ranchers, and sharecroppers. Shed too were particular ways of thinking and being. So Thomas Sutherland affirmed in the very first *Observer*, in which he lamented the commercialization of experience, decried the demise of an older, oral culture, and lauded the good folk of another time.

Those who remained in those "dusty little towns" weren't all beneficent souls, Willie Morris countered in his 1950s sketch of the racism that festered in Boerne. Nor were they shy about embroidering the truth, Bill Porterfield gleaned from the conversations he had with the aging, rumpled men who rocked on the porch of the general store in the shuttered central Texas settlement known as The Grove; their losses were irrevocable, a partial consequence of being cut off from the modernizing impulse the war had unleashed.

Neither were the folk uniformly happy. Impoverished children could die early and hard, as narrated in Américo Paredes's short tale, leaving behind family and friends whose grief was choked off and who acted out in ways at once understandable and inexplicable. Those who hit the road to locate a new life — or simply left for the sake of leaving — found they were bedeviled by the same ills they sought to leave behind. Riding the rails was a powerful thread in the fiction of Amado Muro (Chester Seltzer), whose pen name masked his ethnic identity but did not hide his sensitivity to those who hopped freight trains, and in the cold confines of lurching boxcars gazed out on the twinkling towns through which they rushed, seeking there some measure of the human connection they could not find on solid ground. The hunger for a family of her own led one teenage daughter of Hispanic migrant workers to bolt, marrying her young boyfriend and seeking work to sustain body and soul. In this she was unsuccessful, and Ruperto Garcia shrewdly untangles the layers of response to, and responsibility for, her small tragedy.

True, the people had their moments, and some were right peculiar. Take the experience of trying to order a mixed drink in Texas in the 1960s. In his attempt to explicate the intricate dance between waiter, customer, and the bottle itself, Bill Helmer rings in a new kind of freedom. So does Gary Cartwright in his blow-by-hilarious-blow recounting of the filming of *Viva Max* (1969), a madcap rewriting of the fabled battle of the Alamo that ran into an offscreen (and implacable) foe, the doughty leadership of the Daughters of the Republic of Texas. The Daughters' daughters — real and imagined — could be just as stubborn (and naïve) as their mothers, a point that dovetails nicely with the parting shot in Molly Ivins's recounting of that day in 1970 when Ladies Lib was born in Texas: "Baby, you've got a long way to go."

How far and in what direction wasn't clear, for either gender. But that the contours of life were being redefined, that nothing was sacred, was clear from the *Observer*'s coverage of changing social mores. Buck Ramsey challenged the conspiracy of silence that enveloped the nuclear bomb-driven industrialization of Amarillo; David Denison's wide-eyed narration of the state's goofy ambition to bake the world's largest cake to honor its sesquicentennial gently mocks that aspiration; the haute bourgeoisie of Forth Worth find their comeuppance in Dave Hickey's parody of their antics, as does the National Park Service when in 1990 a group of Chicano militants, led by Rodolfo Acuña, takes an irreverent tour of the Alamo shrine. Another group on the margin sought to rewrite its place in the social order, and in Lars Eighner the homeless of Austin find a skilled advocate who knew their plight because he was one of them. Of all the local moments that went international, none could top the fiery end of the Branch Davidian compound in Waco. Robert Bryce evokes its aftershocks in his eulogy to Dan Mulloney, the cameraman who caught on tape the initial, fatally flawed ATF attack; although uninjured in the melee, Mulloney's psychic wounds festered, leading to his premature death; he was as much a victim of an overreaching government as the Davidians themselves.

Char Miller

Pushing Back the Loneliness About Their Fires at Night . . .

THOMAS SUTHERLAND

DECEMBER 12, 1954 — There is a proverb of the Texas border folk that says: "Se que la burra es parda porque tengo los pelos en la mano," and this freely in English means "I know the donkey's color because I have her hair in my hand."

Here in America especially, as a regrettable by-product of the general dissemination of reading and writing, we are much inclined to place our faith in organized communication and to buy that which is presented to us with pictures and bold print. The folk in their wisdom are much more cautious and are inclined to wait until they have the hair of the animal in the hand.

That is one reason why I place much faith in the folk and believe in the importance of the study of their ways.

I should like to define folklore as embracing everything that we learn from experience but not from school — all of man's ways and works that are not consciously demonstrated through his organized, literate means of communication.

As a result of the activities of folklorists, beginning little more than a century ago, we now have a body of folklore preserved in their collections of stories, songs, superstitions, rhymes, games, jokes and proverbs.

It is good to have this lore set down for us to read, for it is being drowned out by the machines and commerce of mass communication — by newspapers, radio, cinemas, and television, which seldom produce anything really amusing or very meaningful, being tolerated by the public only because their product is what comes to hand when the bored and suffering spirit seeks to escape, just as sick men do when they count the rafters in the ceiling or the panes in their windows. It is good, I say, that because of folklorists, when old men die a part of their experience will be kept for our children to remember as well as Mickey Mouse.

The ways, the customs, the lore that are not in the books may be found in all human activity. Even the schools, whose function is to improve and clarify the folk mind, cannot escape folklore. Rhymes are shouted year after year, generation after generation. Marbles and tops suddenly appear at a certain time of the year. You play hookey, go up the creek, and pick pecans, and tear off the green hulls, staining your fingers deep brown. You catch bumble bees (the kind that have a white dot on their hind end and don't sting you) and tie a string to them and turn them loose at the best moment to interrupt the class. . . . There is a prestige in having pecan stains on your fingers or appearing dumb and untidy, if you are a boy, or neat and intelligent, if you are a girl. All of this is folklore: folk attitudes and folk ways of school.

The world of folk ways and lore underlies everything that we do — all the institutions of men, such as family, church, state, school, and business. Each organism has its roots in the soil and special lore and customs. . . .

The men of folklore have done our urban age a service by setting down these various expressions of the imagination with which our people formerly entertained each other, pushed back the loneliness of their fires at night and reviewed the world as their souls had seen it.

In a Refreshing Provincial Way

WILLIE MORRIS

AUGUST 15, 1958 — A few days before the election, I went into my then-favorite liquor store to get a couple of six packs. The man behind the counter, an old Jewish fellow, was friendly enough. And I asked how he was voting for governor.

"I don't know," he said, with a heavy German accent. "How about you?"

"[Henry B.] Gonzalez," I said.

His eyes suddenly narrowed, his body tightened, he looked at me sharply and with hate. "Don't you remember the Alamo?" he said.

And then, more recently, over in Boerne, I was having breakfast on the porch of the Kendall Inn at a table next to a nice, talkative middle-aged couple from Houston, he a lawyer, she just graduated from college and proud of it, and of the Phi Beta Kappa key she wore on her bracelet. In the conversation I unwittingly suggested that school desegregation with all deliberate speed is now the law of the land. I was advised forthwith:

1. People with such radical ideas should have sore consciences.

2. Bright young men should know that the fourteenth amendment is unconstitutional.

3. The press is owned by the Jews, and the Jews above all others want mixing.

4. The department of education at the University of Houston isn't radical like the department of journalism, and besides it has all

the figures — blacks make lower grades on tests and are
basically inferior.

I left my eggs half finished and strolled over to the Boerne school-
house, where that very day the good old keep-'em-in-their-place philosophy was upheld by that touchstone of all else, the democratic process.
A community registered its decision: two (2) perfectly normal, reasonably bright, moderately well-adjusted young children were inherently
unfit to go to school with the community's Anglo-Saxon offspring
because their skin is black.

. . . All the elements of the story were there: a citizenry frightened into
reaction; a school superintendent who believed strongly but chose not to
cause controversy; a liberal young doctor with enough brains and
courage to relate his Christianity and his Americanism; a Baptist minister who said we whites are outnumbered and *better* be nice; a waitress
who said when you are in business you don't discuss controversial
things; a Negro family which watched patiently and submissively from
the sidelines, asking only that their children not be mistreated. (On the
porch of a little frame house we stood in the dark, the Negro grandmother and I. "Do *you* like colored people?" she asked, the irony of it
in her local pedigree, longer and older than the majority of the Germans,
whose ancestors fled old tyrannies and won land and the right of the
great grandchildren to vote on two little blacks.)

The good Anglo-Saxons of Boerne won their victory, just as the German Jew in the liquor store escaped Buchenwald to win his victory, just
as the Houston lawyer and his wife will fight to win theirs, and may win
it yet. History in fact relates many victories, for didn't the Spanish
butcher the Moors, and the Japanese mangle the Chinese, and the Germans murder the Jews, and the Jews mistreat the Arabs, and don't the
Africans loathe the French and the British, and vice versa and etcetera,
mostly in the name of certain folks' genes? In the midst of this great
complexity it should do our Anglo-Saxon hearts good to know that
dusty little towns can nurture such massive instincts and be downright
genetic, too, in a refreshing provincial way. In our dusty little towns,
with the irrelevancies and the sophistications stripped away, what we
see, we see bare and plain. Let simple hearts rejoice that no globes or
atlases or histories are needed when you have Boernes to study. You can

hold race there in your hand. For the truth is sometimes so terrifying in microcosm, why extend it? No need to suggest perhaps Boerne on August 2 was bigger, bigger yet, than Boerne on August 1, or to utter some apocalyptic nonsense that the long anguished march of human beings to something better and more right suffered deeply there.

The Hammon and the Beans

AMÉRICO PAREDES

APRIL 18, 1963 — Once we lived in one of my grandfather's houses near Fort Jones. It was just a block from the parade grounds, a big frame house painted a dirty yellow. My mother hated it, especially because of the pigeons that cooed all day about the eaves. They had fleas, she said. But it was a quiet neighborhood at least, too far from the center of town for automobiles and too near for musical, night-roaming drunks.

At this time Jonesville-on-the-Grande was not the thriving little city that it is today. We tolled off our days by the routine on the post. At six sharp the flag was raised on the parade grounds to the cackling of the bugles, and a field piece thundered out a salute. The sound of the shot bounced away through the morning mist until its echoes worked their way into every corner of town. Jonesville-on-the-Grande woke to the cannon's roar, as if to battle, and the day began.

At eight the whistle from the post laundry sent us children off to school. The whole town stopped for lunch with the noon whistle, and after lunch everybody went back to work when the post laundry said that it was one o'clock, except for those who could afford to be old-fashioned and took the siesta. The post was the town's clock, you might have said, or like some insistent elder person who was always there to tell you it was time.

At six the flag came down, and we went to watch through the high wire fence that divided the post from the town. Sometimes we joined in the ceremony, standing at salute until the sound of the cannon made us jump. That must have been when we had just studied about George

Washington in school, or recited "The Song of Marion's Men" about Marion the Fox and the British cavalry that chased him up and down the broad Santee. But at other times we stuck out our tongues and jeered at the soldiers.

Perhaps the night before we had hung at the edge of a group of old men and listened to tales about Anice-to-Pizana and the "border troubles," as the local paper still called them when it referred to them gingerly in passing.

It was because of the border troubles, ten years or so before, that the soldiers had come to old Fort Jones. But we did not hate them for that; we admired them even, at least sometimes. But when we were thinking about the border troubles instead of Marion the Fox we hooted them and the flag they were lowering, which for the moment was theirs alone, just as we would have jeered an opposing ball team in a friendly sort of way. On these occasions even Chonita would join in the mockery, though she usually ran home at the stroke of six. But whether we taunted or saluted, the distant men in khaki uniforms went about their motions without noticing us at all.

The last word from the post came in the night when a distant bugle blew. At nine it was all right because all the lights were on. But sometimes I heard it at eleven when everything was dark and still, and it made me feel that I was all alone in the world. I would even doubt that I was me, and that put me in such a fright that I felt like yelling out just to make sure I was really there. But next morning the sun shone and life began all over again, with its whistles and cannon shots and bugles blowing. And so we lived, we and the post, side by side with the wire fence in between.

The wandering soldiers whom the bugle called home at night did not wander in our neighborhood, and none of us ever went into Fort Jones. None except Chonita. Every evening when the flag came down she would leave off playing and go down towards what was known as the "lower" gate of the post, the one that opened not on main street but against the poorest part of town. She went into the grounds and to the mess halls and pressed her nose against the screens and watched the soldiers eat. They sat at long tables calling to each other through food-stuffed mouths.

"Hey bud, pass the coffee!"

"Give me the ham!"

"Yea, give me the beans!"

After the soldiers were through the cooks came out and scolded Chonita, and then they gave her packages with things to eat.

Chonita's mother did our washing in gratefulness — as my mother put it — for the use of a vacant lot of my grandfather's which was a couple of blocks down the street. On the lot was an old one-room shack which had been a shed long ago, and this Chonita's father had patched up with flattened-out pieces of tin. He was a laborer. Ever since the end of the border troubles there had been a development boom in the Valley, and Chonita's father was getting his share of the good times. Clearing brush and building irrigation ditches he sometimes pulled down as much as six dollars a week. He drank a good deal of it up, it was true. But corn was just a few cents a bushel in those days. He was the breadwinner, you might say, while Chonita furnished the luxuries.

Chonita was a poet too. I had just moved into the neighborhood when a boy came up to me and said, "Come on! Let's go hear Chonita make a speech."

She was already on top of the alley fence when we got there, a scrawny little girl of about nine, her bare dirty feet clinging to the fence almost like hands. A dozen other kids were there below her waiting. Some were boys I knew at school; five or six were her younger brothers and sisters.

"Speech! Speech!" they all cried. "Let Chonita make a speech! Talk in English, Chonita!"

They were grinning and nudging each other except for her brothers and sisters, who looked up at her with proud serious faces. She gazed out beyond us all with a grand, distant air and then she spoke.

"Give me the hammon and the beans!" she yelled. "Give me the hammon and the beans!"

She leaped off the fence and everybody cheered and told her how good it was and how she could talk English better than the teachers at the grammar school.

I thought it was a pretty poor joke. Every evening almost, they would make her get up on the fence and yell, "Give me the hammon and the beans!" And everybody would cheer and make her think she was talking English. As for me, I would wait there until she got it over with so we could play at something else. I wondered how long it would be before they got tired of it all. I never did find out because just about that time I got the chills and fever, and when I got up and around Chonita wasn't there anymore.

In later years I thought of her a lot, especially during the thirties when I was growing up. Those years would have been just made for her. Many's a time I have seen her in my mind's eye, in the picket lines demanding not bread, not cake, but the hammon and beans. But it didn't work out that way.

One night Doctor Zapata came into our kitchen through the back door. He set his bag on the table and said to my father, who had opened the door for him, "Well she is dead."

My father flinched. "What was it?" he asked.

The doctor had gone to the window and he stood with his back to us, looking out toward the light of Fort Jones. "Pneumonia, flu, malnutrition, worms, the evil eye," he said without turning around. "What the hell difference does it make?"

"I wish I had known how sick she was," my father said in a very mild tone. "Not that it's really my affair, but I wish I had."

The doctor snorted and shook his head.

My mother came in and I asked her who was dead. She told me. It made me feel strange but I did not cry. My mother put her arm around my shoulders. "She is in Heaven now," she said. "She is happy."

I shrugged her arm away and sat down in one of the kitchen chairs.

"They're like animals," the doctor was saying. He turned around suddenly and his eyes glistened in the light. "Do you know what that brute of a father was doing when I left? He was laughing! Drinking and laughing with his friends."

"There's no telling what the poor man feels," my mother said.

My father made a deprecatory gesture. "It wasn't his daughter anyway."

"No?" the doctor said. He sounded interested.

"This is the woman's second husband," my father explained. "First one died before the girl was born, shot and hanged from a mesquite limb. He was working too close to the tracks the day the Olmito train was derailed."

"You know what?" the doctor said. "In classical times, they did things better. Take Troy, for instance. After they stormed the city they grabbed the babies by the heels and dashed them against the wall. That was more humane."

My father smiled. "You sound very radical. You sound just like your relative down there in Morelos."

"No relative of mine," the doctor said. "I'm a conservative, and you know that I wouldn't be here except for that little detail."

"Habit," my father said. "Pure habit, pure tradition. You're a radical at heart."

"It depends on how you define radicalism," the doctor answered. "People tend to use words too loosely. A dentist could be called a radical, I suppose. He pulls up things by the roots."

My father chuckled.

"Any bandit in Mexico nowadays can give himself a political label," the doctor went on, "and that makes him respectable. He's a leader of the people."

"Take Villa now — " my father began.

"Villa was a different type of man," the doctor broke in.

"I don't see any difference."

The doctor came over to the table and sat down. "Now look at it this way," he began, his finger in front of my father's face. My father threw back his head and laughed.

"You'd better go to bed and rest," my mother told me. "You're not completely well, you know."

So I went to bed, but I didn't go to sleep, not right away. I lay there for a long time while behind my darkened eyelids Emiliano Zapata's cavalry charged down to the broad Santee, where there were grave men with hoary hairs. I was still awake at eleven when the cold voice of the bugle went gliding in and out of the dark like something that couldn't find its way back to wherever it had been. I thought of Chonita in Heaven, and I saw her in her torn and dirty dress, with a pair of bright wings attached, flying around and round like a butterfly shouting, "Give me the hammon and the beans!"

Then I cried. And whether it was the bugle or whether it was Chonita or what, to this day, I do not know. But cry I did, and I felt much better after that.

Night Train to Fort Worth

AMADO MURO (CHESTER SELTZER)

SEPTEMBER 15, 1967 — One night I got on a Texas and Pacific mainline run at Toyah with a one-legged rover nicknamed Sticks because of his crutches. When the engineer eased the train out, picking up the slack without a bump, we were in an empty with open lathes about six cars behind the Big Jack engine.

A damp soft snow was falling, and we bundled up with carlining. But the wind blowing straight and steady from the northwest made us feel the snow's wetness on our foreheads. Sticks, small and spindly with a gray-streaked beard that didn't hide his sickly complexion, shivered. "You feel the cold more when you're hungry, buddy," he mumbled apologetically.

Near Pecos the freight train thundered over a highball stretch so fast it skipped on rail joints, and the rocking boxcars hit back on their coupling pins with a wrenching jerk. We sat with our legs apart and our heads down, bracing for sudden jolts of slack, with our hips numb from the pounding. Then the train began to bounce with a staccato roll and we stood up to ease the punishment. The double-track roadbed was speeding away beneath us, and the barren alkali land swung in a semi-circle around the boxcar's metal door. Sticks lurched forward but the train jarred him straight. He blinked owlishly and showed his worn-down teeth in a grin.

"This boxcar's like a leaping tuna — it's got eight flat wheels, and should have gone to the shops a hundred years ago," he said.

When the boxcar's jarring rattle lessened, we bundled up with carlining again, and Sticks, shivering in a raveled button sweater with the collar turned up around his face, told me he'd sold whole blood and plasma in Los Angeles.

"My arm's like a dopehead's with needle marks — I was puttin' down twice a week there," he said. "I was blowing 'n' goin' though. I eat one of those 51-cent meals at Jake's on the Nickle Street skid row every day, and I slept warm in that tramp dormitory above the Hard Rock Bar at Fifth and Wall every night. That plasma's a good deal — it ain't like the four-dollar blood banks. You can give it twice a week and they never take the needle out of your arm. They get the plasma and then put your blood back in and give you Dextrose besides. It takes about an hour — like a operation. But the last time I went to the plasma center they turned me down — not enough iron. It don't matter though — I'll make it in Texas. Where there's hundreds of stiffs waiting in LA soup-lines, there's only dozens in Fort Worth."

Out in the open, the wind was blowing harder and the snow was heavier. The train was running faster, and the suction scooped up cinders from the roadbed and pelted them against the steel cars. Sticks rolled up his sleeve and showed his biceps. His arm at the elbow was pock-marked with little white dots.

"A nurse give me a bottle of iron tablets," he said. "I taken all those tablets so I'll be ready to sell blood again in Fort Worth. I'll bleach the four-dollar blood bank's finger marks off with Clorox so I won't have to wait six weeks to put down again, and then make the plasma center, too. If I'm still low on iron, I'll go to Scotty's Blood Bank — they just take your temperature and a sample and don't ask no questions there. Me 'n' you'll fill up with Oklahoma-style black eyes when I get my passover money. You can make it in Fort Worth, buddy — you're on both feet."

He passed me a tobacco sack and one of the brown paper bags that hoboes roll cigarettes with when they run out of the regular book issues. After that he rolled a cigarette himself, packing the tobacco carefully so no grain would fall and then guiding his lips along the edge of the bag paper with his forefinger.

"I been on the rail all my life — I got to hear that train rolling and the wheels clicking," he said. "Hardships ain't broke me of the habit — I was born with a goin' spell and I got rambling in my blood. When I got to go with my backroll and skillet, I'll ride any kind of a load. I got it from my Daddy — he was a horse trader in Antlers, Oklahoma, and went around from place to place. Once I tried to get off the tracks and I worked at the pay desk in a big walkup flophouse that had 300 wire cages. But I quit because I had to climb a section ladder and pick fruit so I could eat and sleep good — just settin' was killing me. I've gandied and saw-milled and worked on ranches, too — that's how I lost my leg last year. A steer kicked me and broke it in two places."

The train's thunder rolled, and a wire fence beside the tracks took up the vibration and hummed with it. Then the road-bed turned on a banking curve and down the tracks we could see a highway town's hazy lights, clean and beautiful in the snow. The strung colored lights on the town's main street illuminated an empty thoroughfare. The stores were closed; the depot dark. A big lighted community Christmas tree glowed greens and reds and yellows. The sign at the edge of the sleeping town read: "Fort Worth — 310 miles." Sticks compressed his lips and closed his eyes.

"After I lost my leg, I tried peddling needles I bought for seven cents a box in San Francisco," he said. "But the Bay Area's hilly and you got to climb up eight or ten steps to a house. I got used to dogs barking and grabbing me by the britches-leg. But all that climbing with the sticks made my thigh gall me so, and my shoulders, arms, and ankle ache and hurt so much I had to give it up. After that I was hittin' it pretty rough. I was hungry and couldn't find a sleeping place so I had to carry the banner. One night I stopped to get warm in a bowling alley near Sacramento's Two Street skid row. But they could tell I was on the Dog because I was raggedy and smelled of smoke so they run me out. After that I taken to selling my blood."

Monahans was a snow-blurred sprinkle of lights pushing towards us like a mammoth postcard. Just west of the town the freight train took the siding to let a westbound manifest pass, and we stood in the boxcar's wide doorway looking out at the mesquite-clumped prairie. The mesquite trees were thick and made a fence for a clearing on which an old derrick rose. Its timbers were gray as an old mop; away from it a little piece lay a huge wooden bullwheel with rusty bolts.

Somewhere dogs were baying. It was a vibrant sonorous sound like the musical notes of a deep reed instrument. Wind gushed in the trees with the sound of a distant river and the tops of the cotton-woods, silhouetted against the sky, whipped and threshed like tiny Christmas trees in a storm. The rails began to murmur and a locomotive's light showed, tiny as a lightning bug. It began to swell and the earth trembled as if the railroad cut's sides were going to cave in and carry us under the train. Then the manifest's pounding wheels thundered and crashed and, after a long while, the red marker lights of the caboose passed. Sticks pinched off the burning end of his cigarette and, breaking the paper, poured the tobacco into a sack.

"I'm pretty well beat down, buddy, and I ought to get down on my knees for some help," he said. "But I'd rather be on my own and not on the mercy of missions. A stiff finds a little companionship running up and down the railroad tracks. On every train there's a new buddy to pal with and in every jungle there's a boabout going your way. I made it better during the depression though. The older you get, the tougher it gets — people start calling you Pop."

The locomotive wheels spun slowly, pulling hard, and the coupling pins knocked against each other and connected. Then the boxcars moved and the slack ran out of the drawheads. The freight train was going east again. The brown grass along the fence lines bent flat in the wind and snow sprayed through the boxcar's latticed sides. Sticks shuddered and clenched his teeth. Beneath the white skin of his neck, the muscles were limp and trembling.

"The road gets in a man's blood, but there are times when he wants shelter and a roof over his head," he said. "I'd like to get me a little old tin and tarpaper shack near the railroad yards and just squat for a while. A hobo when he ain't traveling just likes to sit and watch yard engines work boxcars around."

He dropped his head to his chest and then came up straight with a shudder, jerking his closed eyes open. "Soon's it gets warm, I'll freight up to Sioux City — they pay $20 a pint for O-Positive blood there," he said. The locomotive whistle whined back through the snow.

The Itty-Bitty Bottle Bill

BILL HELMER

JUNE 21, 1968 — My startling exposé of Governor [John] Connally's plot to bankrupt liberals and other heavy drinkers has apparently succeeded in alerting thinking people everywhere to the threat posed by liquor-by-the-drink legislation. Yet the very magnitude of the conspiracy has made it difficult for some of our slower citizens to grasp, and our enemies are as crafty as they are treacherous. Reacting to the groundswell of enlightened opposition, our governor, in a stroke of evil genius, now seeks to stun us into helpless confusion by introducing legislation whose provisions are a monument to madness. I refer to the Itty-Bitty Bottle Bill.

Until now the threat was a simple and straightforward one. Liquor-by-the-drink, while in many respects desirable, would double or triple the cost of on-the-town boozing by banishing the old brown bag. Thousands of people foolishly voted Yes in the mixed-drink referendum because they didn't realize this; myopically, they were able to see no further than the big, juicy carrot of "mixed drinks" being dangled before their eyes. Like bait in a trap, the mixed drink can be obtained at the cost of calamity, and only when it is too late will the victims come to know what evil lurks in the hearts of men! Especially the men of the Texas Legislature, which as the *Observer* has often warned, abounds in scoundrels, blackguards, and rascals of every description.

The exhilarating prospect of mixed drinks has blinded many people to Connally's chief reason for proposing a liquor-by-the-drink law in the first place. Did anyone ever think he wanted to modernize and civilize the law, so a man could, as the Good Lord clearly intended, get in out of the hot sun and order himself a cool relaxing daiquiri or whiskey sour? Great garbage, no! He wanted to wring extra money out of every poor soak in the state by taxing not only the bottle, but every drink poured out of it. *The power to tax is the power to destroy!*

But not even the Establishment politicians can shove mixed drinks down the throats of adamant Baptists, even for the purpose of taxing drinkers. Consequently, the mixed-drink proposal is currently masquerading as a liquor "reform" law designed to "clean up" the state's liquor laws. Already the bill is a mountain of minutiae and impossible provisions ("drivel," according to one of our more perceptive legislators) that would reform not drinking, goodness knows, but only the drinkers. To get past the fanatical drys, any mixed-drink bill is going to have to provide enormous licensing fees, drastic enforcement provisions, and unreasonable penalties against a bar or restaurant owner who gets faked out by a cleverly forged ID card. Thus the good governor would render unto God and Caesar equally by taxing sin, and things are tough enough on sinners under the present system, where Liquor Control Board rulings cannot be appealed and agents can raid private parties in private homes.

Since politics is the art of the possible and since nothing is possible in this state without concessions and compromises, the prospects of any sensible mixed-drink law have already vanished. What we have now is the Itty-Bitty Bottle Bill. Under its arcane provisions, no one still is going to walk in, sit down, and be served a whiskey sour. He is going to be served a tiny bottle on a tiny tray. He will then be asked to witness a bit of ceremony — the breaking of the seal! — whereupon the waiter will patiently (or not so patiently, one may expect) truck the tiny bottle back to the bar so the bartender can mix a drink with it. Imagine the fun this is going to be in a crowded bistro on a busy Saturday night when it takes thirty minutes now just to get a beer.

The ultimate compromise is yet to come. The mixed-drink provision may be stricken from the bill altogether, leaving only the highly-taxed, itty-bitty bottles. If brown-bagging seems hypocritical now, the practice will have reached the *brennschluss* of idiocy when Texans find themselves carrying not one big bottle, but many tiny ones, strung around them in cartridge bandoliers, Mexican bandit style.

None of this trouble would have come up had Texans not gotten exposed to big-city ways that made them feel inferior, and they shouldn't feel that way, at all. Granted, there is something primitive and uncivilized about lugging around a bottle, but at least it's honestly primitive and uncivilized — a quaint regional custom that has endured out of service to cultural needs. Tourists from New York might sometimes snicker, but they have to concede that, by God, it works. The possession of a full fifth of firewater protects the natives of this state against a variety of day-to-day hazards: exhaustion of funds, the early closing hours of bars and liquor stores, the dry counties that can slip up on an unwary traveler at night. "Aren't Texans cute, always carrying their bottles with them? You know, we ought to start doing that!"

But now alas, the natives have gotten self-conscious and are ashamed of their customs. They are not able simply to abandon them, of course, and adopt civilized ways — the open saloon. No, they must preserve at least the rituals that their high preachers and political witch doctors have traditionally prescribed to combat evil spirits. . . .

The wholly bloody bushwa of itty-bitty bottles is going to make Texas, among other things, the laughing-stock of the civilized world, and somewhere in the background will be the unregistered lobbyists for the communist-controlled itty-bitty bottle industry, grinning smugly at their latest coup. Yes, folks, write your legislator today! Texas cannot afford [gubernatorial candidate] Preston Smith and a Liquor Reform Law both in the same year.

The Third Battle of the Alamo

GARY CARTWRIGHT

MAY 9, 1969 — When *Dallas Times Herald* city editor Jim Lehrer visited San Antonio in 1964 researching his satirical novel *Viva Max!*, what impressed him most was that there aren't any public restroom facilities in that shrine of liberty, the Alamo. Liberty has its restrictions; please don't squeeze the liberty.

He even asked about it, and a member of the Daughters of the Republic of Texas (DRT), who was sitting darkly behind the information desk, informed him: "It isn't done." She was firm, her face was turgid with history, and Lehrer went away thinking she was right, in her circle it probably isn't. Somehow he resisted the temptation to pursue the subject, thus exercising a discipline that he could not fully appreciate until a few weeks ago when they began filming the movie version of his book.

The third battle of the Alamo, as it came to be called, started with a routine exchange of correspondence in the fall of 1967. Mrs. Maude Crenshaw, then president of the Alamo chapter (San Antonio) of the DRT, agreed to allow the movie company the same privilege any tourist takes for granted; they could film freely on the city-owned plaza in front of the chapel and courtyard so long as they didn't actually *touch* anything. Producer Mark Carliner, who had already constructed a replica of the Alamo (complete with San Antonio skyline) in Rome, understood, or thought he did. Since 1905, when the DRT rescued the shrine from greedy businessmen who would turn it into a brewery, cameras are on a list of things not allowed inside the Alamo. The Daughters maintain the Alamo as they would their good china: when the State Legislature appropriated $5,000 for repairs in 1911 it took a State Supreme Court

order to get the carpenters inside. The Daughters prefer to do it themselves. At issue in the 1911 case of *Conley vs. the DRT* (Conley was
state superintendent of shrines) was not a new roof for the ruins of the
battle of 1836 but a clear statement specifying just who the hell's Alamo
this was.

Producer Carliner was understandably relieved when Mrs. Crenshaw
not only agreed to accept his proffered $10,000 donation, but suggested
that the money be earmarked for the construction of public restrooms.

The trouble started a few weeks later when the DRT's president general, Mrs. William Lawrence Scarborough of Corpus Christi, got wind
of the goings-on. She wrote Carliner that since the novel from which the
movie grew "is of a satiric nature" all bets were off. Dangling like a man
whose parachute is caught on a powerline, Carliner replied that Mrs.
Scarborough was absolutely right, that "we consider [the novel] to be an
offensive, unpleasant, misdirected satire," and for that reason special
care was taken to make the screen version "a genuinely warm human
comedy." Then he repeated the $10,000 offer. But Carliner underesti-
mated the intrinsic nature of satire; he was promptly informed that the
DRT board of management had met and rejected among other things
the idea of public toilets in the Alamo.

"I knew then," cracked Carliner, "that we had entered into the Land
of Oz."

Despite the example of 1911, Carliner seemed to be on safe grounds.
All he really needed to push his cameras into Alamo Plaza was permission from the San Antonio city council, a formality at worst. If the sanc-
tity of his legal position wasn't enough Carliner could also address his
appeal to art and free speech: the script in question might well have been
written by Sen. John Pastore's great-aunt.

In the movie version, Max (actor Peter Ustinov) is a modern-day
Mexican general whose girl has jilted him for an American pole vaulter.
When she tells him in front of his assembled garrison that "your men
wouldn't follow you into a whorehouse," Max sets out to prove just
how wrong a woman can be. Marching his 87 men across the border
and north to San Antonio, General Max recaptures the Alamo, over-
powering its three defenders — an elderly gatekeeper, a Baylor coed
(actress Pamela Tiffin), and a little old lady who sounds suspiciously like
a DRT. At this point, according to the Lehrer imagination, the superpa-

triots of Texas are trumpeted to the counterattack. On paper it is pretty wild stuff.

No sooner had the film crew arrived in San Antonio than the cast of characters stepped out of fiction and into the first available meatgrinder. Mrs. Scarborough, who wears the startled turkey gobbler expression of a Norman Rockwell painting, flew in from Corpus Christi, establishing her command post at the Menger Hotel next to the Alamo. Calling a press conference in front of the Alamo, she spoke of them "making a mockery and desecration of our heroes who died for us at the Alamo," referring specifically to a scene where the Mexican general "takes that pretty little blonde girl [Pamela Tiffin] to the hothouse and seduces her." You could see the flags of no-quarter flapping in Mrs. Scarborough's eyes, where nothing had stirred for years. "Why can't they make a nice movie like John Wayne?" she asked.

Mrs. Scarborough pointed out that: "We are *not* little old ladies in tennis shoes." And several of her companions, one of whom had come straight from the country club and still wore golf shoes, nodded solemn agreement.

Ignoring advice from two lawyers who resigned one after the other during the three-week confrontation, Mrs. Scarborough tried and failed to get a court injunction which would halt the movie making. Rumors then circulated that the Daughters would drape the Alamo in black. Much as the original defenders of the Alamo came to sense that they were indeed out there alone, Mrs. Scarborough fell back on any tactic available. When General Eisenhower died, she ignored a warning from her public relations man and made plans for a news release which noted: "Sometimes the Lord moves in mysterious ways. Sometimes a death brings alive a cause."

She explained to me that this was by way of recalling that Eisenhower "was another glorious Texan who gave his all for liberty. He was born, I believe, in Abilene." He was, in fact, born in Denison; a year later his family moved to Abilene, Kan. But you could see what she was driving at, that this was God's way of making good for that mistake, and if Ike had been around he would have been there with Travis, Bowie, and the other boys, dying for the DRT.

The response was predictable. In a letter typical of those printed in the *San Antonio Express* about the situation, a writer who signed her name Nerna Skidmore Eller objected to carpetbaggers filming anywhere around "the blood soaked ground." A crippled war veteran who also happened to be running for city council protested at such length that he had to be removed from the council chamber. He was waving a crutch and reciting the pledge of allegiance to the flag as they took him away. A man from Gonzales, one of several towns whose citizens refused to come to the aid of the besieged mission in 1836, told the council that the movie company was "lowering morality to its lowest point in history." Another patriot took the direct approach. He showed up on the set carrying a loaded rifle and threatening to cut down anyone who tried to raise the Mexican flag in the plaza.

A Bexar county politician, Dist. Clerk Elton Cude, protested to the council that allowing a film in front of the Alamo would be "like writing a comedy and letting somebody raise a foreign flag over Kennedy's grave." Cude is president of the William Barrett Travis chapter of the Sons of the Republic of Texas; he is also a member of the Lions Club International, the American Legion, the Marine Corps League, the Sons of the Confederate Veterans, and is a man who traces his ancestry to the American Revolution. On top of that he is an amateur historian. He told me: "You know Santa Anna was a hophead, don't you?" I said that I didn't. "Sure, sure he was," said Cude. "During the final big battle he was in a room with a mulatto woman."

Partly through the efforts of the Sons and Daughters (actor Jonathan Winters coined a collective name for them: "The Mothers"), many details of the Alamo are blurred in Texas history books. There is strong evidence, for example, that Davy Crockett was not killed in battle, that he was discovered later hiding under a stack of mattresses and executed. Two local memorials lay claim to the ashes of the heroes of the Alamo — one under the floor of the Alamo chapel, and a much more pretentious one some blocks away at the San Fernando Cathedral in a marble casket purchased in 1936 from funds solicited for that purpose by the Archbishop of San Antonio. These memorials most likely contain dirt shoveled from a site approximating the burial place, which has never been located but frequently exploited.

For that matter, the Alamo itself, with the exception of the chapel, which contains the only authentic ruins of the original mission, is slightly east of the genuine battleground. The true "bloodsoaked ground" is across the street, about where the National Shirt Shop, Askins Credit Clothing, F.W. Woolworth, and Alamo Savings and Loan are currently situated.

The DRT has steadily resisted efforts to install a sound and light "spectacular" in the shrine. "What the hell," a Texas historian told me, "they won't even let kids under 12 in the Alamo research library." It has even been claimed that the Daughters were recently instrumental in getting Crockett a haircut and deleting from textbooks reference to the fact that his cough syrup recipe contained "Tincture Cannabis India, three ounces."

While the outside agitators filmed and the patriots fumed ("This has all the earmarks of a publicity stunt!" Mrs. Scarborough observed at one point), actor Peter Ustinov maintained the detached calm of a man reading the *Wall Street Journal* through the wrong end of a telescope. He recalled that there was no fuss or bother when the movie company of *Is Paris Burning?* raised the Nazi flag over the Arc of Triomphe. "And that of course was a *national* shrine," he remarked. "Surely Texas is now a part of the United States. Otherwise they should be in permanent mourning over the U.S. occupation of the Republic."

Despite the rhetoric, most citizens of San Antonio seemed pleased to have the movie folks in town. Eighty-seven unemployed Mexican-Americans signed on with Max's "army," and about 40 Anglos answered a call for "local bigots" to play the rightwing militia that rushes to the scene of the siege. The "Mexican soldiers" were especially receptive to the opportunity. They stood around all day in the sun, and in the evening you could find them still in their khaki uniforms and drinking in the private club of the hotel where the crew and cast were quartered. When a local civil rights leader picketed the set protesting that "Peter Ustinoff [sic] Hires Cheap Non-Union Mexican Labor," the soldiers attacked him.

Mayor Walter McAllister, himself a member of the SRT (to be a member one must have had relatives in the State before annexation), eventually led the fight to permit the movie company to erect a fake wooden gate in front of the iron-rail gate separating the Alamo's manicured courtyard from the public plaza. And some of the city's leading citizens, including two newspaper publishers and the architect who designed HemisFair, agreed to sit in as extras. Carliner paid them $1.50 an hour, same as the Mexicans and bigots.

Threats to drape the Alamo in black soon dissolved. On Mrs. Scarborough's command the iron-rail gate was padlocked and wrapped in black plastic, an act that hardly bothered director Jerry Paris since the fake gate was more authentic than the gate it concealed. The DRT also locked the main door to the chapel, inadvertently helping production by preventing tourists from wandering out in the middle of a take.

While DRT photographers catwalked the garden walls hoping to gather evidence in the event the movie people actually touched state property, Max's "soldiers" pushed through the spectators and hustled color Polaroid snapshots of Pamela Tiffin in a miniskirt. I asked Carliner what ever happened to the Marx Brothers, but you could tell that he was tense, especially when in one scene a flare blew off course and landed on the roof of the Alamo chapel. Fortunately, the "policeman" to whom the Daughters registered their complaint was actor Jack Wakefield. There was another bad moment when they lowered the Texas flag (after first determining that the flag pole was on city property) and replaced it with the Mexican flag. In their haste the soldiers rigged the Mexican flag upside down. They had to shoot the whole scene again. When they finally restored the Lone Star flag to its proper place it too was upside down.

Nevertheless it became clear that Hollywood was winning both the battle and the war. Eighty-year-old Mrs. Edith Simpson Halter, the "peer" and unofficial historian of the DRT, admitted to reporters that, "it's upsetting to think we may have brought this on ourselves. We used to have better public relations." Increasingly aware that the DRT would not recapture its glory of '05, one Daughter after another quietly disassociated herself from the cause.

Mrs. Crenshaw feared the worst: she even claimed that she heard on the radio that Lt. Gov. Ben Barnes had proposed legislation to "take the Alamo away from us." And another Daughter put the whole thing in focus, explaining that the reason one of her sister Daughters objected so strongly to the movie was that "She thought the picture put the Mexicans in a bad light."

"Is that a fact?" I asked.

"Yes," she said, lowering her voice to a whisper. "You realize of course the woman has Mexican blood."

Ladies' Days

MOLLY IVINS

SEPTEMBER 18, 1970 — On Aug. 26 approximately 150 women gathered on the grounds of the state capitol to discuss job discrimination, abortion law reform, and child care centers. About 40 men stood on the edges of the crowd, waiting for a bra-burning.

In Houston, a crowd of 300 gathered to listen to, or jeer at, feminist speakers at a downtown, noon rally. A group of 35 women who went on to lunch in a men's grill at Foley's department store received front-page coverage in the local papers.

Nothing happened in Dallas.

One witling observed, "in Texas the Women's Strike was a bust."

The movement for women's liberation was a prime target for cheap-shot humor in the 19th century and it still is. The leaders of the Austin meeting responded with almost angelic patience in interview after interview: "No, we do not burn brassieres. Or study karate. Or hate men."

Judy Smith, a science student at the University of Texas and one of the spokeswomen for the liberation movement in Austin, said quietly, "We have such a very bad image in the media that we can't come on strong, use a lot of rhetoric or show hostility. We are concerned with attitudes and economic problems that affect all women, but so many women have read about militant, man-hating feminists that it's rather hard to get the message across that we are not against motherhood."

Miss Smith's pains to explain the serious concerns of women were rewarded the next day in an *Austin American* story that referred to bras or the lack of them seven times in a 33-inch story. The Austin daily's report of the women's activities included the following phrases: "with shaggy legs, Baggy chests, and free-flowing hair," "the braless look," "bra-burning," "I don't wear a bra," "braless" and "bras were rare."

The *Dallas Morning News* ran a story on local women who disapproved the whole idea of women's liberation on the grounds that it is "unladylike." Reporters were apparently unable to locate any feminists in the area who might reply.

About 75 Austin women attended a potluck supper at a Congregational church the evening of the 26th and participated in a meandering discussion of women's problems.

Job discrimination there was not a meaningless phrase over which editorial writers could cluck. It was a divorced mother of three saying in anguish, "I'm a secretary and when I applied for a higher paying position with my firm last month my boss told me, 'Oh there's no doubt at all that you're qualified for the job, but I'd sooner quit than hire a woman.'"

The inequities of the current abortion laws were talked about by women who are risking prison sentences by counseling other women on how to get abortions. "After I had my fifth child, I begged the doctors to tie my tubes," said one woman. "When I had my sixth child, after I had almost died, they did it."

Talk of how to get federal and state assistance in setting up day care centers gave way to plans for arranging cooperative care by working mothers who cannot wait until the government sees fit to help them earn a living for themselves and their children.

The discussion was distinguished by the familiar refrain heard at women's liberation meetings all over the country: "Oh God. I'm so glad to find out someone else has these problems." And the same realistic humor showed itself as the women discussed how to get men to share the housework.

"One solution, not the ideal one, but the only one I've been able to find is to live in filth," said one young woman genially.

"You've got to figure on at least a couple of months of lousy food and sloppy housekeeping until the men learn how to do it," observed another woman.

But unlike their counterparts elsewhere, the Austin women's liberationists were almost painfully aware of the man-hating, bra-burning image of feminists, and they were pathetically eager to avoid it.

One man who attended the meeting inquired of his neighbor, "Don't the husbands of these women work eight or ten hours a day?"

"So do these women," he was told.

"Oh. Yeah. But as secretaries or something that's not so hard."

Miss Smith tried to explain the differences between women's liberation groups and the more established feminist groups such as the National Organization for Women (NOW).

"NOW is issue-oriented," she said. "They work on piecemeal solutions to problems which we believe are symptoms of an underlying cause. The cause is male chauvinism — the unfounded belief that one group of human beings is superior to another."

If NOW was regarded as Establishment by the women's liberationists, it was the far-left antipode at the Governor's Conference on the Status of Women held in Austin on Aug. 29.

Some 1,406 women, invited on the recommendation of members of the Governor's Commission on the Status of Women, attended the conference. No members of women's liberation groups, welfare rights groups, abortion reform groups, or NOW were invited. Two members of NOW appeared on their own initiative. The price was $5 per person.

Women's Lib baiting was a feature of most of the speeches. Bonnie Angelo, of *Time* magazine's Washington, D.C., bureau, set the pace. "A new ferocity has crept into women's protest and some forms of it are not my style," she said. "I don't want to burn my bra." (Applause.) "I think they do unwitting harm to our cause by placing in the hands of our enemies the strongest weapon of all — ridicule. I fear 'lib lash.'

"I do admire the moxie of the liberationists and of course they serve the purpose of making the rest of us look conventional. But I'm against letting the man-haters and bra-burners become women's image," Mrs. Angelo said. (*Time* magazine's cover story on women's liberation last winter was devoted to karate-chopping man-haters.)

Mrs. Angelo surveyed the row upon row of blue rinse perms before her and added, "I believe the real women are here — committed and well-dressed." (Applause.) "We can proceed in that dignified, ladylike manner we have all been brought up to believe is the best way." (Applause.)

Perhaps the strongest statement at the entire conference was made by Cong. Martha Giffiths, D-Mich., who was primarily responsible for the passage in the U.S. House of the constitutional amendment that would give equal rights to women.

She concluded her speech by saying, "My grandmother became a widow in 1890 and said she expected to live long enough to vote for a woman candidate for president. I have no such idealistic dream; I only hope I will live long enough to see the Supreme Court of this country recognize me as a human being."

After a luncheon (fruit salad with tiny marshmallows covered with a strawberry-marshmallow sauce, turkey mornay, broccoli tougher than all the women there, and chocolate cake with nuts) the ladies split up for workshop sessions. Job discrimination was not discussed — employment opportunities were; economic inequities were not discussed — financial planning for women was, with emphasis on investments, real estate, banking and insurance. Abortion was skipped entirely, but a counseling workshop concerned itself with community services, i.e., where to report for volunteer work.

Sex was not mentioned during the entire day.

The workshop that produced the most sensible and effective recommendations at the end of the day was on laws pertaining to women. It was led by federal District Judge Sarah Hughes, a woman with gumption who remarked at one point that she hoped the ladies at the conference wouldn't fall to "studyin'."

"I'm a member of the League of Women Voters," she said, "but I sure do get tired of their studyin'. I'm for action and I think you've got to be aggressive to be successful."

The workshop on laws and women concerned itself with the question of alimony (it should be ended after three years, they suggested), wage garnishment for child support, abolition of "protective laws," equal pay for equal work laws, and the possibility of a revolving loan fund to assist women during the time they sue for equal pay.

Some militant agitator got up and proposed that more women be appointed to the commission who were not white, college-educated, and successful. The suggestion was greeted enthusiastically, but not as enthusiastically as a later suggestion that Gov. Preston Smith be thanked for arranging "this wonderful, wonderful conference."

The major resolution coming out of the commission was that the Governor's Commission on the Status of Women be made instead a legislative commission and be given $100,000 to study all manner of things pertaining to women. The commission also resolved to ask the governor to issue a directive to the state civil service agencies not to discriminate because of sex and to ask him to appoint more women to the 126 positions on the boards of state institutions of higher learning.

Baby, you've got a long way to go.

It's All Over Now

BILL PORTERFIELD

JULY 10, 1970 — J.D. Graham's general store looked like one of those lost little places Bonnie and Clyde used to hit back in the 30's. There was a gasoline pump out front full of high octane cobwebs, a row of old men lounging on the porch and not enough money in the cash register to bother about. This, of course, was a reflection against Miss Parker and Mr. Barrow and not Mr. Graham. If The Grove settlement was flourishing, J.D., being a competent storekeeper, would have been ringing up dollar signs. But it wasn't and J.D. wasn't.

He sat there, a large, gentle-faced man with red ears and a robust belly, swatting dirt daubers and selling red soda pop and white soda crackers to first one kid and then another. This didn't take long because there weren't but seven children (and 57 adults) left in The Grove, which is in the Leon River valley between Gatesville and Temple.

I say left because to hear J.D. tell it, The Grove used to be a place to be reckoned with. E.C. Symm and W.J. Dube operated general stores. Old Man Johnson had a café, that fella Durham ran a candy kitchen, there was a mule barn run by Mr. Glass, Holcombe and Adams were blacksmiths, Profit and Taylor were the barbers, and Collins and Denman were the doctors. And there were enough residents behind these commercial fellows to almost win over the county courthouse from Gatesville. "We lost by one vote," J.D. said, and you could tell it still rankled him.

Except for the Lutheran Church, J.D.'s was the only place of business left. Some of the other buildings were standing, but there was a gray shimmer of yesteryear about them. It seemed to say that these ruins are not inhabited. Only a drunken ghost could have manipulated the sagging stairway to the doctors' second story office.

"Odd of you to say that," J.D. said, unfurling an eyebrow that had gone from red to white. "The last man to navigate those steps was an old feller by the name of T.B. Durham. He moved up there after the doctors left. Stayed drunk all the time. Used to fire boilers at the [cotton] gin. Drunk all the time. Never understood why he didn't break his neck on those stairs."

"What happened to him?"

"Oh, he got sick and died."

J.D. said he guessed the village got sick and died of neglect. After they lost the courthouse fight, the state built Highway 36 around them instead of through them. And then, to make matters worse, the federal government came in at the beginning of World War II and bought up 322 square miles of prime farm land to the west and built Fort Hood. "We lost our big farms," J.D. said. The military base made thriving towns out of places like Gatesville, Copperas Cove, Killeen, and Belton, but it didn't do a thing for The Grove except to further negate it.

E.C. Symm closed his store and W.J. Dube sold his. Old Man Johnson closed his café and died. It got to where a business failure was a prelude to a funeral. Durham, the candy kitchen man, closed up and died and so did Mr. Glass, the mule barn operator, and the two blacksmiths. But they were old anyhow. The younger fellows moved to other towns.

One barber went to Port Arthur and the other went to Gatesville. Nobody remembers where the doctors went.

J.D. was one of the farmers who found himself without a place to plow. So in 1944, he bought the store from Jim Gilbert, who had bought it from W.J. Dube. August Schkade was running the store alone until Dube went into partnership with him in 1908. Schkade died in 1910 and Dube married his widow.

The store is so old no one remembers its beginning. It might be as old as the well out front which Uncle Jim Whitmore dug with a pick and crowbar in 1872. The first 12 feet was almost solid rock. The Grove sits right at the flinty edge of the river valley. The well still gives up sweet water, and the wood stove and the big wall clock in the store are almost as durable. The stove has been burning wood and tobacco juice and warming backsides and shoe leather for about 75 years, and the clock hasn't stopped ticking since W.J. Dube first wound it in 1910.

It is a handsome instrument, encased in a rich, wood cabinet. On its face is the legend: Linz Brothers, Jewelers, Dallas. The four Linz brothers were from Austria. They started out selling diamonds by horse and buggy in Grayson County, north of Dallas. Then they opened stores in Sherman and Denison. By 1898, they were in Dallas in the Linz Building, which for years was the tallest building west of the Mississippi. It was 12 stories and made of marble. In those days, an item from Linz was considered something to strut about, and Dube remembers he got the clock as a premium for selling a lot of something, what, he can't recall. The Linz firm is still in business in Dallas and San Antonio and is considered by the *New Yorker* magazine to be "one of the five finest Jewelers in the world."

They peddled a good eight-day clock. W.J. Dube is a man of unswerving habit, and he began winding his every Saturday morning at 5, the hour he opened the store. Habit became tradition with Gilbert and now Graham. J.D. figures the clock has lasted as long as it has because its gears have never had to fret.

"It knows just what to expect," he explained. "If I got mixed up and wound it on any other morning than Saturday it would probably come unsprung and fall off the wall."

But things do not self-destruct in The Grove. They rust and dry rot. Built-in obsolescence is as unknown as smog and riots. Hinges and habit hang on for dear life and the faces of the men on the porch of J.D.'s store are as stubborn and set in their wrinkled ways as their overalls and boots. Is it atrophy or conviction? Surely they vote like creaking gates swinging backwards, and stand for some things best forgotten, and yet it did not matter. Theirs were the faces of a lost America, which, perhaps only because of its passing, seemed precious now.

The Lutheran Church bell could have been tolling as much for the town as for the funeral of Mrs. Bertha Winkler Hohle, who had died two days before at the age of 76. Yet even in its wake, in its dozing slide to oblivion, there was an illusory sense of permanence about The Grove, and it centered in the general store.

J.D. remained in The Grove because he belonged there. He was born there, and so were his father and his grandfathers. The maternal grandfather, Abram Wyatt, had brought the mail in from Round Rock by pony express. The paternal grandfather, W.J. Graham, had run the general store that Symm later took over. A hicky-looking fellow in a funny hat strolled into the store one day and W.J. and some of the other men began to pick at him. "Hold on, by God!" the stranger growled, putting his back against the bar and facing them. "Do you fellers know who you're talking to? This is Sam Bass!"

"You could've heard a pin drop," J.D. said. "They were right nice to him after that."

J.D.'s wife, Ruby, had been the postmaster for 21 years. Now, since the place is only a branch of the post office at Gatesville, their daughter, Fula Kindler, is the clerk in charge. Fula, who has the red hair her father once had, worked from behind an ornate window in a corner of the store. She said 29 families picked up their mail there and that in the old days, the window in the corner served as The Grove bank.

"The funeral's at 3," J.D. said. He didn't seem to be talking to anyone in particular.

"I know," Fula said. "You ought to close up about 2 so you can go home and change clothes."

J.D. grunted in agreement and watched his daughter. It was easy to see that she was something special in his eye.

"She's balancing the books," he confided. "It reminds me of the old postmaster and storekeeper over at Bland. The postal inspectors were always finding a difference between his books and his cash on hand, but it never rattled the old feller. 'You just check out the books,' he would say. 'If the post office drawer is short any money, I'll get it out of the store cash register. And if the post office drawer has more than it ought to, then I'll take it out and put it in the store cash register.'"

A frail old man in overalls with a frown on his face came in and sat beside the stove, which wasn't lit because of the warm September. The porch thermometer, which had a face like a clock and "Webb Funeral Home, Gatesville" printed on it, registered 93 degrees.

"This is G.E. Wolff," J.D. said loudly.

Wolff looked up at him.

"He had the gin here until cotton got knocked in the head. He used to gin the dickens out of it."

"Wha'd ye say?" Wolff asked.

"I say you been ginning a long time."

"Forty-six year," Wolff said, nodding.

"He's a little hard of hearing," J.D. explained. "You have to talk up to him."

"What's that?" Mr. Wolff stirred again.

"I say you been closed a long time."

"Oh, well. Closed the gin here 10 years ago. But I'm still in business in Burlington. We're partners now, me and my boy."

The two men sat mute for a while.

Finally J.D. broke the silence.

"If the old settlers could raise up and see this country, it'd scare them to death. Wouldn't know where they was."

Wolff apparently heard, because he shook his head as if in agreement.

"Remember how they used to be people come here on Saturday morning and stay till sundown? The street would be so thick with them you could hardly pass. And the dances, Lordy, every Saturday night. And the Fourth of July rodeos, they was something, humph. It's all over now."

G.E. Wolff drove off in his pickup and after a while A.F. Urbantke joined J.D. beside the stove. He was a tall, spare man with a weathered face. He wore overalls. J.D. said he was blind but you couldn't tell it. He made J.D. get up and get him some Beechnut chewing tobacco and a Big Red soda pop, for which he paid cash. J.D. gives credit when it's wanted, but Urbantke has never asked for it.

After finishing his pop, Urbantke began to talk. He asked J.D. a thousand questions and answered them himself. He talked about everything but sports, religion, and politics. J.D. never said a word, just nodded his head once in a while. Finally Urbantke left.

"Why didn't you say anything?"

"I'd be wasting my breath," J.D. said. "Urbantke wouldn't have heard a thing I was saying. He's deafer than G.E. Wolff."

Eula said Mrs. Hohle's body was already at the church, so J.D. closed the store and went to get ready.

The next morning J.D. was open as usual at 5. When the sun warmed things up, the old men began to gather on the porch as they had done the day before and the day before that and the day before on back through the years.

It was as their fathers had done and they wore what their fathers had worn, but they did not talk as their fathers had talked.

The previous generation in The Grove had been optimistic. They spoke of the future and what a man could do in those parts with a little luck and a lot of hard work. Circumstances and events proved them wrong, but not in time to tell their sons to get out while the getting was good. So the sons sit there, old men now, and because the future holds nothing for them, they talk of the present and of holding on, and of the past.

"J.D.," one said. "Did you ever use that old gasoline pump?"

"Once in 22 years. I tried it the first week I bought out Dube. Filled it with 10 gallons and sold on credit, mostly to kids. Not a one of them paid me so I never filled it again."

They talked of the time in '27 when Clyde Barrow and Joe Hancock robbed the bank and put poor old Mr. Brown, a cripple who was cashier and the bank president, in the vault. The loot amounted to pennies, they said. And they talked of the pitiful end to which Mr. Brown came. A bank examiner found he was $10,000 short, and Brown was sent off to prison and the bank was closed, never to reopen. Brown had slipped the money to his brothers, who were about to lose a land deal and needed some cash to save it. He figured to pay it back before it was discovered missing, but his brothers did not come through. The banker served his term, but died shortly after returning to The Grove. Everybody said it was from shame.

At sundown the old men went home to bed and J.D. locked up after letting a lady put a sign in the window advertising a variety show at Comanche Gap.

Time blurred their memory. It has to be said that it was not Clyde Barrow who robbed The Grove bank with Joe Hancock, but Aubrey Ray. If Clyde was ever in The Grove, he behaved himself. The take was not pennies but $1,032. The same duo hit the bank at Copperas Cove 22 days later and were caught. As J.D. said, those were the days. The days of his youth.

Letter from the Panhandle

BUCK RAMSEY

SEPTEMBER 23, 1977 — In 1941 at the start of its unending preparations for modern war, the United States bought about 10,000 acres of isolated farm-and-ranch country seventeen miles east-northeast of Amarillo and built the Pantex munitions plant in the middle of the track. On the western edge, the government constructed a village: symmetrical rows of buildings so uniform there was a nightly problem of entering the wrong apartment by mistake. The war industry, with its promise of regular paychecks and dwellings with gas heaters and indoor plumbing, lured many families from the hardscrabble countryside. Mine was among them.

I sometimes slipped through fences to wander about the forbidden pastures, to lie on my back in the ungrazed grass, watch formations of airplanes roar overhead, and listen to trains rumble away with bombs for Europe and Asia. I thought about the older men in their uniforms — emboldened by the tears of their women. I wished the war would last long enough for me to go off in khakis while women cried sweet tears.

The war ended with me seven years old. For a couple more years, we lived in the village, while the munitions plant deteriorated from the peace. I grew bolder with age and would climb up to survey the area from watchtowers. I walked the barracks porches, and then broke into deserted buildings to steel my nerves against the ghosts inside, preparing myself for some future war. The place did that to people. Made them war-minded. It still does.

Six years after Hiroshima, the government quietly returned to its abandoned Pantex plant, contracting out the work of weapons manufacture to Mason & Hanger — Silas Mason Co. Today, Pantex holds the regional heart and mind as strongly as it gripped my own imagination when I was a child.

A slavish local press has traditionally avoided any mention of Pantex, unless the plant contributed to a charity or a Pantex softball team won a tournament. Pantex plant manager Ross Dunham told a *Dallas Morning News* reporter that "We have a good relationship with the people of Amarillo. They have faith in us." Amarillo Mayor Jerry Hodge later reinforced Dunham by calling Pantex "a civil bulwark of sorts." Hodge added, "Whatever they are doing, we support."

These men, like many with power and intelligence, might have preferred to remain silent about Pantex, but events this year have turned local attention to the munitions plant. On March 30, three Pantex workers were killed in an explosion. Authorities said the accident involved no nuclear materials, and that outside of an electrocution some years back, the deaths were the only fatalities in the plant's quarter-century history.

Then, in late July, the wire services reported that if President Carter approved production of the controversial neutron bomb, the device would be assembled at Pantex.

The neutron bomb is small and ugly. Billed as a defensive weapon, it is designed to bathe enemy soldiers, and presumably civilian bystanders, with streams of radiation able to penetrate walls and tank armor and then rip through organic tissue. However, the bomb would cause little damage to buildings and property beyond the immediate blast area. . . .

International debate on the new bomb has created some public relations problems for Pantex officials and chamber-of-commerce-minded newspaper editors. Plant spokesmen have taken to discussing the bomb's production as calmly as dairy farmers talking about adding new stanchions and milkers to their barns.

"There would be nothing different about our activities on this type of system," plant manager Dunham told the *Amarillo Globe-News.*

The newspaper got into the reassurance act with an August 28 editorial pooh-poohing the "big scare" over the neutron bomb, repeating the story of Pantex's safety record, and concluding: "The people of the Golden Spread have lived without fear for twenty-five years of nuclear weapons manufacturing at Pantex. If we have not been afraid of the work done at Pantex in the past, we have no reason to become afraid now."

Locally, there has been scant protest against the bomb. In Hereford, landowners who think that national publicity will hurt crop sales can sign an anti-bomb petition. Posters in the window of a perpetually locked storefront office standing between two of Amarillo's hardcore beer halls announce that an organization called "People for Social Sanity" is against the neutron bomb. A petition and a few posters are about all.

The strongest private protest I've encountered is a pipedream that some miracle bomb that destroys buildings and spares people could be developed, assembled at Pantex — and then be accidentally detonated on the spot.

Looking for My Sister

RUPERTO GARCIA

JULY 24, 1981 — It had been two years since we'd seen her. Two years before, she climbed out of the car to get us ice cream, walked into the grocery store as we waited crowded in the car in the heat, and she hadn't returned.

We waited until my mother figured it out. Then she had sent my brothers to check. She had eloped.

The next day we all climbed into the back of the work truck, drove toward another ranch, and saw her. She held hands with her young man, his shoes were polished a bright orangy tan and his khakis glistened in the morning light.

When we left, she stayed beside him. We hadn't gone to bring her, we'd only gone to leave her even more. It was only days later, perhaps only one day later, when she married, and she disappeared into the other fields and other roads, and she no longer belonged with us.

There had been no ceremony when we'd gone to see her; only the visit. No one had gotten off the truck, only my father. No one had spoken of it afterward, only he and the young man with the shiny pants. Then we had left.

As we drove now, I could feel something different about the visit. It had been years, not days, nor months, but years. No one else had waited that long to write; everyone else had written sooner.

As we moved across the Texas plains, I could feel the heat, the dryness; could see the vastness of the empty space.

It was not the same, I sensed.

I would look at my mother at times. She would wipe my brother's forehead with cool water as he drove and the sweat beaded on his forehead, then dripped into his eyes. It was not that hot.

Then one time he cried. As I sat in front with them (stood, actually, my mother holding me as I looked forward), I would turn to look at her as she looked at the road. It was different.

The first thing I remember about arriving was the smell. It permeated the air. Stockyards. The aroma of manure was everywhere, the atmosphere as thick as the cattle themselves. For a while I held my nose until I needed to breath, then it was worse. Even the town was one huge cow: Hereford. I didn't know then, but I do now.

There were puddles on every road and over each puddle, communities of gnats. And around and in the puddles, sometimes small children played while mothers watched them from canvassed doorways and watched inside, too, babies in blankets that we couldn't see.

Sometimes a small, red ball would roll out into the street and the children would pick it out of the rancid puddle with their fingers, wiping them on their pants, and go back to their game.

But we moved through it all. Into the middle. My mother watched, then she watched me. My father held his hands on my waist so I wouldn't fall with the bumps.

My sister was one of them.

She stood in the doorway, holding her baby as we approached, the canvas open just enough to let us know where she was and that she knew.

I looked at my mother just in time to see her wipe her face. We had come. I had never seen the letter; we had only come across the state, climbed into the truck, and come.

It had been two years now. My mother wiped the tears on the small white cloth as we descended.

I stayed behind a little while. I stood inside the cab of the large truck and looked around at what I could see. The rest of them walked toward the curtained doorway where she held it open.

And I looked. They were all the same; beside the door another woman looked at us; they reminded me of patients at a hospital, waiting for visitors to come and see them and jealous of the others who have their own.

They looked like people in nursing homes. Small, crowded, with the skinny, undernourished look of passing age.

She stood there, looking at us approach, the small child in her arms.

There were certain horrors to her place. A certain cloud, a miasma of poverty in which the miasma itself begins to spoil and smell, the smell of cattle, and manure, and rancid water. Such is the smell of the poor.

As I walked in, my sister was trying to clean up so that my mother could sit somewhere and so that she wouldn't see. She had seen.

My sister tried to pick up things and explain that they hadn't bought groceries yet. There was no place to put them.

Then she cried. Slowly she leaned forward on her hands, covering her face as she spoke, holding the baby even closer to her, as the words flowed out and she cried. So did my mother.

And then I understood. I could see my brother once again as tears rolled down his face like sweat; and my mother.

The baby had no food, my sister explained. Her husband couldn't find a job. Sometimes he would do odd jobs for a coke or an orange soda, bring it home, and they would put it in the baby bottle.

Then she showed us his teeth. They were yellow, and brown, and rotting. They were small teeth, helpless against the acid of the drink, and when she showed us she began to cry again, quietly sobbing into her clasped open hands.

As she dried her cheeks, I looked around the empty room. The small table, with the bare light bulb hanging over it. The small cot bed with all the clothes piled on top of it. The small mat on the floor, actually two blankets. Then her.

She looked . . . well, she had aged. Gray hair hung lifeless on her head, down onto her face. She was 26, but she looked weak, and tired, from the looks of her bent back. And she looked hungry.

She *said* she was hungry. They wouldn't eat for days because there was no one to ask. He was trying, she said, she didn't blame him.

At times, she explained, he would come home frustrated after doing what he could. In uttermost moments of desperation he would sit on the crumpled bed, his work clothes on, and hold the baby. They he would cry, looking down at the baby as if to apologize to him.

Off to the side of her there was a small stove. It was a kerosene stove they had had for other times. Now it sat there in the corner as a reminder of what they didn't have.

I walked out then.

There is something about being a child, I think, that had something to do with it. In the small world of my existence, the thought of her had entered, and had remained.

She had become part of it, sitting in the corner as she wept and spoke. She had come inside of me, I think.

And everything seems large now; I was a child. It was all important, and I walked out with the large, overwhelming impression of it all, and ran.

Around the long, dull, dirty white camp houses with the curtained doors, the puddles, and the hungry dogs, I ran. They were the skinny dogs of people, with their exposed ribs. I ran, until I stopped to cry.

It was a quiet sob at first. As my small fists would rub against my eyes as tears escaped, I felt a weakling to the force which overwhelmed me.

And as I leaned against the corner of the grimy house, I could feel the women looking on.

It was my sister's face on all the women there. They walked around the place to get water from a central pump, they watched the children play, they watched me cry, then they moved on. They never laughed, nor cried, they just watched.

Even the children were like they were. They didn't play and enjoy the game, they merely played, as if spectators had replaced them on the field.

Almost as if there was a need to play; they were required to play; it was demanded.

And as they played, I began to notice them. Some had six toes, I think. On one foot, on both feet.

Some said they could just have it cut when they got older. They would be fine. The others laughed at them.

There were too many to be laughed at too much. Then they would leave, to play, or to walk through the puddles in the roads between the houses, leaving their footprints to the others, and myself to see. And they wouldn't look back.

I had looked away at first. Someone had mentioned that the boy approaching had six toes, and I had looked away . . . then I had looked down, not knowing whether he would mind or not, and I had seen.

Another had six fingers, and he pointed it out himself, knowing that I knew from the others.

It was from all this that I walked away, not looking back, but knowing that they watched me walk away until I turned the corner of the dull white houses and went home.

She was still there, my sister, but the crying had stopped.

The clothing on the bed had been arranged as if it had been packed, and the sleeves of the large white shirt held it together in the bundle that it was.

We were waiting, I guessed. And as I stood, I could see him coming down the alley that the buildings formed, stooped forward from the weight of things, no longer wearing shiny shoes and golden khakis, merely moving forward.

He walked around the puddles as if he knew where they were, not even looking at them at times, and no longer seeing the women and the children who looked on.

His slim frame walked on, oblivious to what was ahead or behind, so much so that when he finally reached the door, he seemed surprised to see me standing there, not recognizing me at first, then seeing me for only a short while before he entered. In his right hand, well held and hanging at the end of his dark brown arm now caked with mud and smelling of manure, hung the orange soda.

He looked at us as if he knew why we had come, then started to help put things together, the dishes in a small box, the shoes in a bag, and he was through. We had not packed for him; we weren't sure if we should.

Then he went outside. One of my brothers handed him a cigarette that he cherished quietly by the side of the truck, and we all quietly packed all their belongings on.

There were no words.

My sister climbed into the cab with my mother and father; small as she was she didn't displace too much of anyone. My brother got behind the driver's side. The rest of us climbed onto the back, ambled on the front, all except for him, my brother-in-law, her husband.

He went inside again, moving the curtain to the side as he entered, then he walked out, holding nothing but what he had had with him before, a small bag with his shoes, clean and shiny, as if he'd polished them with the same old polish, and he had kept them alive.

Before he climbed on, he stood at the back of the truck, behind it, actually, and looked around him at the puddles and the gnats, and the people looking from the doorways, and the children with the ball that fell everywhere, the only ball, and the toes, and he seemed to see it all together, not one at a time, and he climbed on, sitting quietly towards the very back of the truck as we drove off.

On This Day in Texas History

DAVE DENISON

MARCH 21, 1986 — Whew! We made it 150 years.

Wanting to get in on the spirit, we went down to the City Coliseum to celebrate that we made it 150 years. There was a birthday cake like you'd never seen before. Prince Charles of Wales had been there and had cut the cake with a sword that the governor gave him, and after the prince of Wales and the governor left, they let us all in for free cake. It was on February 20, 1986.

There were security guards all around, trying to keep the people moving toward the exits so as not to make a traffic jam. One of them was pushy and told me to hurry it along. "We've got 150,000 people outside," he said. That was a bunch of fluff — there wasn't even a line outside. I told him just because the cake was big didn't mean he could inflate his figures. So I kept going around and coming back in, so I could look at the world's largest cake.

And it was the world's largest cake. All the banners all over the coliseum said "Duncan Hines. The World's Largest Cake." Here is what it looked like.

It looked like a big ice rink. It was on a platform as high as our waists, and was as big as a hockey rink. "Now that white in the center is the Texas Star," an old man told me. The Texas Star was built up higher than the rest of the cake, way off in the middle. You'd have to eat for weeks to get to it. The newspaper said this cake weighed 45 tons. It was a three-layered cake.

From the side of the cake 'til about seven feet in, the icing was all white. Then there was a ridge of fancy twirls and flowerettes and then the rest of the icing was white with blue speckles all over it. The newspaper said 30,000 pounds of the cake was just the icing. And that it took 93,108 eggs, etc. It's hard to think of so many eggs. If each chicken laid three eggs, that would take 31,036 chickens. If each chicken took up a foot of space and you lined them up, they would stretch for 5 miles. I think that gives you an idea how big this cake was.

All the while I was walking around with a big piece of yellow cake on a paper saucer. There were popular rock songs filling the auditorium. Really, there were people of all colors, creeds, and weights filing through to a background of American pop. Where else in the world would you witness such a thing as this? But you really had to be careful you didn't slip. The floor was dangerously slippery with icing, like you were on ice without skates. There was cake and icing in piles on the floor, like some kind of glorious manure.

This was the truly amazing part. Some people were getting armloads of the stuff. The big cake was made up of a bunch of smaller cakes, cooked up on aluminum trays big enough to take up a normal person's oven. And some people were getting a whole tray of cake. For a while they gave out boxes to carry trays in. Then they quit giving out boxes and people had to struggle with carrying those big cakes. I even saw our representative to the Texas Legislature, state Representative Bill Ceverha with his arms full of cake. He asked if there were any more boxes and they turned him away just like he was anyone. I wanted to tell the security guard, "Do you know who you just refused a box to? State Representative Bill Ceverha, that's who." But I didn't want to get kicked out.

Some guys came in just off the street and obviously hadn't read their newspaper. They looked confused and said, "What was it? Just a big stunt?" They probably didn't even know about the prince of Wales and the governor being there.

Then we helped some guy who looked like the Red Baron bag up some cake. He rode his motorcycle to the coliseum but he was going to take home one of those trays of cake. So he had to stuff it into his backpack. I held the backpack open and he stuffed that two-foot piece of cake in there. "You learn to do things like this," he said. "You take the cake home."

Well, you do. But I felt a little bad for those people. I was walking around with that one piece of soft yellow cake, and by the time I got that put away I was beginning to feel a little sick. The cake was for free all right, but that didn't mean it was worth taking home.

Still, I don't know where else in the world you would see such a thing as this. The smell of the air around that cake was rich, very rich. There were forklifts out back stacking those boxes of leftover cake, just like they did two days ago when they brought box after box in here. *Some*body showed *some*body just what the state of Texas can do to celebrate making it 150 years.

Le Ville des Vache

DAVE HICKEY

What you have to remember about Fort Worth, is that it's a fort.

—*Advice to a newcomer from a lifelong resident*

MAY 29, 1987 — Back in the '50s there was a gambler and minor crime-figure on the west side of Fort Worth, whom I will call "Biggy," who weighed in at about three hundred pounds, favored Elvis pink and black apparel, and drenched himself with industrial strength lilac after-shave. As everyone knew, Biggy had but four passions in life: Losserro's pizza, five-card stud, big-breasted strippers, and this miniature poodle he called Fred and kept clipped in the most artificial and effeminate manner imaginable. So it was not altogether surprising, when "Biggy" fell into arrears with a local shylock, that said shylock — by way of pro-viding incentive for payment — would strike out at one of the objects of Biggy's passion.

In this instance, the victim turned out to be Fred the poodle, whom Biggy found on his front porch one morning with his throat cut. Need-less to say, Biggy paid off the shylock with some alacrity. But not before preserving the body of poor Fred among the steaks and frozen peaches in the brand new Amana deep-freeze locker which he kept out on the back porch. Then, two weeks later, Biggy's shylock was discovered on the kitchen floor of his Samson Park home. He had apparently been beaten to death with the once-frozen poodle now melting into a puddle on the linoleum beside him. Naturally, the pivotal question at Biggy's trial was whether his freezing of Fred constituted premeditation. The defense contended (unsuccessfully, I might add) that it was merely the act of a sensitive man's devotion to his dead pet. Everyone else knew that revenge is best served up cold.

Fort Worth: An aggregation of homes, shops, stores, malls, museums, parks, zoos, honky tonks, office buildings and light industrial areas occupying an expanse of otherwise undistinguished Texas real estate on the lip of the prairie plains, facing west. Not a city, really. (In a city you can get what you want and in a great city you can get what you want *sent.*) Nor a town, exactly. (In a town, you know who your neighbors are, or you know why.) And most certainly, not a community. Probably, Fort Worth is best described as a piece of West Texas, kinda bunched up to keep it from spilling over into Dallas, for, even though the physical distances between structures are not so great as in the rest of west Texas, the psychic distances are, if anything, greater since the place manages to co-extend and compound the alienation and isolation endemic to the Prairie Plains of Texas with the alienation and isolation which is characteristic of American Mass Culture.

To give you an idea: Conceive a marginally civilized, post-war land-and-cattle town full of west Texas autocrats and independent business men going obsessively about their own private businesses; suburbanize it after the manner of the '50s; forget the '60s (in the '60s, local hippies drove Pontiacs); infuse it with a heavy dose of the '70s "Me Generation" self involvement; and intensify that mix with a garnish of '80s "New Greed," and priggish elitism. What you get is a very strange and private place, indeed — where the modalities of social interaction are virtually non-existent and the populace at large is segregated not only according to the traditional race, color, creed, and national origin but also according to age, sex, income, education, neighborhood, mode of transportation and line of endeavor.

There are exceptions however, and on the whole, Fort Worth is not a bad place to live, if you bring a friend. And since there are better pictures in the museums and better bands in the bars, it's certainly preferable to its adjacent metropolis. Also, in Fort Worth and Tarrant County, being an asshole is optional — although it remains a very popular elective. . . .
One afternoon in the early '80s, the matriarch of an old Fort Worth family glanced out the parlor window of her palatial Westover Hills estate

to discover a large and incredibly noisy helicopter settling gently onto her beautiful, manicured lawn. Upon its coming to a rest, who should jump out of the helicopter but her husband, the spirited patriarch of this old Fort Worth family. He was out for a test-drive and wondered if the little wife might like to come along for a spin. When the little wife allowed as how she had to get back to her begonias, the patriarch allowed as how he might drop over and see "Sonny," his son and heir, who lived not far away in an equally palatial Westover Hills estate.

This visit came to no good end, however, since Sonny's prim and not a little paranoid wife spotted the copter as it began its descent and assumed, naturally enough, that it was chock full of Libyan terrorists intend on kidnap, rape and ransom. As a result, the spry patriarch hopped from the copter into his son's beautifully well-manicured lawn only to be greeted by four heavily armed private security guards and three carloads of local police, shotguns, revolvers and M-16s at the ready. As an added precaution, this group was soon reinforced by a contingent of National Guard. Thus do the generations change in *Le Ville des Vache*.

Inside the Alamo

RODOLFO F. ACUÑA

JANUARY 26, 1990 — At a 20-year reunion of 1960s Chicano activists held in San Antonio in December, organizers assigned me the task of leading a tour of the Alamo. When I agreed, I thought the idea of the tour was a joke. So when it began to drizzle, on the day scheduled for the tour, I thought I had an excuse to cancel. But a number of participants expressed interest in the tour and, as the hour approached, some three dozen families showed up to listen to the true story of how Mexicans won the Battle of the Alamo.

Contrary to popular myth, Mexicans were not the aggressors at the Alamo. Texas belonged to Mexico. Nor was the Alamo a defenseless mission. Like other missions of those times, the Alamo resembled a medieval castle, designed as a bastion of defense against those whom the missionaries considered infidels. Missions were usually built on high ground and their adobe walls were a good five feet thick. I painted this portrait for our tour-group, addressing myself to the children of the sixties activists, reminding them that the Mexicans on the outside were the true patriots, since, after all, it was they who were defending their nation's integrity. Anglo-Americans inside the Alamo had arrived in Texas after 1821 (most after 1832), so it was highly improbable that many had been born in Texas.

From the beginning, I made it clear that I had no intention of disrespecting the filibusterers who had died inside the Alamo, but as a historian, I was required to point out that the Mexicans outside the walls of the Alamo had also died — a fact that is often forgotten. As I began to explain this point, three park rangers interrupted our tour and ordered us to leave the premises, advising us that only the "official" story of the Alamo was allowed. They also added that we were subject to arrest. With these words of encouragement, I proceeded with my narration, until the Alamo curator appeared and asked why we were there and, apparently, realizing the implications of censoring us, allowed us to proceed.

My lecture continued: beyond the belief that the Alamo was a defenseless mission, there were other myths, such as the character of the Anglo heroes of the Alamo. William Barrett Travis, for example, was reputedly a fugitive from justice, who, according to prominent scholars, never drew that line in the dirt and asked for volunteers to step across it and help buy time for good old Sam Houston. In fact, the Alamo was considered defensible, though its strategic value is another of many traditions invented by the good old white boys of Texas. Santa Anna should have bypassed the Alamo.

Jim Bowie was yet another myth. No doubt he was a ferocious fighter, whose knife could eviscerate an adversary. But he was also a slave trader, a man who sold other human beings for profit. Hardly the type of person you would want going out with your daughter.

The legend and myth of Davy Crockett also came under scrutiny. Illegal aliens, as I prefer to describe white Texans, generally portray Davy going down fighting. I have seen postcards depicting Mexicans swarming all over Davy—three Mexicans on his right arm, three on his left, and another half dozen at his legs. The unwritten epitaph is obvious: "Davy went down fighting like a tiger!" Crockett, in fact, surrendered and was tried and executed.

By this time we were ready for the tour of the Alamo building itself. A sign instructed us to remove our hats and remain quiet. Great care is taken by the Alamo's caretakers to create a religious atmosphere.

Inside, I dwelled on the architectural features of the building and grounds. And the contradictions between the myth and reality of the Alamo. General Antonio Lopez de Santa Anna's inexperienced soldiers were, in fact, the underdogs, having less firepower and protection than Crockett and company. Like the Panamanian General Manuel Noriega, Santa Anna was an easy man for Anglos to hate.

And then there was the encasement of the bones of some of the Anglo heroes. The irony of white Baptist and other religious fundamentalists who criticized Catholics for praying to the Virgen de Guadalupe and the saints, here praying to the remains of fallen heroes seems amusing. They evidently saw no contradiction in venerating the bones of Davy Crockett — which perhaps in reality are the bones of an unidentified Mexican patriot.

Overwhelmed, we concluded our tour. The parallels between what happened then, and what is happening now, are inescapable. Our government, supported by a duplicitous media, creates its own reality. At the Alamo, only the official version is allowed; of the invasions of Grenada and Panama, only the government's version is allowed. In such a climate, it is only natural that we make heroes of the Contras, based in Honduras and waging war against Nicaragua. We make them the moral equivalent of the "fallen heroes at the Alamo." And all of this is so, not because it is true, but because Anglo-Americans say it is so. So much for epistemology.

We ended our tour paying our respects to the brave Mexicans who had died attacking a well-fortified military post. More importantly, we dedicated our walk through the Alamo to the victims of racism and exploitation that are justified by invention of such traditions as the Alamo.

You Can't Go Homeless Again

LARS EIGHNER

SEPTEMBER 29, 1995 — I thought it likely that I would die before the money ran out. That wasn't my plan, but I am a heavy smoker, at least ten stone overweight, and in my late forties. But it is beginning to look like I will survive my money after all. The money came from *Travels with Lizbeth* (1993), my book about my experiences as a homeless person with a dog. . . . There has been other money too, of course. I've done four books since, despite the traveling I had to do and despite wasting six months on several treatments for an ill-starred movie project, and if I finish the trilogy I am working on now within a month or so, the advance for it may extend my housed condition until sometime in the early spring of 1996. But the prospect of renewed homelessness, sooner or later, is clearly with me. I mention this *à propos* of an ordinance the Austin City Council has passed on first reading and almost certainly will finally pass sometime before Christmas. It is an ordinance to make camping on city lands unlawful. I don't know how afraid of this I ought to be.

"It is a crime to be poor." So the homeless people around the University of Texas told me when I spoke to them as their peer. Even without the ordinance, the necessities of homeless life violate existing laws in several ways. Perhaps like existing laws, the new law will be used arbitrarily by the police to remove individuals that particular officers dislike particularly. Or perhaps there actually will be an attempt to jail all of the homeless — I cannot think there is enough jail space for this, but who knows. Perhaps jail camps will be instituted.

The council has moved against the homeless many times. The main reason cited for outlawing public drinking in certain areas of the city was to cause the homeless to go elsewhere. No doubt the council has discovered that the homeless can do without drink, but everyone must needs be somewhere. Trespassing on private property is already a crime, so perhaps the council thinks that banning the homeless from public property will cause the homeless to vanish. Could the council think the homeless will come to believe that Dallas, Houston, and San Antonio are better places to be homeless?

It is a myth that the homeless are transients who might as well go one place as another. The studies are poor, but almost all studies find that more than 60% of the homeless population in a city became homeless in that city. The homeless are nothing more or less than the poor, made visible by their lack of housing. . . .

Curiously, the latest assault on the homeless occurs just as the housing market in Austin has become tighter than anyone can remember. Austin dropped twenty-odd places on someone's list of best cities in America to live in, and enormous rent increases were blamed for that. Of course the poor fall out of the bottom of the housing market in such a situation, but it is more than that. Some agencies now require prospective tenants to be bonded in addition to providing a large deposit. A substantial rent increase at the renewal of a lease is a certainty and there is almost no hope at all of finding cheaper quarters, so rare are vacancies in affordable housing. It is a curious effect of psychology that the more people who are threatened with the real prospect of homelessness, the more those who are already homeless are despised. William Burroughs has called this the smallest monkey effect. When the big monkey attacks a smaller monkey, the smaller monkey does not strike back, but instead finds yet a smaller monkey to attack.

But at the bottom of the chain is the smallest monkey. When the landlords squeeze the tenants, the rage must be vented somewhere, and the homeless person is the smallest monkey. Is a downtown merchant threatened by the vast malls? Attack the smallest monkey. It is the homeless, he concludes, not his high overhead, that drive away his customers. A silversmith in Austin's open-air market near the University of Texas was interviewed about the homeless. He said they drive away his customers. This was what the merchants in the nearby stores said about the merchants in the open-air market some twenty-five years ago when the market was established. The homeless must be driving away the crafts-man's customers, no matter that business in the market always has been marginal except immediately before Christmas. There is a smaller mon-key for everyone, except for the smallest monkey. It is only logical that as the misery index in Austin rises the city council would pommel the smallest monkey a bit themselves.

I find it very difficult to believe that anyone on the council really can be sincere in saying that help is provided for the homeless in the pro-grams that the city funds. Perhaps I have underestimated the ability of the comfortable to delude themselves. Perhaps I'd be explicit: the city's programs for the homeless are a sick joke. Not as much as a dime on the dollar of the money the city expends on these programs is delivered as something of material value to the homeless. Of course lavish amounts are expended on hiring counselors and social workers to hold the hands of the poor and to counsel them and to give them good advice, but for raising roof beams or dispensing bread and blankets, there is very little. Programs for the homeless are still predicated on the theory that the homeless have some other problem than lack of housing.

When *Travels with Lizbeth* was still fresh off the press and I was con-sidered the golden boy of homelessness, an official of the Clinton admin-istration came to Austin to explain Clinton's plan for dealing with homelessness . . . [and] I was invited to attend an informal briefing in which the plan was laid out for representatives of various agencies.

Of course there would be less money overall — the nasty Republicans were to be blamed for that, but according to the plan there would some block grants and an increase in the earned-income tax credit. A repre-sentative of one agency suggested that much of the money from the block grants might go for WIC, a food program for Women, Infants, and Children. A representative of another agency thought the money might better go for day care. It was, of course, not too difficult to detect that the advocated program was in each case connected to the spokes-person's own agency.

Everyone glared at me when I pointed out that two-thirds was the least estimate of the proportion of the homeless who are single men — some estimates are much higher. (The estimates are lower if homeless-ness is taken to include those in shelters as well as those living in the rough.) Single men are ineligible for the earned-income credit and for the WIC program, and have no use for day care. Or in other words, the three most-discussed aspects of the Clinton plan for the homeless, as it might be implemented in Texas, excluded from any benefit at least two-thirds of the people who are living in the rough. No bureaucrat will thank you for discussing reality when there is a budget to be divvied up.

It is in the spirit of these bureaucrats that the Austin city council suggests that the homeless take advantage of the programs the city funds for the homeless. Such a suggestion is nothing more or less than "Let them eat cake."

At least once a day I look around my writing room and wonder what it will be like this time. What will it be like, when with Lizbeth on her leash and all that we can keep on my back, we step out the door of our home for the last time and are homeless once again. In the early spring Lizbeth and I will both be eight years older than we were when we first set out on our homeless career. . . .

I'll have a few dollars in my pocket when I hit the street. But the fine for existing on public land will be passed and enacted into law by then. It will be five hundred dollars. I won't have that much.

I remember when I was in college, a young man in my dormitory always referred to his birth certificate as his license to exist. We thought that was amusing. But I won't have a license to exist the day I leave home again. I won't have the means to exist on private land. And it will be unlawful for me to exist on public land. What place is there to exist that is neither public nor private?

How long will Lizbeth and I exist on the streets this time? Maybe Lizbeth won't be killed when I am arrested. I think there is an animal shelter in town now that does not kill the unclaimed animals — and surely a very old dog with patchy skin and a cauliflower ear will be unclaimed. Maybe they will take her to that shelter and not to the pound. I don't know where the dogs of the newly criminal homeless will be taken.

Will it be raining that day? No doubt they will know to look under the bridges when it is raining. If I don't set up a camp and I move every night, will they find me? No, no, that won't work. The fire ants will find me if I don't return every night to a spot I have secured from them. How long can I carry my gear on my back these days? I think it is doubtful that I could even make it to a hidden spot along Shoal Creek in one day.

No, probably not anymore.

You see, I just sort of thought we would both be dead before the money ran out.

The Wounds of Waco: The Disaster That Keeps on Killing

ROBERT BRYCE

DECEMBER 21, 2001 — The latest victim of the federal government's assault on the Branch Davidian compound in Waco died shortly before Thanksgiving. There were no gun battles. There were no reporters or TV satellite trucks anywhere nearby. And there will be no high-profile government investigations into his death.

But there is no doubt that Dan Mulloney was mortally wounded at Mount Carmel on February 28, 1993. It just took him eight and a half years to die from his wounds.

Mulloney wasn't infamous in the way that David Koresh was. He wasn't a media star like FBI agent Byron Sage, who did much of the hostage negotiations with the Davidians and later became the FBI's chief apologist. He wasn't a lawyer or a cop. But without Mulloney's hard-nosed approach to his job, the world would never have fully understood or appreciated the deadly beginnings of the clash between religion and government that took place on the rolling plains east of Waco. Mulloney, a cameraman at KWTX-TV, shot the TV footage that was shown around the world, of agents from the Bureau of Alcohol, Tobacco, and Firearms storming the Davidians' home. He risked his life to capture the images of ATF agents as they exchanged gunfire with the well-armed Davidians. Mulloney and his partner, reporter John McLemore, later used their vehicle to transport injured ATF agents away from the shootout.

Mulloney, fellow KWTX cameraman Jim Peeler, and McLemore were the only non-combatants at Mount Carmel that fateful day. And the three became the only independent witnesses in the subsequent trials that attempted to assess blame for the botched raid as well as the subsequent federal assault and fire on April 19, 1993, that left about 80 people dead.

The federal government and the media were quick to blame the TV guys for tipping off the Davidians. They were convenient scapegoats. Shortly before the ATF arrived at Mount Carmel that morning, Peeler had run into a Davidian named David Jones on a road near the compound. Jones, a letter carrier for the U.S. Post Office, had immediately gone back to Mount Carmel and alerted Koresh that something was happening. The TV crew shouldn't have been there in the first place, said the critics.

But why blame the TV guys for the botched raid? The ATF had standing orders to abort the raid if they knew the element of surprise had been lost. Yet the ATF commanders, Charles Sarabyn and Phil Chojnacki, ignored reports from ATF agent Robert Rodriguez, who was working undercover inside the Davidian compound. Rodriguez told the commanders that the Davidians knew the ATF was coming long before the lightly armed agents — hidden inside two cattle trailers — left EE Ranch Road and drove onto the long muddy driveway at Mount Carmel.

Yet the two commanders ordered their agents to go ahead with the raid. The U.S. Treasury Department's report on the botched raid, in which four ATF agents were killed and more than a dozen injured, contains unusually harsh words for the ATF commanders. "Sarabyn and Chojnacki lied to their superiors and investigators about what Rodriguez had reported," says the report. The 200-page document also says the commanders altered records after the raid, in order to mislead investigators. Treasury Department investigators said the officers' attempt to cover their tracks is "extremely troubling and reflects a lack of judgment."

Sarabyn and Chojnacki lied. They ignored a standing order. They altered federal documents. Yet they were never prosecuted for their misdeeds. It was that lack of accountability, that lack of honesty by the ATF and the Department of Justice, says one prominent law enforcement official in Waco, that Mulloney simply could not accept. The fact that he was blamed for an incident that wasn't his fault, "was like a cancer that finally ate him up."

Mulloney watched as his partner John McLemore was forced out of the TV business. He saw his long-time friend, Jim Peeler, who still works at KWTX, torn apart. "He was tormented by it," says the law enforcement official. "I think he basically grieved himself to death."

Mulloney was an average cameraman. But he was an extraordinary news man. He knew almost every cop in Waco. He also knew most of the firemen, lawyers, ambulance drivers, and anyone else who might know things that could help him get a story. That's not braggadocio, it's just true. Mulloney was a better reporter than any of the reporters at KWTX, and everyone at the station knew it.

Those connections allowed Mulloney to hear about the ATF raid on Mount Carmel a couple of days ahead of time. Mulloney knew someone who worked with Waco's ambulance crew who told him about the raid. He later confirmed the tip when he talked to Tommy Witherspoon, a reporter for *The Waco Tribune-Herald*, who had been friends with Mulloney for years, and who had also received a tip about the upcoming raid.

According to Mulloney, Witherspoon named a man in the McClennan County Sheriff's Department as his source. Law enforcement officials in Waco who investigated the incident confirmed that a sheriff's deputy named Cal Luedke was the source of the leak that allowed the TV crew to be at Mount Carmel that day. Yet in the aftermath of the disaster, it was Dan Mulloney—not Witherspoon or Luedke—who became the pariah. Witherspoon has since denied that he ever told Mulloney who his source was. "I deny ever telling Dan Mulloney anything," he told me. Then he added, "Mulloney is a drunk."

There's certainly no denying that fact. After Mulloney left KWTX in 1998, after 15 years at the station, his life began a slow downward spiral. When I interviewed him at his small but tidy garage apartment a few blocks south of downtown Waco last year, he went through several 16-ounce beers in less than an hour. Infected with hepatitis-C due to a blood transfusion he had received several years before, Mulloney's liver was already damaged. He shouldn't have touched alcohol, much less worked in a tavern like Charlie's Corner, where his last job was.

But Mulloney's pain and desire to soothe his life with drink is a bit easier to understand for those who have seen the entirety of the videotape that he shot on February 28, the day of the disaster for which he has been blamed. There are the familiar images of the ATF agents breaking windows on the second story of the Davidian building and of agents exchanging gunfire with the Davidians. But the more haunting images are of the ATF agents carting off their dead and wounded. The entirety of the footage that Mulloney shot that day — the video of the long, slow retreat of the anguished ATF agents with Mount Carmel in the background — has never been broadcast. In one shot, Mulloney captured four agents dragging the limp, face-down body of one of their dead comrades by his arms. Other wounded agents, grimacing in pain, are being carried away from the battle.

At one point, a pair of ATF agents and a group of deputies from the McClennan County Sheriff's Office attack Mulloney, and begin slapping him in the face and neck, kicking him, and trying to wrestle the camera away from him. "Get that fucking camera out of here," one agent yells, while assaulting Mulloney. Mulloney put the camera between his legs and tried to cover his head against the blows. But he kept shooting, kept doing the job he was trained to do.

Mulloney died alone, and that was undoubtedly how he wanted it. His bellicosity and prickly personality had estranged him from most of his friends and family, including his only sibling, Patricia. His heart had begun giving him trouble earlier this year. On November 19, he went to the hospital and had some of the fluid drained from the area around his heart. He drove home and went to bed. Several days later, his landlady became curious and called the Waco Fire Department. On November 24, firefighters climbed through a window and found his body.

As we sat in his apartment last year, Mulloney sorted through a four-inch-high stack of news clippings on the Davidian disaster. And he repeatedly asked why the ATF never disciplined Sarabyn and Chojnacki for their mistakes. "We're tired of being the brunt of this," he told me. "The ATF has had a chance to rebut all of the allegations against us. The problem is they don't want to admit they made a mistake. I don't have an axe to grind. I just want the truth to come out."

Some of the truth about Waco died with Dan Mulloney. He was 52.

THE TEXAS Observer

A JOURNAL OF FREE VOICES   AUGUST 16, 1996 • $1.75

WHERE DO WE GO FROM HERE?

Clinton's Welfare Betrayal • Dugger Declares for Nader
Dubose on Third Party Possibilities • Texas Redistricting Old and New
Dear Governor: Send in the Troops!

Plus: A New Guerrilla Front in Mexico? • *Caballeros* and Jazz
in Texas • An Elegy for San Antonio's Cementville

Cover, August 16, 1996. Despite the Democratic Party's national successes,
the state party was in disarray. The Republicans had already won the executive
house and were poised to take over the state legislature. Cover illustration by
Kevin Kreneck.

IV. THE POLITICAL TUMULT

POLITICS IN TEXAS OF THE 1950S was an ugly affair. Conservative Democrats controlled the one-party state, fending off an emerging Republican Party and the small liberal wing in its own coalition. Governor Allan Shivers and the Shivercrats were particularly adept at keeping their opponents off guard, employing such means as "cross-filing" in elections, which allowed, for instance, a Democrat to run as a Democrat and as a Republican. This tactic stunted Republican ambitions and blocked liberals from securing party nominations. Shivers' dominance was reflected in his three terms as governor between 1950 and 1956 and his control of the Democratic state executive committee, from which he purged even moderate voices.

The gubernatorial race of 1954 proved bitter for those hoping to change these conditions. Eager to topple Shivers, liberals rallied around Ralph Yarborough, as they had two years earlier. Then, Shivers had crushed his opponent by 400,000 votes in the primary, but the incumbent appeared more vulnerable in 1954. Yarborough lashed out at influence peddling in Austin, raised questions about possible collusion between Shivers and bankrupt insurance companies, and alleged that the governor was a Republican dressed in Democratic clothing.

As the charges struck home, Shivers struck back. Playing to cold war insecurities, he denounced "communist labor racketeers" who supported his opponent; when retail workers in Port Arthur set up picket lines, Shivers cried Red, and smeared Yarborough as guilty by association. Then he played the race card in the wake of that May's Supreme Court decision, *Brown v. Board of Education*, alleging that the liberals' darling was a devout integrationist. Shivers carried the primary once again, though by a much smaller margin, 80,000 votes.

It was out of this stinging defeat that the *Texas Observer* was born and its political consciousness was formed. Many of the journal's governing board—Frankie Randolph, Minnie Fisher Cunningham, Lillian Collier, Bob Eckhardt, J.R. Parten, among others—launched the statewide paper so that liberal Democrats could take back their party. Yet because he wanted "no part of some hack party organ, no part of a journalism controlled by a politically motivated board of directors," Ronnie Dugger told the board he would accept the position only if they gave him "exclusive control of the editorial contents." That standard of independence has subsequently defined the *Observer*'s startling news coverage and its (seemingly) counterintuitive political endorsements.

An early editorial set the tone: it chastised public officials whose junkets were paid for by the same lobbyists who wanted political favors or access to the public trough. State Representative Maury Maverick Jr. was not one of those officials, but his insider perspective on the 1955 legislative session offered evidence of land fraud, financial malfeasance, and oil-lobby cronyism in the Shivers administration; still, he remained hopeful that the state would witness better days, "greater harmony," and "the acquisition of more rights for all of mankind in Texas."

Maverick wasn't entirely wrong, as the political arena would dramatically change in the coming years. Insurgent Republicans began to break the Democrats' stranglehold on power, an outcome the *Observer*, an enthusiastic proponent of two-party competition, advanced in its endorsement of John Tower's 1961 U.S. Senate campaign; Republican victories would encourage Shivercrats to switch to the GOP, opening the way, the staff believed, for liberals to capture the Democratic Party.

That vaunted day never happened, but plenty else did. In 1963, five Hispanics ran for the Crystal City council and swept to victory, a signal blow to Anglo hegemony in deep South Texas. Later that year, after John Kennedy's assassination in Dallas, Lyndon Johnson became the first Texan in the White House. But his Great Society agenda received little support from the Texas congressional delegation, who voted against the landmark voting rights bills of 1964–65. This legislation was perhaps Johnson's finest moment, however fleeting, for when he left office in 1968, his legacy was uncertain, with war raging in Vietnam and riots consuming urban America. Worse, his hand-picked successor, Hubert Humphrey, could not carry on the fight, having lost narrowly to Richard Nixon. In this fraught atmosphere, it is not surprising that *Observer* editor Greg Olds had urged Democrats to reject their standard-bearer to save the party from itself. (Olds would later claim that his anti-Humphrey platform cost him his job, an accusation publisher Dugger denied.)

More disheartening news followed. Ralph Yarborough, who had won a U.S. Senate seat in 1957, was outspent and defeated in the 1970 primaries by a flush and vacuous Lloyd Bentsen; no more scintillating was millionaire rancher Governor Dolph Briscoe, who twice vanquished *Observer* favorite Sissy Farenthold. Dispirited and angry, by the early 1980s liberals, led by stalwart Mickey Leland, sought to expel "boll weevil" Democrats such as Phil Gramm so the latter would become the Republicans they were in fact. These turncoats' ideological corruption seemed mirrored in the insider trading and fiscal improprieties that were Texas House Speaker Billy Clayton's trademark. And while Ann Richards appeared to be like a breath of fresh air when she captured the Governor's mansion in 1990 supported by the liberal dream team—farm workers, unionists, women, and minorities—she squandered her mandate and was defeated four years later by a man who would later become president.

At least Governor George W. Bush was good for the *Observer*. Its reporters took delight in skewering his compassionate conservatism, mocking his nonsensical vetoes, and capturing the sheer meanness of his legislative intent. But when Dubya ran for president in 2000, the editor, Nate Blakeslee, following a nearly forty-year tradition, refused to endorse Democratic candidate Al Gore, hoping once more that progressives would rehab the party. That begged the question of whether there was anything left worth rehabilitating. By 2003, a triumphal GOP had restored one-party rule in Austin (and Washington, D.C.); under the direction of U.S. House Speaker Tom DeLay, state Republicans tried to ram through a redistricting plan for Texas that would further devastate Democratic prospects. To stymie this agenda by busting the legislative quorum, Dem representatives and, later, senators, chose the only exit strategy that made sense—they fled the state.

Char Miller

Sitting Ducks

RONNIE DUGGER

DECEMBER 20, 1954 — The two highest officials in the State, at least twelve members of the senior chamber of the Legislature, and several other state officials spent last Sunday, Monday, and Tuesday partaking of the solids and fluids of the celebrative life, boating down the Nueces River on the Texas Company's yacht "Ava," and firing at far-off creatures in the hunting reserves of the Port Arthur Hunting Club.

Such soirees are next to commonplace among Texas politicians. This dangling weekend, paid for by business and industrial interests in the Jefferson-Orange County area, was publicized locally with a shameless candor that speaks eloquently of the insensitive condition of public morality in Texas.

. . . Many of us would rejoice in our legislators' good fortune, and, indeed, would not be averse to sharing it, under somewhat different circumstances. But let the people think upon the subtle dangers of such behavior. . . . Suppose you were a senator and spent a joyous three days cruising, feasting, and hunting as the guest of various business interests, including oil companies, banks, a hotel, and rubber, chemical, and shipbuilding companies. Two months later (in Austin, in the anteroom of the Senate chamber, say) these same pleasant and intelligent but ubiquitous gentlemen would re-appear to discuss with you, man to man, pending legislation regulating oil allowables, or revising Texas anti-trust law, or taxing industrial corporations. We do not know what would go on in your mind, but it is a question worth asking of yourself.

Many are the joys of lunchtime caucuses and cocktail parties, and far be it from us to cast a baneful Victorian eye on good clean fun. We only wish to express our hope that the marksmen of the intercoastal marshes can share with Thomas Jefferson his contentment when he wrote, in a somewhat different connection:

". . . I have in multiplied instances found myself happy in being able to decide and to act as a public servant, clear of all interest, in the multiform questions that have arisen, wherein I have seen others embarrassed and biased by having got themselves into a more interested situation."

Maverick Foresees a Rosy-Fingered Dawn

MAURY MAVERICK JR.

JULY 3, 1955 — I will not say that the dawn of a new era is with us in Texas, but I will say that the dawn of a new era is within the foreseeable future in Texas, and I would not have said that as much as a year ago.

Much has happened in the last year, and even more has come to pass since Jan. 20, 1953, when Governor [Allan] Shivers said in his inauguration speech: "Ineptness or corruption in the administration of a democratic government can and will be corrected by the people, if they are given the facts and opportunity to act upon them. This is a responsibility we must all share."

Yes, much has happened in recent times, and especially since the time when the words I just quoted were uttered — for we have seen shame and disgrace come to the good name of Texas. We have seen 25 insurance companies go broke with creditors and policy holders suffering untold economic disasters. We have seen our [oil-rich] tidelands leased to powerful men and corporations at royalty figures far less than what the Federal Government got for its tidelands, and worst of all we have witnessed the theft of the people's money from the Veterans Land Board.

In the latter part of 1953, the Texas School Land Board consisted of Bascom Giles and stand-ins for Governor Shivers and Attorney General John Ben Shepperd, who did not attend that board's meetings any more regularly than they did those of the Veterans Land Board. The School Land Board leased about 20 percent of the tidelands on a one-eighth royalty basis with minimum cash bonuses of $5 per acre.

It is interesting that when Price Daniel was Attorney General, he demanded that any bid of a lease within two miles of a producing [oil] well had to contain what is known as a high-royalty bidding feature, which meant that the bidder who offered the highest royalty got the bid. This excellent practice was discontinued when Price Daniel left the office of Attorney General and was only re-activated the month before last after the light of publicity turned toward the land office.

Now the important thing about all this is that the Federal Government — unlike the State of Texas — demanded and received bids starting on a basis of one-sixth royalty and with a minimum cash bonus of $15.00 per acre.

In May of this year — for the first time — the State of Texas demanded royalties and bonuses on an equal par with Uncle Sam — and in fairness, a good deal of the credit for this must go to Earl Rudder, the present Land Commissioner.

An important point to remember about the School Land Board is that its members were exactly the same members who made up the Veterans Land Board, one of whom was Mr. Bascom Giles. It is my thought — and prediction — that a great deal can be found out if we really have a thorough investigation of the School Land Board.

An effort was made to have such an investigation during the last session of the Legislature. The State Auditor, a man by the name of Cavness, testified before a committee that it would be necessary that he receive an appropriation of some $80,000 to thoroughly and adequately investigate the Land Board. Through the efforts and leadership of Rep. D.B. Hardeman, such an appropriation was made in the House, but it disappeared when it got to the Senate.

These factors — the veterans' land scandal, the insurance scandal, and what I think will ultimately be an equally important factor — the leasing of the tideland — are contributing issues toward what I believe will be a new era in Texas politics.

But there are other things which must be considered.

It is my opinion that in my six years in the Texas Legislature the immediate past session — with all its limitations and disappointments — was the finest session that I ever served in.

For example, session before last the bill which would have meant repeal of cross-filing under which a man could run as a Republican and a Democrat was defeated in the Senate after a hard and bloody fight. This last session, as lead author, I introduced the cross-filing repeal bill thinking that again we would have a bloody fight on our hands. To my pleasant surprise the bill sailed through the House and Senate with complete ease. Legislators who had once fought and defeated the bill changed their tune and this time voted for it.

That was a good sign. It meant that somehow, someway, the people were making it clear that they wanted intellectual honesty in party affairs — that perhaps we should have a two party state, as I think we should, but above all, let us be Democrats or Republicans and openly make our stand for what we think is right.

In the last session of the Legislature there was no book burning legislation like we had session before last, when a bill was introduced to remove all books from public libraries which degraded Texas history, American history and so on. Much of the credit can be attributed to Texas newspapers editorializing in a way which made it clear that no longer would they tolerate bush-league McCarthys. Thus the atmosphere was devoid of fear, suspicion, and censorship. . . .

Probably the most pleasant surprise of the session for me was the calm manner in which the members of the House and the Senate reacted to the recent U.S. Supreme Court decision on education [*Brown v. Board of Education*]. Frankly I thought that we would see an onslaught of bills all aimed at causing racial tensions and perhaps including features which would attempt to do away with public schools as was done in Mississippi. Yet only on one occasion was the subject mentioned — and that was two days before final adjournment. Not one unfriendly bill, of an anti-racial basis, was even introduced.

Much is taking place in the political thinking of Texas and even more will take place if you who belong to this proud and patriotic organization — the G.I. Forum — will only re-double your efforts.

Up and down the Rio Grande and in connected areas, old dynasties which were the perfection of the so-called patron system are beginning to crumble. Anglo politicians are saying with increasing frequency that you can't hood-wink the Latin-American vote, you can't fool or intimidate them into voting for you, and you cannot take advantage any longer of the lack of education which often so grossly existed. Old time

Latin American politicians, who so long contributed to what I called the patron system, are well on the road to being men who are no longer with great influence and power.

As I said I am not quite sure just what all these things mean, but I am convinced, completely convinced, that we are now solidly on the way to better days, to a greater harmony and to the acquisition of more rights for all of mankind in Texas.

A Vote for Tower

EDITORIAL

MAY 20, 1961 — The choice between John Tower and William Blakley [for U.S. Senate] is not a choice made in a vacuum, nor merely a choice between two personalities. It is more crucially a choice between two men who represent two entirely different organizations through which political power manifests itself.

Because local conditions in Texas, as throughout the deeper South, have their origin in our Confederate past, one of these two organizations — the Republican Party — today shares some decisive political objectives with Texas liberals . . . [while] the very existence of the second organization — the conservative Democratic machine — depends on desperate root-and-branch opposition to the coming power, even of Texas liberals.

Every liberal in this state owes it to himself to consider, calmly and reasonably, the issues raised by this election. We hope he will join us Saturday in voting for John Tower.

A number of reasons point to the conclusion that this is one of the most important races in Texas history.

1. Only in rare circumstances can the will of Texas liberal Democrats be expressed through the state Democratic Party. The reason is quite clear: that party is controlled by provincial Dixiecrat conservatives in "conservative" years, or by accommodating "moderates," well doused in oil, in moderate years.

2. Conservative Democrats primarily concerned with exercising power within the state will never leave the Democratic Party as

long as they control it, no matter how unsympathetic they remain toward the Trumans and Stevensons and Kennedys and toward the aims and objectives of the modern Democratic Party. One of their primary objectives, as only a casual reading of Texas history in the fifties shows, is to keep liberals down within the party and the state.

3. Less provincial and more daring and honest conservatives, however, realize that the impact of their cause nationally is being thwarted in presidential years by the inability of the Republican Party to carry many key Southern states which have no prominent, locally elected Republicans to lead effective GOP campaigns. These conservatives, with the courage and candor to have joined the party which embraces their deepest convictions, have formed the backbone of an aggressive and growing Texas Republican Party.

4. Liberals want to free their party from the dead weight of the Dixiecrats, of whom Blakley is an unerring symbol; Republicans want to reorient Texas conservatism into a source of greater state prestige. At the intersection of these two basic objectives lies a vote for John Tower.

. . . The Republican Party is getting stronger in Texas, a fact which knowledgeable liberals should applaud. It should be common knowledge that one of the most grievous ills of the South since Reconstruction has been its sluggish, narrow one-party system. It has created a reliance on personalities rather than issues in politics; it has encouraged demagoguery and petty ward-heeling; it has spawned groping, formless state legislatures; it has necessitated tawdry, intra-party power grabs; it has been the greatest barrier to a mature political culture, in Texas and in the rest of the South.

. . . It is to be granted, since politics is a game of risks, that when the Republicans have finally accomplished their formidable task, liberals may well be defeated for governor and the state legislature. But they are defeated now anyway, by pseudo-Democrats who would be Republicans in any other state outside the South, and without the state sharing in the obvious advantages of a responsible two-party legislative system. . . .

In many political situations it is necessary to sacrifice for the moment to make possible a meaningful victory in the future. We recognize Tower for what he is: a Goldwater Republican who is so conservative he cannot find a single plank in the Kennedy program he can support.

But losing to Blakley will not merely be a loss to a cynical millionaire racist who has twice served in the Senate without having been elected; who takes pride in Texas' renewed senatorial allegiance with the Eastlands, Thurmonds, and Byrds; who will oppose national Democratic reforms from the position of stronger committee posts. A loss to Blakley, more important, will be the loss of a golden opportunity for reform of the archaic party institutions with which the political climate of Texas has been too long shrouded. . . .

We appeal to reason in urging a vote Saturday for Tower.

New Shapes in Texas Politics

LAWRENCE GOODWYN

DECEMBER 13, 1962 — The coming twelve months promises to be the most important "off year" in modern Texas politics. It may take two to six years for this to become apparent, but by the end of the decade people may well look back to 1963 and say, "That is when it happened."

A two-party Texas, that long anticipated and long postponed development that has eluded the South since the Civil War, exists now: It expresses new forces of change that can be slowed or speeded up, but not halted.

Among them:

1. The conservative wing of the Democratic Party — so weakened by Senator Tower's victory in 1960 that it could barely prevail over the liberal wing in the party's spring primaries this year — was decisively depleted by more defections to the Republicans in November. Henceforth it is unrealistic for conservative Democrats to anticipate victories over liberal Democrats in statewide primary elections. Too many of their troops have gone away.

    As one wag puts it, "You can't have all those little old ladies running around putting up [Jack] Cox signs, staffing telephone committees, and attending precinct planning meetings without creating a social bond that transcends politics. They look upon all Democrats, regardless of other labels, as outside their social circles. They aren't coming back, brother."

2. The tremendous rise in the voting power of Negroes and Latin Americans — a change deeply understood by political insiders

on every side but not apprehended yet by Texans generally —
gives an ever-broadening base to the liberal-labor-minorities
coalition. Leaders of these minorities will play increasingly
powerful parts in the political decision-making of the liberal
wing of the party: Indeed, in the competition from Republicans
and conservative Democrats for the votes of members of
minorities, these voters can be expected to be wooed by a
variety of political types who only five years ago looked upon
race-baiting as a sure vote-getting device. Roughly 100,000
Negroes voted in November in Texas — a statistic to which
politicians respond.

3. The emergence of well trained and energetic Republican precinct organizations in medium-sized cities, small towns, and
even rural areas will keep newly arrived Republicans glued to
the G.O.P. for state races — in contrast to the old conservative
custom of voting Democratic in the spring and Republican in
presidential elections. Together with the increasing muscle of
the liberals, this really kills the old-line conservative Democratic
state machine.

4. Before passing from the contemporary scene, the conservative
Democratic aggregation can be expected to make one and
possibly two desperate and well-financed efforts to stay the
engulfing tides of liberalism and Republicanism. But the San
Antonio precedent could apply here.

First, the liberals, united behind Henry Gonzalez in 1956,
upset the incumbent conservative Democratic state senator,
Ozzie Latimer, by a few hundred votes. Seizing the opportunity
of opposing a liberal, the Republicans ran a well financed but
under organized campaign against Gonzalez in the general election. The G.O.P. lost, but learned some lessons and pledged a
clan of recruits from among Latimer's former friends in the
Democratic Party.

Taking heart from Gonzalez' fortunes, the liberals next swept
in an entire legislative ticket. More conservative money — and
voters — began weighing the G.O.P. The long dominant conservative Democratic machine watched with shell-shocked horror

as the two new machines rapidly organized in their midst — the eager, enthusiastic G.O.P. militants and the faction-ridden but victorious liberal Democratic coalition. . . .

Today, in San Antonio, there is a conservative Republican Party, and there is a liberal Democratic Party. The conservative Democratic tradition that dated back to the Civil War is dead. The whole process took just six years. . . .

All of this adds up to a new premise in liberal politics in Texas. Heretofore, liberals sought statewide candidates who could add enough votes from outside their coalition to make up a majority. Now, the mathematics of the liberal situation calls for candidates who can hold all the elements of the coalition together. This is easier said than done, because the pace of change, in racial attitudes and in racial expectation, is far swifter than most liberal politicians realize.

5. The passing of the poll tax will ensure further strength for the liberals and Negroes and Latin Americans within liberal ranks. This is true whether the registration law replacing the poll tax is super-liberal, moderately liberal, or not liberal at all. Most statehouse observers believe that as a practical matter, a new registration law cannot be whammied enough to neutralize the repeal of the poll tax.

These are the new realities of Texas politics. Only five years ago, in the special legislative session of 1957, Texans wrote a whole series of segregationist laws. None of them could pass today — indeed, they might not even get out of committee. It is impolitic to be openly segregationist in statewide Texas politics in 1962. . . .

This produces a new thesis which 1963 will test: the liberals, to hold firm, must be more liberal, more explicitly integrationist. [Gubernatorial candidate] Don Yarborough almost rode this thesis to a "sleeper" victory in 1962. His fault, if anything, was that he didn't ride it hard enough in the face of adroit competition [from John Connally] in Negro and Mexicano precincts. In any case, Yarborough took the most advanced position on civil rights of any state-wide Southern candidate in memory.

In response, Connally was not explicit on civil rights issues, but he did something no other conservative in Texas has done — he granted positions of status and some authority in his campaign organization to leaders and would-be leaders of the Negro and Latin-American communities. His civil rights pitch to the mass of minority voters consisted of the adroit use of civil rights symbols such as Gonzalez and Kennedy, on campaign literature.

Between them, Don Yarborough and Connally have changed the way the game will be played. Other statewide politicians will have to move much faster on civil rights than they have, just to keep up.

Meanwhile, the conservative Democrats maintain their grip, however nervously, on the helms of state government. Some of their ablest political figures are plotting their courses of action, and several of the more light-footed among them may survive quite a while into the political future.

But for the conservative Democratic organization itself, "quite a while," in the new Texas context, may not be long.

Los Cinco Candidatos

LAWRENCE GOODWYN

APRIL 18, 1963 — The highway signs proclaim the existence of "The Spinach Capital of the World," and a mile or two further on, "Crystal City, population 9,500." It is a long, hot, dusty drive from Central Texas to this forsaken corner of the state near the middle Rio Grande, 50 miles from Eagle Pass and its Mexican twin, Piedras Negras. In the flat, bleak brush country sprawling south of San Antonio to the river there live some one million Texans, only 200,000 of them "Anglos." Of Crystal City's people, about 7,500, or three out of four, are Mexican-Americans . . . or Latin-Americans . . . or Latinos . . . or, as they call themselves, mexicanos. But this year Crystal City has an historic distinction: of the 1,681 paid poll taxes in the town, 1,139 belong to mexicanos. Crystal City has become a special town, undergoing its own special kind of ordeal. Tuesday of last week, five mexicanos formally challenged, by contesting for all city council posts, the government of the town and the spending of the taxes that come in large part from the Anglos who control the economy. Out of this challenge grew the somber trial of a rural people caught up in all the cruel complexities of 20th century racism . . . and counter-racism . . . and counter-counter racism.

It began with an Anglo.

Last October Andrew Dickens got mad at B.H. Holsomback, the mayor of Crystal City for the past 25 years. Dickens says he started a poll tax drive among the mexicanos after he was "taken" by the city fathers on a property lease. "I was taught as a youngster," Dickens says, "there's a difference between Anglos and Latin-Americans, but these officials taught me there can be quite a difference between Anglos and Anglos."

Leaders of the Political Association of Spanish-speaking Organizations (P.A.S.O.) have been building up Texas Mexicans' voting strength ever since the 1960 Kennedy campaign. Albert Fuentes, P.A.S.O. state executive secretary and a noted survivor of San Antonio's storied west side political infighting, is fond of citing the potential political impact in Texas of the two million mexicanos he habitually describes as "the sleeping giant." Mexicano power in San Antonio politics is a permanent face of that city's life. But the head of P.A.S.O., Albert Peña, a Bexar County commissioner, says the mexicano as a political force is still laggard in Texas because he is afraid he will lose his job if he steps out politically and he does not believe he has a chance to win.

Crystal City was a ready-made situation for a local test whether these two conditions could be overcome, because it is an Anglo-dominant town with a mexicano majority, and because a large pocket of several hundred workers at the California Packing Co. (Del Monte) plant in the town belong to a teamsters' union local and therefore have protection from political firings. The teamsters and P.A.S.O. joined in with a will on the poll tax drive, and when the smoke cleared at the end of the last January, better than a two-to-one majority of the qualified voters were people with Spanish names. . . .

Five days after the poll tax drive ended, Martin Garcia, a 23-year-old student from St. Mary's University in San Antonio, drove down from San Antonio to help establish the "citizens committee for better government." Garcia embodies the strange cross of forces here: he is a district director of P.A.S.O. and an employee of the teamsters — he is one of the "outsiders" from San Antonio the Anglos say stirred up all the trouble. When politics permits, he is a law student at St. Mary's.

The "crowd" at this first meeting in early February numbered 23 persons, the retired Andrew Dickens and 22 mexicanos who responded to the call of Juan Cornejo, the teamsters' business agent at the packing plant. All 23 became directors of the committee; the decision was made to run five candidates in the April city elections. In Crystal City all power is vested in the five-man city council that hires the city manager.

Fifty attended a second meeting and, before the third, a sound truck rented from San Antonio was used to promote attendance and 100 showed up. A candidate committee recommended ten candidates, and anyone else who wanted to run was told by Garcia to show up for the next meeting, at which the final five would be chosen. "I told them," says Garcia, "that anybody who filed later, after not coming forward then, would split our ranks — and we would consider it an act of treason."

The theme of this third meeting was discrimination in the Crystal City Boy Scouts. The day of the meeting the local paper carried an account of the Lions Club plan to organize an all-Anglo troop. Fuentes asked the crowd how long they were going to stand for this sort of treatment, the opening thrust in what was to become one of the campaign's most disputed issues.

At the fourth meeting the candidates were announced: Cornejo, the local teamster agent; Antonio Cardenas, a truck driver for an oil company; Manuel Maldonado, clerk in the Economart store downtown; Mario Hernandez, a Modern Homes salesman; and Reynaldo Mendoza, operator of a small photography shop. "It was after this fourth meeting, when we announced candidates, that the obstructionism of the Anglo establishment really began," Garcia says.

"First the boys went down to file and came back empty-handed. They said the clerk told them they had no application forms. So we just typed up our own. Took us five hours. We had them notarized. Then I got a photographer to go with us, and he took pictures as each man officially filed. They didn't like that — they'd never seen Mexicans so 'arrogant' before. But . . . that weekend the paper acknowledged that the five had been duly filed.

"Then," Garcia continues, "we had the voting booth episode. They cut us from three polling places to one and made no provisions for a secret ballot. They wanted people to vote right under the eyes of the election judges. . . . Carlos Moore [teamster political director for the northern district of Texas] helped out here. He told them we either got a voting booth or we'd file an injunction. The law is clear. Well, finally we worked out an agreement for P.A.S.O. to provide the booths. It cost us $42, which we paid for, thanks to the timely arrival of a $50 contribution from the Austin P.A.S.O. chapter.

"Then we got the run-around on poll watchers. Their attitude was 'We've never had any, so that's that.'" Moore showed City Mgr. James Dill the law, and they got poll watchers. They were told they couldn't use a loudspeaker because of an anti-noise ordinance, so they checked and learned there was no such ordinance, and "back to the loudspeaker we went," Garcia says. Fuentes says they were told there would be no help for mexicanos in filling out absentee ballots until they showed that the law required it.

"Each time they said 'no' to the law, and we showed them the law," Fuentes says, "two things happened: the Anglos' morale went down and the mexicanos' morale went up."

Nine days before the election there was a big meeting, 700 people standing in the hot sun, with no attractions — no beer, no tamales, no music — except "*los cinco candidatos*," as the five candidates were now constantly called in the mexicano conversations, and State Reps. John Alaniz and Johnson of San Antonio and Fuentes. Johnson says the audience was "solemn but with a twinkle in their eyes." He told them that life without freedom is worthless, and brought the house down. He asked them to treat his gringo brothers better than the gringos had treated them.

Alaniz says that as they left the rally many of the people in the crowd said to him and to Johnson, "*No nos dejan solos*" — Don't leave us alone. They meant, after the election.

Throughout the two months' organizing drive by P.A.S.O. and the teamsters — from the first meeting of 23 people to the semi-final crowd of 700 — the big fear of the challengers was that the rank and filers would lose their nerve on election day and stay home. P.A.S.O. leaders saw what they regarded as a hopeful sign of solidarity in the success of economic boycotts applied to "*los correctos*," the middle-class Mexican merchants. In the last week, some of them came around and put up signs for *los cinco candidatos*.

But the big test of their followers' final pre-election feelings toward the Anglos — or, as they were called, "*los ojos azules*," the blue eyes — was certain to come on election eve at the climactic final rally. The *Observer*'s on-the-scene coverage of Crystal City began at this point, just before the final rally on election eve.

"The Mexicans are trying to take over our town," the Anglo filling station attendant is saying. A fading twilight gives a reddish cast to everything — the baked land, the dusty roads of the Mexican quarter, the pale stucco houses. It is two hours before the mexicanos' "rally *grande*." The dust billows before the rising evening wind.

A preliminary cruise, alert for overt signs of tensions. A poster flashes by, then another: "Vote for all 5," and the names diagonally across the sign: *Maldonado, Cornejo, Cardenas, Hernandez, Mendoza. . . .* Downtown the central plaza is like any other in this part of the country, but for a curious statue of Popeye opposite city hall. The spinach capital. A car drives by Popeye, signs on all four of its doors, "Vote for all 5."

The rally is to be held at a round slab of concrete grandly named Benito Juarez Plaza, nestled deep in the Mexican side of town. A rude, plank building just off the plaza has been emptied of its chairs, which the early-comers (some 200 people, children mostly, with a few mothers and men) have placed around the perimeter of the slab. . . .

The circular slab was rimmed with people arranged around its edges. The middle of the slab was vacant, emphasizing the solitary pole that rose from the center, supporting the plaza's one light. Beyond the throng, cars and trucks were pulled up on all sides, filled with people. It was a shirt-sleeved crowd, estimated at between 1,500 and (in the *San Antonio Express*) 3,000.

Garcia, in a two-minute address, set the tone of the tumultuous meeting. His remarks, all in Spanish, sent reporters scurrying for an interpreter. Angel Gutierrez, chemistry major at nearby Uvalde Junior College, offered his services. Garcia told the crowd, "We're here tonight because deep in our hearts, we're all Mexicans, and tomorrow we're going to vote for our people."

Fuentes opened in English: "I want to tell our out-of-town guests that tonight they are seeing a people setting themselves free through the ballot box." Then in Spanish he said, "The Anglos want to know why P.A.S.O. is interested in who Crystal City elects to run this town. They want to know why I would drive 120 miles down here. You know what I tell them? I tell them I have three children, their skin is dark and their name is Fuentes. Some day they may come to Crystal City and if they do, I want them to have equal opportunities. . . .

"The gringos say they are not afraid of this election. They say they never worry until the day before the election, then they go out and buy the vote. 'Give a Mexican a dollar and he will sell himself,' they say. But this is no longer true. The mexicanos' eyes are open, and the price is higher now. The man who wants to buy a vote must pay liberty, respect, dignity, education for the children, a higher standard of living for all, and progressive government — that is the new price.

"We're going to have people there in the polling booth tomorrow to help you. Do not be afraid. . . . The victory we win tomorrow is here tonight. The Anglos know this now. More important, we know it too."

Fuentes moved away from the microphone to thunderous applause that rolled over the platform in waves. The candidates were introduced to the crowd. Each wore a small baby's *huarache* pinned to his lapel. The leader, Cornejo, was applauded five times in his two minute talk. The one remark the interpreter had time to pass along: "I am not scared of anything they might do. My life is for the people of Crystal City."

Hernandez was introduced by Garcia as a man with whom he had been kicked out of a restaurant the day before. Hernandez challenged the mayor to show him one paved street on the Mexican side of town. (That night, on the eve of the election, the city council awarded a $250,000 contract calling for the paving of three streets in the Mexican quarter.) Mendoza and Maldonado, nervously adjusting the *huaraches* on their lapels, spoke only a few words each, but both received the roar of the crowd. Cardenas, the fifth candidate, was working that night, driving his truck. . . . Gutierrez, our interpreter, made his way to the speakers' stand. He told the crowd, "They say there is no discrimination, but we have only to look around us to know the truth. We look at the schools . . . the houses we live in . . . the few opportunities . . . the dirt in the streets . . . and we know." The shock waves again, the strongest of the night, perhaps for Angel. One of his classmates explained: they are proud of him. He is an honor graduate of Crystal City, and he is with them, not like the middle-class Mexicans supporting the five incumbents. . . .

As election day broke, Anglos' resentment permeated the town, a living hostility that broke out suddenly in conversation. . . .

City Atty. Jay Taylor's office stood just beyond the crowds queued up to vote at city hall. "Certainly we're resentful of this union bunch coming in here, and stirring up a bunch of rabble," he said. "We never had any trouble before — or any discrimination." He said the local Mexicans had the purest motives, but the union people shoved them into the background and "named their own slate."

Taylor said the pro-incumbent forces were worried but thought that they would win. "Our better Mexican element will not go along with this movement," he said. "This is a good town. Shoot, I've seen some towns in South Texas where they won't even let Mexicans open a business downtown. We've never had that here. We have a number of Mexican teachers in the schools. Our assistant football coach, assistant band director, are Latins. My oldest son . . . has a Mexican teacher for Spanish."

Though the specific campaign charges of discrimination that helped keep the mexicanos heated up were denied, some Anglos conceded what one called "the broad pattern of discrimination." He said there were 1,400 outdoor privies in town, "and at an average of six people to a family, that's practically every Mexican in town."

One incumbent councilman said, "There's no discrimination. There's just too many of one race." But another citizen said, "The Mexican is still the chili-belly, the garlic-eater, the spic, the greaser to the Anglos in these parts. And we are still the gringo — and what else, I don't know — to the Mexican."

. . . At noon Fuentes came in and sat beside me at the counter. He drew a black line down the middle of a sheet of paper. On one side he wrote "542 Anglos"; on the other, "1139 mexicanos." He subtracted 175 from the mexicanos and added it to the Anglos — "the middle-class mexicanos, trying like the devil to behave like gringos," he said. He added 100 over-60 voters to the Anglos and 70 to the mexicanos and came up with a total of 810 on the Anglo side and 1024 on the mexicano side. With an 80% turnout, he figured, the mexicanos would win by three votes; but he said, "The way they count votes down here, we got to win by 100 to win at all. That'll take 90%." He downed his chocolate milk, said, "it's going to be a cliff-hanger," and disappeared out the door in front of a burly Texas ranger. . . .

In retrospect the day seemed to float by like a mist — charges, counter-charges, attitudes, anxieties, drifting out of sequence. The best quotes in the *Observer* notebook seemed to have come from those who did not want their names used, like the kindly Anglo mother, in her fifties, who blurted out in a moment of frustration, "They're just jealous, that's all. These lower class Mexicans are just jealous," and a moment later, in a sudden surge of guilt said, "I don't know, you try not to let it worry you. They don't live . . . too well." With renewed urgency she said, "We have tried to do something. We *have* done something. Thirty years ago, they died like flies . . . They'd get out there in the water in the spinach fields and go home wet and sleep on dirt floors. Now their legs are straighter and they don't all look like they had the rickets." But, a few minutes later: "It's disgusting to see them try to take this power. After the burden we've carried, supporting them . . . they pay no taxes and now they want it all."

. . . Waiting for the count as the evening advanced, about a thousand people gathered on the square, some 750 [mexicanos] on the plaza side, about 250 [Anglos] by the Ranger cars outside the drug store. An 8:30 progress report showed the Anglos ahead for three of the five seats. Toward 10 o'clock the long wait wore on the mexicanos' nerves, and the crowd grew restless. Fuentes said they were nervous because they thought, "it's being stolen from them."

. . . At 10:20 the election judge appeared and said they were almost done. He addressed Garcia and Moore: "We have bent over backwards to vote your people. Illiterates, everyone. I don't see how you can have any complaints." "Thank you," Moore managed. The election judge went back in and in another two minutes, it was apparently all over. As if by magic [Texas Ranger Captain A.Y.] Allee appeared at the steps and was the first one in. He took a quick glance at the results, looked through the glass door at the marshals, and gave a quick, time-honored gesture, an upsweep of his right fist.

"We got the shaft," said a deputy. The official totals: Maldonado 864, Cornejo 818, Cardenas 799, Hernandez 799, Mendoza 795; Ritchie 754, Brennan 717, Holsomback 716, Bookout 694, Galvan 664; the two independents, 164 and 146.

Los cinco candidatos had swept the field. Garcia ran down the street to Fuentes. Within seconds there was pandemonium: the winners were hoisted up on shoulders, so was Garcia, so was Fuentes. Handshaking, horns, a couple of mexicano versions of the rebel yell, and remarkably suddenly they fled to cars and dispersed under the gazes of the Rangers.

A tall, blond-haired man was heard to mutter on the square then, "God damn Mexicans. What chance has a white man got?"

. . . The morning after the election, Maldonado, the quiet one who campaigned the least and led the ticket, was fired from his job at the Economart. His employer said he campaigned on election day instead of working. Maldonado said he did not blame his employer.

The next day Cardenas, the truck driver, was told by his employer, Aubrey Davis of the Davis Vacuum Truck Service, that his salary was cut from $77.44 a week to $35 a week. . . .

The trucks are beginning to move out of the deep valley now, carrying their migrant cargo northward. Two trucks that left Crystal City on the morning after the election still had the sign "Vote for all 5."

Beyond that, one is conscious of the pain of poverty, the tragedy of a town in which decent people are diminished by feelings they cannot suppress, and the fact that in South Texas, the vanguard of a million mexicanos has begun to make their voices heard, as a cry, a plea, or a demand.

The President Is Sworn In

SARAH T. HUGHES

NOVEMBER 29, 1963 — It was 2:15, Friday, November 22. I had just reached home from the Trade Mart, where a large and enthusiastic crowd had gathered to see and hear President John F. Kennedy. We waited in vain, for he had been assassinated as he was leaving the downtown area of Dallas.

Numbed and hardly realizing what had happened, I drove home. There was no reason to go to court. In the face of the tragedy that had befallen us, all else seemed of little consequence.

I phoned the court to tell the clerk where I was. Her response was that Barefoot Sanders, U.S. attorney, wanted to speak to me. Immediately I heard his familiar voice. "The Vice-President wants you to swear him in as President. Can you do it? How soon can you get to the airport?" Of course I could, and I could be there in ten minutes.

I got in my car and started toward the airport. Now there was another job to be done — a new President, who had to carry on, and he must qualify for the office as quickly as possible. He had much to do, and I must think of him, and do the job that had been assigned to me.

There was no time to find the oath administered to a president, but the essentials of every oath are the same. You have to swear to perform the duties of the office of President of the United States, and to preserve and defend the Constitution of the United States. I was not afraid. I could do it without a formal oath.

Police blocked the entrance to the location of the plane, but there was no difficulty. They knew me, and I told them I was there to swear in the Vice-President as President. One of the motorcycle officers went to the plane to confirm my statement and then escorted me to the plane.

It was a beautiful sight, the presidential plane, long and sleek, a blue and two white stripes running the length of the plane, with the words, "The United States of America," on the blue stripe. It seemed to exemplify the strength and courage of our country.

I was escorted up the ramp by the chief of police to the front door, where one of the Vice-President's aides and the Secret Service met me. I was trying to explain that I did not have the presidential oath but could give it anyway when someone handed me a copy.

In the second compartment were several Texas congressmen, vice-presidential aides, Secret Service men, and the Vice-President and Mrs. Johnson. Mr. and Mrs. Johnson have been my friends for many years, but on such an occasion there did not seem to be anything to say. I embraced them both for that was the best way to give expression to my feeling of grief for them, and for all of us.

By that time, a Bible that was on the plane had been thrust into my hands. It was a small volume, with soft leather backs. I thought someone said it was a Catholic Bible. I do not know, but I would like to think it was, and that President Kennedy had been reading it on this, his last trip.

The Vice-President said Mrs. Kennedy wanted to be present for the ceremony, and in a very few minutes she appeared. Her face showed her grief, but she was composed and calm. She, too, exemplified the courage this country needs to carry on. The Vice-President leaned toward her and told her I was a U.S. judge appointed by her husband. My acknowledgment was, "I loved him very much."

The Vice-President asked Mrs. Johnson to stand on his right, Mrs. Kennedy on his left, and with his hand on the Bible, slowly and reverently repeated the oath after me: "I do solemnly swear that I will perform my duties of President of the United States to the best of my ability and defend, protect, and preserve the Constitution of the United States." That was all to the oath I had in my hand, but I added, "So help me God," and he said it after me. It seemed that that needed to be said.

He gently kissed Mrs. Kennedy and leaned over and kissed his wife on the cheek.

Here was a man with the ability and determination for the task ahead. Great as are the responsibilities of the office, I felt he could carry on. I told him so, and that we were behind him, and he would have our sympathy and our help.

As I left the plane I heard him give the order to take off, "Now let's get ready and go." I drove away with my thoughts on this man, upon whom so much now depended.

Fools 12, Folks 8

LARRY L. KING

JULY 23, 1965 — *"Hain't we got all the fools in town on our side?
And ain't that a big enough majority in any town?"*

To answer the question Mark Twain put in the mouth of Huck Finn:
No, we hain't got all the fools in town on *our* side. But we got a heap of
'em in our midst. Mostly they go around posturing as Texas congressmen, and if you've got the stomach to stand it these pages shall soon
reveal the latest perfidy performed by exactly one dozen thereof.

Once I fed my family reasonably often, if not well, through the
sports-writing dodge. And so when I heard how Texas congressmen got
recorded in the House on the voting rights bill, I naturally thought of the
results in sports jargon. Reported in the line scores, the mournful numbers would have read: Fools 12, Folks 8.

Let me call time out in this dirty game to answer the shocked comments of everybody — beginning with my sweet wife, extending through
Editor Ronnie Dugger and reaching out to you, Dear Reader — who will
draw a big breath and declaim, "Mercy! You can't go 'round calling a
dozen Texas congressmen *fools*!"

The hell I can't. Don't stop me until you've heard the evidence.

What exactly one dozen of our native heroes in Congress did was to
come out flat-footed against folks having the right to vote. Oh, for the
most part they perfumed it up and powdered it some, employing sweet
words like States Rights and The Constitution and Local Responsibility
in trying to get the stench out of the thing. But there is no honey in the
rotten carcass of the lion, and the thing still reeks. Plainly and simply
stated so that even your average Neolithic Texas legislator might under-

stand it, the voting rights bill removed the dodges, tricks, skullduggeries, jokes and hitches through which many citizens have long been disenfranchised. The bill zeroes in on six Southern states containing counties in which less than 50% of the eligibles were registered or voted in the last election, and from which enough complaints were received to show that the something rotten wasn't necessarily in Denmark. In short the bill was drawn to scratch where the itchin' was.

Few surprises are found among the dozen Texas congressmen who declared against the voting rights bill. They were, not exactly in the order of their respective brain wattages, Reps. [Lindley Garrison] Beckworth, [Omar] Burleson, [Bob] Casey, [John] Dowdy, [O. Clark] Fisher, [George Herman] Mahon, [Wright] Patman, [William Robert] Poage, [Joe] Pool, [Ray] Roberts, [Walter] Rogers, and [Olin Earl "Tiger"] Teague. Before their names disappear in a puff of public indifference, let us consider together what they voted *against*:

1. Suspension of so-called literacy tests, some of which require applicants upon demand of voter registrars to recite whole pages of the State Constitution, or to name every public official from the President of the United States down to the County Tick Inspector.

2. Requiring local or state governments accused of having disenfranchised citizens to show evidence — in duly constituted federal courts — of having complied with existing laws safeguarding voter rights.

3. Authorizing appointments of federal examiners in areas with histories of chronic complaints of irregularities, to register persons who would be qualified to vote were it not for discriminatory literacy tests.

4. Empowering the Attorney General to institute suits to enforce the 15th Amendment in the federal courts, with federal examiners being assigned to monitor such cases pending a final judgment.

5. Providing criminal penalties for intimidating, threatening, or coercing any person for voting or trying to vote.

6. Providing criminal penalties against fraudulent voting practices.

Those six provisions in the voting rights bill aren't exactly to be confused with the Communist Manifesto, though from some of the hooting and dancing on the House floor against them one might have thought them conceived by Karl Marx at his most diabolical. I can't see how any grown man who stayed in school long enough to qualify for mid-morning recess can offer one common-sense reason why those six basic points should not be employed to protect the citizen's right to ballot — presuming, of course, you think we are serious about holding *free elections* in this Republic.

This apparently is a presumption one cannot make of certain of our mudbog Mikados. There they were out there on the House floor in front of God, Lyndon and everybody, bawling the type of low comedy I sometimes do at parties when the night is full of drink. Somehow they managed to keep straight faces while doing it.

Congressman O. Clark Fisher, who for reasons vastly incomprehensible has been chosen for twenty-odd years to represent an arid section of West Texas full of plain folks and goat herds, railed at one point of "when Martin Luther King invaded Selma, Alabama, with his blood-splattered demonstrations." I should not have been surprised had the learned Dr. Fisher next proclaimed that water flows up hill, the Alamo is in San Angelo, or that canaries chirp bass. For unless I have been seriously misled by the Left-Wing Press, the blood was splattered (a) when Alabama "lawmen" fell on peaceful marchers with clubs and gas, (b) when hooligans struck from behind and killed a minister who had affronted them by walking down a public street and (c) when some gutter-snipe Klansmen fatally shot from ambush a lady whose crime was visiting from Detroit. Dr. Fisher struck similar sparks of unintentional wit before asking of demonstrators "What more do they want?" Well, Clark, they might have the gall to want to vote even as you and I do without having their lives endangered. They might want to use the public facilities for which their taxes help pay. They might want to enter courthouse doors now open only to those persons of lighter hues. And they might even want certain damn fools to remember recent facts of history as they really happened — strange as the notion may appear to all true-blue patriots such as we.

Came next a verbal juggling act offered by Congressman John Dowdy, who cried that mob rule prevails in the street. Democrat Dowdy squawled his message in the same connotation Republican Goldwater applied in the campaign just past, and if that confuses any of you civics students please see me after class. The Dowdy one mentioned a certain comedy he sees in "the hallelujah chorus of We Shall Overcome," and in the figure of (ho-hum!) Martin Luther King. He tried hard, but I could not see where it was funny except when the piney-woods windbag wound up his oration by bellowing how, should the voting rights bill pass, we would become "the land of the slave and the home of the knave." That ain't even good as poetry.

It was hard to discern whether Congressman Walter Rogers meant to be funny or not, so grim-visaged was his presentation of an amendment demanding that all "new voters" swear a special oath to support the Constitution. Professor Rogers lost by a comfortable margin, perhaps because the Members didn't know whether he meant to go by the Constitution the rest of us believe in or the one he seems to assume is his own special property. I will say that even in a losing cause Rep. Rogers appeared appropriately pompous throughout. He lectured on how his amendment would be "a most potent weapon against communism and especially against participation of communists in elections in this country" and solemnly declared that he required of voters not a literacy test but "only a patriotism test." The only person who appeared smitten with enthusiasm about Dr. Rogers sitting in judgment of our patriotism turned out to be Congressman-at-Large Joe Pool, who propelled his girth upward for purposes of proclaiming he backed the idea "100%." As usual, Rep. Pool was backing an idea not enchanting to the majority.

After everybody had their sport the House passed the voting rights bill 333 to 85. This can be bad news only to folks who stomped around muttering over the dangerous trend toward majority rule, of communist plots unknown at this moment even in the Kremlin, and maybe to eighty-five somebodies in Congress who may face a day of reckoning at the polls when the new law bears its fruit of additional free men armed with the ballot. Some twenty-odd congressmen from The Old Confederacy proved pliable enough to change their ancient views and vote for the bill. The diehards who did not largely voted on racist grounds no matter their protestations to the contrary. One has but to read the Congressional Record to find all the hateful, snide little references to Martin Luther King, We Shall Overcome, freedom marches, and the like to really see what lurks in the hearts of men. It is a sad commentary that a dozen Texas congressmen, and Senator John Tower from our state, chose to cast lots with the bigots and mountebanks who would probably bring back slavery if they had a choice.

Well, that's my case in calling the score Fools 12, Folks 8 — except for one minor point. Brother Webster informs in his dictionary that a fool is "a person who lacks judgment."

The defense rests. . . .

Humphrey Must Be Defeated to Save the Democratic Party

GREG OLDS

NOVEMBER 1, 1968 — The division among members of the *Observer* staff and the mixed emotions each of the staff members has as to how best to proceed in the November 5 elections is reflective of the ambivalent feelings these days of many Texas liberals. The editor believes Hubert Humphrey should be defeated; the associate editor and the editor-at-large (who also is the publisher) have come 'round, after some time, to believe Humphrey must, after all, be supported. Inasmuch as editorial policy is the prerogative of the editor, the *Observer* hereby expresses its support for the defeat of Humphrey and the discredited Democratic party—the while acknowledging disagreement with this recommendation on the staff of this paper and a considerable body of dissent from this conclusion within this community of the Texas left. The *Observer* suggests that write-in votes be cast for Sen. Eugene McCarthy for president and New York Mayor John Lindsay for vice president, or for whichever two candidates the voters prefer to the Democratic ticket.

It is not at all easy for the *Observer* to suggest such a course: the effect of such voting is to add to the support Richard Nixon will have in Texas. So be it. The reasons for our advocating such a course among supporters of the progressive movement in Texas are complicated but, we believe, persuasive. This election, more so than any other in at least this century, will be affected — and probably decided — by factors other than which candidate is favored by certain types of voters.

There are other issues at stake this year. There is a large body of the electorate who believe the question is not which candidate will come the closest to running the government the way they want but, rather, how can the Democratic party be restored to its 20th century role of being the key instrument of American social progress? This concern is precisely why many progressives are not going to vote for Humphrey in 1968 and why the *Observer* recommends Humphrey's defeat.

If the choice is merely which man, Humphrey, Nixon or Wallace, most nearly approaches embodiment of the liberal and progressive values, the choice for those on the left in Texas and nationally is simple. Humphrey, of course. If, as the *Observer* believes, the choice is more complicated than that, then deciding how to proceed is a source of complex anguish.

"The lesser of two (or three) evils." "Consider the alternatives." These are the slogans the Humphrey campaign has centered on. These are slogans that have had much effect on liberals in the nation; Humphrey has gained ground by their use; he is looking better and better to those on the left as election day nears. Many McCarthy and Kennedy and McGovern backers who, before Chicago and immediately thereafter, said they would not vote for Humphrey have changed their minds and now freely say they will back him. Others, who remain silent, will find in the voting booth, that they just cannot vote for Nixon or Wallace and will, reluctantly and sadly, vote for Humphrey. These are people, these liberals, who are worried about the next four years in America and in the world. They do not want Nixon to decide nuclear equations, to name Supreme Court justices, to determine the future of domestic social legislation, to set the tone and tenor of American society, social justice, intellectual pursuit or cultural advance in the years just ahead. We cannot, these liberals say, have Nixon until 1972 or 1976. The poor must be seen to, the inhabitants of the ghettos and barrios liberated, the Vietnamese given peace, the nuclear sword removed from suspension above the head of humanity. Humphrey best can do this, Nixon will not, Wallace will not, so it is said.

The *Observer* is worried less about the next four years than about the next twenty-five. If the Democrats are kept in power under present circumstances, then hope for restoring the Democratic party, the nation's key instrument of social progress and justice, to its historic course of progressive reform will be grievously undercut. The cynicism and cruelty of Chicago exemplified the nature of many of those who currently run the party, and this nation. That party must not be rewarded by Humphrey's succession of the discredited Johnson administration. If Humphrey is elected the men who now run the party will remain in power; they will influence the new president as they have influenced the present holder of that office — and Humphrey has shown himself a good deal less able to resist the entreaties of powerful men than has Johnson. As Jack Newfield has written in the *Village Voice*, Humphrey, after four years in the White House, is a "moral eunuch." "If he couldn't stand up to Mayor Daley, how can he deal with the joint chiefs, the CIA and the Pentagon?"

Humphrey has shown himself to be a man of crucial moral weakness. If truly he doubts the wisdom of our Vietnam policy, as his apologists tell people who yearn for peace, then why did he not use his influence as vice president towards that end? He could have resigned; he could have demurred; he could have remained silent. He did none of these. On the contrary, he became perhaps the most outspoken, enthusiastic advocate of American murder and atrocity in Vietnam. His mushiness on the issue to this day bespeaks a misunderstanding of our nation's tragic role in Asia.

Humphrey sought, in his September 30 TV address, to assuage the feelings and ease the concern of those who want us out of Vietnam. In substance, however, he said nothing that Johnson has not been saying since 1965: we will de-escalate if the other side makes some step in good faith to de-escalate. Specifics as to what would constitute good faith de-escalation by the Viet Cong are not forthcoming.

Moreover, while Humphrey has remained publicly silent on the matter, we have not stopped the bombing while the Paris peace talks drone on, though many sources tell us that such a stoppage would greatly enhance the chances of the negotiations. Why has not Humphrey urged a bombing halt now? Lately, there is word that instead of stepping down the U.S. military effort in Vietnam our country is preparing a final push before Johnson leaves office; the president appears yet intent on winning military vindication of his murderous policies. Tristram Coffin, in a newsletter he publishes from Washington, advises that the Pentagon now plans to put some rear-echelon troops into combat in Vietnam. "This was revealed," Coffin writes, "when a source on Capitol Hill 'leaked' the import of a letter from Defense Secy. Clifford to Chairman Richard Russell of the Senate Armed Services Committee. . . . Under the Pentagon plan, perhaps as many as 90,000 additional Americans will be in combat." What is Humphrey doing to stop this? Surely he has heard the talk of a final American push in 1968. Humphrey has done nothing.

Has Humphrey really changed his mind about Vietnam? Has he departed from the Johnson administration policy? His September 30 address has been represented as a departure from the LBJ policy, as an appeal to people who want to get out of Vietnam. But as Mary McCarthy (no relation to the senator, though she backed McCarthy) wrote in the *New York Review of Books* recently, "You can read anything you want into Humphrey's recent remark about stopping the bombing if elected; it is like a big Rorschach blot." Other commentators have agreed.

And, just three days before that address, Humphrey wrote one Texan, a man who wants us out of Vietnam, saying, "You ask that I modify or change my policy on Vietnam. There are two reasons *for my not doing so.* First: we are having trouble enough in Paris, Hanoi and Saigon without complicating it further by suggestions from presidential candidates. Second, *my position has not changed* and I will not change it to gain political advantage. I believe we should conclude the war as soon as possible but that we cannot simply fold up our tents and go home. The detailed arrangements are not in my hands at the moment. When they are you can count upon my concluding the hostilities as soon as possible." (Italics added.) Thus three days before the TV speech which HHH people have represented as Humphrey's moving away from the LBJ war policy the vice president was writing that his position has not changed from what it was. What it was, as we know, was to stand with Johnson in Vietnam.

Why, then, should we believe Humphrey has changed his mind? We are being inundated, once again, with words, obfuscation. There may be a change in degree in the Humphrey stance, it is true; if so, it is a movement towards peace of inches rather than of the miles our nation needs to travel. There is no genuine advantage in having Humphrey instead of Johnson running our nation's foreign policy if HHH is to persist in the same policies, representing those policies in words, rhetoric, that are more pleasing to the ear while the bombs continue to fall in Vietnam.

The case against Humphrey (really against retaining the Democratic party in power) was stated most eloquently in a recent article by Christopher Lasch in the *New York Review of Books*:

. . . Those who hate what Humphrey stands for must not be seduced once again into the familiar mistake of voting for the Democrats on the grounds that the Republicans are even worse. If anything, the Republicans are the lesser evil in this election. Both parties, having repudiated their moderate wings, are thoroughly militarized; both are committed to the war; neither has any program for dealing with poverty and racism except force. Nevertheless the Democrats, as the party in power, must take the greater share of responsibility for the disasters of the last eight years. The antiwar forces should combine in refusing to vote for any of the major presidential candidates; if the election appears to be close, as now seems unlikely, they might even consider voting for Nixon.

The main thing is to defeat Humphrey, not because Nixon is more likely to end the war nor because, even if he tries to carry it on, he will at least have to face a Democratic opposition in Congress — although both these things may be true — but simply because it is unthinkable that the Democratic party, after embarking on a war it promised to stay out of, highhandedly putting down a popular uprising in Santo Domingo, suppressing dissent at home (as in the Spock trial), letting the cities decay while maintaining a multi-billion-dollar budget for defense, and conducting its convention over the bodies of young people protesting a war the Democrats themselves once agreed was not to be countenanced — it is unthinkable that any party with such a record be rewarded with reelection. A Democratic victory, moreover, would prove that the Democratic Party can flout the popular will with impunity. A Republican victory would preserve at least a façade of democracy. . . .

The aim of those on the left and in the center who seek a Humphrey loss on Tuesday is the restoration of the Democratic party as the key progressive force in American life. We cannot rely on the Republican party for progress: that we have seen often in this century. But right now we cannot rely on the Democrats for progress either; so committed to this disaster of a war is that party that social reform so desperately needed here at home is a fiscal and psychic impossibility. The choice of Americans this year is a wretched one indeed: between a party committed to an atrocious war and a party that has failed to provide an alternative to that war policy.

The Democratic party has become a bastion of reaction; its rhetoric is reminiscent of its better days of the recent 36 years (though it is a rhetoric now badly outdated); but its deeds are woefully inept, insensitive, antihuman and irrelevant to the needs of the times. A Humphrey defeat will restore the party to control of its better elements, those who are ideological descendants of Roosevelt, Truman, Stevenson and Kennedy — men who have kept their liberal and progressive ideologies up-to-date with the fast-changing times; men on the frontiers of leftist progress; men who, unlike Humphrey, have stayed aware of what is going on in America and the world.

All this leaves us with Nixon, then, doesn't it? Sadly, it does. But consider the argument of Mary McCarthy, again, in the *New York Review of Books*: ". . . Nixon, if willing, will be able to withdraw from Vietnam with greater ease than Humphrey, since the Democrats as the opposition party will hardly be in a position to accuse him of surrendering to communism. . . . Looking behind the candidates, we can see that Wall Street is against the war and that organized labor is for it, which gives hope that the victory of Nixon may contain a consolation prize for those who, more than anything else, want the war to stop. . . ."

Will Nixon be willing to stop the war? We don't know. But neither do we know about Humphrey. Really, it's a tossup. But Nixon has not been tied to the present war and, astute politician that he is, Nixon must realize well that this country will be ungovernable if the war is not stopped in the first twelve months or so of the next president's administration.

To adopt another argument against the Democrats and for the Republicans, the arguments of columnist Walter Lippman: Humphrey rules a grievously split party; Nixon's is more united and, Lippman believes, will thus be able to grapple with the problems of governing our nation.

Another, quite secondary reason the Texas left should oppose Humphrey is that the defeat of the Democrats nationally will wreck the Austin-Washington axis that has worked effectively against progressive change in Texas. This is not a reason that should be primary in the minds of those on the Texas left in deciding how to vote, however: national matters are far too important to yield even in Texans' minds, to provincial considerations. With the Democrats out of power, the conservative wing of the Texas Democratic party will have far less stroke in Washington than otherwise. The result will be that the state's business establishment will turn to Texas Republicans for influence in Washington, working most likely through Sen. John Tower for what they want from the federal government in the next four years. That will strengthen the fledgling Texas Republican party and hasten the day many liberals have helped work for — a two-party Texas.

All the foregoing is a complicated argument for liberals to follow and for the *Observer* and other public voices of the left to propose. But as we said at the outset, this year's election, more than any other in this century at least, is to be determined by factors other than which candidate most nearly represents the views of blocs of voters. Rewarding the Democratic party after its vile and vicious war policy; after nominating a candidate who has championed that policy and not foresworn it in this campaign; after permitting the crushing of the legitimate revolts of the young and the disaffected, is quite unthinkable. Humphrey will not be able to govern well this country. We have no reason to believe or expect, as we are being entreated to do, that he will become his own man upon election; at the very latest (and, indeed, it would have been very late, even then) he should have achieved "own-man" status on August 28, when he was nominated.

No, let us have four, even eight years, of Nixon, rather than lose the hope of recalling the Democratic party from reaction.

Last Flight to Johnson City

BILL HELMER

JANUARY 24, 1969 — Unlike most of my friends, I was never a Lyndon Johnson man or a Lyndon Johnson hater. Often I agreed with his critics, and shook my head in disapproving wonder at how this president, for all his political skill and craftiness, could so blindly (it still seems) follow his advisors to disaster in Vietnam, or how he could so lose control of Kennedy's and his own domestic welfare programs. But I always found myself defending him on the very grounds that disturb so many people: that he was playing to the history books. Being slightly cynical anyway, I always prefer the leadership of a shrewd and world-wise scoundrel to that of an idealistic intellectual who has little working knowledge of human nature and no idea of what the hell is really going on. Especially if the scoundrel wants to earn himself a place in history as a good and great leader. It seems to me no better motive could be attributed to any man.

I pondered some of these matters on inauguration day as I made what I shall call, purely for the sake of dramatics, the Last Flight to Johnson City. Through well-connected friends in high places, I managed to score a free ride to Austin aboard the executive-size Jet Star that accompanies Air Force One carrying Secret Service men and surplus dignitaries. It is also used (because of its small size) to carry Johnson from Bergstrom Air Force Base in Austin to the landing strip at the LBJ Ranch. After the Washington ceremonies late Monday morning, Johnson was on his way back to Texas — more or less for keeps — and I was going along.

The ride itself was thoroughly uneventful. Having watched the swearing in of Richard Milhous Nixon and Spiro Theodore Agnew I was in a mood of deep despair, and managed to avoid the plane's more talkative passengers by sitting in a corner beside an inscrutable Oriental gentleman and across from a dozing Secret Service man. My only significant communications in the plane concerned the booze and sandwiches and how to operate the marvelous vanishing toilet in the passageway between the cockpit and the passenger compartment. All I could see out the window was a white sea of clouds.

I have no idea of the mood in Air Force One, but sitting there in Air Force "Two" I imagined it to be one of mixed relief and melancholy. One of history's most colorful, controversial, and sensitive presidents was through, and on his way back home. From persons close to him I had learned that his last days in office were extremely unhappy ones; that he seemed inwardly obsessed with the fear that he was unpopular — almost in the high school sense — and that Americans were thinking he had not tried his damnedest. Almost alone among my friends I had come to view him as a man whose road to hell was paved with good intentions; as a man who, in a way like Kennedy, had all the power and money and prestige anyone could ever want, and could now afford to expend his remaining energies altruistically like a good king in the service of his people. (My charitable view of some controversial people is based on the personal belief that all altruism is motivated by self-interest: people do good things essentially because it makes them feel good. Profound Thought No. 22.)

But the worry of the Johnson staff (and doubtlessly Johnson himself) on Jan. 20 was that the retiring president would land at Bergstrom and find no one lining the Cyclone fence.

Thank God the crowd was there: several thousand homely nondescript Texas types holding up their Kodaks and their crudely lettered signs balancing kids on their shoulders yelling and waving, stretching their necks and their toes to glimpse their descending world leader who was coming home, bloody and somewhat bowed. No hecklers were on hand this time, and probably few thinkers: only a sentimental mob of what an old style, unscrupulous, pragmatic American politician would look upon as "The People."

Squinting through a telephoto lens, I could see Johnson clearly as he emerged at the door of Air Force One. He stood there with an almost tearful smile for a minute or more, surveying the throng of people. The Longhorn band played a "Hello Lyndon" that was a little too fierce and brassy for the occasion. For the mood was pretty solemn. The happiness that afternoon was not that any victory had been won, but that a battle was over.

The sky was overcast and getting dark, and the portable TV lights at the foot of the passenger ramp gave Johnson's face the radiant glow of a cheap religious painting. For the first time in years he looked genuinely happy. He spoke briefly from a small black platform, that this time had no presidential seal, showed off his family and his ornery grandchild, Patrick Lyn Nugent, who had spent the previous days testing the patience of Secret Service men and everyone else in the White House. As his grandfather spoke, he labored to disconnect the microphone.

But nothing very important was being said anyway. A photographer beside me in the camera platform chuckled when Johnson said of Richard Nixon, "I hope you will be as good to him as you have been to me." He must have been thinking as I was, that Nixon could hope for more.

Afterwards the former president, smiling grandly, stepped over to the cyclone fence and began shaking hand after hand after hand. Then he took the little Jet Star on to Johnson City.

Ten or twenty years from now, I'm convinced, the history books will treat Lyndon Johnson with great sympathy, judging his failures in the context of their time and circumstances. Scholars will rush to vindicate his efforts and intentions, if not always his judgment. In recent conversations with some of his harshest critics, I myself detect a mellowing that I consider extremely hypocritical. But I suppose it's Liberal not to kick the body of the vanquished foe and even more Liberal to treat his wounds.

So now, with sorrow and regret, I must turn anti-Johnson just to rile my friends. We now look ahead to at least four years (God willing) of Richard Milhous Nixon and his glittering galaxy of Agnews and Hickels and the like. I expect the 1970 model cars to sprout tail fins. I am going to get drunk frequently and argue belligerently that the new administration is merely another plot engineered by Lyndon Johnson to make himself look good in retrospect.

Lloyd Bentsen's Fortune

KAYE NORTHCOTT

APRIL 3, 1970 — When Lloyd M. Bentsen, Jr., retired from the U.S. Congress [in 1955] at the age of 33, he explained that he was leaving politics because he wanted "to establish financial independence" for himself and his family. Seventeen years later, his business interests include banking, insurance, farming, oil, gas, and defense contracting. He may or may not be independent, but he certainly is wealthy.

Many Texans are under the impression that Bentsen, Senator Yarborough's Democratic opponent, has always been rich. "Well, that's not true," he quietly told the *Observer* during a telephone interview. That was all he offered on his early financial status. One hears estimates that he is worth as much as $20 million, but the candidate is reticent about his wealth. He says he will make public his financial statement when he is elected, and not before. "I assume the reason we want to give financial statements is to show what a man's worth is when he is elected and what his financial losses and gains are when he gets out," Bentsen said, as a means of explaining why he sees no reason to reveal his net worth during his candidacy.

Bentsen is the son of a millionaire. His father, Lloyd Senior, made a fortune selling land in the Lower Rio Grande Valley. When Lloyd Junior abandoned politics to launch a career in business, "Big Lloyd," as his father is known around the hometown of McAllen, most assuredly provided some ballast for the venture.

Today Bentsen is president of Lincoln Consolidated, a holding company with offices in Houston. His father is chairman of the board. The company was formed in 1967 as a parent for Lincoln Liberty Life

Insurance Company; Funds, Inc., (which manages five mutual funds); Compensation Programs ("specializing in deferred compensation planning and administration," according to Standard and Poor's stock exchange report); and Benjamin Franklin Savings Association. Ben Franklin, a Texas concern with $58.7 million in total assets and $53.9 million in total savings, was purchased by Lincoln Consolidated in June of 1969. In mid-1969, Lincoln Consolidated reported a total income of $1,482,848 and $765,982 in net income. According to Standard and Poor's, Lincoln Consolidated paid $32,000 in federal income tax in 1969, and no income tax in 1968. Bentsen told the *Observer* that the company paid "substantially" more in income tax in 1969 but that he did not have the records handy.

Lincoln Liberty Life is headquartered in Lincoln, Nebraska. It writes a variety of ordinary life insurance on a non-participating basis plus accident and health insurance and group life insurance. Bentsen, his father, and four other Bentsens are on Lincoln Liberty's board of directors. In 1969, the company's total assets were $75,617,295.63. Its net gain for the year was $444,293.49.

The insurance company is a prime example of the type of bank holding company that Texas Congressman Wright Patman has been working to bring under more stringent federal control. According to Lincoln Liberty's annual report for 1969, the company owns stock in the following Texas banks:

- First National Bank of Edinburg - 1,498 shares worth $112,353.60.
- First National Bank of McAllen - 16,601 shares worth $222,184.48.
- First National Bank of Mission - 4,560 shares worth $110,345.15.
- Security State Bank of Pharr - 5,750 shares worth $68,717.
- Texas City National Bank - 2,310 shares worth $69,300.

In July of 1967, the House Banks and Banking Committee issued a report on control of commercial banks and interlocks among financial institutions. The report cites as its most interesting case "Lincoln Liberty Life Insurance Co. of Houston, which has between 15.1 percent and 41.28 percent of the shares in each of six Texas banks. All of these banks except Texas City National Bank are in the same geographic area known as the Lower Rio Grande Valley. . . ." It is interesting to note that this insurance company has in all except one case kept its percentage of bank stock holdings in these banks below 25 percent, thus avoiding the necessity of subjecting itself to regulation under the Bank Holding Company Act. How close Lincoln Life has become to a regular bank holding company is seen in that if it owned just one more share of First National Bank of Edinburg, it would come under the Bank Holding Company Act. If it had one more share, it would be required to divest itself of the bank or the insurance company.

At the time of the report, the company had 24.97 percent of the Edinburg bank stock and 41.28 percent of the stock of the First National Bank of Raymondville. The Raymondville stock may have been sold during 1969.

The U.S. House recently passed Congressman Patman's revised One Bank Holding Company Bill, and the bill is awaiting a hearing in the Senate Committee on Banking and Currency. If the measure passes, Lincoln Liberty Life may be required to get out of the banking or the insurance business. The new bill allows the Federal Reserve Board to break up bank holding companies when it can establish that a company controls a bank, even if it owns less than 25 percent of the stock.

Jake Lewis of the House Banks and Banking Committee told the *Observer* that, if the Patman bill passes the Senate, the interlocking directorates among the Rio Grande Valley banks, Lincoln Liberty Life, and Lincoln Consolidated could lead the Federal Reserve Bank to conclude that the Bentsens do indeed control the banks. The boards of directors of the banks, the insurance company, and the parent company are saturated with Bentsens. According to the Texas *Banking Redbook*, Lloyd M. Bentsen (it does not say whether it is junior or senior, but is presumably senior) belongs to the boards of five Valley banks—the first national banks of Raymondville, Mission, McAllen, and Edinburg, and the Security State Bank of Pharr. Both Lloyd Senior and Lloyd Junior are on the boards of directors of Consolidated and Lincoln Liberty Life. Elmer Bentsen, a brother of Lloyd Senior, is on the boards of three of the Valley banks in which Lincoln Liberty has stock, and he also is on the boards of Lincoln Liberty and Lincoln Consolidated. Calvin P. Bentsen, Donald Bentsen, and Ted A. Bentsen are board members of both Lincoln Liberty and the McAllen bank. And R. Dan Winn is a member of the boards of both Lincoln Liberty and the McAllen bank.

Bentsen told the *Observer* he will resign from Lincoln Consolidated if he is elected. "When I went to Congress before, I withdrew from my law firm and never accepted another legal fee again," Bentsen said. "That's the sort of ethics I think should be displayed when you enter into public office."

Bentsen also has a financial interest in the U.S. farm subsidy program. Although the candidate has endorsed a limitation of $20,000 a year in cash subsidies to individual farmers for not growing certain crops, Bentsen was one of 331 farm owners in 1967 to receive more than $50,000 a year in crop subsidies. The government paid him $108,904 that year for reducing crop production on his property in Hidalgo County. In 1966, Bentsen received $152,352 in farm payments. The 1968 list of farmers in the over $50,000 category does not include Bentsen, and the 1969 list is not yet available.

The day before Bentsen announced his candidacy, he quietly resigned from the boards of directors of Continental Oil, Panhandle Eastern Pipeline Co., Trunkline Gas Co., Houston's Bank of the Southwest, and Lockheed Aircraft Corporation. Bentsen said he sold 1,000 shares of Lockheed stock at the time he resigned from the board. "I resigned because I wanted to make a total commitment to this race," the candidate said.

Bentsen told the *Observer* that his resignations leave him free from any conflict of interest. Still, be might be expected to be sympathetic to the problems of his former companies. His relationship with Lockheed might be particularly sticky, since the aircraft company is in considerable trouble over its $600 million cost overrun on the military contract for the C-5A jet transport. Lockheed, which is this country's leading defense contractor, recently asked the Department of Defense for conditional release of more then $500 million in contract disputes. Lockheed's financial crisis will not be solved overnight. It is bound to be a topic of debate in the Senate next year, and so are crop subsidies, bank holding companies, insurance, oil, and gas.

A Way to Go from Here

BOB ECKHARDT

MARCH 26, 1971 — After the election of 1970, Texans interested in progressive legislation were asking, "Where do we go from here?" Now, less than two months into 1971, a new organization gives promise. The Coalition for Honest Government is still in its formative stages, but its beginnings have been more portentous than those of any similar organization of the recent past in Texas.

The underlying premise of the organization is the concept that the people can have influence on the direction of government other than just at election time. By active, intelligent support or opposition of legislation there can be tangible and appreciable results. We can convince some of those we oppose at the polls to see the value of at least certain progressive ideas and then pick up the vote, on that issue, that we lost at election time. If we pick up enough votes, we may change our minds on the office. If we don't we may show the public why we should change the incumbent.

The independent liberals, labor, minority groups and conservationists cannot afford to limit their political engagement just to election time. It is the forces that are working year-round — issue to issue, legislative vote to legislative vote — that win the battles. Legislators are constantly made aware of the presence of special interest representatives all during the session of the Legislature. These legislators should be made as aware that those interested in the people's interests are present, aware and vocal, too.

You may say that an active people's group or lobby, if you wish, could do little more than just occasionally swing an undecided vote or change a committed one. But, if we form this nucleus of public concern, those who believe in progressive government will feel more like speaking up since they will know they have active support from around the state. And between those who are organized and those who join us ad hoc on certain issues, we can be a strong force for good and honest government.

In the election season, personalities tend to crowd out issues. Personalities attract people, but they can also distract and repel. In addition, there can be, and frequently are, many influences, social and business, exerted at election time.

People frequently are opposed to a progressive candidate for any of many reasons, perhaps primarily because people are conservative in general. But they are, I think, liberal in particular.

For instance, they have supported my Open Beaches Act in great numbers, and they are willing to support strong, specific reforms in the area of preserving the environment.

As we push forward on issues, more liberal leaders and more potential candidates will emerge, not by design of the organization, but as a matter of course through the process of involvement itself. We will discover new resources, new support, new potentials for victory.

This sounds optimistic. Some of the embittered may say this is old-fashioned outmoded stuff. But it is not. What we used to do was to avoid the dangers of faction by avoiding involvement in the big issues, and then we scrapped over personalities and nursed our grievances in defeat. I do not believe you support an issue, advance a cause or win an election while crying over a defeat.

I think now is the time to dedicate ourselves to the ends and purposes that we espouse, in common, such as a fairly based state tax system which precludes more regressiveness, fearless enforcement of environmental protection, and constant insistence that government "put the jam on the lower shelf," as Ralph Yarborough has said. And this says a lot. It means that consumers should have the benefit of class actions to bring honesty to the marketplace. It means the benefits of a generally good and sound economy should not be drained off by crooked stock manipulations that doubly work against the people by also bribing their representatives to act against the people's interest. It means that people who are not rich should be able to enjoy clean air and people who are poor should have sewers and streets and parks.

These matters do not divide us. To choose among the many good aspirants for the presidency to defeat Nixon in 1972 would divide us. And to vie for an early position in the camp of a candidate for governor or senator is a divisive exercise.

As I see it, this is the rationale and direction of the Coalition for Honest Government. If you agree, join us. If you disagree, try, from your vantage point, to set us straight.

Leave It to Dolph

JIM HIGHTOWER

FEBRUARY 17, 1978 — If simple competence rates a five on a one-to-ten scale of gubernatorial ability, Dolph Briscoe is about a two, and that's giving the fellow the benefit of all doubts.

Recently the governor flubbed another simple task, this time possibly undermining two years of effort by a broadly based citizens committee that had worked with Land Commissioner Bob Armstrong to develop a plan to cope with some of the growth problems along the Texas coast. It was Briscoe's responsibility to appoint a Natural Resources Council and advisory committee to administer a state coastal management program, hire a staff for the council and then serve as its chairman. Less than a month remains before the NRC is supposed to issue a comprehensive report on coastal problems, complete with recommendations for action, but the council has yet to meet, its staff has hardly done a lick of work on coastal matters and the advisory committee — filled with Briscoe cronies — has only just been appointed.

The coastal management issue, as complex as it is important, cries out for state officials who are politically adept problem solvers. For some years now, industry and population have been surging down Texas' 367-mile coastline, and clashes among competing interests over proper uses and care of the area have been taking an increasingly hostile turn. The challenge to state government is somehow to balance the conflicting needs of shrimpers, oil companies, hunters, chemical firms, ranchers, developers, conservationists and others so that all might live and work together without destroying the very region that attracts them in the first place. It is the kind of issue that will confront Texas officials more and more as our population spreads and large extractive and polluting industries put an ever greater strain on the state's natural resources.

Under the terms of the 1972 federal coastal zone management act, states were encouraged to face up to such growing pains. The feds promised that their own coastal development regulations would be adjusted to conform to approved state problems, and that U.S. money would be made available to help administer them: Land Commissioner Armstrong was designated by then-Gov. Preston Smith to develop Texas' plan.

To help him do the job, Armstrong convened a 40-member advisory committee in 1975, pulling together all of the diverse interests at odds on coastal development. Included were representatives of the Texas Farmers Union, Exxon, the League of Women Voters, Dow Chemical, the Texas Environmental Coalition, the Mid-Continent Oil & Gas Association, the Texas Nature Conservancy, Tenneco, the Sportsmen Clubs of Texas, Houston Lighting & Power, and the Texas Shrimp Association. To the surprise of everyone, these naturally competing elements were able to work together on each other's problems and reach final agreement on a legislative package, which was introduced in Austin last year. The Legislature passed the proposals without dissent in the Senate and with only one "nay" vote in the House. Everything was moving ahead, and there was optimism all around.

Enter Dolph Briscoe. First he delayed signing the legislation, apparently because he was unaware of its history and because he has a sort of involuntary impulse to veto any bills that suggest a coordinating role for government (unless it's to build highways, coal slurry pipelines, or such). But the industrialists who supported the measures straightened him out, and the laws were signed, taking effect last Sept. 1. The NRC act required the governor to appoint 16 voting members to the council, which was easy, since the law specified the 16 state agencies that were to be represented on the body. He made these appointments in September. Things went downhill from there.

The governor was to serve as NRC chairman, though he could designate a full-time alternate to officiate in his stead. Briscoe named Al Askew as his surrogate, so demonstrating that he either still does not understand the purpose of the NRC legislation, or that he has no intention of making it work. No doubt Askew is capable and as concerned as the next person about coastal problems, but he is the head of the governor's Energy Advisory Committee, a responsibility that gives him neither the time nor the broad perspective the important work of the council demands.

The governor also hired a staff for NRC, as the law allowed him to. He brought Frank Sheffield home from Washington, where he was working in Briscoe's federal relations office, to be NRC staff director. That was fine, but the governor then added seven people to the NRC staff and promptly put them in Askew's office, four miles away from Sheffield, who appears to have control over their activities. It turns out that Briscoe has been playing a bureaucratic shell game with the people of Texas by using the NRC to hide employees who actually work for the governor's office. One of the seven, John Huggins, told the Associated Press that he was the fuel director for the state's emergency fuel allocation office, a job that has much to do with Askew's energy assignment and next to nothing to do with coastal problems. Huggins, who is salaried at about $20,000 a year, was quoted by AP as saying, "I work for Alvin [Askew]. We work for energy resources, I think. I'm kind of hazy. I don't know."

When the Associated Press uncovered the hidden employees on Feb. 1, the governor suddenly took a powerful interest in the Natural Resources Council. After five months of inactivity, Askew tentatively scheduled the Council's first meeting for Feb. 21, even though the founding legislation had required the members to convene quarterly. Then on the day of the AP revelations, Briscoe made the first of 13 appointments to a 15-member advisory committee mandated by the NRC law. Askew termed the governor's timing "coincidental."

But it is not the late date of the advisory committee appointments that really has upset those involved in coastal management problems; rather it is the lack of experience, qualifications or demonstrated concern of most of those named. Said one flabbergasted observer who had worked hard to help develop the coastal management program, "This committee looks like [Briscoe] pulled a list of campaign supporters out of his desk drawer and picked a dozen names at random."

The NRC act requires that advisory committee members "shall be chosen to represent a balance of economic, social, and environmental interests."

Briscoe, however, mindlessly stacked the committee. He named people who may be capable, but who show no special disposition for this particular duty, save maybe their pro-Briscoe political sympathies. The single exception is John B. Armstrong, a member of the Kingsville ranching family, who also served on Armstrong's committee. Four of Briscoe's appointments represent oil or chemical interests, three are attorneys and another three are ranchers. Not one person named in the first round represents commercial fishermen, farmers, the ports, labor, sportsmen or environmental interests. The decided lack of balance has more than angered some; at least one environmental group that was active in developing the legislation is contemplating a lawsuit against the governor.

Briscoe's appointments secretary George Lowrance, however, says, "I just flat don't think it's true" that the committee lacks balance, adding, "You don't have to be a member of an organized group to be an environmentalist. I consider myself to be a strong environmentalist. I'm damned interested, damned concerned." He said the governor's choices added up to a well-rounded group. Just to be on the safe side, however, on Feb. 3 the governor named a card-carrying environmentalist as his 14th appointment to the advisory committee — Galveston city councilwoman Edna Fuller.

Nobody had asked or expected Briscoe to fill the committee with bird watchers and liberals. There were plenty of quite suitable possibilities who lean far to the right, including some of the corporate members of Bob Armstrong's committee. Indeed, the land commissioner was asked to submit a list of 15 nominees, which he gave to Askew about two months ago. "I tried to name people [Briscoe] knew," Armstrong told the *Observer*. "I didn't want him to take my whole slate, but I did want to sprinkle in some of those who had been through this issue — who could give some continuity." Except for John Armstrong, Briscoe ignored the commissioner's recommendations.

So the NRC advisory committee will have to start over, forced to cover much of the ground that Armstrong's group traveled two years ago, but lacking the diversity of interest that made the previous committee's effort so successful.

This isn't a case of gubernatorial malfeasance (even Briscoe's failures are uninspiring), but merely another instance of gross ineptness, of opportunity lost or at least stalled. The advisory committee could have been exceptional from the start, and the NRC could have had a cracker-jack staff capable of making Texas' coastal management program a model for the nation and a boon for the people who live, work and simply enjoy the Gulf Coast. All this may come to pass, but if so, it will be no thanks to Dolph. But, as Armstrong said, "I used to be surprised by things like this, but nothing surprises me anymore."

The Tumor in the Texas Democratic Party

MICKEY LELAND

JULY 10, 1981 — I am going to talk very plainly and directly to you today about a problem within the Democratic Party that threatens our survival, and one which we must take the initiative to correct. I speak of the traitors in our Party, the "boll weevils" who have taken our help, and our votes, and our trust, and have deserted us and have embraced Ronald Reagan and the Republican Party. . . . Last month on the budget vote 63 Democratic members of the House abandoned the House leadership and the Democratic platform and voted for the Republican budget. Moreover, ten of the Texas Democratic delegation jumped ship too.

Now, I want to carefully distinguish between those members of Congress who have or will vote contrary to the Democratic position either out of personal belief or because their districts demand it . . . and those few members who go far beyond a vote and undertake a leadership role in sponsoring and working for the Republican program. Namely, I am alluding to Phil Gramm and Kent Hance, who have crossed the line of acceptable political conduct by actually sponsoring the Reagan budget and tax programs. . . . Hance and Gramm deserve a forceful, immediate response from the Democratic Party — they ought to get punished.

It is bad enough that the Texas Democratic Party is being embarrassed nationally by these two turncoats . . . [but] what is even more outrageous is that they expect to get away with this. They expect to come back to the well again, and receive Democratic money, party assistance, and our votes, as if nothing had happened.

. . . We cannot and must not tolerate this. . . . Do you think that Sam

Rayburn or Lyndon Johnson would have stood for this violation of party loyalty? I can assure they would not. So I am carrying on the best of traditions.

It is really quite appropriate that black Democrats take the first step. Even when a Democratic President and a Democratically controlled Congress turned their backs on us and cut our badly needed social programs and put us out of work, we still went to the polls and were the only traditional Democratic constituency who stuck by the party. Moreover, we have the most to lose. We see first hand what the current right-wing, conservative trend is actually doing to our people. And now, we must have the moral courage to speak out and say *no* to any attempts to move the Democratic Party any further to the right: It has already gone too far.

. . . I plan to introduce a resolution . . . that would condemn Hance, [Charles] Stenholm [chair of the House Conservative Democratic Forum], and Gramm for their actions and would call on the State Democratic Executive Committee at its next meeting to censure them and officially deny them any future party assistance, including campaign funds . . . We should also seek *real* Democrats to challenge them in next year's primary election. . . . As an individual, I intend to make my views known, regardless of the political repercussions. . . . I was not elected to go to Washington to roll over and play dead. You didn't elect me to represent you on the Democratic National Committee to keep quiet. The black caucus did not elect me chairman to grin and shuffle and be a good boy. I have to represent myself and my people — and if that means fight, then by damn, I intend to fight with all of the strength and energy I can muster. This is a case where I have chosen to draw the line — I have chosen to fight — because it's right and I invite you to join me today — to reaffirm our dignity and our sense of justice — to say "No More!". . .

A Tale of Two Speakers

JOE HOLLEY

JANUARY 29, 1982 — Away from the nostalgia of [recent] centennial tributes, it's worth recalling [former U.S. House speaker] Sam Rayburn's shortcomings — his skepticism toward organized labor and advanced civil liberties legislation, his distrust of big-city liberalism. But these days, I'd rather ponder the man's bedrock honesty. As LBJ biographer Robert Caro points out, lobbyists could not even buy Sam Rayburn a meal, nor did he ever indulge in that time-honored (dishonored) tradition of the junket. (At this writing, Cong. Charles Wilson of Lufkin is in the midst of a taxpayer-financed trip to Persian Gulf countries, his second visit to the area in a month; Cong. Richard White, who announced his retirement last year after nine terms, is one of six members of the House Armed Services Committee visiting Venezuela, Brazil, Argentina, Chile, Peru, and Mexico.) During his 48 years in Congress, Rayburn took exactly one trip — to inspect the Panama Canal — and he paid for that trip himself. He refused not only fees for out-of-town appearances, but he also paid his own travel expenses. When he died, his savings totaled $15,000. That's all.

And that brings me to Billy Clayton [Texas House Speaker]. Like Sam Rayburn, Clayton seems never to have forgotten who he is or where he came from — they're both sons of the Texas soil — but Clayton seems scared to death there'll come a day when once again he'll be scratching out a living on a windblown Panhandle farm. Perhaps that helps explain his latest public service peccadillo — attempting to use inside information to obtain a mineral lease from the Lower Colorado River Authority, a state agency. How he gets away with such improprieties I don't know —

it may be that voters harbor a measure of admiration for his country-boy cunning.

Last September the Speaker invited LCRA general manager Elof Soderberg to lunch in the Speaker's capital apartment where Clayton handed Soderberg a lease proposal and a check for $167,504.28. Soderberg says he declined the offer because the river authority had not decided whether it would lease the land adjacent to the Fayette Power Project. Clayton later mailed the proposal to the LCRA.

LCRA Board Chairman Harry Shapiro of San Saba said the offer was rejected Sept. 16 by the LCRA's power and energy committee. He said he told Soderberg to "return the damn thing." Shapiro said he believed anything the Speaker of the House would have brought the LCRA board would have been unethical.

Clayton called the whole thing "just a straight-up business deal." He said it never occurred to him that ethical questions might be raised because "it would just be like leasing a lot from the city."

I know a bald-headed, granite-faced man I wish he could tell that to. When Sam Rayburn lost his temper, people say, the blood crept forward from his neck to his head, turning the head red. If really mad, he'd turn purple. Billy Clayton, I suspect, would turn Sam Rayburn purple.

Farmworkers for Richards

LOU DUBOSE

MARCH 9, 1990 — Near the back door of Palmer Pavilion [in McAllen], Ann Richards was stopped by a young woman who for most of the morning had been observing the United Farm Workers convention from a table at the back of the hall. Richards, who had just addressed the farmworkers, still had to speak to the Valley Interfaith Convention in Edinburg before traveling to a Founders' Day celebration at the Edgewood school district in San Antonio. But she stepped away from her entourage and for a few minutes listened to the young woman.

Then, while Richards' son Dan and Austin Rep. Lena Guerrero stood waiting, Ann Richards and the young woman moved yet farther away from the crowd and the conversation continued. The discussion grew more animated until finally, some 25 minutes later, Richards shook hands with the woman and left the convention.

Unable to catch up with Richards, and uncertain of whether she would be available at the Interfaith convention later in the afternoon, I approached the other party to the discussion and inquired about the topic.

"Social work," she said. "I saw [Richards] at a national convention of social workers in Corpus Christi and thought she was interested in social work. So I wanted to talk about social work in the schools, especially in the lower grades."

Rosie Lopez is 23 and completing a masters of social work at Pan American University in Edinburg. What she conveyed to Richards, she said, was the importance of hiring social workers for the public schools. "We lose too many [students] by waiting 'til it's too late, by not giving them counseling. We need to have, at least here in the Valley, social workers in the low grades."

The discussion, it seems, is noteworthy. For here was a young woman, a former UFW member who two years ago was thinning sugar beets in Wheaton, Minnesota, and detasseling corn in Williamsburg, Iowa, pitching social-work-in-the-schools to a gubernatorial candidate who was willing to listen. And not just to listen in a perfunctory sense, but to ask questions, to demand examples, and then to respond.

It was, if only for 25 minutes, the way it's supposed to be. Where better to find insight into public education than from a woman who, despite the interruptions posed by the migrant life, had made it all the way through the system.

"She listened to everything I had to say," Lopez said of Richards.

Richards had come to the convention to accept the endorsement of the UFW. In accepting the endorsement, she reaffirmed her support for the farmworker cause and for their agenda in the Legislature. Twenty-two years ago, Richards said, when the farmworkers union was preparing to march on Austin, she joined them in McAllen. She told the convention that her daughter, Cecille, had attended her first dance then, "a union dance in this building." And Richards predicted that her granddaughter, the daughter of union organizer Cecille Richards, would attend her first dance in a union hall.

But beyond symbolic gestures, Richards promised to support the legislative agenda of the UFW and insisted that when elected, she would support and sign such legislation as the bill outlawing the short-handled knife—a bill sponsored by Lena Guerrero, passed in both chambers, and vetoed by [Governor] Bill Clements. "I will support a living wage, safe work, and decent living conditions for our children," Richards said in her speech to the convention. "*Juntos*," she concluded, "*sí se puede.*" Together, we can do it.

None of the other gubernatorial candidates addressed the convention; but then neither of the other Democratic candidates [Jim Mattox and Bill White] was recommended by the executive committee for the union's endorsement. And though it was only one day in a long campaign, it served the purpose of reaffirming our commitment to Richards as the best of the Democratic field.

Bad Bills Roundup: The Beat Goes On

BY THE BAD BILLS GIRL

JULY 18, 1997 — *At the close of the 75th Texas Legislature, the Bad Bills Girl was looking forward to a well-deserved vacation, perhaps counting de-commissioned nuclear war-heads in Amarillo. Unfortunately, the Bad Legislative News just keeps rolling out of Austin, so before she took off for cooler climes, The BBG filed the following report.*

The Guv's Hammer

S.B. 823 (Payroll Deductions)

H.B. 2915 (Privatized Workers)

H.B. 3116 (Subsidized Workers)

S.B. 1514 (Colonia Initiatives)

S.B. 414 (Death With Dignity)

As St. Peter will tell you, it's difficult enough trying to keep track of sins of commission. Yet the sins of omission — like Governor [George] Bush's punitive, post-session vetoes — have their own dismal consequences. The Guv vetoed thirty-seven bills in all, saying they were "counter to [his] philosophy of local control and limited government, or they duplicated existing legislation." But less public-spirited motives are also apparent in several vetoes: he went after some bills that would ever-so-slightly protect the rights of labor against management, one that might provide some social services to poor communities, even one that would allow citizens the right to choose a natural death.

S.B. 823 would have allowed a municipal employee (e.g., a firefighter) to *choose* to have his or her "employee association" dues deducted directly from his or her own paycheck; the Guv said the bill *mandated* "payroll deductions for union dues and therefore violated the principle of right-to-work." He was equally out to lunch on H.B. 2915 and 3116, which would have provided some protection to state and private employees whose jobs are now threatened by the headlong rush to privatization and state-subsidized welfare-to-work programs. Bush said he wanted to retain employer "flexibility" (i.e., the absolute authority of management to lower wages and standards of employment).

Bush also vetoed a colonias initiative (S.B. 1514) for agency coordination that had the support of the entire Senate and all but one House member, and he vetoed the excruciatingly detailed S.B. 414, allowing people to *choose* to die without being subject to unnecessary technological measures — apparently the bill offended the Guv's hard right-to-life constituency.

Pricing Pollution

S.B. 633 *(Sponsor: Brown)*

How can you tell a good environmentalist bill from a bad one?
The bad ones pass.
This is not a foolproof rule of thumb for the Lege, but it works far too often. Another one might be, look out for any bill sponsored by Lake Jackson's favorite son, Buster Brown. The impact of S.B. 633 — mandating burdensome "cost-benefit analyses" of any new "Major" environmental regulations — promises to make environmental protection much more difficult, and to generate frivolous and costly obstructions to any attempt to prevent environmental outrages. The law is part of a national conservative attempt to convert all environmental issues into bottom-line economic ones, leaving clean air, land, and water (haplessly priceless) in the lurch, every time. "The real intent of S.B. 633," says the Sierra Club, "may well be to have a 'chilling effect' on state agencies so that they do not even consider rules not specifically mandated by law."

Kick the Poor

H.B. 1439, 2508 (*Sponsor: Hilderbran*)

Most legislation is cloaked in confusing euphemisms, but occasionally it's possible to see the shamelessly punitive motivations leaking through the legalese. So it is with Harvey Hilderbran's H.B. 1439, whose primary purpose is to make the lives of people on welfare just a little more miserable. The law mandates that the Department of Human Services foreclose any attempt to use cash assistance for anything but DHS-defined "essential and necessary goods and services"; it also gratuitously makes it more difficult for a welfare client to receive a cash withdrawal from a benefits account. No longer can a client, like every other customer, get cash at a cash register; now she must go to the "customer service department."

What's the matter, Harv? Did one of your inflamed constituents see a food stamp recipient actually get *change* at a grocery store? Such outrages must stop!

The ever-vigilant Hilderbran also managed to attach H.B. 2508 as a rider to the Appropriations bill; it will mandate "finger-imaging" of welfare clients — despite the fact that, according to the Center for Public Policy Priorities, pilot programs have shown that such police-state policies cost more money than they save. But that's not really the point; the point is to treat poor people like criminals, so they remember that poverty is the only unforgivable crime.

George Jones, R.I.P.

H.B. 1 (Appropriations)

Anti-Rap Rider (*Sponsor: Ratliff*)

Senator Bill ("Obi-Wan") Ratliff wants to prevent any state investment in that nasty gangsta rap, so he attached this rider to the omnibus budget bill. Constitutional questions aside, the ban would prohibit investment in any music that "describes, glamorizes, or advocates" a host of unsavory activities, including crime, pedophilia, insults to women, "illegal use of a controlled substance," "ethic" [*sic*] or religious violence, etc. Is Snoop Doggy in trouble? Maybe — but then so are Cole ("I get no kick from cocaine") Porter, Maurice ("Thank heaven for little girls") Chevalier, Marty ("I feel the bullet go deep in my chest") Robbins, Johnny ("I killed a man in [Reno] just to watch him die") Cash, Jimi ("I shot my woman down") Hendrix, not to mention the collected works of George ("I gotta get drunk") Jones. For that matter, what about "Onward, Christian Soldiers"?

It seems the wisdom of Elder Ratliff — certified by *Texas Monthly*'s Paul ("Jabba the Hut") Burka — is considerably overrated.

It's worth remembering that Ratliff's idiotic rider may well be the least offensive provision of the budget bill, which — in the frank assessment of Patrick Bresette of the Center for Public Policy Priorities — "failed to meet the critical needs of the state."

At the *Observer*, that's what we call a Very Bad Bill.

Chronicle of a Death Foretold

LOU DUBOSE

MAY 28, 1999 — "I can't live with this," Plano Senator Florence
Shapiro blurted out, shortly before she walked from a Thursday, May
13 evening meeting of the Senate Criminal Justice Committee, to a
Republican Senate Caucus meeting in Buster Brown's Capitol office.
"They're doing the same thing they did to us on vouchers." After two
days of intense negotiations, in which Waco Republican David Sibley
tried to negotiate a deal between the four Republicans and three Democrats on the Criminal Justice Committee, the two parties had finally
agreed to hate crimes language they could support. Before a final vote,
however, the committee Republicans had to take the compromise to a
specially called caucus meeting in Brown's office.

The meeting came at the end of two days of protracted negotiations
on the Hate Crimes Bill, also called the James Byrd Jr. Bill in memory of
the nation's most prominent recent hate crime victim, the African-
American man murdered in Jasper last June. On Wednesday, two of the
Democrats on the Senate committee, Royce West and John Whitmire,
had repeatedly met — at times in conference rooms and at times in the
hallway — with the bill's Senate sponsor, Rodney Ellis. Committee
Republicans Florence Shapiro, Jane Nelson, and Robert Duncan had
begun their Wednesday meetings in a conference room, but abandoned
it after several hours because it was too accessible to the press.
Republican freshman Mike Jackson was usually nowhere to be seen,
and Sibley (not on the committee but one of the most powerful members
of the Senate) shuttled back and forth between the two groups. But it

eventually became apparent that no shuttle diplomat could have moved Republican ideologues Shapiro and Nelson.

What could be gathered from observing the meetings, from hallway conversations, and from sources close to the unending negotiations, was that Shapiro and Nelson refused to allow the inclusion of gays and lesbians as a protected category in the Hate Crimes Bill. At one point on Wednesday, the Republicans responded to Democrats' entreaties to vote a Republican version of the bill out of committee, agreeing to do so — only if the Democrats would promise not to attempt to amend the gay and lesbian category back into the bill when it reached the Senate floor. Whitmire wouldn't respond to questions about that particular Republican offer. But speaking to the press, he was as intractable as the Republicans. "I can't support a bill that takes sexual orientation out. This is about hate crimes . . . 20 percent of the hate crimes are committed against gays. It's the second largest category."

By late Wednesday afternoon, Ellis realized he did not have the vote of Lubbock Republican Robert Duncan, and promised to return for a vote on the following day. Duncan was the only Republican on the seven-member committee that the three Democrats could hope to move to their side. He is known as a thoughtful lawyer-legislator who will listen to logical, factual, and emotional arguments before reaching decisions. "The guy's got a heart," a public interest lobbyist watching the process said. "And he's trying to live up to Montford's legacy." John Montford was the conservative Democrat who held the seat Duncan now holds, and during Wednesday's negotiations, Duncan approached the bill as Montford might have — looking at the legal technicalities such as burden of proof, and how prosecutors might use the bill if it were to pass. And looking for a compromise.

But Bob Duncan doesn't have the power that John Montford had, and Senate Republican Caucus Chairman Buster Brown isn't known for either intelligence or negotiating skills. In the absence of the leadership of the Governor or the Lieutenant Governor, David Sibley would have to broker a deal. On Thursday evening, before his caucus met, he must have thought he had succeeded. But after the caucus, Sibley walked into the committee room and quietly told Democratic Committee Chair Ken Armbrister, sitting alone on the dais: "It's a no go." "When he said that," Armbrister said later, "I realized there was no reason to wait any longer."

So Armbrister summoned the committee, which slowly convened into a somber and dramatic tableau. At stage left sat a sober Senfronia Thompson, House sponsor of the bill the Senate committee was about to kill. Below her, in a seat usually reserved for a committee clerk, sat Austin Representative Glen Maxey, the only openly gay member of the Legislature. To Thompson's right sat an expressionless Rodney Ellis. Next to Ellis, with a pained look frozen onto her face, Florence Shapiro. Then Mike Jackson, John Whitmire, Kenneth Armbrister, Robert Duncan, Royce West, Jane Nelson.

Duncan, pale and drained, appeared ill. West, a huge and usually robust man, looked down at the microphone with a lugubrious expression on his face. Even before Nelson began to make the argument that "if this bill could end hate . . ." and Shapiro followed with her rationalization that "categories divide us rather than uniting us" — there was no need to vote.

The Republicans had gone to their caucus with a bill they said they could vote for, and returned only to kill it. No one expected Shapiro, Nelson, or Mike Jackson of LaPorte (an unreflective Senate freshman) to vote with the Democrats. Thursday night was Bob Duncan's moment. After asking several questions about procedure, in an almost inaudible voice, he voted "Present-not voting" — as did his three Republican colleagues. The Hate Crimes Bill was dead.

Immediately following the vote, West argued that the bill could be revived. "We're not through. It's not dead," he said to Ellis and Whitmire. "We're going to State Affairs." West quixotically hoped to bring another version of the bill to the State Affairs Committee, which had suspended its meeting so that its chair, Florence Shapiro, could participate in the negotiations on the Hate Crimes Bill. In the Senate chamber, where Shapiro's committee was still at recess, West and Whitmire spent an hour with Jeff Wentworth — arguably the most moderate Republican in the Senate. When the Democrats felt they had their votes lined up, West attempted to be recognized. Rather than allow Royce West to have the floor, Shapiro gaveled her committee to adjournment.

The Hate Crimes Bill was again dead. On Friday, in a day of parliamentary tactics unlike anything seen since a group of senators known as the Killer Bees shut down the Senate twenty years ago, Ellis, Whitmire, and West would try unsuccessfully to revive it.

What killed it? "There are only two differences between today and 1993," Whitmire said, recalling the year when the current hate crimes law (so vague that it will likely be ruled unconstitutional) was enacted. "There have been more hate crimes. And we are in a presidential campaign." It has been widely reported that the Governor said he would consider signing the bill if it made it to his desk. But if the bill, overwhelmingly passed out of the House, were indeed to pass the Senate, Presidential Candidate Bush would be confronted with the prospect of signing a bill that would outrage the Christian right — whose support he believes he needs to win the Republican nomination.

Senate passage of a hate crimes bill would also be a liability for Lieutenant Governor Rick Perry. James Leininger, a Christian-right multi-millionaire and Perry's biggest financial backer ($1.5 million), has two abiding interests: vouchers and tort reform. Perry has failed to get a voucher bill onto the Senate floor, and one of the session's two major tort reform bills is dead in a Senate committee, while the other passed the Senate but is moribund in a House committee. Like Bush, Perry loses should a hate crimes bill pass.

"You want to know what this is about?" asked a Senator who requested anonymity. "See that little lady lobbyist from the Eagle Forum? She's been all over the Republicans on the [Criminal Justice] committee. The right-wing, the 20-percent, Republican Christian right, are driving this whole train."

On Friday the train arrived at its terminus. Democrats began the day with a walkout and thirty minutes of group prayer under the Capitol rotunda. Then, through a creative "filibuster by personal privilege speech," they shut down the Senate. Perry realized he had lost control, and the Senate stood at ease for nine hours of additional back-room negotiations. The Democratic Caucus (excluding Eddie Lucio, Frank Madla, and Armbrister, who do not participate in the caucus — and Greg Luna, at home in San Antonio recovering from surgery) held the Senate hostage on the final day for bills to be either voted out of committee or die. During that nine hours there were deals, rumors of deals, compromise language supposedly sent over (at last) by the Governor's office, and speculation. "We're keeping hope alive," Ellis said to reporters.

Hope died at 8:45 P.M., when no compromise was forthcoming, and

Senate Democrats agreed to return to the floor. Bob Duncan delivered a speech that proved that he is no John Montford. Rodney Ellis eloquently held forth on the Constitution. And Royce West looked at Florence Shapiro and told her he still worries when "my son or my son's son go out at night, that they are going to be the victim of a crime perpetrated on them because of the color of their skin."

Just before Senators raced to committee meetings, where they would push through as many bills as they could get out before the midnight deadline, George W. Bush appeared.

Not in person, but in a press release, handed out by an aide to Senator David Sibley. Sibley had been negotiating since Wednesday, he said, only because Governor Bush had urged him to break the impasse. The compromise language offered up on the last day, Sibley implied, was the Governor's work. And Republicans spread the word that Vance McMahan, the Governor's criminal justice aide, had sat in with the Republicans for part of the day.

Ellis wouldn't buy it. Nor would Senfronia Thompson. "The Republicans killed this bill," Senfronia Thompson said. "We would agree on one line, and they would come back and move the line." As for the Governor, Ellis found the rumors of his last-minute arrival hard to accept. "Governor Bush?" Ellis said before racing off to a committee meeting. "Governor Bush never put no paper in my hand."

Vote Your Hopes

NATE BLAKESLEE

NOVEMBER 3, 2000 — The last few months have seen a spirited exchange . . . in these pages concerning Ralph Nader's candidacy and its putative effect on the Democratic Party. Texas progressives do not have to wrestle with this dilemma, since they cannot harm Gore's chances regardless of how they vote on November 7. Texas' thirty-two electoral votes are already in Bush's pocket, so Texans are free to vote Green with a clear conscience. Swing states are a different matter. Voting Green in those states could very well split the liberal vote and give the election to Bush.

Voting Green under these circumstances, one common argument goes, is a luxury of the middle class, who will more or less fare equally well materially under either major party. Yes, there are social issues to consider, abortion rights chief among them. It's a genuine issue, but keep in mind that Bush was chosen as the GOP's dream candidate in part because he is soft on abortion. Middle-class women are the key swing voters in this election, and there are a lot of pro-choice soccer moms who lean Republican. The most active segment of the GOP base is pro-life, but the majority of people in this country are not, and the Republican thinkers and money-men know it. Bush is not a "stealth" candidate; he comes from Eastern moneyed Republicans; his dad despised the Christian GOP activists (and the feeling was mutual). Gore knows this, which is why he feels the need to protest (too much) that Bush really is pro-life — it's been the Democrats' hole-card for so long, he can't bear to feel the tactical advantage slowly slipping away from him.

It's the working class and the poor who will really suffer if the Greens hand the presidency to a Republican, the argument goes. Thus, in the weeks leading up to the election, responsible middle-class liberals will urge one another, in the interest of working people, to vote Democratic. And what do the working people themselves say? Surprisingly little: roughly two in three in this demographic are not expected to vote in the election at all. If there were a movement afoot in the Democratic Party to champion the working class, surely the workers themselves would have heard about it by now, and responded accordingly. Is it a secret? Go back and watch the debates again and focus on Gore: does he mention the decline of unions? The rights of welfare mothers? Insurance redlining, which is as bad as it's ever been? Last year saw the highest number of layoffs in the last decade. Is Gore even aware of that fact? Go over the transcripts: amidst all those promises to the middle class: does he even once utter the phrase "working class"?

Give working people credit for understanding where their own interests lie. They can spot a movement when they see one. In the last twenty years, a grassroots uprising of evangelical Christians took over the GOP from the precincts on up. They came close with Buchanan's candidacy in 1988, but thankfully they never brought their dreams to fruition; Pat Robertson's endorsement of Bush this time around was quietly seen as a sellout by the rank and file. But at least they made a go of it; at least they made the party into a genuine movement. The Democratic Party has not been a movement for a long time, and no quadrennial ad campaign, test-marketed and tightly focused on swing voters, is going to convince the stay-at-home majority of erstwhile Democratic soldiers otherwise.

Remember the Holiday Inn!

JAKE BERNSTEIN

JUNE 6, 2003 — The last opportunity for the mayor and City Council of Killeen, Texas to try and influence the House Committee on Redistricting occurred about an hour before midnight on Tuesday, May 6. The delegation had traveled to the Capitol before noon the previous Friday. They had waited all day and into the following morning for their turn to testify, to no avail. The committee had pushed on till dawn Saturday, listening as one witness after another pleaded with them not to go forward with a proposed Congressional redistricting plan. As the hours dragged, the witnesses grew angrier, excoriating the committee for crafting a map in secret. They called it an "embarrassment to the state," and "a debasement of democracy." They used words like "hubris" and "gerrymandering." Witnesses cited press reports that pinned the plan on U.S. House Majority Leader Tom DeLay (R-Sugar Land). Those testifying questioned whether the committee had the guts to stand up for their constituents against the interests of a Washington, D.C. politician. Are you more Republican than Texan, one demanded? Occasionally one of the nine Republican members on the 15-person committee would question a witness, or attempt to make a point, but mostly they just sat impassively waiting for the endgame.

The Killeen delegation got home around 3 A.M. Saturday. They slept a few hours and piled back into their cars to return to Austin. That Sunday at 1 A.M., they finally had the opportunity to testify, but on a map everybody knew would change. The real map, crafted by Tom DeLay, would be sprung on the whole committee right before they were to vote.

Tuesday evening it appeared as a committee substitute offered by Rep. Phil King (R-Weatherford). And so the folks from Killeen returned to plead their case. By the time Scott Cosper, council member at large for the City of Killeen, rose to speak, 121 people had voiced their opposition to the bill and 11 had testified for it. More than a thousand had signed cards, mostly against.

Unlike the witnesses from Austin, who were the majority of those that testified, Cosper represents an area of central Texas that consistently votes Republican in statewide races. But there is an exception to the voting patterns in the Killeen area. For the past 12 years they have sent U.S. Rep. Chet Edwards, a Democrat from Waco, to Congress. White Texas Democratic Congressmen like Edwards are the ones that Tom DeLay has marked for extinction. Under the proposed map, DeLay would accomplish his goal by yoking vast swaths of rural Texas to densely populated enclaves of suburbia. It's estimated the redistricting plan would eliminate from five to ten Democratic incumbents.

Cosper explained that Killeen votes for Edwards in part because the city is home to Fort Hood, one of the largest military bases in the world. Edwards has used his seniority in Congress to become the ranking Democrat on the Military Construction Appropriations Subcommittee. From this powerful perch, he works hard to safeguard a military installation that pumps $49 billion a year into the Texas economy. Under the map presented by King, Killeen would be severed from Fort Hood and placed in a district anchored by suburban San Antonio about 100 miles away. Edwards would likely lose his seat to a freshman Republican. "It is drawing the largest single site employer in the state of Texas [away from] the strongest Congressman who has the power and seniority to support that base," Cosper told the committee. "It is actually very confusing to me why we would want to lose any seniority on either side of the House, but maybe I don't understand the issues."

Or maybe the issues just don't matter. Cosper was learning a hard lesson about the 78th Texas Legislature. In the Texas House, the merits of the arguments don't count. It's a reality the Democratic minority learned quickly this session. And it's what drove them to an unprecedented act of resistance. Whether it was tort reform or the budget, the Republican majority voted as a bloc all session long, sometimes against the very interests of their own constituents. Most often they did so because the leadership, usually acting on behalf of campaign contributors, ordered it. Implicit in their stance was the promise that, come election time, Republican leaders would flood their districts with enough special interest money that only one message would prevail — their own.

Shortly before the final midnight vote on the King map, the folks from Killeen were treated to another revealing spectacle. Committee member Rep. Vilma Luna (D-Corpus Christi), who had absented herself from most of the testimony, suddenly appeared with an amendment that would slightly move a line on one district on the map to favor her county. This session, Luna has been a consistent stalwart of the Republican leadership. In exchange for her allegiance she obtained a key role in the budget process. Her ability to demand the slight alteration of the map appeared to be another bonus. At no time did Luna express public concern that the new map, if passed, would ensure Republican control of Congress for decades to come.

Luna's perks were not extended to Rep. Kino Flores (D-Mission), another Hispanic Democrat who gave his vote to Speaker Tom Craddick (R-Midland) at the beginning of the legislative session. In the room behind the committee chamber, away from public view, Flores and Luna had fought over the map. Under the new plan, there would be three new Hispanic districts in the Rio Grande Valley, Flores was told. One belonged to State Sen. Eddie Lucio (D-Brownsville), to win his crucial vote for the map in the Senate. The other followed Luna's preferences. That left Flores with a district that stretched from Hidalgo County all the way to Austin. It was not a district that a Hidalgo politician like himself could win. "I don't want anything less than what everybody else gets," he would gripe the following day.

A greedy scramble for the crumbs left on the Republican table had been the Democrats' fare the entire session. Craddick had co-opted enough disgruntled blacks and Hispanics to neuter the Democratic caucus, fostering an every-man-for-himself attitude. The "cross-dressers," as some of their colleagues snidely called them, made it exceedingly difficult to organize the Democrats.

Back in the committee room, Flores refused to go quietly. "How come I didn't get an opportunity to try to go and cut this up and change my vote around," he wheedled to the Republicans in charge. He then asked about the "protected" district without mentioning Lucio's name. Audience members snickered as the farce played out before them. The group from Killeen grew increasingly frustrated. Luna glared at her fellow Hispanic Democrat. Despite the drama, in short order both her amendment and the map itself were voted out of committee.

That night it seemed as if Congressional redistricting was as inevitable as sunrise the next morning. The Republican leadership held a firm command. They would ram their plan through the House, and with the right enticements, it would pass the Senate. There was only one hope — a quorum-busting walkout — but that would take a degree of coordination, unity, and resolve House Democrats seemed unlikely to muster.

Elected as Democratic House Caucus leader at the beginning of the session, Rep. Jim Dunnam (D-Waco) found himself in a particularly unenviable leadership position. For the first time in 120 years, Democrats were in the minority in the Texas House. The caucus was divided. A number of its members owed their allegiance to the Republican leadership — a radical band of ideological zealots whose goal was to destroy the Texas Democratic Party by attacking its three main funding sources: unions, trial lawyers, and Democratic congressmen. And Dunnam had nothing with which to threaten or promise his troops. He couldn't deny them chairmanships or provide money for their reelection. Furthermore, he declared himself, on principle, opposed to a heavy-handed style of leadership. "If we threaten or pressure our members we are just as bad as [the Republicans] are," he said after the caucus failed to hold together for a vote on a tort reform constitutional amendment in April.

But unwittingly, the Republican leadership had strengthened Dunnam's hand. Craddick deliberately excluded many of the caucus' most experienced Democrats from his team. Unencumbered by the responsibilities of leadership, representatives like Pete Gallego (D-Alpine), Scott Hochberg (D-Houston), Garnet Coleman (D-Houston), Richard Raymond (D-Laredo), Senfronia Thompson (D-Houston), and Yvonne Davis (D-Dallas) could use their extensive knowledge to resist the Republican onslaught. Throughout the session leading to the walkout, Dunnam operated the caucus as a collective where anybody who could contribute was invited to do so. The result, in the end, was a genuine dream team: a mutually complementary blending of diverse, individual talents which truly reflected the face of present-day Texas. Together they were stronger than the sum of their parts.

"Dunnam has an interesting mix of leadership styles," says Rep. Aaron Peña (D-Edinburg). "He involves everybody; he understands the big picture; and he is not self-aggrandizing."

Dunnam's approach proved to be ideally suited to the redistricting fight.

After the redistricting committee hearings ended, members of the caucus had informal conversations about engaging in a walkout to break a quorum and prevent the bill from being heard, but with only days before it was to come to the House floor for a vote, not much had been finalized. "There was no real plan," admits Dunnam. "On Thursday I said, 'I have to get off my rear and start talking to people.'"

In a sequence that has been reported widely, Dunnam and a rotating core group of leaders: Coleman, Gallego, Raymond, Thompson, and Rick Noriega (D-Houston), began to meet with small groups of Democratic representatives. In meetings held in Coleman's office, a discreet location since it was near a key elevator, Dunnam would lay out the situation. Everybody knew the new districts would likely rob their constituents of representation. They had been made aware that, despite his public insistence to the contrary, Senate Democratic caucus Chair Sen. Gonzalo Barrientos (D-Austin) couldn't guarantee that his 12 members would stand together to block a redistricting vote. It would be up to the House. If they failed, Texas would be a domino for the rest of the nation, as DeLay pushed redistricting in every Republican controlled legislature. "If we can stop them now, then my six-year-old will have an opportunity to have a Democratic Congress in her lifetime," says Dunnam.

Then Dunnam would take the members through different scenarios until they could see that the only workable alternative was a walkout. Dunnam insists it was not a hard sell. In particular, they talked with the Democratic chairmen who had cast their lot with Craddick. "There were competing values," remembers Noriega. "It was a gut check — am I part of the leadership versus realizing the egregious nature of what was being attempted."

Noriega, whom Dunnam had tapped at the beginning of the session to poll members and manage floor debates, knew that some in the caucus had a tendency to be extremely flexible when it came to their positions. "Jim rightly had the insight to bring them in by groups and look eyeball to eyeball and talk about what our commitment to each other should be," he says.

Parallel to the conversations, Dunnam, with the help of rules expert Hugh Brady and Keith Hampton, the legislative chair of the Texas Criminal Defense Lawyers Association, explored various possible outcomes to the project. Originally they had wanted to go to Louisiana but Hampton pointed out that the state had a Republican governor, who after a phone call from the White House, might be inclined to expedite an extradition. So instead they chose Oklahoma after discreet inquiries to the state's Democratic governor and attorney general. They talked with a former Texas Department of Public Safety agent to get a sense of what the agency might do. The logistics would be impossible if everyone went somewhere different, so they decided to stay together. "There had to be some way of guaranteeing that everybody could see everyone's cards," recalls Gallego.

Brady's answer for how to prevent Republicans from voting on the machines left vacant by the Democrats provided an unanticipated key ingredient to the success of the plan. Each member would have to sign a letter asking the clerk to lock his or her voting machine. The letters would be distributed to the clerk, the leadership, and the press precisely at 9:15 A.M. on Monday, May 12. They originally decided to quietly take the letters to members on the floor to sign that weekend but they then thought better of such a public maneuver. So, instead, one by one, each representative came to Coleman's office to sign. It turned out to be a significant, albeit unintentional commitment ritual as each signed the document in the presence of the others. Some hesitated. In the end, all those who had initially promised to support the plan signed. "That solidified it in my view," says Noriega.

While the Democratic representatives took incremental steps toward their goal, the Republican leadership knew that a walkout was being planned. House Calendar Chair Beverly Woolley (R-Houston) purposefully scheduled bills by Democratic representatives for Monday as a way to entice them to stay. But the leadership clearly did not believe the Democrats could be successful at such a bold step.

The story of representatives anxiously awaiting the arrival of their peers for the late departure by bus from the Embassy Suites the Sunday night they left Austin has already entered Texas political lore. Some pessimistic members kept luggage in their cars while they waited for the others. Dunnam dispatched someone to the parking lot to watch for the DPS. Several diehard Craddick Democrats had declined the invitation. Luna would tell reporters on that Monday that she had not been invited, but Gallego insisted he called her cell phone and left messages on Sunday. They received a psychological boost when an ailing Rene Oliveira (D-Brownsville) came to see them off before heading for the Mexican border. Then 47 Democratic representatives took a leap of faith and boarded two buses, armed with the promise that four more reps would join them in Oklahoma to reach the magic 51 they needed to break the quorum.

Few but Dunnam knew they were bound for Ardmore, Oklahoma, just over the Texas border — the least likely place to be portrayed as a vacation spot by the media. Beyond their destination, the extent of Dunnam's plans were the rough drafts of two press releases; one if they made it successfully, and the other if the DPS stopped them at the border. "I had confidence that if we got on the bus and crossed the line we had plenty of smart people who could figure out what to do next," he says.

The spot where the 51 Democrats spent the bulk of their time while in Ardmore was a conference room at the Holiday Inn they dubbed the war room. Since every army needs sustenance, conveniently, it was attached to a Denny's restaurant by a swinging door. The room couldn't be locked, so Democrats took turns guarding it through the night. (They were not being overly paranoid, as two men with cameras not affiliated with any media organization took a room at the hotel, apparently to catch Democrats in compromising shots.) Sentries stood ready to eject nosy reporters. Photographers and cameramen were only allowed entrance for brief spells to take footage.

Dunnam set the tone for what would occur in the war room the very first day, recalls Noriega. "Jim said, 'I'm not negotiating unless we all agree. There will be no cutting of deals. It's all of us or nothing.'"

The caucus leader resisted any attempt to portray the situation as a standoff between him and Craddick. Dunnam says there were some that felt that he should be the one to call Craddick to see if the Speaker would negotiate. Dunnam argued successfully that the call should come instead from someone close to Craddick. And indeed, Robert Puente (D-San Antonio), a Craddick-appointed chairman and one of the first Democrats to sign on with the Speaker, ended up making the call. When the group held press conferences, those picked to speak would rotate by region or area of expertise.

"Throughout this the attitude [was] to spread the wealth, be as inclusive as possible, and get everyone involved," said Pete Gallego.

Remarkably for 51 headstrong politicians, every decision was made by consensus. Sometimes it took hours in the war room to decide the proper wording of a letter or the exact response to a Craddick press conference held in Austin. But everyone needed to claim authorship of whatever response they made. "Everybody was important," recalls Dunnam. "If everybody had not gotten on the bus, nobody would have gotten on the bus."

If the group hadn't bonded sufficiently simply by boarding the buses, once again the Republicans inadvertently aided their cause. Back in Austin, they were vilified, called names like "chicken" and "coward." Long after the DPS and reporters found them on Monday, their families were followed and questioned by police ostensibly searching for them. These tactics simply drew them closer together. "When they started calling us names, it showed a lack of character and a lack of leadership," said a visibly angry Senfronia Thompson, sitting on a couch outside the war room.

Dunnam couldn't quite believe that his group was so united, even after a tornado scare forced them all into a shelter in the middle of the night on Tuesday. "When we had the tornado, I expected the next morning to walk in and have everybody mad at Jim Dunnam," he recalls. "But everybody was in a great mood."

Gov. Perry and Craddick knew all they had to do was peel one Democrat away from the group. But this time, no amount of coaxing swayed any of the 51. The governor called at least one freshman, Rep. Timoteo Garza (D-Eagle Pass), allegedly urging him to "be a hero." Garza acknowledges that he received a phone call from the governor's office but won't discuss the content of the conversation.

At the time, Rep. Miguel Wise (D-Weslaco) expressed the confidence everybody felt. "Nobody will break," he said. "Who wants to be remembered that way?"

When they had arrived, the group had hoped to spend a few days filing cryptic media dispatches "from somewhere in Oklahoma" before revealing their whereabouts to the world. Instead, a *Dallas Morning News* reporter found them on Monday, followed shortly by the DPS, who had no jurisdiction to force their return.

On Tuesday, the media battle over the event commenced in earnest. While the Democrats had expected some interest, they were overwhelmed as 23 cameras lined up for their first press conference. "We were penned up yesterday and now we get to hit back," said Rep. Barry Telford (D-DeKalb) at the time. "It's an atmospheric change and it's kind of fun to watch."

They spread out, working their cell phones, talking to every media outlet that would listen. While some had help back in Austin, most simply winged it by themselves. Hispanic legislators held press conferences and interviews in Spanish so their communities would be informed. "[By mid-week] we saw the Republicans rev up their media machine," remembers Aaron Peña. "They have a Rolls Royce and we have a Volkswagen."

The Republican message, synchronized and disseminated with its usual efficiency, was a simple sell: Why won't they work? It appeared everywhere from CNN's *Crossfire* to the carefully crafted talking points Republicans in Texas parroted for the local news. Democrats had a much harder message to convey, involving as it did complicated issues of representation and process.

From the beginning the Democrats made their target Tom DeLay, not the colleagues they left behind. Some worked the sound bite better than others. "We will not be accomplices to a partisan, gerrymandered, Washington, D.C. plan," Steve Wolens (D-Dallas) told the assembled press corps.

And indeed, their stand captured the imagination of the Democratic base everywhere. "The overwhelming reaction from Democrats all over the country is not in response to the principle of the thing," believes Dean Rindy, an Austin-based political consultant who advises Dunnam, "but joy that someone had the courage to stand up to Tom DeLay."

Toward the end of their stay, the war room looked like a battle zone. Scattered everywhere could be found gifts from grateful Democrats across the nation. A toy superhero action figure, one of the ones sent to each member, lay on a table. In a corner floated a cluster of yellow balloons. On the far wall someone had draped an American flag. A box filled with stacks of a book entitled *Profiles in Courage for Our Time*, a gift from North Texas Congressman Martin Frost, covered a chair. And everywhere, messages of thanks.

"Destalló la bomba (a bomb went off)," said Rep. Paul Moreno (D-El Paso), who had flown in from his hiding spot in Las Cruces, New Mexico, to be with the group so they would have 51 present. "This is going to have an impact nationally."

"I will always remember being [part of] 51 who had a common cause and who shared conviction," says Rep. Jim McReynolds (D-Lufkin). "The experience was the richest I've ever had in terms of my political life."

Inside the war room, Anglo Democrats (who called themselves WD-40s for White Democrats Over 40 until the owner of the trademark sent a threatening letter urging them to stop), urban blacks, and South Texas Hispanics found common cause with each other for the first time. Some discussed the future. In coming elections, they pledged mutual aid. "We talked about ways to support each other and how to see ourselves as a team instead of different tribes," says Peña.

Dunnam says throughout the week he watched as those who had been ready to oppose the reelection of certain caucus members decided to put aside their differences. "It was a unique opportunity to heal wounds created during the session," says Wise.

The result is an infinitely stronger Democratic legislative caucus. It created trust and goodwill where precious little had existed. "Obviously you will never have complete consensus on most issues, but what we at least demonstrated with our members is that we can do it and people will respect the opinions of others," says Dunnam. "And that will help later on when we can't agree."

In the 2004 election there will be no significant statewide Democratic candidates. The key races will be legislative, and that is where resources will be focused. It is likely the caucus will form a political action committee to support fellow members. Increasingly, they will play a larger role in an ineffective Democratic Party battered by repeated defeat.

"There is a new group in town and those who have exercised leadership in that group will now exercise leadership in how we rebuild the Party," vows Garnet Coleman.

Even several weeks after Ardmore, a battle is raging over how the walkout will be defined. Republicans have targeted Anglo Democrats seen as vulnerable with political ads that portray them as scofflaws fleeing their work responsibilities. They have received help from friendly media like Fox and *Time* magazine. Still, Dunnam believes that if they can get their message out, the walkout will work in their favor. He mentions, for example, Patrick Rose (D-Dripping Springs), who represents Lockhart, which would be carved into four different congressional seats under the proposed redistricting. Jim McReynolds' Lufkin district would be controlled by suburban Houston, which covets the rural area's water. The same could be said for Barry Telford's district in DeKalb, which would be dominated by suburban Dallas. "Forget about all the fundamental democracy issues," says Dunnam. "If [they] say, 'By God, I'm not going to let anybody steal all our water, and I'll go to Maine, if that's what it takes' — you can win that all day long."

The night before the Democrats returned, a package arrived for them from Texas icon Willie Nelson. Along with red bandanas and whiskey, the country star sent a note that read "Stand Your Ground." Democrats had captured the imagination of the foremost expert on the populist theme of the renegade standing up for his community. It's a story line that happens to be a Karl Rove special.

When DPS agents tried to enlist the Department of Homeland Security to hunt the absent lawmakers down, Democrats received a significant boost in their effort to portray the walkout as the resistance of the common man against an imperious outside authority. With a grand jury investigation underway, the outcome of that tale has yet to be concluded.

Whether the walkout presents the Democrats with a new sense of purpose for the future remains to be seen. Jeff Crosby, a consultant for the Texas Democratic Party, believes it won't likely be an issue in the next election, but instead an undercurrent. Regardless of the spin that Republican-dominated media will put on it, the walkout has injected hope into a Democratic base starved for signs of life from its leaders. And the caucus knows they can't afford to be complacent. DeLay has already vowed to continue to push redistricting. Gov. Perry could include it in a special session. He has already pledged to call at least one in the interim. While it is more likely, post-Ardmore, that Democratic senators will hold together to block redistricting, the outcome is far from certain. And the avalanche of Republican election money is already on the move. "We've peed in the lion's face," says McReynolds. "The lion is not just going to lay around."

The Texas Observer

JULY 24, 1964

A Journal of Free Voices   A Window to The South   50c

Photograph by Russell Lee

J. Frank Dobie of Texas

Cover, July 24, 1964. One of the essential figures in the intellectual culture that supported the *Texas Observer* was J. Frank Dobie. So crucial were his contributions that when he died in 1964 the magazine dedicated an entire issue to his impact on Texas life and letters. Cover photo by Russell Lee.

V. CULTURAL AFFAIRS

IN 1984, EDITOR GEOFF RIPS made an important change to the structure of the *Observer*, launching a section tagged "Books and the Culture." Because the "operant mode of the *Observer* has been and will continue to be democratic, we plan to have [it] serve as a marketplace for the exchange of ideas and information among writers and readers." In its pages, writers have celebrated and damned the day's literary achievements and cultural productions, previewed films and documentaries, and published poetry, opening up for discussion "the new orders and understanding they bring to our time and place, the new symbols they glean from our culture and those they help to create." Although in the abstract these subjects seem at odds with the *Observer*'s decidedly political cast, the reviews, critiques, and poems could be just as engagé. In expanding the journal's coverage, Rips signaled that there was more to Lone Star politics than riveting exposés of a pliable legislature and its sugar-daddy lobbyists.

Cultural analyses had always made good copy, and as part of its early commitment to tilting with the powers that be, and cracking through the state's provincialism, the *Observer* had always published editorials and articles that challenged everyday assumptions. Subjects abounded in the early 1950s. When trustees of the San Antonio Library Board banned books based on their authors' putative politics, editor Dugger, a native of the city, blasted these "cultural vigilantes" for attempting to brainwash the citizenry and invoked Justice Oliver Wendell Holmes's defense of free speech, the "freedom for the ideas we hate."

Among those precious few who seemed to embody this righteous conviction was that Texan troika, Ralph Bedichek, Walter Prescott Webb, and J. Frank Dobie. In their varied investigations of their native ground as a state of mind, and in their efforts to open up that mind through unfettered intellectual inquiry, they embodied what Dugger believed was an essential democratic mission; no wonder that when each of them died, they received special-issue send-offs from this journal of free voices.

There were other cultural concerns that the *Observer* touched upon, including the increasingly widespread distribution of television, a funny thing, thought satirist Billy Brammer. The idea of televised political commercials set Brammer's heart racing when he contemplated their impact on electoral campaigns. Yet what he took for their hilarious (if sideshow) possibilities would become the main act soon enough, as the media savvy former *Observer* editor, and incumbent agriculture commissioner, Jim Hightower acknowledged following his 1990 electoral defeat.

There were other unanticipated turns. The *Observer*'s once-reverential treatment of Bedichek, Webb, and Dobie came crashing down when it published what is arguably its single most important piece of cultural criticism, Larry McMurtry's "Ever a Bridegroom"(1981). Blowing off the "Holy Oldtimers" as "bucolics," dismissive of all other pretenders to the literary throne, and discouraged by Texans' lax reading habits, McMurtry ended on the downbeat: "Until Texas writers . . . stop looking backward, we won't have a literature of any interest." Yet New York City was not the sole source of all things cultural, Geoff Rips cautioned. Sculptor Donald Judd's self-important geometric constructions, plopped down in the Marfa high country, shrank beneath the big sky of West Texas, a stark failure of East Coast chic to colonize this arid land. This was a small victory, perhaps, for the larger picture remained grim, Rod Davis opined in the mid-1990s, because the "first-rate voices" of Texas writers were increasingly being drowned out by the "white noise of Prozac publishing."

Happily, an appreciation for the absurd has leavened the oft-brooding *Observer*, as is revealed in Brammer's send-up of Austin's hippie culture and Molly Ivins's wicked look at Texas-sized pretensions and Texans' outlandish presumptions. Not least of these was the construction of the world's biggest airport, Dallas–Forth Worth, which architect James Stanley Walker deftly skewered shortly after it opened in the late 1970s. And when Dagoberto Gilb and Debbie Nathan poke fun at their literary ambitions and political vocabulary respectively, they remind us just how much the *Observer* has benefited from writers who have been convinced — and have convinced us in turn — that words have a remarkable power to persuade, trouble, transport, and crack us up.

Char Miller

Stacked Stacks

RONNIE DUGGER

JANUARY 10, 1955 — When we were about twelve, we used to haunt the children's section of the San Antonio Public Library looking for P. G. Wodehouse's books about his aristocratic butler, Jeeves. Later we heard about Wodehouse's trouble because of association with the Nazis, but it never occurred to us then that anyone might use that as a basis for keeping his books out of the library.

Now comes a group of cultural vigilantes, riding the crest of the present hysteria wave against all things leftist and they censor out of the purchase list of the library the writings of authors who are mentioned in indexes of the California or House un-American activities committees. For example, we have learned that they have refused to purchase books by Nobel Prize-winner Pearl Buck and Pulitzer Prize-winner Oliver La Farge.

A more vicious un-Americanism cannot be imagined. It amounts to adoption by the library trustees of a censorship list of the worst kind. The reports of the committees in question are made up in part of the unproved and often unprincipled allegations of demagogues, ex-communists, and fanatics tossed around in the heat and passion of unjudicial and publicity oriented hearings. That any library in a free country would engage in such a narrow-minded procedure is really alarming.

We the people have the right to read what we want to read and to learn what we want to learn. We do not elect our public officials to give them an opportunity to brainwash us. The stacking of the stacks of San Antonio's library should cease at once. A man's politics, rightist or leftist, inside or outside of his books should not be a deciding factor in their purchase by a public library. Book-buying should be left to librarians who have dedicated their professional lives to library science and who follow the responsible reviews, know the public's wishes — and even read the books.

We have confidence that the people of San Antonio will depose the misguided trustees now mismanaging their library's affairs and re-assert the faith all thoughtful Americans have in Justice Holmes's rule that ultimately freedom of speech is freedom for the ideas we hate.

Thoughts on TV and Things to Come

BILL BRAMMER

AUGUST 10, 1955 — There's no getting around it, men, next year is going to be 1956 and elections in Texas roll around on these even numbered years with depressing, almost alarming, regularity. And, well, to tell the truth, I can hardly wait.

We here, right here on this here *Observer*, will, of course, be bringing you the exclusive, on-the-spot developments of the various state-wide races. But that's not what sets my pulse a-clanging. What gets me excited, what makes me all queasy inside, is the importance of television in next year's races. Picture, if you can, the four or five gubernatorial candidates who can afford it — or even the four or five who can't afford it — appearing almost nightly for our living room edification. Why the 1954 TV blitz seems pale, almost austere, in comparison.

Think of what we're in for: All manner of candidates, their press agents wracking their ulcers, searching for some new way to present their clients to the people. It's not too wild a dream to think of seeing Ralph Yarborough taking a milk bath, or Jimmy Phillips killin' himself a bear, or Reuben Senterfitt swimming with Esther Williams, as the cameras grind away. If the press agentry is resourceful and imaginative enough, there might even be commercial sponsors bidding for John White's or Wil Wilson's or maybe even Governor Shivers' show before the campaign is over.

I've talked this over with Jack Summerfield, who ordinarily ponders the clarity of our channels on page six of this publication, and he agrees that all things would be possible with television in this best of all possible campaigns. You can probably tell by now that I'm not one of these television snobs: I like TV; I like its narcotic effect; I watch everything. I like hard-selling commercials, for instance. The harder the better. It's my fond hope that someday the fellow who sells Gleem Toothpaste (Adv.) is going to step out from behind his "invisible protective shield" and get drenched by a garden hose, impaled by a javelin, or mortally mangled by a bowling ball.

Meanwhile, Ah simply want to make mah point clirr. There are going to be a good many people trying to save Texas in our living rooms next summer. They'll be saving Texas for Texans, or saving it from the CIO or the Eastern radicals or the Wall Street interests. The monster in the parlor is going to hold out the bright promise of lower taxes and more highways and higher pensions. It will also inform us that the rascals are going to be thrown out of the State house, although a few misguided souls may try to clutter up the shows with specific issues.

In the interim, I am going to hold fast to the chaise lounge, my little pig eyes glued to the screen. I mean the least we can do is cultivate the habit. Just the other night, for instance, a locally-produced quiz show was beginning to pall on me until one of the prettier panelists, trying to find out about a "mystery guest," asked: "Do you have a tendency to buy dark suits?"

Well, I had the tendency to hurl a crucible through the screen, but with patience I held on to my sense and soon it was all worthwhile. Another panelist immediately inquired if the guest was "dark, or light complected."

Ordinarily, I don't allow such language in my home. It has always been my firm conviction that only Tex Ritter should be permitted to use the word "complected" — and then only when he's singing "Boll Weevil." Television is so broadening, though, and we have to make certain allowances; we should all cultivate the habit looking toward the bright promise of 1956 and our summer entertainment.

My Friend, Roy Bedichek

J. FRANK DOBIE

JUNE 27, 1959 — Nature is the complex of all complexities. One part of a man may be as simple and serene as the cow chewing her cud in the noonday shade of a tree a thousand miles and a hundred years away from any milking machine; and yet the whole of this same man may be as complex as the genius of Shakespeare — that is to say, the greatest genius in the world — ever penetrated. It will be a great deal easier to show Roy Bedichek in the simplicities of naturalness than to express him in the naturalness of the highest intellectual and emotional complexities.

His going to bed with the chickens in summertime and not too much later in the wintertime and getting up with the morning star at all times made his friends smile. He favored several kinds of independence common to the country. . . . He liked to cook outdoors, eat outdoors, sleep outdoors, look and listen outdoors, be at one with the unexplaining wind from the south, with the swing of the Great Dipper around the North Star, and with the first bob-whiting at dawn. He preferred camping on a hill so that he could watch the firmament, rather than down in a shady valley by water.

The last car he bought, in 1951, was a Dodge pickup truck in which he could carry enough water to make his camp on a hill comfortable for a day or two. This pickup was for camp purposes, but he used it to run about in also, his wife owning a sedan. He got an immense satisfaction out of trucking in cow manure, also occasionally chicken manure, for his compost pile, with which he annually fertilized his garden. He got a satisfaction out of hauling his own wood in from the country; he liked especially cedar stumps that he wouldn't have to cut for the fireplace. He had complete camp equipment, including a tent-fly to go with the truck. Part of the equipment was a field guide to the flora of the country and a field guide to the birds. He always took along something to read as well as to consult; above all, he took along the most richly and variously stored mind I have known. Not for him the dream of retiring to some private land and mating with "some savage woman" to rear his dusky race. For him back to nature was not back to the primitive, there to be saved from poring over miserable books.

His father, James Madison Bedichek, an ex-Confederate soldier, quoted philosophers and talked philosophy at the family dining table. He proved up on a quarter-section of land near the village of Eddy, not far from Waco in central Texas. Here he and his wife ran what they called the Eddy Scientific and Literary Institute, dubbed the Bedichek School by the public. Mrs. Bedichek boarded and roomed some of the pupils. Roy's aptitude for books was as congenital as that for milk. The atmosphere of literature and of thought was as natural to him as the atmosphere in which a lone buzzard soars over a cedar-covered hill or in which a coyote trots through the mesquite, sniffing for a woodrat's trail. I would not call his taste exactly austere. He took pleasure in witty limericks, even though bawdy; he could talk for hours with some cedar-chopper whose literary vocabulary was limited to the printing on a bottle of Levi Garrett's Snuff. I've heard him say a dozen times that he could no longer read American fiction because it is so pallid and insipid compared to the great Russian fiction rammed to the breech with vitality: Turgenev, Dostoyevsky, Tolstoy. He admitted Balzac into their company. During a long span of his life he read the greater part of Shakespeare about once every two years.

The Walt Whitman that he knew by heart and had absorbed into his very marrow was not the sentimentalized "good grey poet" but the tough poet of democracy. "He is our greatest exponent of Democracy among the poets," Bedi wrote me in a letter. "The reached hand, bringing up the laggards — could there be a more expressive phrase of the true inwardness of Democracy than that?" Along with Whitman, his favorite American writer was Thoreau, acid, with the wild taste, a rebel. Bedichek gloried in the influence that Thoreau's "Civil Disobedience" had on Gandhi and India and is still having over the world.

While he was writing *Adventures with a Texas Naturalist*, or maybe it was *Karankaway Country*, he made a habit of reading pages of Plato with his pre-dawn coffee. Plato helped start the day for him on a noble plane and put him into a creative mood. At this time he would not wilt the freshest part of the day with the littleness and banalities of a morning newspaper. For no man writing a book has morning ever been, to quote a 1945 note from Bedichek, a time to "stoke the furnace of indignation against numerous manifestations of Fascism in this country." He never learned the Greek language, but his ideal of a balanced life, of a just proportion of the elements that make up a human being, was essentially Greek. In reading Homer, he compared several translations. As hundreds of quotations and allusions in his books and letters would show, the immortal essence of the Greeks was in his veins.

It seemed to me that the philosophy of Henry George had a more determining effect upon his economic views than any other writing. Henry George advocated a single tax and did not consider it just that an individual owner of real estate should collect the unearned increment given to it by population and labor. Bedichek believed in the single tax but would justify buying a piece of land by saying, "It's better to run with the hounds for your dinner than with the hare for your life."

Immanuel Kant's categorical imperative was his golden rule: Do only as you would have others do; or, act only as if you would have the act become universal law. The categorical imperative is contrary to the ways of greed and lust; so was Bedichek. He was as unenvying and as free from greed and jealousy as any man could be. Anybody who knew him would as soon expect apples to fall up instead of down as for him to misrepresent a fact. . . .

As newspaperman, chamber of commerce exponent, and director of the Interscholastic League of Texas, Bedichek had done a vast amount of hack work. Anybody who works for a living spends the majority of his energies in hack work. But though Bedi was a university man, specializing in the humanities, he had never been deflected by the Ph.D. system into the inferiorities of literature. He had spent a lifetime reading the best before he turned author with seventy just over the hill for him. While H. Y. Benedict was President of The University of Texas, I heard him say that Bedichek should be teaching literature. "Why not put him to teaching it?" I asked. "Because every Ph.D. professor of English would have a colt if I did," he replied. That was the truth! Sawdust never yearns toward vitality.

We all learn with wonder of the feats in memory performed by the Macaulays of history, but I've never known anyone else in the flesh who held in memory so precisely so much of what he had read as Roy Bedichek. . . . I despair at getting into print the felicity and fitness with which Bedichek was forever drawing out of his storehouse. Many writers, perhaps most, read in order to suck in something that they can feed out. During most of his life Bedi read to delight and enlarge his own mind. Now how in the devil had he come to remember those lines from Burns' "On the Late Captain Grose's Peregrinations thro' Scotland"? (He had to tell me the source.) And how in the devil could they lie down there in the cellar of his memory for a generation or two and then, just as occasion arose for their application, jump to the surface like an empty corked bottle released at the bottom of a pool?

On February 24, 1957, I paid Bedi a visit in his shack, taking with me for him a paperbound copy of A. E. Taylor's *Socrates, the Man and His Thought*. On the fly leaf I had written:

> Dear Bedi, I give you this book because I would be as bereft if you
> went away as Crito and the others were when Socrates went. As one
> of them said of him, I can say of you, my friend, "the wisest and
> justest and best man that I have ever known."
>   —DOBIE, 24 February 1957

Two days later I received this letter:

> Dear, dear Dobie —
>
> After I had been about an hour at work this morning, I glanced
> up and saw the volume "Socrates" you gave me yesterday. I remem-
> bered that I had seen some writing on the fly-leaf which I didn't take
> time to read while you were here. I had dismissed it momentarily as
> a "good wishes" inscription and so had let it escape my attention.
>
> I reached up and got the volume in my hand "just to see." I was
> affected to tears, and I don't mean metaphorical tears but a real
> secretion from the lachrymose glands. One got loose from the inner
> corner of my left eye and it felt wet and warm, so I know they were
> real.
>
> The old Greeks (bless them) were not ashamed of tears. That
> shame was a part of the sentimentalism and masculine assumption
> of superiority of that romanticism which assigned tears to women.

I am profoundly affected, (stirred emotionally in that nervous plexus situated in the abdomen) by your placing me in a unique position in your affections. Truly, I have felt towards you a friendship I never felt for anyone else except for Harry Steger, who died 44 years ago.

Bless you for recording this where I can turn to it when sometimes: "the world is dark and I a wanderer who has lost his way."

Yours,

Bedi
February 25, 1957

Two or three years before this, standing in a group of friends, I said to Bedi, "You are as good as grass."

"Don Quixote," he said, "once told Sancho Panza, 'You are as good as bread. Nothing but the sexton and his spade will ever part us.'"

Now the sexton and his spade have come. Something has been sheared off of me.

Freedom and "Fatheads"

BOB SHERRILL

FEBRUARY 2, 1962 — The state legislature this week granted funds that could extend indefinitely the work of the special textbook investigation committee. Members of the committee indicated that after wrapping up their Austin inquiry, they may move their base of operations to Amarillo and San Antonio and other cities where groups of citizens are unhappy with the content of school library books and textbooks, alleging pornographic and subversive content.

But it was the consensus of many who have followed the textbook dispute all the way that this week's session will probably be looked back on as the climax of a running wrangle . . . [over] a wave of book censoring across the state.

Anticipating a record turnout, Committee chairman W. T. Dungan moved the hearing from the main committee room to the much larger old supreme court chambers, but even so the crowd clotted at the doorways and spread into the hall.

Many were there to hear one man: J. (for James) Frank Dobie, folklorist extraordinary. . . . Though the text of his address showed his earnestness, Dobie appeared to enjoy the fray, as he squinted benignly at the audience, pushed back the white lock that kept flopping across his forehead, and waved to help the photographers. A red plaid tie fluttered around on his chest like a small toreador's cape. A sporting fighter, Dobie went out of his way to shake hands with his ideological enemy, J. (for James) Evetts Haley [head of Texans for America], before laying into him.

Earlier in the day, Dobie told the *Observer*: "Evetts is sometimes a mean fighter. He'll kick you in the b——s. But I'll say this, if he thinks he's right, he'll stand there alone, in the blizzard, and the rain, and fight for what he believes in."

(That evening, when Dobie wasn't present, Haley called Dobie a supporter of subversive organizations and a liar. Advised of this the next day, Dobie sounded grieved: "We've known each other for many years," he said. "I didn't think he would attack me personally.")

Excerpts from Dobie's talk:

"All we are asking for is to leave freedom free to combat error. We don't any of us think that wisdom will die with us. . . . A censor is always a tool. Or, as Hitler called Mussolini — a utensil. Not one censor of history is respected by enlightened men of any nation. . . . Any person who imagines he has a corner on the definition or conception of Americanism and wants to suppress all conceptions to the contrary is a bigot and an enemy to the free world.

"The more censoring of textbooks, the weaker they become. Their publishers are so compliant that most of them would print the texts in Hindu if the buyers preferred. Their aim now is to offend nobody. The result is negative — something as dull as a Ph.D. thesis in a department of education.

". . . The book burners are rising again. The Minute Women, The Ku Klux Klaners. Yesterday, they took 10 books off the shelves in Amarillo. . . . Tomorrow, what?

"I've been in the cathedrals of England mutilated by the Cromwellians — all in the name of conscience. There is a vast difference between having an ignorant conscience and an enlightened conscience. Merely being conscientious isn't enough."

He said he had read *Lady Chatterley's Lover* and *Tropic of Cancer* before they were allowed in the country, and "I did not find a single four-letter Anglo-Saxon word I hadn't heard from older boys before I had arrived at the age of puberty. I've been hearing them ever since. Hearing these words and reading them has had little influence on my thinking.

"School kids aren't fools. They aren't going to be fooled by some dull, tail-twisting and flag-waving propaganda.

"I'm for textbooks selected on the basis of strength, vividness, justness, and the beautiful."

. . . If the students and university professors on hand rewarded these statements [by Dobie and others] with considerable applause and cheers — reactions that Chairman Dungan met with continued patience and continued gaveling — much of the audience showed its hostility, as did the opposition witnesses, such as M.F. Gabler of Hawkins who said that since the "Bible blackout" that took effect in California . . . "crime has pushed far ahead of what it is in the state of New York." Some young people in the room laughed, and Dungan gaveled them silent. . . .

And Mrs. A.A. Forester was back. She is chairman of the textbook committee of the Daughters of the American Revolution and of Texans for America. When Rep. John Alaniz asked her to name specifically the textbooks she objected to, she asked: "Do you have a list of the textbook adoptions of this year?" Alaniz: "Yes." Mrs. Forester: "Well, all of them."

But the clashing of weapons was heard again in earnest after the supper break, when [J. Evett] Haley took the stand to rebut his scholarly and student opponents. Frequently he raised his voice and spoke with bitterness to the young people who "sit there and grin," and called them "supercilious." He said the professors had argued "it is all right to write anything you want to, but if we don't want to buy it, it is censorship." He said "even the fatheads at the University of Texas" should know that. He called the professors "leftwingers," said Dobie "is a member of a number of subversive orders and movements" . . . [and] said he himself had been fired by the University of Texas years ago, and, he asked, "where was that bunch of bleeding hearts" when "I was fired for teaching the truth?" He also called the Dobie group "long-haired, super-intellectuals, super-sophisticates." He said Dobie associates with the "authentic liars of Texas."

(Thursday, the *Observer* checked with the payroll department of the University of Texas to find out when Haley taught at U.T. and if he was fired, as he said he was in Wednesday's testimony. The payroll department says he was not on the staff as a teacher but as a "collector." It was explained that this meant he went around the state soliciting manuscripts for the university's historical collection [from 1931 to 1935]. The payroll department does not record his having been fired. Some of the older professors at the university say they had not heard of the "firing" until several years after he left when Haley himself first publicly described his exit in this way. They said it was their opinion the funds just ran out, that being the bottom of the depression.)

. . . Testifying on Haley's side at the night session was Dr. Medford Evans, a [member of] Texans for America and, by his unsolicited admission, the organizer of the John Birch Society in Louisiana and Mississippi.

He said the future does not belong "to those who talk about it so much. Eleanor Roosevelt is no longer young. . . . Max Lerner is not young. Norman Thomas is not young."

A young man in the crowd called, "What about [John Birch Society founder] Robert Welch?"

Evans took it in stride: "The question is pertinent. Neither does the future belong to Robert Welch." It belongs, he said, to the Young Americans for Freedom. There was applause, but not from the college group.

He added, "This is more obviously true in the Ivy League than in the imitation Ivy League." . . .

Free of Both Hate and Fear

GLEN L. EVANS

AUGUST 9, 1963 — I first saw Walter Prescott Webb in the middle 1930's when I was a student at The University of Texas. We exchanged a perfunctory greeting; I was struck by the solemn expression on his face, and I guessed him to be a severe and unapproachable man. Several years passed before I realized how mistaken this was. I did not have him as a professor, although, in an informal sense, I was always his student. From the time we first became well acquainted, around 1940, until I moved away from Austin in 1954, we met for long or short talks perhaps once or twice a month. Thereafter I saw him only once or twice a year. Most of our meetings were over a cup of coffee or at lunch, but occasionally they were in his office. Sometimes I made notes on what he had said. . . .

In a stimulating group Dr. Webb was not an aggressive talker. More often than not he would sit quietly, listening intently. Now and then he would break in with a pertinent remark or a short, illustrative story. He knew . . . as most people do not, how to contribute to a conversation without dominating it. At times when something was said that amused him he would burst out in a roar of laughter that was utterly contagious.

Despite the mournful expression he wore, Dr. Webb was a skilled dispeller of gloom. In 1959, after we had attended the funeral for Roy Bedichek, Webb, Mr. Dobie and I went out together for lunch — a meal for which we had no appetite. Mr. Dobie was suffering in his depths. I, too, felt the loss acutely and was becoming terribly depressed and lonely. Dr. Webb had known Roy Bedichek much longer and more intimately than I, and was certainly not less conscious of his loss. Yet he talked more freely than usual, recalling cheerful and witty things that Bedi had said. He reflected that the only way that life might be thought to have a happy ending was when death came, as it had come to Bedichek, suddenly and painlessly after a long, happy, and useful career. His statements were logical and soothing, and as free of inanities and sentimentalities as always. I feel sure that he intended to help lift our spirits, and he succeeded.

He was a deep and complex man. I suspect that he had the quality of greatness within him. About a year before Bedi died, he remarked to me, in substance if not exactly, "Webb shows no sign of mental aging. Instead, he gets stronger every year. He has a source of inner power that the rest of us don't have — or if we have it we don't know how to reach it." Thinking for him seemed as natural as breathing. It gave him dignity and serenity, and freed him from emotional strains. In the time I knew him I don't believe he feared anything in or after life. He seemed free of both hate and fear, but I don't believe that he had ever made a conscious effort to divest himself of either. It seemed that acts or events that normally incite hate or fear got digested in his thinking processes and never entered the emotional part of his being.

The last time I saw him was around the middle of February, shortly before his death. I was in Austin for the day, and he invited me to join him and his wife, Terrell, whom I had not met previously, for lunch at the Night Hawk cafe near The University of Texas campus. During the hour or so we spent together he was brimming over with enthusiasm. He talked mainly of *Washington Wife*, the book which he and Mrs. Webb had helped bring out, and of which he was inordinately proud. His unconcealed devotion for Mrs. Webb and the joy he derived from her companionship was as pleasing for me to observe as it has been for his many other friends. When I left him I knew that he was happier than I had ever seen him before. His death was a shocking loss to all of us who knew him, but according to his own standards, his life had a happy ending.

A Letter from Texas

RONNIE DUGGER

FEBRUARY 7, 1964 — I shall try to spin out of this typewriter and this closed hotel room in Dallas of the President's death, the subject of what can be said about Texas, the home state of the new President, known to me as the place I live.

Let us be done with the stereotypes, please. Let us be done with them. Writers the magazines ask to go do tooth-sucking sniggles on Texas gaucheries ought to say no, I will do what I see, but not what you expect me to see. Texans in the East ought to have better sense than to do the absurd things that are expected of them, and we Texans who will stay here at home, as I will, for I love it here and belong here, an animal that feels best when he knows where he is, we have the duty now to communicate what it is and has been to be here. . . .

Consider the stereotypes about Texas against certain facts known to us who live here. For instance, does it strike you odd that a guy named Hank Brown, a plumber from San Antonio, could become the most liberal state labor president on civil rights in the entire South? That there are intellectuals born and bred Texans? That a thin blonde babe in tight black slacks and a waist-length leather jacket may have character that is personally her own and admirable? That a water color artist in Houston may be doing work that is truly valuable and may never be appreciated? That the fiercest defender of underpaid Mexicans in the United States is the Archbishop of the Catholic Church of San Antonio? How can anyone honestly tell you what Texas is? Lyndon Johnson will have to show you, himself, who he is, and Ladybird, she, and Katherine Anne Porter has shown you who she is, and Sam Houston showed, he, and that is all any Texan can do.

I can tell you marvels. Have you ever been startled in a hotel lobby by the face of a cross-eyed cowboy under a Stetson hat? Can you imagine a professor at the University of Texas marching against a S.A.C. base outside of Austin on Easter? Does it vaguely surprise you that Texans get sent to mental hospitals? Have you ever met a Negro intellectual in a country farmhouse? He has been hiding there. What would you make of it if populism awakened again in Texas? Have you ever seen a river that runs over rocks ruined by real estate agents who've divided the banks into lots? Then there are Texans who are pragmatic and insist on finding out for themselves how it works, or does not work, to make love on a night on the coast among the dunes. There are Texans who are dogmatic and don't make love at all. There are children at the beaches as lovely as Gitanjali's and places in sanctuaries where even thorns caress, and forests like islands, and great vacant plains whose whole power is meaning nothing. . . .

I can tell you that we breed real people here, because I have met them, and continue to. Some friends and I used to have a floating discussion club. We would gather for weekends at clubhouses on lakes, in a tourist court in Rockport on the Gulf, in a forested place near Houston, and once at the late Walter Webb's Friday Mountain camp in the Hill Country, and we would talk our dreams into tatters, and tell each other what each other ought be doing instead of what each other were. That's all over now, we do not meet any more, we got tired talking to each other about the same things that worried each of us, but in big places like Texas, you come and go with your friends, meet and stop meeting and still go on being friends across distances that often these days become physically insuperable for any casual purpose. If the stereotypes have done Texans no other favor, they have helped those of us who are friends hold on in an awareness of our common place, even across continents.

It is an eerily visceral thing to love your home place. I first noticed it powerfully in the way I feel about the gravel play-yard and the exit from it through an alleyway at Bonham elementary school in San Antonio. I can pass there, where I went to school and played and came home through the alley, and although all I remember on the school grounds is drinking from the water fountain, being called a sissy, and being afraid of being beaten up, I am overcome with nostalgic wistfulness.

The same thing happens now when I leave Texas a while and return: when I came back from California last, I did not have Texas on my mind, and was not even here — I was in Juarez, the border town across from El Paso, eating *cabrito* — when suddenly I thought, "I'm home," and a kind of strangeness and displacement left me. . . .

To a Texan a car is like wings to a seagull. Our places are far apart and we must dip into them driving. For an often traveling man like myself, the junctions in the highways and the towns are like turns in a city well known.

We must drive fast from Austin to El Paso to make it in a day. One time another family and the one I am in set out for there, but ran out of light, so we doubled back to an old railroad car watering place that happened still to be by the side of the road. We built a fire and ate and slept there the night, and woke to the dawn too literally rosy to be a good thing to try to describe. You have to feel a fire by a railroad siding in the West Texas desert to know what we felt together, how casual and friendly it was that night and morning, on that desolate and sunbitten land.

One of the drives I like to take is the ferry out of Galveston up the coast past High Island and into Port Arthur. You drive along, the waves almost laving your right tires, you could drive on in if you'd had enough, and then you veer away from the water into Port Arthur through the gothic fantastics of an oil refinery. Workmen in orange helmets walk and chug around amidst the legs of these giant spatial structures, orbs, catwalks, skeletal obelisks, the technological dreams weighing down the men who sleep and work within them.

Texas: back to Texas. (Where is this place? This can't be Texas. No millionaires, no oil derricks, no Stetsons, no government scandals. Lightolier fixtures — piped-in music — pink ceiling — pastel-lemon light bulbs — well, yes, it is named the "Eatwell Café." Fit name for a cattle town.) But we don't have any more cattle towns. Try Fort Worth. Or worse, try the restaurants near the stockyards there, one of which is the nearest New York will ever get to the fragrances of cattle ranching. . . .

I have long had a romantic idea of the shrimp boats and the bait sellers, all that having to do with the people who live at the edges of the sea off the fish and the fishing. They seem to have found a way to be of the world, and out of it, too; they can dream off into the Gulf as they stand in the blinding sun by their bait stands, or if they're shrimpers, they can go out a couple weeks, come in, sell their catch, live it up until they're broke, and then go out again. Once I was going to leave journalism and go to work on a shrimp boat, where people are close-quarters and the work is lively and hard. I must have 500 clippings now on things that have happened to Texas shrimpers — boat wrecks, storms, Mexican gunboats firing on them, fleet blessings, washed-overboards, brawls at waterfront. You don't have to be far away from a thing to fail to experience it.

The beach, the long Padre Island, now a national park, all that sand and whiffy grass and those gentling dunes, blurs together in a man's comprehension and is just there. . . . Now, of course, there also are the crowds, the beer cans and the strewn bodies; the sand in your teeth and ears irritates more because it's no longer a private hardship. In Texas, too, we are going now toward too-crowdedness. What will we do? Our leaders do not understand yet that the beauties must be made sanctuary for all of us in collectivity. Soon it will be too late. At least most of Padre was saved, thanks mostly to Sen. Ralph Yarborough.

I will tell you a little about our senior senator. He is a kind of a butt of the cocktail circuit in Washington and he is a better man than nearly all of them. He has a fineness of character that is utterly personal to him.

And about Sen. John Tower, also, a few words. To a liberal he is worse than Goldwater and he seems like a throwback to a right-wing Utopia on an island out of Daddy Warbucks, but he had the courage to run against Lyndon Johnson, and he has the courage yet to stand where he does, even if it's upside down; which it is.

I do not mean to be truculent, we have plenty of cowards, and it's a good thing, but there is something in the history of the state, Indians, Alamo, grand old Sam Houston refusing to secede from the Union, Jim Hogg ramming the railroads with his own personal bulk, that makes all of us, even us cowards, understand that courage really is the question.

Speaking very personally, I think of State Rep. Bob Eckhardt of Houston in company with Sam Houston. From much knowing his mind and his responses I am sure he is a statesman and a wise man. In the urbane clarities of his thinking, the calm way he is honest, and the plain nobility of his frame and his unkempt mane, he is the Texan I think of when I look through a book of photographs that were made of Lincoln. . . .

I beg your indulgence to tell you what worries me most about Texas. I fear that the concentration of wealth in the control of a few people may constipate and befoul our democracy. I fear that our democratic politics is being corrupted, and legally, by the high costs of running for office and the high cost of getting re-elected. I describe Texas, but sense the same in the country. Why are we not hearing a great debate about it? Perhaps the question contains its answer and democracy is in trouble. . . .

There is a hard kind of conservative in Dallas who seems to me opportunistic and unscrupulous, willing to use cruel methods as long as the results are right. Perhaps because of this, I don't come to Dallas much; it reminds me of a prison, its skyscrapers full of cells, and forming below and between them the windy courtyards of honking and desolation.

I do not like to drive in Houston, which sprawls like a neon jungle except that it has some sections of spectacular mansions with lawns so large and foliage so elaborate, full time gardeners are required. Walking in River Oaks I wonder how this would appear to a poor man from Peru, or an African intellectual, and sense in such affluence a coming trouble for our country. Yet inside some of the homes there I have met people with no harm in them, and warmth and courtesy toward everyone of whatever bearing.

I would not have you think I claim there is anything discrete or unique in things and people worth seeing and knowing in Texas. We do not need that or any kind of specialness in my state any more. We are becoming strong enough as a culture to know that we will most of the time fail as individuals, against our highest goals, and to be able to accept this, and honor the more those who do not fail, against our highest standards. We are not so uninformed about the razz-ma-tazz nightclub life and the frenetic business pace in Arizona and New York, Chicago and California, that we feel any generically Texas shame about our own gaucheries and vapidities. There seems to be enough of these to go around without our making special stock of ours.

But you know, the race will be in a hell of a shape if we lose our sentiment. If the sneer ever overpowers the hope that someone will get the message — well, do you know what Lee Oswald told a Dallas Repub-

lican about his visit to Russia? He said Russia is "incredibly boring."
Texas is not. It's credibly real and it's full of willingness for sentiment.
People love here as though we've just discovered love and there's a future for it. We haven't learned to believe yet that everybody, down deep,
is a son of a bitch, or the prospective mother of one. I think we're right,
and I fear we're wrong. I hope you who do not live here will let us who
do join you as ordinary equals in the attempt to keep life, and to keep it
from being incredibly boring. Say whatever you like about any one of
us, we will, too. But say not "about Texas," for as it is not anything in
particular, so, to we who love it and are here, it is everything that surrounds us, and the places our intelligence lives, and hears, and grows.

The Best Name I Know

JOHN HENRY FAULK

JULY 24, 1964 — In 1953, when my son was born, I wanted to give him the best name I knew. The best name that I knew then was Frank Dobie. It belonged to a good and honest man, in fact, one of the best and most honest men I have ever met. I figured that the man who had made it such a good name should have some say-so about its use. So I called Mr. Dobie down in Austin (I was living in New York at the time) and asked him if he minded sharing his name with my son. He said that he didn't mind in the least. Thus it was that there came to be a Frank Dobie Faulk.

A couple of months later I brought Frank Dobie Faulk down to Austin to show him off to my family. A pious old sister, a member of my mother's quilting circle who had taught me in Sunday school years ago, in the Methodist church, called me up at my mother's home. Ostensibly she called to tell me how glad she was that I was back home, that she hoped to see me in church next Sunday, and that it rejoiced her old heart to hear that I was doing so well with my radio and television career. She covered those matters in less than five seconds. Then she launched into the real purpose of her call.

"Jist wondered, honey, why on earth you would saddle that pore little baby of yours with such a name as Frank Dobie. Seems sich a pity when there's so many good *Christian* names around."

"It was the best name I could think of," I replied. Her voice took on that quavery whine, condescending and self-righteous, which characterizes her particular brand of religiosity.

"Johnny, you've jist been away from Austin too long. That ol' Frank

Dobie has got to where he's a outright disgrace. When he ain't blessin' out the gov'mint, he's ridiculin' religion an' pokin' fun at preachers. Jist disgraceful the way he goes on. I've heered and don't doubt fer a minute it's so" — here her tone became conspiratorial — "that the old sinner never put a foot inside a church in his life." I could have told her that as a matter of fact, Mr. Dobie as a boy had been watered at the same spiritual spring from which she drank, the Methodist Church. But I told her goodbye instead.

Mama, when I told her of the call, commented a bit apologetically, "Pay her no mind, Johnny. She's a simple-minded old ignoramus who has nothing to do but sit around and feed her prejudices with misinformation. If she knew Mr. Dobie a little better, she would love and respect him as much as you do."

Mama was right about ignoring the old lady's remark. Her kind of criticism of Dobie had long since ceased even to anger me. I knew that Dobie pays it no mind at all. But mama was wrong about the old lady liking Dobie if she knew him better. If she had known Dobie better, what he really believes, she would have liked him even less. There is not a religious or political fraud in Texas who can stand J. Frank Dobie. He makes them too uncomfortable. Hypocrites and humbugs offend him and he says so with a cheerful directness.

Dobie got the way he is, I think, by being a prospector in the world of ideas. He started prospecting in the Southwest a long time ago, and he has widened his territory steadily ever since. He wasn't prospecting for gold and lost treasure, but for the rich stores of folklore, for the tales and the songs of the people who lived close to the earth, people who bore the authentic stamp of the land in their hearts and their faces. He leaned his ear close to the earth and caught its subtle sounds and rhythms. He listened and he absorbed. Listened and absorbed, not with just his ears, but with his heart and his mind. As his intellect and his emotional field expanded, his horizons grew ever wider. He was always a thinking man. But he became more than that. He evolved into what Emerson called "man thinking." As a "man thinking" prospector, he has become an unfailing expert on the real gold in the limitless world of ideas: he can smell the difference between real gold and fool's gold.

Dobie's mind continues to explore, to expand. If he has any god, it is what he calls the Liberated Mind. He is not a denouncer, either by nature or by inclination. But he has prospected and mined out so much that is of real value, he has little time or use for dross or synthetics. This, coupled with the hearty readiness with which he will affirm ideas and facts, regardless of their popularity, has earned him the enmity of the timid and the prejudiced, but it has endeared him to a great number of informed and civilized minds.

Two persons who possess such minds are Edward R. Murrow and Carl Sandburg. Both have known Mr. Dobie for a number of years. Ed Murrow became very fond of him over in England during World War II, when Dobie was a guest professor at Cambridge and Murrow was broadcasting from London for CBS. Ed told me, "Mr. Frank moved around England and talked to the people and he listened to them. They got to know him. He did more to win British respect and affection for Americans than our entire diplomatic corps and propaganda program combined." Mr. Carl Sandburg told me, "*Whatever's* the matter with America, Frank Dobie ain't."

In 1953, the best name I knew to give my son was Frank Dobie. It's still the best name I know.

Apocalypse Now?
A Sensitive Sounding of Today's New Youth

BILL BRAMMER

> Give me an old wall and a garbage
> Can and I can by-god sit there forever.
>
> — William Burroughs

> Show me a rose,
> And I'll show you a girl named Sam,
> Show me a rose,
> Or leave me alone.
>
> — Groucho Marx

NOVEMBER 1, 1968 — As I recall it now in the neurotic glow of middle age, the golden era of my own Radical Youth could be characterized as a dull, headachey interlude generally occurring between high school and graduation and the onset of stupefying installment debt. Radicalism was a mean, grinding, no-nonsense business, by God. We worried ourselves sick about "reasonable" anti-lynching legislation . . . And Taft-Hartley . . . And parity for the farmers . . . And tidelands oil. Wow. Friends jeopardized appointments to Officer Candidate School by publicly supporting freedom of speech for alleged security risks. We took a lot of chances like that. Fraternities wouldn't pledge us. Girls wouldn't date us. Life was hard. I tell you, hard.

But we were responsible revolutionaries. We kept our blue suede shoes mostly on our feet, our ducktails a respectable distance from the spine. Certainly none of us were remotely interested in parading 'round the streets after dark looking to get our skulls leavened by police. I myself was busy most of the time writing devastating editorials critical of the poll tax and the oil depletion allowance.

I indulge in this nostalgia, now, by way of offering credential for what follows: A dispassionate, desperately authoritative report on today's New Youth. Read it, and . . . well, take heart or fall into despond as your taste and rampant anxiety dictate. For myself, I am tuned in, turned on and almost entirely bereft of any emotion save for such as might apply to geriatric disorders.

An aging hippie friend is our principal source of intelligence: long in the tooth, yes, but longer still in the hair. I got to know him years ago during his pre-hippie, post-beatnik days around the University of Texas, a time when I was attempting to determine the identity of a genius poet responsible for a fragment of monument-sized graffiti in evidence along an expanse of concrete retaining wall flanking Lamar Boulevard.

"REGENTS IS PIGS"

Belaboring the obvious, conceivably: I found it inspired, all the same. It proved to be the work of my hippie friend, at that time a mere 18-year-old anarchist. Call him Harry He-Who-Flies. Not his real name, of course, but it is one he assures me he can live with.

I looked in on Harry's scenic, psychedelic slum digs the other day. He was standing out back with a few friends, obviously still searching for new graffiti coups, gazing overhead at a small biplane towing a message exhorting everyone down below to "PRAY FOR ROSEMARY'S BABY."

"Outta sight," Harry said. "Except I don't happen to believe in the efficacy of prayer. Just another establishment game." Whereupon he expressed a vast longing for possession of a biplane. I asked him how come.

"Oh, like first off I'd compose a groovier commercial message," Harry said. "Then I'd just fly around some 'til they shot me down."

I asked him what sort of message he had in mind.

"How about, for starters, how about . . . AUSTIN SUCKS?"

"Very nice. Ought to make folks proud to live in this great country."

"Yeah. Sock it to 'em. Through the stupendous medium of my own famed monument-gauge graffiti."

He looked up at me, pensive and red-eyed. My visits with Harry often as not coincided with instances of national peril such as presidential abdications, assassinations, nominating conventions. "What the hell's gone wrong now?" Harry said. "You come to sound me out again on the temper of the times?"

I plugged in my tape recorder.

"Ordinarily," Harry began, choosing his words with great care, "I would prefer to remain anomalous. There comes a time, however, when decent citizens got to stand up for America and tell it like it is."

"How is it, Harry?"

"It's like, the American people are very uptight man."

"About what?"

"Law and order, baby. Violence in the streets."

"How do you feel about it?"

"They're right, man. Never saw so much violence. I myself no longer venture out after dark. Never can tell when you're going to be poleaxed by rioting troopers or melancholy spades or overreacting rednecks pursuing you with pipewrenches and calling you a dirty, freaky long-haired queer."

"How about other issues?"

"Permissiveness among cops," Harry told me. "I'm thinking about staging a hair-burning ceremony at Zilker Park, a sort of Burn-In, to protest. Nothing pretentious, you know, nothing flamboyant like with incinerating draft cards and Buddhist monks. Still I been considering a nice little barber shop singe. Burn it up off my shoulders."

Harry explained that he regards this as a matter of conscience: "I really couldn't live with myself, man, if I got sort of stomped to death by my fellow man."

I asked him about the candidates.

"Hard to say. I mean take Wallace, for example. I dig what he puts down about violence on the streets and all. Except when he says he's gonna run over long-haired hippie anarchists with his car. Presumably he would do this on some *street* or other. Now it may be stretching it some, but we figure that qualifies as a somewhat violent act."

"Possibly. What about the other candidates?"

"I like Humphrey. I mean, I think he's on record as being opposed to running hippies down in the White House limousines. As a matter of public policy. But Nixon—he's something else. Nixon refuses to comment at all on whether he might, as president, run us all down in his new car. He says he's reluctant to say anything which might upset or compromise the American position in the delicate peace negotiations in Paris."

I asked Harry if he had any concluding comment. The tape was running out.

"If I had the courage to go out at night like in the old days," Harry said, "I'd get my paints and put up a few slogans, pithy fragments like graffiti wisdom, flipped-out metaphysics and like that."

"Like what?"

"How about APOCALYPSE NOW? OR NEXT WEEK? How about a number of hip reminders as concerns the drug peril, you know? I wrote some down the weekend of our First Annual Therapeutic Indian Madras Peyote Chewing and Free-style Hallucinations pageant. My way of dramatizing my own determination to quit taking drugs altogether. All kinds. Or most kinds. Or at least cut down a lot. I mean anything that tastes as unspeakable as peyote can't be *all* good. As for acid, I am hugely bugged by the possibility of even so much as *annoying* one of my chromosomes."

"How do you propose to curb drug abuses?"

"Gonna warn all these kids — leadership, man. These kids coming up are just outta-sight irresponsible nuts! They've had it too easy. So I intend to lay down the law to 'em. Bridge this generation gap. Like, do not carry any more dope on your person than can be ingested in an instant. See? Also, do not carry dope if you are subject to insulin shock, epilepsy, or coronary occlusion. Also, do not drink while doping. Very dangerous, as we all know. Also, do not sell or give dope to undercover narcotics agents (the gravest drug abuse of all); nor to little kids, unappreciative friends, unresponsive chicks. Finally, do not attempt feats of skill and daring while stoned, such as walking on water, racing heavy machinery, wandering into police stations, crawling into theater lobbies or giving ten percent of your stash to church poorboxes."

Apocalypse now? Or next week? Our party nominees should be so straightforward in their campaign rhetoric.

Our examination of the awful, unwashed hippie peril degenerates into obsession and polemic: the shift from a whiskey culture to a drug culture among great numbers of the American middle class.

A regrettable tendency, of course, though not without its mitigating factors. Nice boys and girls do not lightly commit felony crimes every day of their lives without exhibiting some disproportionate concern with the felonious act itself — let alone great destructive heaps of paranoia. It's one thing to argue that the Law — good or bad — ought to be respected; it's quite another, however, when some incorrigible lump of draft bait suffers a longer stretch in prison, as a second-time offender for possession of a killer weed, than the otherwise respectable-looking contemporary who has merely chopped up his parents into little bits and pieces of prime London Broil. Anti-social acts are relative affairs.

My friend Harry is genuinely intimidated and more than a little fearful. And he is unqualifiedly appalled that the great majority of Americans appear to approve of Chicago's solution to such social problems as unpleasantness created by freaky-looking protestants. Even a routine weekend hippie picnic or outdoor dance invariably draws more secret agents, establishment *provocateurs*, outraged police, militia and federal gangbusters than the best-advertised Mafia conventions.

It's possible, of course, that America would forgive its youth, provided young people trim their hair, dress respectably, get some sort of job, and exhibit sufficient patriotic zeal for incinerating Vietnamese peasants. Still one is reminded of Scott Fitzgerald's observations from another time and place: "Don't get to thinking this is a real country just because you can assemble a lot of high school kids in gym suits and have them spell out BANANAS for the newsreels."

Texas Observed

MOLLY IVINS

DECEMBER 27, 1974 — The rest of the country is in future shock and in Texas we can't get Curtis's Clean Crapper bill through the Legislature. Curtis Graves is a state representative from Houston who introduced a bill to provide minimum standards of cleanliness for public restrooms in this state. It was defeated. Solons rose on the floor of the House to defend dirty johns. The delights of peein' against the back wall after a good whiskey drank were limned in excruciating detail. In New York City, Zero Mostel gets up on a stage and prances around singing "Tradition!" while the audience wets itself with nostalgia. In America, the rate of change shifts from arithmetic to geometric progression. In Texas, where ain't nothin' sanitized for your protection, we still peein' against the back wall.

What this country really needs, along with a new government, is a stiff dose of Texas. Things still are the way they used to be down here, and everybody who thinks that's quaint is welcome to come dip into the state's premier product. Like Johnny Winter sings, "They's so much shit in Texas you bound to step in some."

. . . Texas is a dandy place, in short spells, for anyone suffering from *nauseé de* Thruway Hot Shoppe. It is resistant to Howard Johnson, plastic, interstate highways and Standard Television American English. But the reason it's resistant to such phenomena is because it's cantankerous, ignorant and repulsive.

The reason the sky is bigger here is because there aren't any trees. The reason folks here eat grits is because they ain't got no taste. Cowboys mostly stink and it's hot, oh God, it is hot. We gave the world Lyndon

Johnson and you cowards gave him right back. There are two major cities in Texas: Houston is Los Angeles with the climate of Calcutta; to define Dallas is to add a whole new humongous dimension to bad.

Texas is a mosaic of cultures, which overlap in several parts of the state and form layers, with the darker layers on the bottom. The cultures are black, chicano, southern, freak, suburban, and shitkicker. (Shitkicker is dominant.) They are all rotten for women. Humanism is not alive and well in Texas. Different colors and types of Texans do not like one another, nor do they pretend to.

Shitkicker is pickup trucks with guns slung across the racks on the back and chicken fried steaks and *macho* and "D-I-V-O-R-C-E" on the radio and cheap, pink nylon slips, and gettin' drunk on Saturday night and goin' to church on Sunday morning and drivin' down the highway throwin' beer cans out the window and Rastus-an'-Liza jokes and high school football and family reunions where the in-laws of your second cousins show up.

You can eat chili, barbecue, Meskin food, hush puppies, catfish, collard greens, red beans, pink grapefruit, and watermelon with Dr. Pepper, Pearl, Lone Star, Carta Blanca, or Shiner's, which tastes a lot like paint-thinner but don't have no preservatives in it. People who eat soul food here eat it because they can't afford hamburger. Since last year, you can buy a drink in some bars, but a lot of folks still brown-bag it cause it's cheaper and Chivas and Four Roses look alike comin' out of a brown bag.

The frontier is what John Wayne lived on. Most Texans are Baptists. Baptists are civilized people. Beware of Church of Christers.

Texas is an unself-conscious place. Nobody here is embarrassed about being who they are. Reactionaries aren't embarrassed. Rich folks aren't embarrassed. Rednecks aren't embarrassed. Liberals aren't embarrassed. And when did black folks or brown folks ever have time to worry about existential questions? Lobbyists, loan sharks, slumlords, war profiteers, chiropractors, and KKKers are all proud of their callings. Only Dallas is self-conscious: Dallas deserves it.

Texas is not a civilized place. Texans shoot one another a lot. They also knife, razor, and stomp one another to death with some frequency. And they fight in bars all the time. You can get five years for murder and 99 for pot possession in this state—watch your ass.

The only thing that smells worse than an oil refinery is a feedlot. Texas has a lot of both. Legend has it that ecology in Texas started with a feedlot. So many people in Lubbock got upset with the smell of a feedlot there that they complained to the city council all the time. The city council members didn't act like yahoos; they took it serious. After a lot of hearings, it was decided to put up an Air-wick bottle on every fencepost around the feedlot. Ecology in Texas has gone uphill since then.

The two newest members of the Air Pollution Control Board were up for a hearing before a state senate committee this June. E.W. Robinson of Amarillo told the committee that he was against allowin' any pollution that would prove very harmful to people's health. A senator asked him how harmful was very harmful. Oh, lead poisonin' and such would be unacceptable, said Robinson. What about pollution that causes allergies and asthma? Well, you don't die of it, said Robinson. While the air of Texas is entrusted to this watchdog, the water is in good hands too. Not long ago, the director of the Texas Water Quality Board was trying to defend what the Armco Steel Company is dumping into the Houston ship channel. "Cyanide," he said, "is a scare word."

Art is paintings of bluebonnets and broncos, done on velvet. Music is mariachis, blues, and country.

Kinky Friedman and the Texas Jewboys cut a single recently with "The Ballad of Charles Whitman" on the one side and "Get Your Biscuits in the Oven and Your Buns in the Bed" on the flip. Part of the lyrics of "The Ballad" go like this: "There was a rumor/about a tumor/nestled at the base of his brain . . ." Kinky lives on a ranch in West Texas called Rio Duckworth.

There is a radio station just across the border from Del Rio, Texas. It plays hymns during the day and broadcasts religious advertisements all night. They sell autographed pictures of Jesus to all you friends in radioland. Also prayer rugs as a special gift for all your travellin' salesmen friends with a picture of the face of Jesus, on the prayer rug that glows in the dark. And underneath the picture is a legend that also glows in the dark, "Thou Shalt Not Commit Adultery."

Texas is not full of rich people. Texas is full of poor people. The latest count is 22 percent of the folks here under the federal poverty line — and the feds don't set the line high. The rest of the country, they tell us, has 13 percent poor folks, including such no-account states as Mississippi. Because Texas is racist, 45 percent of the black folks and the brown folks are poor.

Onliest foreign thang that approaches Texas politics is Illinois politics. We ain't never left it lyin' around in shoeboxes, elsewise, we got the jump on everybody.

Texans do not talk like other Americans. They drawl, twang, or sound like the Frito Bandito, only not jolly. Shit is a three-syllable word with a "y" in it.

Texans invent their own metaphors and similes, often of a scatological nature, which is kind of fun. As a group, they tell good stories well. The reason they are good at stories is because this is what anthropologists call an oral culture. That means people here don't read and write much. Neither would you if the *Dallas Morning News* was all you had to read.

Texas — I believe it has been noted elsewhere — is a big state. Someone else can tell you about the symphony orchestras and the experimental theaters and those Texans who are writing their Ph.D. theses on U.S. imperialism in Paraguay and 17th-century Sanskrit literature. I'm just talking about what makes Texas Texas.

So I will tell you about my friend John Henry Faulk, who, back in the McCarthy era, which is still going strong here, was accused of being a "premature anti-fascist," and that, he notes, made him as popular as a sick whore tryin' to get into SMU Theology School. John Henry favors the Vietnam war on religious grounds — he says that if we don't bum 'em, they not gonna bum theyselves. Besides, he doesn't like them. "We go over there to bum them Veetnamese — send our best boys over in million-dollar airplanes, in broad daylight, wearin' pressed uniforms, and what do them Veetnamese do? They come out at night. On their bicycles. Wearing' pyjamas. Not even Christian. If they don't like what we're doin' for 'em, they should just go back where they come from."

I will tell you about the radical president of the Texas labor movement Roy Evans, who spat, as it were, in Mr. Meany's eye and said he damned well would work for George McGovern. And the Archbishop of San Antonio who is a chicano militant and about Miz Seay, my landlady, who only rents to good hippies. And Anders the Mad Dane, who takes us on canoeing trips so we can set around the fire at night and get drunk pickin' and singin' "Faded Love" and "Honky-Tonk Angel."

I will tell you about the Dirty Thirty, a group of legislators who don't think it's all right for the speaker of the House to do a bribery number, even if he can see to it that none of them are ever elected again. And about Zarko Franks, son of a Yugoslav bootlegger from Galveston, who believes that Baby Jesus never made an ugly woman. And Whiskey Bob Wheeler who lives in Tilde, Tex., and has read 37 books on Chairman Mao and the Chinese Revolution, not to mention the *New York Review of Books* every month. He says there aren't too many people to talk to in Tilde. And about Jose Angel Gutierrez who ripped off Crystal City from the *gringos* and about the judge in Dallas who gave an extra-heavy sentence to a black kid because he thought the kid had shouted, "Riot on!" at a demonstration.

There is a person named Ima Hogg; her daddy was governor once and she is (the usage is deliberate) a fine lady. I will tell you about a woman I know in Abilene who is too smart, too aware to spend her time at bridge and ladies' do-good groups. She tried to do something "political" once — to get fluoride in the city's water supply. The John Birchers almost ruined her husband. Now she stares at the prairie a lot with dull eyes and is sometimes merry in bars.

I will tell you about the librarian in Lockhart, who lets the kids read J.D. Salinger, even though they said they'd fire him for it. And about Amando Muro who lived in El Paso and was supposed to be a young chicano writer, and we all thought he was better than Hemingway, but he turned out to be 56-year-old *anglo* and the story of his own life was better than any story he ever made up. And Tonya Childs, who died the way a Texan should in a car wreck, and who taught a lot of salesmen and mechanics in night school how to care about Spanish existentialists.

I will tell you about Dobie and Ayres and Arrowsmith and many, many more who had a better vision of Texas. Or a vision of a better Texas. They always get investigated by the Legislature for alleged commie ties and fired by the University. The University rhymes with thirsty.

I will tell you about William Brann, the iconoclast, a newpaperman who lived in Waco 80 years ago and who attacked cant, hypocrisy, and the Baptists, for which reason he was shot in the back one day — right where his galluses crossed. But that story has a happy ending; Brann managed to draw his pistol as he lay on the sidewalk and killed the man who'd shot him before he died himself.

Concrete Theology

JAMES STANLEY WALKER

AUGUST 26, 1977 — Lewis Mumford in his 1959 *New Yorker* review of Frank Lloyd Wright's only New York building, the Guggenheim Museum, concluded that it was one hell of a structure, but a catastrophe as a picture gallery. Mumford's main complaint was that patrons were forced to meander down a spiral ramp and view paintings on a slant — an architectural element that inhibited, rather than enhanced, art appreciation. The Guggenheim's shape sabotaged the only purpose of a museum.

The Dallas/Fort Worth airport has a similar problem: it is one hell of a site for flying machines, but a horrible place for human beings who want to board planes and go somewhere. It may be the only airport in the world that is bigger than Manhattan and almost impossible to find. Travelers searching for the secret flying field on the miles of Texas plain between the metropoli encounter the frustration of the negative: there are no signs, no pointers, nothing to say, "Dallas/Fort Worth Regional — This Way." If by chance or instinct one comes upon the place, trouble has only just begun.

DFW is an exercise in horizontal confusion, the ground-level equivalent of a crazed elevator with no floor numbers or push buttons, racing up and down a high-rise and stopping at random. You never know quite where you are. The signs at DFW aren't directional aids; they're enigmatic symbols. "Recirculation," says one; "Terminal Parking," reads another that is particularly threatening. Motorists searching for The Way drive up and over curbs; those who have already been terminally parked in "Remote" are led into a labyrinth, a tunnel left over from a Kubrick movie that feeds into . . . another parking lot. Escape from the maze of underground tunnels, automobile graveyards, and Airtrans tracks is a matter of luck, not design.

DFW's double spine and double runway design is that of a two-way autobahn with doughnut-shaped arms — much like an endless dollar sign. From the ground, DFW's turnpike ambience calls up memories of the cluttered road to Galveston Island or the single asphalt strip on South Padre. The airline terminals — all vapid architectural efforts with the backwater and surf of thick concrete behind them — blend into the empty North Texas prairie. Only from the air is it possible to see that down there lies a self-contained statement, as distinctly defined as the crooked Rio Grande.

But architectural insensitivity has struck again, and the unworthy terminal buildings are identical, bland pebble-finished exercises in the Le Corbusier International Style that have become a common post-WW II sight. These neutral drone structures have only one redeeming feature: they give some focus and stability to the horizontal confusion.

. . . Sometime during their extensive academic training, architects are supposed to be taught that there is some relation between function and form — a church ought not look like a warehouse; a cotton gin ought not resemble a monastery. DFW fails to be practical; it is instead a species of religious design.

. . . The irrationality of DFW's design and its ultimate triumph over its ostensible purpose suggest an outbreak of religious fervor, a cultish exultation. The Dallas/Fort Worth Regional Airport is the flat, horizontal, commercial church of a Texas cargo cult. It expresses the same faith that inspired Melanesian worshipers to slaughter their precious pigs and erect mock telegraph systems of bamboo and rope, in the belief that soon Great Pigs would appear from the sky, signaling the onset of a South Pacific millennium.

DFW's flares to the heavens [will] no more lure the Great Pigs of prosperity than did the islanders' bamboo electronics. Cargo tonnage from 1974 to 1975 actually decreased; the 1975-76 increase was a modest 14 percent. The massive growth predicted for the area adjacent to the flying field never occurred; dozens of developers with plans for new housing and industrial cities have been forced to sell out or go bankrupt.

DFW remains our decoy for the future, our unorthodox chapel, provincial and denominational, an infuriating example of over-design in reinforced concrete.

Ever a Bridegroom:
Reflections on the Failure of Texas Literature

LARRY McMURTRY

OCTOBER 23, 1981 — About fourteen years ago, as I was trying to force several rather disparate essays to join hands and look like a book about Texas, I complicated the problem by adding an essay called "Southwestern Literature?" — emphasis on the question mark.

At the time the piece was thought to be harsh, not because I had questioned the existence of a Southwestern literature but because my attitude toward the Holy Oldtimers — Dobie, Webb and Bedichek — was less than reverent. In fact, it wasn't much less than reverent: the books of all three men were given more in the way of praise than they really deserved. Time has begun its merciless winnowing; today the sheaves these three men heaped up look considerably less substantial than they seemed only fourteen years ago.

J. Frank Dobie, by far the most prolific and most popular of the three, has fared much the worst. It is now clear how much his book needed the support of his forceful and infectious personality. Like Will Rogers and other raconteurs, he was better in person than on paper.

In years to come Roy Bedichek's *Karankaway Country* and *Adventures With a Texas Naturalist* are apt to give more pleasure to readers than all the books of his friend Dobie — merely because they are written well. I don't think Bedichek had much to say, but his eye and his whimsy were served by an excellent, flexible prose style. He is as appealing — if as minor — today as he ever was.

Nonetheless, I am not sure that the Bedichek influence has been wholly benign. The bucolic essay may be a sweet form, but it is also a limited one — indeed, almost a retrograde form, the most likely route of a nostalgic retreat from our increasingly urban realities. I think we have too many bucolics. Now what we need is a Balzac, a Dickens, even a Dreiser. Texas writers have paid too much attention to nature, not enough to human nature, and they have been too ready to fall back on the bucolic memoir or country idyll rather than attempting novels, poems, and dramas. Minor forms only rarely prompt major books, and the lack we suffer from most is a lack of major books.

. . . Our literature is not *evenly* minor — some Texas books are better than others — but none of it is major.

Were I set the task of seeking an exception to that dictum, I would probably try and make a case for Walter Prescott Webb. Unfortunately, I think the case would fail. Webb's achievement was genuine, but small. He had a first rate mind and he continued to extend its reach throughout his life, but the yield, finally, was two important books, *The Great Plains* and *The Great Frontier,* the latter being by far the more impressive. It is one of the few Texas books that bespeaks a true intellectual vitality. By contrast *The Great Plains,* comprehensive though it is, seems dull and rather wooden. Webb lost much of his energy to academic store-keeping, and more of it to his huge romantic work on the Texas Rangers. Though he matured late, he matured fully, and might finally have delivered a masterpiece had he not been killed. The longer Webb wrote, the greater seemed his potential, an unusual thing. In writers late growth is not the norm, in Texas or not.

When I say that Texas has produced no major writers or major books, the exception I most expect to hear argued against me is Katherine Anne Porter. Again, I think the argument would fail, but hers is a subtle case and merits more prolonged address than I can give it here.

Alone among Texas writers of her generation, Miss Porter thought of herself as an artist and had the equipment to be one. Though often sharply critical of modernism, she touched most of the modernist bases, usually at a time when no one else was occupying them. A large part of her artistic equipment was dedication — or stubbornness, as she called it. Another part was what might be called a high neurosis, driving her from place to place and prompting her to leave, like dumped baggage, a remarkable body of evasions and misrepresentations, through which her biographers will be sorting for the next few decades. . . .

Oh, the whole talent was there, and a fine talent it was: but a talent seldom either fully or generously put to use. Miss Porter believed in a pure style; hers, at times, is purified almost to the vanishing point. By her account, she did this in the name of an aesthetic, removing the local and the immediate in order to reach the timeless and universal.

Unfortunately for her aesthetic, and unfortunately too for many of her stories, the local and immediate is the true street of fiction — at least of the sort of realistic fiction she was trying to write. The great ones, the Dickenses and Balzacs, Flauberts and Hardys, Faulkners and Tolstoys, wasted none of their time attempting to boil the accents of their own times and places out of their fiction. . . .

Gertrude Stein, whom Miss Porter did not like, once made a famous remark about — I believe — Oakland, California. There was no there there, she said. I feel very much the same way about the fiction of Katherine Anne Porter. The plumage is beautiful, but plumage, after all, is only feathers.

Despite its criticism of the Holy Oldtimers, my fourteen-year-old essay seems on the whole a surprisingly optimistic document. It was written in the mid-sixties, when there was every reason to think that Texas was about to experience a literary coming of age. There were at least a dozen young writers loose in the state whose potential everyone was ready to welcome. [John Graves'] *Goodbye to a River* had appeared, and [Billy Lee Brammer's] *The Gay Place,* and [Vassar Miller's] *Adam's Footprint,* all interesting beginnings. A flowering seemed not merely imminent, it seemed already to have occurred.

One reason for my optimism was my sense that the country — or Western, or cowboy — myth had finally been worked through. It was clear by then that this myth had served its time, and lost its potency; insofar as it still functioned it was an inhibiting, rather than a creative, factor in our literary life. The death of the cowboy and the ending of the rural way of life had been lamented sufficiently, and there was really no more that needed to be said about it.

Moreover, this realization seemed widespread. Most of the young Texas writers I knew were quite willing to face the fact that they were city people; they all seemed well aware that the styles which would shape their lives and sustain their fiction were being formed in Houston and Dallas, not back on the homeplace, wherever it had been.

For reasons I don't fully understand, my mid-sixties optimism was unfounded, generally as regards our literary flowering, specifically as regards the Western myth. At a time when the latter should have ceased to have any pertinence at all, drug-store cowboyism became a minor national craze. Boots became trendy in New York just as the last of the real cowboys took to wearing dozer caps and other gear more suitable to the oil patch and the suburb.

I recognize now that in the sixties I generalized too casually from a personal position. *In a Narrow Grave* [1968] was my formal farewell to writing about the country. It had dominated four books, which seemed enough, and I began rather consciously to drain it from my work. I proceeded to write three novels set in Houston, one set in Hollywood, and — most recently — one set in Washington, D.C.

I didn't deplore country living — still don't — but I had no doubt at all that urban life offered me richer possibilities as a novelist. Granting certain grand but eccentric exceptions, virtually the whole of modern literature has been a city literature. From the time of Baudelaire and James, the dense, intricate social networks that cities create have stimulated artists and sustained them. No reason it should be any different in Texas, since we now have at least one or two cities which offer the competitions of manners upon which the modern novel feeds.

It was thus something of a shock, as I started looking at my shelves of Texas books in preparation for this essay, to discover how few of them deal with city life. Not only are there few readable city books, but many of the country books are filled with explicit anti-urbanism. Writer after writer strains to reaffirm his or her rural credentials.

Why? The vast majority of Texas writers have been urbanites for decades. Many are veterans not only of the Texas cities, but of the cities of the East Coast, the West Coast, and Europe.

Where has this experience gone? Where are the novels, stories, poems, and plays that ought to be using it? Why are there still cows to be milked and chickens to be fed in every other Texas book that comes along? When is enough going to be allowed to be enough?

Part of the trouble, I am afraid, lies with Texas readers, who, if my experience is any indication, remain actively hostile to the mere idea of urban fiction. Virtually every time I give a lecture in Texas I find myself being chided by someone in the audience because I have stopped writing "the kind of books I ought to write."

Evidently, in the eyes of these readers, only my first three books were the kind I ought to write — the ones that happened to deal with small towns and cowboys. *Leaving Cheyenne* forever is what my readers seem to want. . . .

This is an understandable prejudice, but one which any healthy writer will ignore.

Unfortunately, not enough Texas writers are ignoring it. Too many of them love repeating themselves — after all, it's easier than thinking up something new to say. Many seem to find offering up an endless stream of what might be called Country-and-Western literature, an agreeable way to make a living. Easier to write about the homefolks, the old folks, cowboys, or the small town than to deal with the more immediate and frequently less simplistic experience of city life.

What this amounts to is intellectual laziness. Most Texas writers only know one trick, and seem determined to keep from learning another. The result is a limited, shallow, self-repetitious literature which has so far failed completely to do justice to the complexities of life in the state. . . .

If some of the above seems overstated, it is because I've concluded that nothing short of insult moves people in Texas. This is perhaps another aspect of clinging frontierism. Gentle chidings go unheard. In these parts the critical act has never been accepted, much less honored: literary criticism generally means two writers having a fistfight in a bar.

Not only do we need critics, we need writers who are willing to get along without one another's approval. Literary comradeship is a fine thing up to the point at which it begins to produce a pompous, self-congratulatory, and self-protective literary culture. In Texas, rampant good-old-boy-and-girlism has produced exactly that: a pond full of self-satisfied frogs.

In my opinion the self-satisfaction is entirely unjustified. There are as yet *no* solid achievements in Texas letters. Those who fancy otherwise probably haven't tried to reread the books. Cyril Connolly felt that the minimum one should ask of a book was that it remain readable for ten years. When this modest standard is applied to one's Texas books their ranks are immediately decimated indeed, almost eliminated, in a view of which it seems the more unfortunate that our in-state literary culture has begun to exhibit the sort of status-consciousness characteristic of literary society in New York or London, without the excuse of talent or anything resembling the intellectual density to be found in those cities.

The hunter who is reluctant to use a gig might as well avoid the frog-pond of Texas letters. Gigs are what's needed. As it is, most Texas writers work for a lifetime without receiving a single paragraph of intent criticism, and if they should get one now and then it will usually come from out of state. Anything resembling a tough-minded discussion of Texas books by a Texan is thought to be unneighborly. The writers get reviewed, but reviews are merely first impressions. Criticism begins as the second impression, or the third, and even the thumbnail variety, which is all I can offer, is almost never practiced here.

The need for hard-nosed, energetic, and unintimidated local critics is plainly urgent. It's one thing that our literary society had gotten so clubby and pompous, quite another that the books which constitute the reason for having a literary society are still predominantly soft, thin, and sentimental — not to mention dull, portentous, stylistically impoverished, and intellectually empty. The large majority of them are dead where they sit, and reading them is about as pleasant as eating sawdust. . . .

The problem is not so much shallow talent as shallow commitment. Our best writers' approach to art is tentative and intermittent: half-assed, to put it bluntly. Instead of an infinite capacity for taking pains they develop an infinite capacity for avoiding work, and employ their creativity mainly to convince themselves that they are working well when in fact they are hardly working at all. The majority of our most talented writers have not yet produced even one book with a real chance of lasting. Forget second acts, in Texas literature: so far we have only a bare handful of credible *first* acts.

Meanwhile, as the cities boom and the state changes, a great period is being wasted. Fiction in particular thrives on transitions, on the destruction of one life style by another. Houston and Dallas have sucked in thousands of Rubempres, but where are the books about them? These cities are dripping experience, but instead of sopping up the drippings, and converting them into literature our writers mainly seem to be devoting themselves to an ever more self-conscious countrification.

There is no point in belaboring the obvious. Until Texas writers are willing to write harder, inform themselves more broadly, and stop looking backward, we won't have a literature of any interest. . . .

Marfa's Lesser Lights

GEOFFREY RIPS

AUGUST 17, 1984 — Sixty miles southeast of El Paso, IH-10 leaves the Rio Grande and heads due east for Van Horn. At that point the land becomes as desolate as a moonscape. Short, rust-colored mountains — the Quitman and Finlay ranges — Sierra Blanca peak at 6900 feet. The desert in all directions is gray, gray stone and sand, gray brush growing to a height of no more than three feet.

Just past Esperanza, the last marked settlement on the Rio Grande for the next 100 miles, where the highway parts company with the green strip along the river, past the site of old Fort Quitman, the road begins to climb heading east. It is July and hot. Every rock, every pebble reflects the sunlight.

Then, ten miles past Esperanza, at the foot of a rust-colored mountain, there is a small stone building covered in green. Trumpet vines wind around the stone pillars of the terrace and provide a shady arbor. Inside, a bar and café. The building is a maze of small concrete rooms, each built as if an afterthought to the room in front of it. In one room are cases upon cases of Coca-Cola. This is an oasis of Coca-Cola in the desert. In another room two pool cues are crossed on a green felt table. In the main room of the café, a soap opera blares on a large color TV. The walls of the room are dark blue. There are five or six metal tables surrounded by chairs. No one is sitting there now. A man sits at the bar talking to the proprietors — a husband and wife in their fifties. She speaks English; he uses Spanish. The room is dark and cool. The conversation is lively. There is no intimation of the desolation outside.

Five miles farther on IH-10, now on the other side of that rust-colored mountain, we see two small men running hunched over through gray brush. There is a small plane circling overhead. There is a green-and-white border patrol car parked off the highway and a patrolman running up a hill. The two small men have no chance.

Some lives are unbearably hard.

Two miles farther east, we are stopped at a roadblock while the border patrol looks into our car. Then the town of Sierra Blanca.

From Van Horn southeast on Highway 90 the desolation gives way almost immediately to green irrigated fields. From Valentine to Marfa, the fields are so lush they'd probably send most Central Texas dry land farmers into a dead faint. For miles around Valentine, gates announce entrances to the Ryan Ranch.

The town of Marfa surrounds the Presidio County Courthouse. The courthouse itself revolves around the light provided by its glass cupola mounted above its elegant wooden stairway. A Swedish salesperson has passed this way. In the restrooms the old wooden stalls are appointed with huge, orange, Swedish high-tech toilet paper dispensers and next to the sinks is another Swedish device for dispensing towels.

In the city hall, I ask directions to the Art Museum of the Pecos. "Oh, Donald Judd," a woman behind the counter exclaims. "You go down past the blinking light and the road curves to the left," she says, using her left hand to motion to the right. "Oh, I mean it curves to the right. I'm left-handed," she explains. "Go past the border patrol office up to a little sign on the fence that says, 'Art Museum of the Pecos.' There's a row of old apartments, and the office is right there. Or, if you go down [Highway] 67, you can see a field with concrete blocks on your left — no, I mean your right."

It was just as she'd instructed. Up the gravel road, past the border patrol office was the gate for the Art Museum of the Pecos and the row of apartments. To the left, between Highway 67 and the row of buildings that were once Fort D.A. Russell, an army post, was a long string of concrete boxes, each about eight feet tall and fifteen feet on a side, arranged in small clusters, some providing a framed view of the landscape beyond, some obstructing that view with three walled sides. It was unmistakably work by Donald Judd, a leader in the Minimalist epoch of American art.

Now, I've walked around Donald Judd boxes in New York galleries —

both the simple plywood variety and the glitzy shiny metal constructions. Each can provide an imposing presence in the cramped lofts of
New York. But here, in what is romantically called the "antelope field,"
the blocks form an inconsequential series of cold geometrics in an imper-
fect world of water troughs, gravel roads, and semis barreling down
Highway 67. In a way, this is nice. The work is like a string of abandoned
Marfa sheds. It is not overlarge nor does it inhabit a landscape that is
otherwise uninhabited by humankind: it cannot be accused of that kind
of cultural imperialism.

At the same time, the Judd boxes and the museum—set up by the Dia
Foundation of Philippa de Menil of the Schlumberger fortune and her
husband, collector Heiner Friedrich—seem to work best not as aesthetic solutions but rather as solutions to the age-old questions: where
are you going to put a bunch of oversized boxes and how are you going
to get paid for them in the manner to which you are accustomed?

 . . . [If] Judd's work were in an open field far from the Art Museum
of the Pecos, it might begin to approach the Stonehenge it purports to
be, to proclaim more loudly its survivalist aesthetic. But that would put
it beyond the confines of the museum world, of the non-profit Dia
Foundation and its tax write-off afforded by public access, beyond the
financial security Judd requires, while eschewing the commercialism of
the art world.

Meanwhile, Judd has built a walled compound in the middle of town
and has helped the Dia Foundation acquire buildings in Marfa and out-
fit the barracks and large brick and glass warehouses of Fort Russell. In
the process, the art world is providing some local employment: carpenters to restyle the old barracks into guestrooms, studios, and offices;
masons and concrete pourers to pour and shape the cubes designed by
Judd; secretaries; a curator (imported) and building and grounds crews
for the Dia properties.

Nevertheless, the so-called "Marfa project" is, in the end, an attempt
at colonization of the Big Bend region by representatives of New York
chic. There is little evident exchange with local residents, except for the
purchase of lands and buildings at relatively low prices. A lone attempt
to mount a public program consists of a tour of the grounds by wealthy
art patrons shipped in from El Paso. These patrons were regaled by
New York art dealer Leo Castelli with tales from his stable of artists.

According to *Texas Monthly*, Judd and Dia Foundation may be parting ways, arguing as they are over money and power. Some lives are unbearably easy.

As we left the "antelope field," a tow-headed kid rode a motorbike around the concrete structures, raising clouds of dust. A nice touch.

Along the road north to Fort Davis, the Marfa Flats are rich with tall green grass. Twenty inches of rain in the previous six weeks, fourteen inches in one stretch. Here's where the antelope really play. They lift their heads from the grass as the car goes by.

The next day, on the hot dry Edwards Plateau near Junction, four small, dark men, with blankets tied across their backs, hunker down in the shade of a live oak not far from the highway and wait for the sun to go down.

Jim Hightower: The Media and the Message

DAVE DENISON

DECEMBER 21, 1990 — The day after the long night in which Jim Hightower found himself 50,000 votes short of victory in the campaign for another term as Texas Agriculture Commissioner, he stood in front of television cameras and reporters at a Capitol press conference and offered explanations for his defeat.

The fault, he said, was his own for failing to raise enough money to counter his opponent's televised attacks. But he was galled, nonetheless, by the role television plays in electoral politics.

"I heard that a TV reporter last night had said, well, that Hightower hadn't, after all, campaigned for this office, so no big surprise with this result," Hightower said. "In fact, of course, I campaigned all across Texas, in just about every place that had a zip code," he said. "What she really meant was that I didn't have TV ads. I guess that's what politics kind of comes down to today."

Long thought of as one of the most media-savvy of Texas politicians, Hightower seemed, in the days following defeat, to entertain conflicting sentiments about the media. On the one hand, he adhered to the belief that if a politician has a strong and appealing enough message, the message will be heard through the media. On the other hand, he admitted he was frustrated with the political process and the media's role.

I met with Hightower 10 days after the election in the Department of Agriculture office he will vacate next month. Following are excerpts of our conversation.

DD: . . . The question becomes, if that's what modern politics is, namely television advertising, and some television sound-bite wars, do people like you have a future in it? Can you talk substance on television?

JH: I think we can. I think if I were running for governor or U.S. Senate, I would have gotten those issues covered a whole lot more. . . .

DD: It sounds as if your argument is that even given what politics has come to, a populist message could win just as successfully in the war for sound bites, symbols, and images.

JH: Oh, absolutely. I think it does. And sometimes not populism, but anti-establishment right-wing candidates. George Wallace and David Duke, they tap that anti-establishment anger that is out there and twist it to their advantage. The media didn't like them but they were fascinated and they cover it. Jesse Jackson did it [in 1988] just with the power of his message, as well as his rhetorical ability, but the message was so powerful. And that's the only way I see to counter the insipidness and trivialization of politics, is to have a message so powerful. I mean, you're talking about things that people care about. . . .

DD: You're saying the problem isn't really with the media, it's with the message.

JH: The problem is with both. It starts with the message. If you don't have a message, if you're not choosing sides, who you are for, who you are trying to help, what's your vision, what do you want to get done, and who you are against . . . If you don't have that, then why should voters vote for you? And the solutions are not only candidate media, but the much larger electoral reform needs. The candidates need to be able to go directly to the people. I believe there should be free air time for all the candidates. That'll change the TV right there. . . .

But that's not the [only] problem. Something's wrong with the system of coverage of the elections, and something's wrong with the system of candidates putting themselves forward. I could have sat there and done nothing but be on the telephone for three months, raised my money and made the occasional appearance here and there, and then been ready and got on TV in those last three weeks. And that's probably what I should have done.

Books Suck

DAGOBERTO GILB

NOVEMBER 25, 1994 — Imagine this: one day you're pronounced a writer. I'm not talking about a book being published — even after all those years and years of waiting for that — but when they — you know, *they* — say you've won an award for it and they fly you above the Chihuahua desert, across all of Texas and over the Mississippi River, and then above all these roads and highways you've never driven on — never seen a single billboard sign from the airplane window — to a city as expensive sounding as Boston, Massachusetts. And they're paying. You've decided to take your son, who's 15. Fifteen, those jerk years. The years when you can often look at him, once a soft sweet baby, as tender as your first true love, and you are faced with the age-old fatherly question: Does he want me to kick his ass? Is it right to kick his ass? Despite internal and external protestations to the contrary, would it be GOOD to kick his ass?

But you're taking him because you've always promised yourself that this day would come. You imagined it differently. You imagined that you would go hiking up Glacier National Monument, that sacred Indian place of emerald lakes, beneath pearl mountains of ice, risking the hazards of sudden snow drifts and grizzly bears. You got real though. You are a city guy. You have to wait for some nature friend to take the two of you sometime — something like that.

So, instead, Boston. As a writer. That's official language, upheld by a panel of wise judges (whether they'll regret it or not). You take your son because that right moment has come. Father and son, dad and boy, pops *y m'ijo*. The two of you together. And he's gonna see this you, the writer you. That you you were those years he pointed to his empty mouth and bare feet and wondered why you weren't really working right then. It's like a rite of passage thing for him to go with you to Boston.

Here's the secret part, the worm at the bottom of the bottle: Your son says — he says often, very often, so often it doesn't sound as funny as it does when you say it just once or twice or so — he says, books suck. Try meditating on that for about a day and you'll get the impact. I mean this. For one full day, every time you see or hear about a book, you utter it. Whenever you think of a book, think, books suck.

Imagine how it is if you write books. And that voice is your son's. Your first son's, the cute baby all grown up. And you don't think he's kidding.

And so when you get to Boston you decide to sneak over to Annie, the Pulitzer Prize and National Book Award winner, who you admire so much, and warn her beforehand. You don't know her well, so you're a little worried about impressions. Annie, you whisper, I want to tell you, so that it doesn't come as too much of a shock — my boy, my handsome son over there, if he happens to say books suck, well, you know, please forgive me, forgive him. How old is he? she asks, and she nods her head when you tell her. She says she understands. She has two sons. But do you believe her? *N'hombre!* You think she probably had sons who liked her for being a writer. She doesn't realize that your boy means it. That he really means it.

So one day your son comes home from the mall with his friend. They saw a movie and guess what, he bought a book. A *book*. You are a little suspicious. It's called, *This Book Sucks*. A magnum opus featuring Beavis and Butthead.

How do you like that, dad? he asks, and he's smiling sarcastically, proud, like he wrote it.

You look at the price. Twelve bucks! Of his hard-earned money? Money he soaked from you, now that you think about it. Easy money, you might say. But . . . his own money.

So whadda you think, dad?

It's a tough call, a real tough call. You ask if he'll let you read it. Sure, he says, and for the moment he's actually pleased with you.

The Fate of the Texas Writer

ROD DAVIS

JULY 26, 1996 — Not long ago I learned that Lars Eighner was in danger of returning to the same fate that, for a time, had made him famous: homelessness. He was in poor health and had spent most of the money from *Travels with Lizbeth* and some of his friends were trying to organize a modest fund-raising effort.

A few weeks later, in a Dallas newspaper gossip column, I read that a Dallas fitness promoter was about to enter a lucrative new book contract, coauthored by one of the new breed of celebrity-chasing writers for *Texas Monthly*. That very same week I was interviewed by a headhunter for a large software company about an editing job and was told that they were looking for someone with more on-line technical experience, and that I was only a "content provider." Somewhere in the course of all this an old terror began to reassert itself in my mind. The writing world, the one I've inhabited all my post-military professional life, seemed to be contorting into something I'm not sure any of us completely understands. . . . When I mentioned Eighner's plight to one of his old friends, an award-winning author supporting himself as a substitute teacher in the Dallas Independent School District, he replied, "This is what happens to us. You can't make a living here being a serious writer."

At the close of a century in which the voices of Texas writers have risen from the thinnest soil to find a place in the richest lairs of the national culture, that's a pretty sorry assessment. But true. The expression of original, first-rate voices is now all but supplanted by the white noise of Prozac publishing. Today, Eighner's books can't even get reviewed in *Texas Monthly*. The labor movement developed a term for the slow, subtle, systematic destruction of an entire industry of workers: "silent violence." Writers like to think we're above that kind of assault. We're not. The ongoing, accelerating suppression of our best efforts, our sharpest minds, our toughest investigators, our most courageous and compassionate spirits, and almost all our minorities, is neither benign, nor accidental. . . .

The real terror is that the juggernaut against us may have gone too far. At the hard level of jobs it may have . . . and magazines, let alone TV and radio stations, have been cleaning their houses of trouble-making and boat-rockers with great efficiency. The state of journalism in Texas is a scandal as great as the state of politics — and of course goes unreported. There is scarcely a staff job in the state open to or held by a writer of integrity; or a major one held by a black or brown. Exceptions won't run to the fingers of both hands. We are now guerrillas, exiles, hold-outs, nay-sayers. Who are "we"? We are the opposition. We are everything not permitted. There can be no other position for a writer, within any culture. To examine and objectify and re-create as narrative is to stand apart from the thing considered; opposition is implicit. It can be the loving opposition of a baby to its mother, or the blood stance taken by slave against master. But, for writers, it must be conscious. Opposition is the key to our future. Otherwise we do not have a future.

Is it any worse here than elsewhere? Does a writer in New York or Washington or Florida or California have it any differently? Probably not. The nationalization and the globalization of the economy has put the same economic pressures on all workers — writers are workers, for wages. Even screenwriters in Hollywood. The forces that shape the writer's mind and spirit are likewise no stranger to our brothers and sisters in Calcutta or Bogotá, Tokyo — or Lagos, where writers are literally, not symbolically, executed these days.

. . . Always, writing in Texas has been a colonial enterprise. Sometimes more so. Except for a brief Golden Age — bookended, roughly, by the founding of *The Texas Observer* in 1954 and the collapse of city magazines and two-newspaper towns in the early 1990s — serious writers living in the state had to publish serious work somewhere beyond our borders. The *Observer* itself often sent its best elsewhere. Later, the *Texas Monthly* [TM] did the same. The question today is not whether the Texas writing industry has sunk back to its old colonial status, for that question is moot. The New South has come with a price.

The fate of the Texas writer in today's neo-colonial economy is set against a tableau of simulation and deception more dangerous and sophisticated than at any time in the past. Despite excitement about the growth of electronic communications, the outlets, within the state, in which writers can grow, mature, find voices and endure, have all but dried up. The robustness and combativeness that characterizes periods of creative energy have been replaced by corporate caution and individual cynicism. Most of us are forced into what Martin Amis calls "left-handed writing," the kind one does for pay, at the specific direction of the editors who manage the simulacra.

Real writing, by which I mean free inquiry, seriousness and integrity of intent, devotion to substance as well as style, and a disregard for consequences, is allowed almost nowhere. To be a serious writer in Texas, to place yourself in opposition . . . means you set yourself apart. For which you make professional enemies, lose friends. You risk your livelihood with every manuscript. Real writers accept this risk. . . .

But writers have always needed intermediaries. I don't mean editors. Most editors are meddlers, young massahs or trade careerists. One in a hundred adds, rather than subtracts. Many in Texas aren't even from Texas: *TM*, of all places, has long imported East Coast young massahs for its senior editorial slots — a mark of colonial insecurity, not devotion to cosmopolitan meritocracy. I know a writer who contends that it is writers who should constitute the staffs of magazines, with editors as the freelancers, chosen by writers, rather than the other way around. This would be the natural order of the expressive process, but that would put writers in control, and, in or out of Texas, that's the last thing the corporate culture that has replaced democracy wants.

No, the intermediaries for writers are the sellers of writers' goods: publishers. Publishers tolerate what writers say if it is either good for business or not terribly bad. When publishers can't do either, writers either get fired, or, even more silently, not hired at all, as happened to journalists in San Antonio, Houston and Dallas in the past decade when their publications were closed down and single-paper monopolies took over. "The story of all of us," in the deeply corrupt superpower world of conglomerates like the *Dallas Morning News*, became the story of a few, getting rich for keeping the story of the many so deeply buried. Legion are the tales of writers at Texas newspapers punished for doing their jobs. At the upper levels, the silent violence of the *Dallas Morning News* and *Texas Monthly* controls writing by fist-in-glove paternalism (security for loyalty), on the one hand, or diamonds-and-denim Brahminism (loyalty for insecurities), on the other, but further down the food chain the repressions morph into the more conventional brutalities. It's the difference between being fleeced by a slick savings and loan president or having your legs broken by Pinkertons.

Alternative publications such as this one, or the *Austin Chronicle*, or the *Dallas Examiner* (one of the state's few black-run publications) offer respite, but not volume or power. Ad sales are tough if you want to give voice to all the publics, not just the white, pro-business, anti-labor middle class hegemony that permeates the Texas media. . . . Small and university presses certainly help at the book level, but the volume is low there, too, and most Texans don't even know about them. . . .

Many important Texas writers have observed the development of this media oligopoly — with its tethers deep into government, the political parties, the surrounding business world — unfolding. Yet their objections on this matter have no real venues. They can't even mention, in a Texas publication other than this one, that economic dislocation and consolidation of industries are a function of the monopolistic tendency of finance capitalism — because they are prohibited from saying "capitalism" in the sense of calling attention to it as a system. . . .

And there are also the more subtle, powerful, alliances of common ideologies. In Dallas, the new *D Magazine* of religious right publisher Wick Allison caters almost exclusively to the elite, white Park Cities neighborhoods where executives of the *Dallas Morning News* make their homes. The once-upstart independent weekly, *The Met*, is now a business partner with the *News*, whose publisher Burl Osborne, in turn is good friends with the *Monthly*'s Mike Levy. And so on, a pattern replicated in city after city, print and broadcast, advertising and telecommunications. These are not conspiracies, they are communities of interest, and their interests are not ours. They are neither the interests of the average Texan whose real struggles, triumphs, concerns and tastes are so betrayed and contorted as to be unrecognizable.

Three decades ago, it was possible for Larry McMurtry to conclude that all this petty but profitable grab-ass was evidence of a backwater culture. I'll give him grudging credit for that, but today his critique would miss the point. We're not culturally deprived; we're culturally censored. And not by hicks. The previously mentioned media have re-engineered; gone high tech. Lean and mean. Most have deep pockets, thanks to takeovers by conglomerates whose money in turn comes from off-shore manufacturing, price gouging, and the massive layoffs of American workers begun under Ronald Reagan, continued nationally under Massah Bush and still going on here at home under Young Massah Bush and his friends, like *Morning News* publisher Osborne. Well-financed, ruthlessly managed, impervious to labor, consumers, and conscience, the Texas media and allies at the close of the century are nearly ready to eliminate the need for writers altogether. . . .

With so much at stake, the media aren't much interested in self-criticism, and writers are afraid to bite the hands that feed them. I can already guess the potential freelance work this essay will cost me. I don't care anymore. In my two decades here as an adult, and as an editor or writer, I have worked in just about every possible writer-compatible staff job: four magazines (three now defunct), one TV station, a wire service (purists to a fault, bless 'em), a PR agency, a state agency, two universities, and this publication.

I have freelanced, hustled new projects, even tried to re-start a small worker-operated Chicano sewing factory in West Texas (killed by Dallas sweatshop labor). I have turned to nonprint formats, such as film and documentaries, I have cannibalized savings, borrowed against life insurance, used up advances. I have wondered what it is I am trying to get at, why the voice inside looks for its own way of finding itself. I am familiar with the hells of fear and anxiety. I have had it better than many of my peers: I have yet to be homeless. And I love to write. . . .

Every writer who has decided to leave [Texas] in order to get a clear mind or to be published has paid a price. Has seen why the fight to keep Texas writing alive within a Texas publishing context is critical. Has seen that going away can dilute the voice of whatever it is that we need to say, each in our own way. Something happens to Texas writers out of state; it happens just sending work out of state for publication. What happens is the heart-breaking re-shaping of consciousness to adjust to the expectations and stereotypes of the empire-at-large.

Case in point: in the mid-'80s, a number of Texas writers, including me, were asked by *Esquire* to write a major piece about Austin. None of the stories ever appeared — not because they weren't any good, but because they "weren't what we're looking for," which was editor Lee Eisenberg's way of saying he had a stereotype of Austin that was different from what Texas writers kept sending him. You may remember that problem with reporting from Vietnam.

. . . The issue at stake in re-directing our fate is therefore not just an esthetic quest for expression of general truths or individual visions, but a call to see into the stultifying nature of the process by which the truth and visions are expressed. This is not an abstract issue. It is about real control of real power, of real ideas and real minds in real bodies. Of some import. We are not a backwater. We are the nation's second-most populous state. We are full of problems — health care, poverty, racism, education, colonias, etc. — but our citizens are as sophisticated as those anywhere else. And as thick-headed. We do not want for content: Texas-based stories fall out of the sky like cinders after a bomb blast.

Why, then, are our writers in the economic position Frances Fitzgerald famously described as "cheap intellectual labor"? Because the economic elites of Texas — the eight-hundred-pound gorilla to whom the "invisible hand" really belongs — make the backwater an enduring presence. Rio Grande Valley agri-conglomerates, High Plains industrial ranches, Houston banks and hospitals, Dallas/Fort Worth multinational corporate headquarters, Amarillo chambers of commerce, Austin lobbyists, elected bagmen — the real Web of Texas — have pressed their arch-conservative ideological tableau into every sanctuary of white- and blue-collar life.

. . . If what I believe is true, that of each thing comes its counterpart, then the fate of the Texas writer may yet evolve a measure of greatness proportional to the pogrom. I believe in dialectics, in balance, in yin and yang, in payback. What seemed so close at hand after Brammer and McMurtry, and then the first explosions of Gary Cartwright (now trimmed back to half-time), Bill Broyles, et al. when *TM* was truly something, pushing past the vastly overrated humdrum of local color minstrels like Dobie and Graves, might come back. It might break forth again simply because there is too much here to tell and too much talent to tell it and even Prozac journalism cannot stop it.

It must also survive the future. Computers and digital technology are the next wave of "public prints." In some ways this opens the dialogue between writer and reader as never before; but the same force which corralled and then impoverished writers in print will do the same thing in the electronic world, only more efficiently. Indeed, despite its anarchistic origins, the Internet has been absorbed into the white noise marketplace almost without a trace of its original form. The development of software and computers has always been corporate in nature and conservative in ideology.

. . . The decentralization brought by the computer, and seemingly ideal for writers is, when mediated through corporate ownership, also an extremely effective means of dividing and conquering. Content providers and other home workers can't really confront the power of the managers and accountants. There aren't any brawls in the digital office, because there is no office. There aren't many blacks or browns, either. Why should there be? The only place minorities have edged into the Texas media at all is in broadcast, because ratings depends on image, and if you're selling products to black or brown folk you got to put up some nonwhite reporters. Newspapers do this to an extent, to fend off discrimination suits. Magazines are virtually lily-white across the board. In print, nobody sees the faces of your staff, and cyberspace is similarly "color blind." . . .

One, two, many malcontents! Who else but the dissatisfied to break the silence of the violence, to say the fix is in, so that when it isn't, we can be believed. The fate of the Texas writer is to prevail. At some level, I still think we have to. We all have a role in our fate. Our fate is made as we go along. That's why it's fate, not immutable law. What can be done? Mao said, never fight a battle you can't win, because you lose. I say: Win. I say: Write. I say this is our fate. . . .

Power Spelling

DEBBIE NATHAN
(DEB-BEE NAE-THUN)

MAY 19, 1999 — After I moved to San Antonio from El Paso, people said I should write something comparing the two cities — both with majority Mexican-American populations, but each with its own palpably different character. For months I searched for the perfect metaphor to capture the contrast. Recently I found it, at a spelling bee.

Spelling bee?

You may never have been to a spelling bee, unless you were a contestant in grade school or middle school, or unless your child is a contestant. Remember the practice word lists? Standing at the mike, shaking, trying to get every letter right? The bell dinging when you messed up? The judges' stern eyes following your doleful walk off the stage? And remember the "pronouncer"? Much of your success, or failure, depended on whether this distinguished elder spoke your word loudly and well. Otherwise, you had two choices: ask for a definition, or take a blind stab at spelling a mumble.

My twelve-year-old son has been a bee freak ever since he won his school contest in El Paso in the fourth grade, and advanced to citywide (where he bombed out in the second round). He still drags me to contests where kids compete to see who'll go to Washington, D.C. for national finals. So this spring, early on a Saturday morning, we went to Trinity University for San Antonio's big bout. It was sponsored by the *Express-News*, and followed the hallowed format of spelling bees everywhere: big stage, nervous kids, sober judges, officious pronouncer.

But there was one difference: in El Paso last year, a bad pronouncer almost caused a riot. In San Antonio this year, a woman with equally questionable diction raised nary a ripple of protest.

The El Paso guy was introduced as "a prominent local actor." Like every Texas border burg, El Paso is so economically depressed, and therefore so lacking in professional theater, that "local actor" is synonymous with incipient homelessness. The phrase also implies you're from out of town, since no sane homey would try to make a living as a thespian.

Sure enough, the pronouncer turned out to be a bearded, vaguely scruffy-at-the-edges fellow who'd obviously been raised in Brooklyn. His voice was resonant, stentorian — and totally incapable of pronouncing "r" at the end of a syllable. "Lodge," he said to one of the first contestants. "Lodge?" echoed the Chicano kid. "Lodge," repeated the pronouncer. "L-O-D-G-E," spelled the kid. Ding! went the bell. "Sorry," said the judge. "The correct spelling is L-A-R-G-E."

Soon moms and dads were rushing the stage to file pronunciation protests. At first the judges honored them and put the kids back in the bout, while warning the humiliated pronouncer to say his "r" and "s." He promised to, but it was no use — he just couldn't control his accent. By the end of the bee, irate parents, most of them Hispanic, were buzzing with indignation about the Anglo interloper. "Hey," one said. "What right does this guy have to bring his accent here and mix up our kids?"

At this year's San Antonio bee, Latino kids were also in evidence. But the Anglo pronouncer was no down-at-the-heels immigrant. Instead, her helmet-like blonde hair and good suit marked her as heir to a 78209 zipcode pedigree. The two pink-faced male judges also looked like denizens of the Stewart Building on Broadway.

It wasn't long before the woman used the following pronunciation to say the word that means "arranged in a cross": CRUCIFARM. "Crucifarm?" said a puzzled child, and proceeded to give the Old MacDonald spelling for what should have been C-R-U-C-I-F-O-R-M.

The pronouncer's diction exemplified what UTSA provost Guy Bailey, who is also a linguist, has identified as typical speech of aging Texas Anglos. My father, a Houston native, is a model: he says "carn" for corn, and his "war" rhymes with "bar." Texas Anglo kids don't talk like this anymore. Chicanos hardly ever did.

The blonde pronouncer lady obviously was doing the Texas Anglo thing to her "o" in "cruciform." Yet none of the parents — not even the

Hispanics — registered a word of protest. Another kid came up and got "darsal" for "dorsal." "Mommy! Do something!" begged my son.

So I walked to the stage and, in respectful whispers, protested that "crucifarm" and "darsal" were non-standard pronunciations.

The judge just looked at me. Then he lectured the audience that indeed, the pronouncer was correct. During an intermission, he kindly sought me out to explain. "You see," he said, pointing to a phonetic guide in the spelling bee word book, "the 'o' has a dot over it. That means the word is pronounced 'CRUCIFARM.'"

I tried to reason. "What's the vowel symbol for 'farm' like where you raise wheat?"

"That's an 'a' with a dot."

"Well then, how can an 'a' with a dot be the same as an 'o' with a dot?"

"Because they're homonyms!" Again he was all patience and self-confidence and hubris. I gave up.

"Boy," my son said later. "I've seen people pronounce things wrong before. In El Paso they'd admit it. But here, they're stubborn!"

"It's not about stubborn," I tried to explain as we left Trinity. "It's about power. That's the difference between where we used to live in Texas, and where we live now."

He didn't quite understand. I started to elaborate: stuff about Anglos and Hispanics and conflict and politics, and when I got to hegemony, I realized I'd lost him way back.

Then I said something like, "But things are better now — before, they were really horrible."

He didn't catch it, but I did. I'd said "harrible."

I shut up and let him talk the rest of the way home.

SPECIAL ISSUE

THE TEXAS OBSERVER

May 29, 1987   **A Journal of Free Voices**   *One Dollar*

Photo by Alan Pogue

URBAN TEXAS

Cover, May 29, 1987. This stunning image of automobiles racing through Dallas perfectly captures the emergence of Texas as an urban state. It is now home to three of the nation's nine largest cities—a dramatically different landscape than when the *Texas Observer* first appeared in 1954. Cover photo by Alan Pogue.

VI. SOCIAL DIVIDES

SILENCE MAY BE GOLDEN, but not in the civic arena. The less said about social problems, and the fewer voices raised over political inequities, the greater the oppression, the more intense the misery. Democracy functions best when civic debate is at a raucous pitch.

The *Texas Observer* was born to raise a racket. That's what Franklin Jones Sr., editor of the *East Texas Democrat* (est. 1953 and folded into the *Observer* the following year), meant when he called it "an obstreperous, boisterous and mischievous child."

Its mischief making has ever since been directed, in Ronnie Dugger's words, to breaking the "silence in Texas about poverty, discrimination, and economic power." Labor was the first to benefit from this attention with the inaugural issue's headline — "Shepperd Urges Port Arthur Truce." With top-of-the-fold coverage of the Shivers administration's belated mediation efforts, the *Observer* chronicled the dispute's evolution, set the strike in its state and national contexts, and printed street-level viewpoints. To harass picketers, hardware store owner Fred Miller played at high volume a recording of human laughter, a vivid detail that speaks to the complications of economic strife.

These disputes only became more tangled when race was factored in, for segregation was not checked at union-hall doors, undercutting the movement's recruitment drives, a point the *Observer* made in defense of the rights of black labor. It was as quick to support brown power in the fields, extensively tracking the Starr County strikes of 1966 that led to a march on Austin; when marchers stopped in San Antonio for Archbishop Robert Lucey's blessing, he apologized for sanctioning their demand of $1.25 an hour, a "ghastly recompense for exhausting labor under the burning sun of Texas." His words remained relevant thirty-five years later, after a wildcat strike at an Amarillo meatpacker. Karen Olsson homed in on the plant's blood-splattered high-speed work environment, and on a disengaged union, hostile management, and the workers who fought for their rights because they loved their jobs.

Every bit as complex was the quest for civil rights, and the *Observer*'s coverage of it is among the finest of any U.S. media. Reading a 1955 AP squib about the murder of John Reese of Mayflower led Dugger to interview the teenager's family, locate witnesses the police had ignored, unearth crucial evidence, and write reams of hard-hitting copy that kept the investigation, trial, and final proceedings in public view. But discrimination could also be found in more benign locales: in a 1960s Texarkana beauty parlor, race determined who shampooed, cut, and swept up the trimmed tresses.

By the 1970s, the most blatant Jim Crow laws had vanished, yet racial tensions were palpable. They exploded in Pittsburg in July 1970 when the mutilated corpse of Conrad Rogers was discovered on Farm Road 993. Determining whether he had been murdered or accidentally run over kicked off rumors among blacks and whites that revealed their immobilizing distrust of each other. Nothing much had changed by the late 1990s in Tulia, Texas, when officers busted a disproportionate number of black males for drug violations; Nate Blakeslee broke the story of overly aggressive law enforcement, judicial bias, fraudulent witnesses, and an aggrieved black community.

That the pace of social change is glacial would come as no shock to student activist Carlos Guerra, but the story had its funny side. In 1967, while attending Pan American University, he learned that the U.S. Office of Education had reclassified Mexican American students as "Others," prompting him to chortle over the confusion this term would sow among racists, whose anti-Mexican clichés would have to be recoined ("I have nothing against Others"). Laughter alone would not secure Mexican American political rights: El Paso protesters launched silent vigils to convince a slumlord to provide gas hookups for his tenants, and in so doing discovered their voices. Larger-scale awakenings, though, depended on mass organization, and Raza Unida, a political party which grew out of

1960s South Texas voter-registration drives, was running candidates statewide a decade later. Powerlessness remained, however, and is excruciatingly portrayed in the Aguinagases' cradling of their dying son while racing between Panhandle hospitals that refused to render aid unless paid in cash. No amount of electoral clout could have compensated for their grief.

Nor could it have compensated for the loss of natural environments buried beneath Texas's postwar industrialization. Since the 1950s, the *Observer* has offered comprehensive analyses of the state's water woes, befouled skies, and polluted terrain, the sources of which have often been well-connected corporations insulated from meaningful regulation. Propelled by an *Observer* editorial, for instance, Senator Ralph Yarborough labored diligently to preserve Padre Island as a national seashore. In 1970, Kaye Northcott asked whether our despoiled environment would be cured, and nearly thirty years later the answer came in Michael King's "Who's Poisoning Texas?" — no.

Stewardship vanished in other realms. Perhaps the most terrifying evidence of its loss lay in those whom Charles Whitman gunned down from the University of Texas Tower, a killing spree that did nothing to promote the pragmatic gun controls the *Observer* had long advocated. Violence of another kind permeated Amarillo, home to Pantex, a neutron-warhead assembly site; local Bishop L. T. Mattheisen urged Pantex's workers to square their labor with their faith and seek more "peaceful pursuits." This call is akin to Demetrio Rodriguez's demand that the state reconcile its constitutional obligation to provide equal education with the gross disparities in school-district funding. Beginning in 1968, Rodriquez was lead plaintiff in federal lawsuits that ultimately forced Texas to develop a more equitable sharing of educational monies. But then social services in general have never received high priority, as manifest in the life and death of Larry Robison, a severely troubled killer on whom the state lavished more funds to arrest, try, imprison, and execute than it did to treat his mental illness. His is a cautionary tale of retrogressive public policy in an atomistic society that no amount of silence will ever correct.

Char Miller

Miller Opposes Union Until Retailers Unite

DECEMBER 12, 1954 — "I've got a sign: 'Remember the Alamo,' so that's the way I feel about it."

So says Fred Miller, white-haired and jocular proprietor of two struck hardware stores in Port Arthur.

"I don't think the retail trades in Texas ought to be organized as long as the retail merchants are not organized," Miller told the *Observer*. He said that his appliances carry only a 10-percent markup, and until competition is lessened, he doesn't see any room for organized labor.

. . . The issue in the strike, Miller says, is recognition of the union. Standing behind his counter in the middle of the clutter characteristic of hardware stores, Miller said:

"If those people had got their union here I'd have made it so uncomfortable for them they'da had to leave."

. . . "This is a union town," he said, "and the pickets have hurt. I can't send goods to other merchants: they won't take them. Only one freight line will deliver freight here. You've got to go out and get your own coke. I've had to liquidate one warehouse. But none of the salesmen have stopped calling, and no one has turned me down on credit." He says he is now breaking even again.

For about a week in front of his stores he played, over and over very loudly, a recording of human laughter. "I finally had to stop it when the stores around complained," he said. But even now the record plays over and over again, but softly, on the sidewalk in front of his store where the pickets walk to and fro.

And he has two signs in front of his store. One of them reads:

"Our employees ARE NOT on strike." Miller here is making the point that the persons picketing his store are not now his employees, for some of them did not formerly work for him — and those of them who did are fired now, anyway.

The other reads:

"Remember the Alamo. Help us win our Independence."

Miller belongs to the group of merchants among those struck who say they have no intention of ever giving in on the recognition issue. He told the *Dallas News*:

"I'd feel like a traitor if I signed up. I'd never sign up. I'd liquidate before I'd sign."

Asked if he feels there are Communists among the strikers now, Miller said: "I don't know, but birds of a feather flock together. If you ask me they are here too."

He thinks that either the strikers will quit or the State Legislature will pass a few laws to put them out of business. He says those laws, as being discussed now by various legislators, would provide that only employees of a firm can picket it, and that a union cannot picket a store for recognition.

". . . You tell 'em [the strikers] I feel good now about this strike. For a while it was pretty bad, but we feel good now. We're only guinea pigs but we feel like we're in the front lines."

A Negro Boy Murdered in East Texas

RONNIE DUGGER

NOVEMBER 2, 1955 — A 16-year-old Negro boy has been murdered and two younger Negro girls shot in a rural East Texas area ridden through with race tension.

A black 1950 or 1951 Ford sped past a cafe where they were drinking soda pop and dancing and somebody in the car pumped nine bullets through the walls and a window.

The boy grabbed onto the girl he was dancing with, but she was hit too. She tried to get loose, screaming, and he let her go and fell to the floor.

The night riders sped on down Highway 149 and turned onto a farm road heading to the Negro community of Mayflower. They sprayed more bullets right and left into a Negro school bus and the bus driver's car, a Negro's mailbox, a Negro home, and the Negro school at Mayflower.

Two of the bullets almost hit a middle-aged Negro woman who was kneeling by her bed around midnight saying her prayers. A clutch of them smashed into another room where three young children often sleep.

Police say 27 bullets were fired, possibly from an automatic .22 pistol.

The theory immediately developed that the killing was an expression of white resentment about a $200,000 bond issue that had been passed for a new Negro school building at Mayflower. In three separate outbursts during the six months since the election, three Negro homes, two Negro cafes, and the Negro schoolhouse in Mayflower have been shot into at night. The same school bus was fired into the night after the election confirming the bond issue.

Sheriff Noble Crawford of Gregg County called the shooting "a thing that's pretty hot."

"It's a nasty situation, I tell you, for sure," he said.

He said about the killers:

"It could be whites, just as well as could be niggers, no point to duck it."

Deputy Sheriff Caven Penney of Rusk County told the *Observer*:

"The lead we got we think it's white. We haven't got enough to pin 'em yet."

However, a Negro leader, J.C. Beckworth, principal of the fired into school, said the local law enforcement agencies are working "pretty slow" and are not providing "proper protection." He said he wants the Federal Bureau of Investigation to enter the case.

R.A. Shaw, white superintendent of the Tatum School District, said: "We need a good detective, that's what we need."

Willis Gene Thompson, a Negro who saw the car as it passed the cafe, says he did not see if the people in it were white or Negro.

The killing happened Saturday night . . . October 22, ten miles from Longview in Gregg County on Highway 149. The rest of the shooting was along farm road 782 in Rusk County.

The boy's name was John Earl Reese. He was a good boy and had harmed no one. The morning of the day he was shot he had returned from three weeks of cotton picking and turned over $30 to his guardian grandmother. They went to town together to buy him some school clothes for Monday morning. The clothes were never unfolded.

The wounded girls were sisters, Johnnie Merl Nelson, 15, and Joyce Faye Nelson, 13. They were both shot in the arm. Joyce Faye was dancing with the boy, who is their cousin, when the shooting began.

The story has been reported very briefly in the Longview paper, with no mention of the racial implications. It was described in a similarly cryptic Associated Press story.

The boy was buried Thursday.

Of the possible connection between the school bonds and the shooting, Beckworth, the Negro principal, said:

"I am positive that it had to do with it. I know that's right. They don't want us to have no school. They have robbed us from the beginning and don't want us to have nothin'."

Shaw, the white superintendent, said of the first shooting of the Negro school bus:

"That was an aftermath outburst of tempers. That's the way we felt. Kind of a scare deal, that's the way we felt about it."

Sheriff Herman Orr, of Rusk County, asked about the motive for the first school bus shooting, said:

"We thought the motive was the school thing."

On the recent shooting, Shaw said:

"It's possible that it could be the same set up, the same people inspired the other thing, and the possibility that the people got drunk and went too far with it.

"I don't think, believe there was race hatred a part of it," Shaw said. "The white opposition dislikes Professor J.C. Beckworth, they feel like he leads his people, they vote in elections, something tells me they might have thought they were shooting into his house when they shot into his brother's."

. . . "There is no race hate" around Tatum, Shaw said, "except there might be some animosity against that nigger leader out there."

Sheriff Crawford seemed angry about the killing.

"Sons a bitches drivin' along a highway," he said. "If it was one man against another you could weigh it, but they were nothing but kids, that's the bad, the sad thing."

Asked about possible motives, Crawford replied:

"Well some figger it was the school bond election. All right, suppose it was. The only ones interested in that would be grown men. You can take that and fit in well an' good if you're looking for somethin'. If a man blew up the school bus or dynamited the school, all right — but a man interested enough in civic things to be interested in a bond election taking a .22 and shooting a bus or car and into people's homes and into a cafe with a bunch of kids dancing . . . It's hard to put it together."

. . . The fatal day began for John Earl Reese with his return from the cotton fields near McDougal. He paid the man who hauled him home $10 and gave the balance of $30 to his grandmother. (He told her he averaged $7 a day.)

His grandmother raised him. His father had not lived at home in seven or eight years and Mrs. Hughes says he did not work when he did. Mrs. Hughes took [John Earl] in three months after he was born so his mother could go off to Longview and earn money as a cook. She has since died of a stroke.

. . . Late Saturday evening . . . Mrs. Anne Lewis, 47-year-old aunt of [Johnnie Merl and Joyce Faye Nelson], decided she would go to town and drop the girls off at Buddy Hughes's place, a Negro cafe on Highway 149, ten miles from Longview.

"On the way we saw him (John Reese), he wanted to go. He looked so pitiful, so we took him with us — an' look what happened to him!" Mrs. Lewis said.

On the way to the cafe, Johnnie Merl recalls:

"We saw four boys in a black 1951 Ford when they passed us on the bridge going toward Longview. They were hollerin' something out the window, but we couldn't hear what it was, they was running so fast — I guess 95." Joyce Faye, the younger sister, agreed about the speed. They said it was 9:30 at night. Johnnie Merl said they were white boys.

Mrs. Lewis dropped the youths off at the cafe and went to town. On the way, she said, she saw the same car stopped, with two white boys working on it at the back. "Now I think it was about wheah the license plate would be," she said. "If they waz fixin' to do what they did they might'a been takin' them off."

Tatum Drive-in is a cafe for whites near the edge of Longview. The *Observer* made inquiries there. "Mama" Tatum, wife of the proprietor, said of the night of Oct. 22:

"Two men came in here about 11 and I wouldn't serve 'em." Her daughter, Janice, a waitress at the cafe, said these two men, who she said were from Tatum, are mean characters; one of them once hit her over the head with a gin bottle when she refused to take a swig, she said. Janice said they drive a dark-colored 1950 or 1951 Ford and have a .22 rifle.

The *Observer* notified Sheriff Noble of the Tatums' testimony, and he sent a deputy there to check. He said Monday there was a lead and that it is still "in progress."

Eight or ten miles down the road, at about 10 or 13 minutes past 11 o'clock that same night, a similar Ford passed Buddy Hughes's place, and bullets spewing from its windows killed John Reese and wounded the two sisters.

Some Negroes were standing around Mrs. Hughes's porch talking over the shooting. Henry Hendrix, a 55-year-old Negro, said he was outside the poster-plastered cafe that Saturday night. It is a lonely little place half a stone's throw off Highway 149. The roof is corrugated tin.

The inside is of varnished pine with a couple of side tables, a juke box by a support column in the middle space for dancing.

"They had put on some little ol' dancin' song, and he (John) pulled the little ol' gal out there and they had jus' started to dancin'," Hendrix remembered.

"Bullets [began] fallin' and shinin' lak fire, red and blue. . . ." Mrs. Hughes said.

"There was no way to get out of the way," said Hendrix.

"Just lak lightnin'," Mrs. Hughes said.

"When he fell, she broke an' run," Hendrix continued. ". . . I got back out of the way and let John and them down," he said.

Anna Mae Hughes, 20-year-old wife of the proprietor, said at the cafe that it was "like somebody done lit a pack of firecrackers."

. . . Deputy Sheriff Sweatt said there was no beer in the cafe that night. "It's a dry precinct. I looked in the ice box and everywhere but there wasn't any," he said. "We've had no trouble with beer or liquor in that district," Crawford added.

After shooting up the cafe, the people in the car drove down Highway 149 across Cherokee Lake into Rusk County and turned down the farm road leading to Mayflower.

With the cold moon the only witness, they fired nine times beneath a persimmon tree into the Negro school bus and driver H.C. Thompson's car. He, his wife, and their six children were inside the house, frightened.

"All six were in bed the second time," Thompson said. "If they shoot at that house they cain't miss all a us."

. . . The killers drove on and reached the house they may have thought belonged to the Negro school superintendent and fired into it seven times. . . .

The Negroes along the highway and the farm road and even in nearby Easton, the only all-Negro community in Texas, live now in mortal fear. At night it is not entirely safe to drive up and stop in front of a Negro's home. Guns are loose in the land, and guns await in reply.

Some white residents of the area seem to know much more than has been published in the papers. Some expressed indignation about the shootings. In Tatum, about nine miles from the scene of the killing, a woman who runs a drugstore said: "Well, I hope they catch 'em. It was all uncalled for."

A waitress at the B&N cafe there said: ". . . Anybody that crazy got no business runnin' loose. Anybody that crazy liable to shoot at anybody."

A teen-age boy in a cafe said: "Well, that's just one less of 'em."

John Reese slept in the same room with his step-grandfather, 69 year-old Lee Hughes. His grandmother had laid his new school clothes on a couch in this room. His books were on the iron double bed he slept on. He had filed his old school papers and some cherished magazines in a cardboard box.

In 1954, when he was in the eighth grade, he wrote: "I study my lessons so that I can help myself in life, and learn how to [introduce] a person to someone, and learn to count so that no one won't beat me out of [nothing]."

. . . Mrs. Hughes is a stoic woman. She is the daughter of two former slaves who lived, worked, and died in the same east Texas area she has known all her life. She and her husband live in a modest home on a winding red dirt road back from the Mayflower school. A blue sign on a wall in the living room says: "God bless our home and the people there in."

She cried softly as she sat on the front porch and talked about her boy.

"I can't get myself reconciled," she said. "Just the one child [my daughter] had. I thought a lot of him, I was partial 'im."

She rocked a little.

"He's dead. I won't let them bury him with the bullet in his head even if it cost $100 to take it out. Lawda mercy, I don't think I'll ever get over it." . . .

The Shootings

RONNIE DUGGER

NOVEMBER 2, 1955 — The death of a child is always unbearable. The senseless murder of a 16-year-old boy and the wounding of two younger girls, quite possibly because of their race, leaves one's humanity prostrate and wordless. The evidence surrounding the death of John Earl Reese points to a simple conclusion: that some East Texans who were angry about the adoption of a bond issue for a new Negro school went on a wild shooting spree. Not only did they shoot into the Negro cafe and hit three innocent children; they shot into the old Negro school and the Negro school bus — two miles apart — and into a Negro's home and a Negro mailbox. Testimony from the two wounded girls and their aunt also points to the conclusion that the marauders were white.

Let us hope that the incident was not racial. The evidence is not certain: it is merely obvious. But if it was racial, let no white man in East Texas think he or the system of discrimination in which he lives can take comfort in the hope that the killers were "young thugs on a spree." For six months Mayflower has been terrorized — bullets into three Negro homes, two Negro cafes, the Negro bus, the Negro school — and not a voice raised against it, not a man, not a woman, not a newspaper. If they were, indeed, teenagers, then their parents must answer for them, and [so must] every man in East Texas who is an accessory to the climate where a Negro is held as less than a man and only slightly more than a mule.

Ordinarily, a newspaper is proud of its exclusives. This week we are ashamed. In three separate outbursts at night, the Negro community was riddled with gunfire from passing cars. The very Negro boy who now lies dead from the latest shooting was in another Negro cafe that was shot up months ago — and nothing was done about it. How is it possible for these things to happen over a period of months without the newspapers reporting them and their social context? As long as the journalistic cowardice continues in East Texas, that long will the racists be heartened. Look well, then, colleagues, at the picture of the boy on his slab, and think upon the future.

Unions and Race

RONNIE DUGGER

AUGUST 9, 1957 — Prejudice is the same among union people as it is among farmers or merchants or doctors. This fact the state labor convention collided with last week. We have little but praise for the way the union responded to it.

By a heavy vote the convention — made up of delegates who are directly answerable to the workers in their locals — affirmed their opinions that all men and women are entitled to equal rights and integrated schools.

The platform the civil rights committee wrote included a good condemnation of job discrimination, which persists in a number of Texas locals, and union segregation, which while negligible in Texas labor, persists in a few locals.

Over this issue the convention broke. There were some wound-up threats of withdrawal from the state AFL-CIO, and confronted with them, the convention leaders decided to bargain for the much-stiffer enunciation of civil rights of the national AFL-CIO in return for side-tracking the specific condemnation of outmoded practices persisting in Texas unions.

There was a good deal of truth in one observer's reaction. "They are for every general right but balk at the one that's immediate."

It is also true that unions have made appreciable headway against race hate in their own ranks. The voting was itself proof that members of organized labor in Texas are more enlightened on the issue than their fellow citizens. . . .

As for the AFL-CIO in Texas, . . . [it] will be judged by performance.

We know the union leaders of the state council, and we are certain of their fundamental commitments to democratic processes and to the welfare of working people. Politicians who have held unions in contempt now must suffer more serious consequences, and toward this development we can feel nothing but delight. We find it inconceivable that the influence of labor in Texas politics could be anything but desirable for many years, Texas having suffered so, in her government, under essentially corporate rule. If, in the future, Texas labor abuses its power, why, men not committed to it will still be around to say so, and the people will still have the final vote.

The Bounty of Nature

RALPH YARBOROUGH

DECEMBER 12, 1962 — I have many memories of hunting, fishing, and camping. Growing up as a boy in East Texas between the Neches River and Kickapoo Creek, on the western edge of the eastern timber zone, I watched the pileated woodpecker hammer, saw the great flights of ducks and geese and blackbirds that filled our skies fifty years ago, and marveled even as a boy at their numbers. The frogs, the copperhead, the moccasin were near the borders of our sloughs and ponds there, and the gar and trout were near their surfaces, herons and egrets and cranes waded their shores or perched on lookout points, kingfishers and water turkeys sat on the bare boughs of dead trees over the water, more patient than human fishermen. The virgin hardwood forest was unfenced. Not old enough to possess a gun, I roamed the woods with my fish hooks and my dogs, alone, and watched the birds as I fished for catfish and perch. I feared only the wild, razorback hogs and the scrub cattle which ranged the river and creek bottoms. I muddied the waters and grabbed for fish in hollow logs and holes in the bank and got hold of loggerhead turtles and snatched a powerful moccasin, and came out of all of it without being bitten, although a few times I was very much shaken up.

On fishing trips when I was a boy, we just slept on the ground under the trees, without benefit of any camping equipment, and slapped the mosquitoes all night. I enjoyed camping ever after that until World War II, when I had to sleep on the ground, even though in a sleeping bag, for a hundred consecutive nights on Louisiana maneuvers during the coldest recorded winter since St. Denis camped at Natchitoches in 1717. Ice-covered limbs broke off of trees, killing several of our men in our division and injuring a number of others. While I still camp out on deer hunts, I do it for the hunting, not for the camping.

Before I announced for governor ten years ago, I spent something like four to six weeks each year hunting and fishing. Since the day I announced for governor against Allan Shivers on May 1, 1952, I have spent only six days hunting and fishing, one day for deer, one day for turkey, one day for doves, one day for ducks, one day for geese, and one day fishing. Six days in ten years are not enough. I want to hit the fishing and hunting trail again.

But I don't want to create the impression that I am only interested in hunting and killing animals. Nature is greater than the chase. Man's habitat is the outdoors and all living things, and if he destroys a part of it, he destroys a part of himself. If he recklessly kills off species of birds and animals, he impoverishes the human race forever. Although a fenced-up America has ended wild, free, open, uncrowded woods forever, I still feel akin to the things I saw, hunted, lived with, and loved in those East Texas woods half a century ago.

There was food in the woods for a boy, wild plums and mulberries in spring and summer, grapes in abundance in summer and fall, muscadines and persimmons, red haws and black haws, chinquapins and hickory nuts, mayhaws and the kernels of nettles. Wild birds sought all the wild fruit, and I raced with them for choice bites. I ate from the field and forest and fried my fish on the river bank, carrying only salt with me. As I sat alone on the banks of spring branches or creeks and fished and watched the birds and other wild life, virtually as free as an Indian boy except for my store bought clothes, the wind rustled the leaves of trees, and I imagined, as a boy will, that the trees were talking to me, but they seemed to be saying Indian words, like I had heard from Hiawatha, that I didn't understand. But now I understand, they were crying out for the salvation of our trees, our wildlife, our heritage.

It has been disappointing to me that so few of the candidates for the governorship of Texas have seemed to have much recognition of the need for a large number of parks in Texas to serve our more than ten million people, not to mention the millions that we hope to lure into our state as tourists. If we expect them as tourists, we must have something for them when they reach Texas. Some Texans seem not to have realized that. Texas screams for tourists, but our state government will do nothing to attract them. People will go where there are attractions and opportunities for recreation.

Someone with vision is needed in the state government who will push a program of state parks to supplement and complement the one national park that we now have and the second that we are about to obtain. With our population and an area of more than 265,000 square miles, Padre Island, the Wheatley Ranch, if it is available, and the Big Thicket area combined will not accommodate all of the recreational needs of Texas for the future.

Of the 110 recognized independent nations of the world, Texas is larger than each of 78 of them and has more population than each of 84 of them. Texas is incomparably richer in gross national product per annum, or average per capita wealth, than each of more than 80 of them.

Such being the case, Texas needs parks, schools, universities — facilities for people. We have had a few great and generous souls who have donated money for universities, but far too few, and virtually none who have been willing to give money and property for outdoor recreational facilities for the people, so badly needed in this urbanized, industrialized, mechanized age. The Wheatleys are among the first forward-looking Texans to recognize the need of repose and natural surroundings as an offset to the rackety-clackety environment in which people are forced to spend most of their lives in our urban living.

After four long years, the Padre Island bill passed the Congress. I remember the *Observer*'s editorial for a national park on Padre back in 1958. The late Bob Bray, my press man [formerly the *Observer*'s associate editor], brought it in. Bob and his father once owned a newspaper on the Texas coast. He wanted me to introduce the Padre Island bill, and he advocated it strongly. He was very fond of fishing; I didn't introduce it at first, but he buttressed the editorial with other ones from the *Corpus Christi Caller-Times* and the *Houston Press*. I knew something about the Padre Island fight of 1936, when James Allred was governor, and wanted to look into that and study the legislation over title to Padre Island that went to the Supreme Court. We finally pitched the bill in the hopper on the 27th of June, 1958, in the 85th Congress. I re-introduced it in January of 1959 in the 86th Congress and re-introduced it in January of 1961 in the 87th Congress. We had four senatorial hearings, and it has taken an almost incalculable amount of work to get it through.

The bill as passed does not preserve as large a part of the island as I had hoped for, but it is approximately 90 percent as long as we had asked for; most of the island is included. I am glad that at least there will be an 81-mile-long seashore recreation area, 78 miles fronting on the Gulf of Mexico and 66 miles covering the island from the east shore to the west shore. It will be the longest national seashore area in the United States and has been described as the greatest undeveloped and largely unspoiled beach in the United States. Furthermore, the South Gulf of Mexico coastal area is the bottom of a huge continental funnel in bird migration. It is said that some 400 species of birds use portions of the island at some season of the year.

It is acknowledged that national recognition of the island will have a favorable economic impact on Texas. However, as those of us know who have lived close to the land and have a natural knowledge of the relationships to be found in nature, there is a sense of rhythm in the sights, the sounds, and the vast stillness of these open reaches of sea, sand, and grass that once lost can never be recaptured. To preserve all this is a matter of fundamental importance.

A bill must be passed by the state legislature, which holds title to the tidelands. It is inconceivable to me that the people of Texas would miss this great opportunity, this bounty offered them by the federal government, to achieve and own and hold forever a strip of land as the great forces of creation built it. . . .

Shampoos and Segregation

FRAN BURTON PRESLEY

NOVEMBER 27, 1964 — Some Negro youths went to a white barber shop here [in Texarkana] and were turned away. Mrs. Brown, who works for my husband Jim and me, laughed about the incident. "Our hair is coarser than yours," she said to us. "That barber wasn't trained to cut those boys' hair."

"Some white men have coarse hair, too," Jim said.

Mrs. Brown nodded absentmindedly, then continued, "And our beauty parlors are different from yours, too."

During our conversation, Mrs. Brown and I discovered that the same beauty operator, Mrs. Reese, worked for both of us. Mrs. Reese, who runs a beauty shop in the little Negro community where she and Mrs. Brown live, doesn't make enough money there. She works at a beauty parlor serving whites during the day and at her own at night. I sometimes go to the beauty shop where Mrs. Reese works as "shampoo girl."

In almost all the beauty parlors I've patronized, a Negro woman has the job of shampooing and keeping the floor clean and the supplies handy. Sometimes she is a licensed beautician. At one beauty shop the shampooer was busy when I went in for my appointment and the white beautician had to wash my hair. The pretty, platinum-haired girl fumed. She said to me, "All niggers are alike. They won't do anything they can get out of."

"She was busy with another customer," I said.

"Ha!" she spat. "You oughta haveta *work with one*."

At still another beauty parlor I overheard a conversation while waiting in the anteroom. The tall, sun-tanned beautician was putting her customer's hair up on rollers between puffs of a cigarette. Her customer was a slim, middle-aged woman, well dressed.

Beautician: I sure do need some help here and I put an ad in the paper the other day. You know what? The phone rang the next morning and this girl said she was a qualified beauty operator and would like a job. I could tell by her voice she was a nigger.

Customer: Yes, you can tell.

Beautician: I could hardly keep from laughing but I told her I'd already hired somebody.

Customer (laughing): They wouldn't know how to fix our hair. Say, have you ever had any colored girls come ask you for a shampoo and set?

Beautician: No, but they did at one place in town. They didn't get it. I know what I'd do if they came here. I'd say, "Sure, I'll take you. A shampoo is $50 and a set and comb-out is another $75."

Customer: Better not do that. The NAACP'd pay it.

Beautician (laughing): Shoot, I'd go ahead and do it for that kind of money. I'd turn y'all out and fix their hair.

Blood-Soaked Textbooks

BILL HELMER

AUGUST 19, 1966 — The man on that Tower was no berserk killer. He was more a mad craftsman. Charles Whitman carried out his work methodically, soberly, and with extraordinary skill not found in an impassioned murderer. Alone on that parapet, viewing the world below him through the cross hairs of a telescopic sight, he single-handedly turned a quiet campus into a battlefield littered with dead and wounded. It took time to realize what that man was doing, and it took even longer to appreciate how well he did it. Some died looking up at him, not yet believing.

I was walking across the northwest corner of the campus a few minutes before noon, on my way to the Student Union to get a sandwich. I had heard two or three blasts coming from the direction of the Main Building and they reverberated like gunshots, but I thought it was merely a workman somewhere using a nail-driving gun. The explosions came regularly, only a few seconds apart. Then I noticed sirens off in the distance, getting louder, and saw a campus policeman running in the direction of the Main Building. I decided the sandwich could wait until I found out where the action was.

I walked up the drive toward the Main Building and noticed that the next shot came from the top of the Tower. I could see a rifle lying on the rim of the observation deck, barrel sticking out better than a foot, not moving. It looked like a .30 caliber Army carbine from the way the stock completely surrounded the barrel. Nobody could hit anything at any great distance with a little open-sight carbine. Then I saw another barrel poke out over the west edge, fire, and pull back in. A few seconds later it fired again, toward the southwest. I was sure he wasn't doing any damage, except maybe to windows. Just some nut trying to get himself in an awful lot of trouble.

I looked around and saw several persons huddled in the west door of the Main Building, and some others standing by the pillars on the covered walkway around the Academic Center, just across the drive. One of them yelled at me: "You'd better get your ass out of that street. A bullet just hit this pillar." I suddenly felt very naked.

On the walkway a student told me there was a crazy rifleman on the Tower, which I had already figured out for myself, and that he had hit several people. "There're bodies all over the front mall." I was too used to news work to put much stock in second-hand spectator reports. Alarmed but still rather skeptical, I worked my way around the back of the Academic Center and made a dash for the Student Union building where I knew a good, safe window on a stairway landing to peek out.

Three people were already there, a girl and a man on the right side of the window, and another man on the left, whom I joined. The window opened outward and was nearly as wide as the landing. Someone said, "There he goes, see him?" I saw something move quickly along the parapet under the big clock on the west side, then a puff of smoke, followed by the echoing report. Seconds later another shot, toward the south. The man was dashing from one position to another, firing downward. Everyone was talking in cliches: "My God, what is he doing?" "This just can't be happening!" "I just don't believe it!" A bullet exploded into the window frame, blowing glass and stone everywhere. I dropped to the floor and saw the girl stagger backwards, clutching her face: The shot had struck right where she was standing, and I thought she was hit. I started to crawl toward her and put my hand down in blood. The man beside me on the floor was bleeding heavily from a hole through his right forearm. I yelled, "Get down!" which was quite unnecessary, and grabbed his arm above the wound and squeezed with both hands to try to slow the bleeding. I called for a handkerchief to tie off his arm, and he pulled one from his own back pocket with his other hand. I began to worry about my legs, which were stretched out on the small landing in full view of the Tower. Someone began pulling on the wounded man's feet. I let go his arm and helped guide him under the low window to the stairway where several persons were waiting to help.

Then I crawled under the window, over blood-soaked textbooks, and went down to the main lobby.

The girl was unhurt. I saw her standing by the foot of the stairs, still trembling, with someone's arm around her. A man told me I had blood on my neck and asked if I had been hit. The question seemed a little stupid since I also had blood on my hands and arms and pants, but when I went down to wash off I found a small cut on my neck from a fragment of glass or bullet. It occurred to me how absurd this all was. I saw myself in the mirror, ignoring the sirens and the booming rifle outside, craning my head to one side and dabbing at the scratch with toilet paper like I had cut myself shaving.

I was tense, still incredulous, but the bullet through the window seemed to have the effect of dispelling fear. The uncertainty was gone. Now I understood the situation. There simply was a madman on the Tower, and he was shooting accurately and to kill. I knew exactly what to do: keep my damned head down.

It was about 12:15 when I walked back to the lobby, and I found the mood had changed. The people there no longer talked of the gunfire outside as a bizarre, impossible joke. There was too much blood on the floor. Someone was yelling for a first-aid kit and cloth and water. A girl standing in the front door vestibule cried, "He's shot an ambulance driver." Another student came in from outside saying a policeman had been shot, that several people were lying on the Main Building mall, and that people had been killed and wounded all up and down Guadalupe. I went back downstairs to look for a way to get back to the Academic Center next door. A student ran past me in the hall, yelling for a policeman. He kept saying, *"That man is dead! That man is dead!"* as if he couldn't quite believe it. I got into the Academic Center auditorium through a back door and found a wounded girl stretched out on a table, being cared for by some students. Upstairs, from the protected walkway, I could see a girl crouched tightly against the broad base of the flagpole in front of the Tower, where the sniper was not shooting. Directly across the wide sidewalk from me, an elderly woman stood trapped in a sheltered corner of the Main Building steps, face in her hands, sobbing. Almost every tree had someone crouched behind it.

The shooting had turned into a full-scale battle. The sniper's rifle boomed less frequently, but now there was answering gunfire from everywhere. I could feel the shock of a large-caliber rifle firing somewhere nearby, and I saw pieces of stone falling from the top of the Tower as bullets struck the parapet. How strange it felt to stand there in such comfortably familiar surroundings, hugging a marble pillar I walked past every day, listening to the constant banging of rifles and the sound of real bullets whacking and whining off stone.

The worst feeling, and one I think everyone felt, was that of helplessness — the feeling of being pinned down, with no way to help the people out on that blistering hot concrete, and no way to fight back. Finally an armored truck arrived, the first evidence of any kind of organized action.

More than an hour had passed and people were starting to relax, to accept the gunfire and casualty reports as routine, under the circumstances; the way I imagine an infantryman quickly learns to accept bullets and death as a normal part of combat. Within the glass-walled lobby of the Academic Center, the building nearest that deadly Tower, students crowded around transistor radios, listening without much emotion as the toll rose into the twenties and thirties. The expressions of shock and disbelief and fear were changing to speculation on how long the sniper could hold out, how many shots he had fired, how the police would get to him. Now that everyone understood the rules, the whole grim affair was turning into a tense game. Finally, in one dramatic move, the cops won.

Without the sound of battle and the combat atmosphere the entire episode began to seem less shocking than depressing. I watched them carry some of the blood-covered dead and wounded out of the west door of the Main Building, and down the same drive where earlier I'd stood looking up at the Tower, not realizing that those shots I saw were killing people. The thought that I had been such a good and stupid target bothered me a good deal more than the bullet through the window. It had missed. The others had not missed; they just weren't fired at me.

During the next few hours I began to learn all that really had happened, and, for the first time, began to appreciate the enormity of the crime and the uniqueness of that one man with a rifle. A crackpot, a nut, a maniac almost never possesses the skill of a Whitman, or the manner. He was cool, efficient, and totally rational in every way except his impulse to kill, and in that he was determined, unflinching, and extraordinarily competent. He planned his deed with more good sense than most people can bring to bear on the job of packing a suitcase for a trip. He executed his plan with no sign of indecision or compromise. Another sniper might have indulged himself in shooting into the bodies on the mall, or knocking out a tempting plate-glass window, or lobbing a few bullets into the Capitol or downtown Austin. Whitman did absolutely nothing for dramatic effect; he labored only to kill, in the old "one shot, one man" military tradition.

When the armored car rolled in to rescue some of his victims, he wasted not a shot on the driver plainly visible to him through the bullet-proof glass, or on the truck or its tires. A friend of the driver told me Whitman fired only at the police officers trying to pick up the wounded. Earlier he shot an ambulance driver. Most madmen cannot totally escape certain deeply ingrained qualms toward killing children, unarmed rescuers, or obviously pregnant women. Whitman saw them in his telescopic sight and shot them.

He had the right tools for the job. The 6mm Remington was ideal: a high-velocity soft-nosed hunting bullet, extremely accurate over long, clear ranges. With a four-power scope the chief factor in hitting a distant target is the human ability to sight in and hold steady, and Whitman possessed that. He apparently even knew to allow for the downward angle of his shooting, which required less sight compensation for bullet drop because of gravity. He hit his victims mostly in the head and chest. His .35-caliber Remington pump had less effective range and no telescopic sight, but its big bullet crashes through almost anything without deflection. Hunters call it a "brush-buster." (A bullet from the ground disabled it as Whitman aimed through one of the drain spouts.) His automatic shotgun, purchased and sawed off in gangster fashion on the morning of his rampage is unexcelled for the fast, deadly, close-quarter shooting he apparently anticipated in the Tower itself. Austin police cars carry these weapons racked against the dashboard. They "clear the air" without much aiming. When finally cornered and killed, Whitman was waiting with his light, short, fast-firing .30-caliber carbine, which holds up to 30 rounds.

And he was expert. In 90 minutes he fired about 150 shots. During the first 15 or so minutes very few of his bullets missed, even on moving targets, even at ranges up to 400 yards. Later, with conspicuous targets scarce and police bullets striking all around him, forcing him to bob up and snap-shoot, he still could hit. His over-all average was better than one hit out of three shots. Amazing. Other riflemen might shoot that well, but not when under emotional strain and heavy fire. Such a performance in combat would have earned him a chest full of medals instead of police bullets.

The enormity of his crime seems to have disqualified Whitman as a fiend, or even a villain. I have heard no one, not even the friend of mine who that day was sickened enough to vomit, express hatred toward him. Only pity and dismay. It is hard to hate a pain-tormented animal that strikes out indiscriminately as it dies. To have seemed such a splendid fellow to his friends, to have seemed the respectable, responsible citizen who certainly could have bought a high-powered hunting rifle under the strictest law — what agony he must have gone through before he broke.

And once he did break — my theory — he turned all responsibility for his actions over to the beast within, to the demon with whom he could no longer cope. The human Charles Whitman requested an autopsy to possibly discover why he did what he did, and instructed that his life insurance go to mental health research. The helpless Charles Whitman then put his terrible skill and dedication at the disposal of the demon that possessed him, and set to work.

The only man who showed more selfless dedication that Monday afternoon was a young cop with a revolver who led the way around that parapet. Ramiro Martinez did not go up there wanting to die.

"Ghastly Recompense" Under the Sun

ARCHBISHOP ROBERT E. LUCEY

SEPTEMBER 2, 1966 —

My dear brethren:

The presence here of so many Texas citizens of Mexican descent is a symbol of a new era in human relations throughout the Southwest and in other parts of our nation. Until a few months ago, a Mexican-American was expected to be docile in the face of injustice inflicted on him by certain powerful groups. Historically our Spanish speaking citizens have endured poverty, discrimination, scorn, and contempt from unworthy employers who have forgotten the law of love. It has often happened that honest working people did not dare complain when they had to work for starvation wages because they were in a vulnerable position; they could be dismissed from their employment and they had no one to defend them or plead their cause. Some sort of wage, even an unfair one, was better than losing one's job and having no income whatsoever. Through the years our Spanish speaking people have suffered in silence the injustices heaped upon them either by individuals or by a badly organized social order.

But now our citizens of Mexican descent have learned that there is a law of justice in industry and agriculture which should be applied to them; they have learned that they should not suffer cruelty and discrimination without protest or complaint; they have learned that they have a certain dignity as human beings and they must not sell their souls to servitude; they must stand up and defend themselves against discrimination and oppression. . . .

It is with a large measure of reluctance and regret that we endorse and approve your demand for an hourly wage of a dollar and twenty-five cents. No sane man would consider *that* a fair wage in these days when the high cost of living requires a much better return on your labor, and we join you in desiring that this inadequate wage be granted to you only because you have known the sorrow of cruel wages in the past and this objective of yours is a step in the right direction. We would hope, however, that the conscience of America, the power of the government, and your own determination will persuade your employers to behave like human beings and grant you steadily increasing wages so that you and your families may live in decent and frugal comfort.

A wage of a dollar and a quarter an hour is ghastly recompense for exhausting labor under the burning sun of Texas. This explanation and this apology are necessary because I have approved this brutal wage scale.

May God be with you as you march to Austin, the capital city of our state, and may your reception there be in complete harmony with your dignity as human beings, American citizens, and children of God. May He bless you abundantly in the years that lie ahead.

Discourse by an Other

CARLOS GUERRA

OCTOBER 27, 1967 — The U.S. Office of Education recently issued a policy directive to school districts and colleges that henceforth Mexican-Americans would be classified as "others" in the racial category on student censuses. Defying anthropology, the office has created a new race, and this is bringing screams. Almost immediately the Bonilla brothers, Corpus Christi political leaders, sent off a telegram to the office saying, among other things, "Shame, shame, shame." And all over South Texas many people of Mexican ancestry, who sometimes speak in various grades of Spanish, and whose skin tones range from white to dark, found themselves being labeled something new. A few were pleased, why, I'll never know. Many were indignant. I am still confused.

A wise white once said that a Jew was he whom a Gentile called a Jew. Updating, I suppose we can now say that an Other (and I guess that should be capitalized) is one whom the Office of Education calls an Other — confusing as that may sound. We used to be called Mexicans, until the powers-that-be decided we could be citizens. Then we were Latin-Americans, until someone decided our contributions to the Roman Empire were negligible, at which time we magically became Mexican-Americans.

Throughout the whole time, of course, we were called other names, too, too numerous and too derogatory to list. But we were still considered White — not lily-white — but nevertheless, legally White. Now we are officially Others.

As one might expect, this change is not one to be taken lightly. After the initial shock has passed there will be problems. Once again we

Others will suffer another chronic attack of acute identity crisis. After all, we will have to ponder the fact that we are not White anymore.

South Texas Whites, on the other hand, will have to alter their cliches. They will soon be saying, "I have nothing against Others." And then there will be the classic, "Some of my best friends are Others, but would like your sister to marry an Other?" Really unfortunate, the ring is lost on that one, but how about, "Why we used to have an ol' Other boy working on our farm." And it will certainly be confusing to hear them say, "There's bad and good in every race. There's the Greasers and then there's them Others." It will sound like stating the obvious.

And the old White political hacks will not be spared. Somehow, it just won't be the same to hear them at an Other political rally proclaiming, "Ah want yew nice folks to know jus' how much Ah like this Other food o' yours." But won't they sound extra-benevolent when they begin their speeches with "Ah like all Other people."

. . . I wonder if the Washington bureaucrat who pulled this off realized what a mess he was going to cause. Perhaps he didn't realize that he was making the second-largest minority group in the country non-White. Intentions aside, this move was like giving us license to start screaming "get whitey," or something similar. And I wonder what LBJ is going to think when, while rushing past an anti-war demonstration, he hears someone scream, "No Vietcong ever called me Other."

A March in El Paso

ELROY BODE

APRIL II, 1969 — El Paso has never seen anything like it. It was only a march, yes, but a march of old women in blue canvas shoes and green stockings, little kids in ripped coats, babies in their mothers' arms. It was a demonstration by The People, *La Raza*, and their supporters — white, black, brown.

The gathering spot for the march was the corner of Fifth Street and Campbell in South El Paso — opposite a tenement owned by Dr. Owen Vowell, a local osteopath. The purpose of the march was to focus attention on the fact that the tenement dwellers did not have natural gas for cooking and heating and thus were forced to use kerosene, which they considered dangerous and unhealthy.

For the previous month Dr. Vowell, who operates a maternity clinic next door to his tenement, had refused to meet with representatives of the South El Paso Tenants' Union and had indicated he would not yield to the Tenants' Union's request that he install gas lines into his tenement. Also during the previous month — for 23 consecutive nights — southside residents held prayer vigils in front of the house of Esteban Alba, Dr. Vowell's rental agent. Mr. Alba would not meet with the tenants either.

Thus at three o'clock on March I — on a day when elm trees were starting to bud, the sky was clear, the afternoon pleasant to walk in — the march was held. Four hundred and fifty people were in a line, moving down the sidewalks of South El Paso behind flags of the United States, Mexico and Our Lady of Guadalupe: 450 people walked along with the casualness of fans going to a football game. Blondes, beards, Brown Berets; students, professors, lawyers, housewives; VISTA workers carrying cheerleaders' megaphones; dapper men in suits, with their daughters; two carloads of MAYO (Mexican-American Youth Organization) youth from Del Rio and Uvalde; members of MACHOS, an anti-poverty group of South El Paso, and friends of MACHOS; cripples, old women (San Tiago Roche, born 95 years before in Chihuahua, Mexico) and women getting old; women who had worked the previous day as maids, gone home, cooked, taken care of the family, gone out with their candles on another prayer vigil in front of Mr. Alba's house, returned home in order to get up at four in the morning to start the day again. . . .

The demonstrators carried signs, of course: "Mr. Alba, You Go To Church But What For? Help The Poor"; "God Loves People, Why Don't You?"; "It Is People Like Dr. Vowell Who Make The Che Guevaras Necessary."

Yet the march was relaxed and easy-going. There was no tension in the air. The police escort was unobtrusive, efficient, sensible. People in the shops read the handouts, as they stood in their doorways. Some smiled. Some returned peace signs. And some stared critically. ("They've seen too much TV," said one man who was watching from inside a bar; "they just want to draw attention.") At the barber college on South El Paso Street there were good-humored yells from the barbers as they gazed out at the more Christly-looking marchers: "Hey, you guys shouldn't pass up a chance for a free haircut." But there were no hostile encounters, no bricks thrown, no hecklers. Even the wise-guy soldiers on the streets, trying to pick up girls for a Saturday night, seemed a little awed by the procession. . . .

In the center of town the marchers stopped at San Jacinto Plaza and made a circle around a speaker's table on which a gasoline stove from the Vowell tenement had been placed as a centerpiece. Attorney Jesus B. Ochoa, Jr., serving as master of ceremonies, was the first to speak to the marchers and to the crowd that had gathered. . . .

[Later,] the flag bearers led the demonstrators north from the plaza toward the home of Esteban Alba, who lives in Sunset Heights near the UTEP campus. . . . By now the marchers were tired but few strayed from the group. Aging women in worn coats and scarves, barely able to move along, would look bashfully and ask the person nearby: "How far is that man Alba's place?"

... At 230 Porfirio Diaz, a very comfortable Spanish-style home on a quiet hillside street, the marchers stopped. Several young men, perhaps not fully understanding the purpose of coming to Alba's house, perhaps irritated a bit by the too-peaceful cast of the march, began to shout toward the closed windows and doors. But the leaders — those who had been coming to the Alba residence night after night — began to move through the crowd, calling out in high, almost melodious voices: "Silencio ... silencio ... silencio." Even as the crowd obediently quieted, the military-minded young men still did not grasp the meaning of the call or else did not think it was to be taken seriously. They apparently couldn't believe that a group of tenement dwellers had not come to yell "fascist pig" at Esteban Alba but had gathered one final time before his elegant Italian cypresses to symbolize their discontent in a prayer vigil.

The prayer was given — the leaders chanting from the rear, the tenants responding together: the hymn was sung ("Tu Reinas": "You Shall Reign"), and then as the rising west wind began to whip the flags the people turned slowly away and, still singing, began their two mile walk back to South El Paso.

It was a sobering and significant event. The people of the southside — usually thought to be somewhat passive, accepting, enduring — and those who had understood the harshness of their daily lives — had gone on a march.

Jose Aguilar, director of Project MACHOS in South El Paso, was realistic after the march. He knew that Dr. Vowell might remain just as firmly set against making improvements in his tenement as he had been before. But that was not the significant point of the demonstration, he felt. "It is not as important," he said, "that we win this specific battle as it is that we have finally got the people together. That's what counts."

An Ecological Armageddon

KAYE NORTHCOTT

FEBRUARY 6, 1970 — Even on clear days, a temperature inversion often traps industrial crud and automobile exhaust, turning humid Houston a dirty brown. The polluted air stings the eyes and beclouds the lungs. All over town one's nostrils are offended by a chemical stench emanating from hundreds of smokestacks. It was on just such a day recently that President Nixon's Water Pollution Control Advisory Board met in Houston to see what kind of progress the state has made in improving its environment since the last time the board met in Texas two and a half years ago. Other than a new sense of urgency on the part of the state's citizens, the board could not detect much progress.

The citizens' board listened to two days of testimony on [Biochemical Oxygen Demand] content of Ship Channel waters, confusing technical results of estuarine research and glowing reports of the pollution control activities of a myriad of overlapping local, state and federal agencies. But when it came down to simple and vital questions, such as whether Galveston Bay and the Houston Ship Channel are in better condition than they were two and a half years ago, the board could get few straight answers from the experts.

It was from their own on-site investigation and from private citizens that board members learned just how serious Houston-area pollution is. After looking at the Houston Ship Channel, board chairman Carl L. Klein, assistant secretary of water quality and research for the Department of Interior, said that the stinking liquid contained practically no water at all, just industrial and municipal effluents. "It's too thick to drink and too thin to plow," he observed.

From persons unfortunate enough to live in or near the Gulf Coast industrial area — in Galena Park and Pasadena east of Houston, south to Nassau Bay and Clear Creak, all the way down to the coast — the board learned of an approaching ecological Armageddon.

Claire Hooper, a NASA employee who owns a house on Clear Lake, appeared at the Houston meeting with a jar of bilious dark green fluid which he took from the dying lake that borders his front yard. He said that on calm days there is six inches of foam on the Clear Lake shore. Nowadays when he goes sailing, his little boat leaves a sudsy wake. Thermal pollution makes the water uncomfortably hot in the summer. The water stinks so much that Hooper and his wife keep their windows closed most of the time. And the odor becomes unbearable when industrial and municipal emissions cause giant fish kills. Even when fish are able to survive in the lake, it is hazardous to eat them. "A friend of mine took a fresh fish out of his freezer for dinner," Hooper said. "My friend said it smelled like it had been marinated in kerosene. Actually it had been — since birth."

A housewife who lives on Clear Creek, which empties into Clear Lake, showed slides taken of her backyard during the past year. The creek's color varied from murky brown to green to black, depending on the type of industrial trash being emitted upstream. The year's worst case of pollution came from a styrene tar spill which the incensed housewife said covered her yard and felt like "black bubblegum." Fumes from the tar caused blisters on house paint. "If it can blister paint, what can it do to your lungs?" Hooper asked.

"The most frustrating thing in fighting the problem is to find whom to hit," Hooper complained. He said the government is only "paying lip service to the problem."

Board member Edward P. Morgan, an ABC newsman, agreed with Hooper. He said the existence of a confusing array of pollution control agencies in the state actually is a subtle technique of passing the buck. Morgan's assessment of the Texas situation has not changed much since August, 1967, when he wrote in the *Observer*: "The men who run the Lone Star State, through a tacit but powerful interlocking directorate of politicians and corporation executives, are perpetrating and perpetuating a monstrous deception on the public — they have created a facade of corrective measures which is deliberately self-defeating. Progress gets lost in the labyrinth of boards, commissions, committees, foundations, and study groups which virtually cancel each other out in jurisdictional disputes, allowing The Establishment to do business virtually as usual."

Indeed, a large number of weak governmental agencies are responsible for various aspects of the state's environment. The Water Quality Board was established in 1967 as the big brother agency to set up water quality standards and coordinate control with federal, state, and local agencies. This year the WQB has approximately 150 employees. During the past two years it has received $4.3 million in state funds and about $600,000 in supplemental federal funds, a paltry amount to police water polluters through this vast state.

Until very recently, the board concentrated its efforts on setting up pollution standards and issuing some 2,399 waste permits to release effluents into the state's waterways. In addition to the regular permits, which conform to WQB pollution standards, there are 1,323 statutory permits loose in the state. These permits were issued before the Water Quality Act took effect and they allow higher rates of pollution than the regular permits. As part of Operation Clean Sweep, the water board will review many of the statutory permits.

Texas' clean air and water quality acts provide fines of up to $1,000 a day for polluting without a permit or variance. But to date, the WQB has officially asked the attorney general to initiate action under the water act against only three firms, and the legal agency has completed and won only one of the cases, that against ABC Rendering Co. of San Antonio. Vince Taylor of the attorney general's office estimated that all told, Texas cities and counties have filed an additional half a dozen suits against water polluters under the Water Quality Act. He guessed that there have been so few legal actions because "local governments have not yet come to understand the act."

One obvious reason for the pollution boards' reluctance to get tough with industrial polluters is that, often as not, industrialists have ruled the boards. Gov. John Connally got into trouble for appointing John Files, who owns the Merichem Company of Houston, to the Air Control Board. Files had been named "Polluter of the Month" by the *Houston Post*.

Nor has Gov. Preston Smith been averse to appointing foxes to the henhouse. One of his Air Board appointees, H.B. Zachary, Jr., owns an asphalt plant that is now under fire from Dallas citizens for excessive dust. It is not the first time that Zachary cement and asphalt plant emissions have been cited as pollution hazards.

Under a new board chairman, Gordon Fulcher of Atlanta, the WQB is showing a new aggressiveness. Soon after his election as chairman late October, Fulcher initiated "Operation Clean Sweep," a review of chronic water polluters. His first step was to call together representatives of all the industries and municipalities along the Sabine River, which marks the eastern border of Texas. He warned them that the state plans rigorous enforcement of its anti-pollution laws. Fulcher plans similar meetings throughout the state. The federal board elicited a promise from him that Galveston will be the next area to be put under serious scrutiny.

"Our visit to Galveston demonstrated an amazing situation — an island city polluting itself into extinction by threatening its tourist industry and its own beaches," the President's Water Pollution Advisory Board stated in a release at the end of its hearing on the Texas Gulf Coast.

Board members were shocked when representatives of the Galveston Chamber of Commerce, which is critical of the city's sewage program, showed them where the city is dumping 1.5 million gallons of raw sewage daily into West Galveston Bay, an area popular for swimming and fishing. The unusually frank C of C members also took the board to a city dump where trash is simply thrown into the bay.

Carl Klein, the hot-tempered assistant secretary of the interior, reacted by announcing that present and future federal water pollution control funds to Galveston would be withheld until the city takes steps to stop dumping its untreated sewage into the bay. But to Klein's embarrassment, he later learned that Galveston does not receive any federal water pollution funds. The order, however, will keep the island city from getting any in the future. Both Gordon Fulcher, chairman of the state water board, and Sen. Ralph Yarborough were angered by Klein's decision to hold up federal funds, since it blocks the best possible money source for Galveston's pollution ills. "I thought it was a thoroughly irresponsible act of shooting from the hip," Fulcher said.

Galveston city officials seemed surprised by the board's disgust with their sanitary operations. Lind Nelson, director of city utilities, said, "I didn't realize they thought we weren't going fast enough in this pollution thing. Why, in five years we hope to be able to have all our sewage treated." Nelson insisted the city cannot afford to do anything about its pollution situation right now. (Fulcher promised the federal board that the WQB will hold a show-cause hearing in Galveston first thing in February to ask the city why it should not be forced by the state to start immediate work on additional sewage treatment plants.)

A day before President Nixon's board arrived in Texas, the WQB held an emergency session and decided to initiate legal action against eight of twenty-seven cities and districts in the Clear Creek area which are dumping sewage into the Clear Creek basin. The fortuitous timing of the WQB's action made some persons cynical about the board's true intentions, for pollution — like everything else — has become embroiled in politics. Gov. Preston Smith reportedly invited the Nixon group to visit Texas in hopes that he could convince the experts that the state is cleaning up its own mess and that there in no need for federal intervention. (Under certain conditions, such as the endangering of commercial shellfish production by polluters, the federal government can impose its own anti-pollution standards on an area.) The federal pollution advisory board is limiting its investigations almost exclusively to Democratically controlled states, as the Johnson board did to Republican states; so, ironically, a federal interest in pollution abatement is considered a political insult, no matter how desperately a state needs help. Although the federal group was far from impressed with Texas' pollution control attempts, its threats of taking control of the Ship Channel and the Galveston Bay area proved to be hollow. Chairman Klein admitted that the board's strongest weapon in fighting pollution actually is publicity.

Among the proliferation of water agencies to which the Nixon committee was referring is the State Health Department which has some independent pollution control duties of a public health nature and the Texas Parks and Wildlife Department which is empowered to enforce provisions of the Water Quality Act when they affect aquatic life, birds, and animals. In addition, the Water Development Board investigates all water quality matters concerning groundwater in the state and plans for further water resources. The Railroad Commission is the sole pollution control agency to handle oil and gas leakage. . . . On the local level, municipalities, counties and water districts operate their own waste disposal plants and carry out water pollution control measures to protect their drinking water. And a number of federal agencies have at least statutory authority to control certain types of pollution. These include the Corps of Engineers (which is responsible for controlling ships' pollution, but actually relies on Coast Guard tips to spot pollution at sea), the Bureau of Commercial Fisheries, and the Bureau of Sports Fisheries.

The Texas Air Control Board mainly is responsible for keeping air quality at desirable levels. Although its activities have received more publicity than the water board's, it has an even smaller budget and staff than the WQB. During the past three years, the TACB has received only $238,717 from the state and $397,122 from the federal government. That is only 4.7 cents a year per capita for the Texas pollution. The state has authorized 50 employees for the clean air agency this year, as compared to 150 for the water board.

Until very recently, both the state air and water boards were reluctant to prosecute polluters. Their policy has been to go very slowly, first setting up anti-pollution standards, waiting for polluters to identify themselves and then giving them ample time to install anti-pollution equipment. Only within the last few months have the boards begun to get tough with chronic violators of environmental standards.

Critics of the boards justifiably have accused them of simply licensing pollution. As of October, the air board has granted 289 variances — 185 from smoke and particulate matter regulation, 86 from outdoor burning regulations, and 18 from sulphur compound regulation. (The variances allow concerns to continue to emit illegal amounts of pollution while installing pollution equipment.) Since there are some 15,000 industrial plants in Texas and only 357 have petitioned for variances, it can be assumed that thousands of others are polluting the air without the TACB's knowledge.

The Air Control Board has won two substantial court suits against corporate polluters. A $17,000 fine against International Minerals is believed to be the highest civil penalty ever levied for air pollution in the United Sates. The state also won $10,000 from the Hooker Chemical Corporation. But the TACB has asked the attorney general to take legal action against alleged polluters in only 32 cases to date, and the attorney general initiated action in only ten of those cases. A lime company, a fertilizer producer, and two lumber companies have shut down operations because of TACB regulations.

The air and water boards' stated policy is to comply with local governmental decisions on granting variances and permits. Traditionally, county and city officials have been as lenient as the state boards in giving industry ample time to install pollution equipment. But in January, reacting to a new public militancy against polluters, both the Houston City Council and the Harris County Commissioners Court asked the TACB to deny all future variances. In its first meeting of the year, the air board ignored the requests and extended four variances to Houston area companies (USS Agri-Chemicals, Inc., Intercontinental Steel Corp., Olin Corp., and AMF Tuboscope). The action was vehemently criticized by Houston politicians, but the TACB justified the variances on the basis that pollution control installations are virtually complete at the industrial sites. The four variance extensions are each for less than three months. Air board members argued soberly that each variance must be judged on its own merits. At the same meeting, the board denied a six-month variance to Occidental Chemical Co. of Houston. Occidental immediately closed down, putting 55 Houstonians out of work.

In a recent interview, Charles Bardon, TACB executive secretary, said the board will begin to make extensive use of show-cause hearings, an administrative play in which representatives of a polluting concern are subpoenaed to show cause why they should not be prosecuted. He said the board also plans a helicopter survey of the Houston area as part of a crash program to identify air polluters in the area. Such an investigation is vitally necessary . . . [but] unfortunately, the TACB's staff is far too small to police the whole state to apprehend polluters.

All in all, the pollution picture in Texas, especially along the upper Gulf Coast is exceedingly grim. The multitude of weak pollution abatement agencies was especially disturbing to members of the federal board. It was complimentary of the Gulf Coast Waste Disposal Authority which was created by the Legislature last year to allow Harris, Galveston and Chambers counties to call a joint bond election to obtain funds for regional waste disposal. (One other county, Montgomery, dropped out of the regional proposal because of industrial opposition.) In a summary statement, the board said authorities which can make regional attacks on pollution are much more effective than the proliferation of water agencies. What it failed to point out, however, is that Governor Smith has yet to name members to the Gulf Coast board, and so it has yet to take any action at all.

None of the anti-pollution agencies have adequate staffs or funding.

Congressman Bob Eckhardt pointed out at the hearing that the state would be better off financially if the Legislature would appropriate funds to match federal pollution control grants. He said the state has ignored the growing ecological crisis because the Legislature still is rurally dominated and insensitive to the problems of Texas' municipalities. This year, Eckhardt said, Texas will be allocated $40 million in federal aid for construction of sewage treatment plants. Pending applications from Texas, however, total only $22 million because under the matching system municipalities and water districts pay 70% (about $51 million) of the cost of a project, the government paying only 30%, bringing the federal and local cost to $73 million. If the state would participate in the grant program by putting up $18 million, the federal government would pay a higher percentage of the total bill — as much as $40 million — leaving a remainder of only $15 million for local government to pay. That is, cities would get the same program they will pay $51 million for under present standards at less than a third that cost. The total cost to state and local government would be $33 million instead of $51 million, a savings of $18 million to Texas taxpayers.

No matter where the money comes from, millions more will have to be spent to save the state's environment. Such an outlay would have seemed impossible a few years ago, but now improving, or at least maintaining, quality of the environment has emerged as the most urgent quest of the decade. Ecological concerns are in vogue, and whether due to a sincere desire to save the land and wildlife and air and water or an opportunistic understanding of the national mood, politicians, from President Nixon on down, are taking the issue to heart. The question is whether politicians and bureaucrats and industrialists will actually seek ways to salvage our despoiled environment or whether they will attempt to hoodwink the public with placebos rather than honest-to-God cures.

About That "Lynching"

MOLLY IVINS

OCTOBER 16, 1970 — Early in the morning of July 12, 1970, the body of Conrad D. Rogers, 31, a black man, was discovered on Farm Rd. 993 seven miles southeast of Pittsburg, Texas.

Both his legs were broken, his guts were torn up, the lower portion of his face was missing, his genitals were later found several yards away, his skull was cracked, one arm was damaged, and all the fingers of one hand broken. There was very little blood at the scene and no trace of broken glass or strips of chrome, as might be expected had Rogers been hit by a car. Rogers is listed at the Camp County Courthouse as a pedestrian fatality.

The black citizens of Pittsburg, about 35% of the population, seem to believe to a man that Rogers was murdered. His father, Leonard Rogers believes it. Black investigators sent to Pittsburg by both the NAACP and the SCLC believe it. C.L. Bolton believes it. And C.L. Bolton is not your average outside agitator. He is a worker, a preacher, and a member of the Pittsburgh school board. Even the man at the *Pittsburg Gazette* said of the Bolton family, "They'se a good bunch a niggers."

Nevertheless, it is both plausible and probable that Conrad Rogers was the victim of a hit-and-run driver.

L.E. Bell, Jr., Camp County attorney, describes himself as a doubting Thomas. And when he first saw Rogers' body in the Johnson Funeral Home that Sunday morning he firmly concluded that Rogers was the victim of a particularly vicious axe murder. "I called Doc Pendergrass to come down right away," Bell said, "cause I figured I'd need his testimony if I was going to try this axe murderer. Well, when he told me he thought Rogers had been hit by a car, I told him he'd have to prove it to me. And he did, to my satisfaction. I've been over and over it and I don't see any other explanation."

R.K. Pendergrass is a general practitioner and surgeon who also serves as the county medical officer. He reminds people that he is not a criminal pathologist and no formal autopsy was performed on Rogers. Autopsies are extremely rare in Camp County. Pendergrass is ready to stand on his judgment that Rogers died from a hit-and-run accident.

The evidence supporting Pendergrass' decision lies in the fact that Rogers was struck twice that night. What hit him the first time is a mystery. According to Pendergrass, it was a motor vehicle going at a high rate of speed. According to Bell, it must have been something like a cement truck or some vehicle with some kind of all metal front attachment — a tractor? — a tow truck? — some front end that would not leave shattered glass on impact. There are medical reasons for the fact that Rogers bled so little.

About the second vehicle there is no mystery. A 17-year-old Pittsburg boy drove his girlfriend home from a dance a little after midnight on the 12th and saw nothing on Farm Road 993 on his way to her house. On his way back about 45 minutes later, he saw something in the road (he thought it might be a bundle of papers and tried to straddle it with his car). He hit it hard enough to go back and check on what it was. On glimpsing Rogers' body, he went home for help and the town's constable was called.

Department of Public Safety officers have checked the boy's car and found no evidence that it caused Rogers' death; there were no marks on the front of the car. However, they did find bits of flesh and some pubic hair on the undercarriage of the car, indicating that the boy's car had further mutilated the body.

The case is now with the D.P.S. which has not been able to get a trace on any vehicle damaged as one that struck Rogers might be, despite extensive checking with repair shops in the area. Bell is fully prepared to prosecute the driver of such a vehicle should it be found.

There are still some questions. What would something like a cement truck be doing barreling down [Farm Road] 993 after midnight? But the questions that arise if Pendergrass' judgment is not accepted are even more confusing and give rise to even less likely scenarios.

Meanwhile, rumors continue to run rife in the black community of Pittsburg ... rumors that Rogers' genitals were found in a sack, that there was a gunshot wound in the back of his head, that his clothes were in a bunch stuck into his stomach cavity. None of them are true.

The separation and alienation between races in Pittsburg are not so terrible that a black man could have been murdered there with official connivance in covering it up. They are just great enough that no one in authority seems to have considered telling the black people of Pittsburg just what has been discovered about Rogers' death.

Leonard Rogers said gently, "You know, I'm just a colored man. I ain't got no colored friends that can help me, defend me. A white man gets into trouble, and they all come, the whole shoot 'n push. Now that sheriff, I thought he was my friend. I worked for him, you know, to get out the votes for him, but it looks like he's done forgot me." The sheriff has in fact been in the hospital after a serious operation.

Bell is also something of a friend of Leonard Rogers. "Oh, he gets busted every now and then for bootleggin' and gets a fine, but it's not personal between us. You might call it a business risk for him. We've always gotten along well. We get along fine. If he believes these rumors ... I can't understand why *he* hasn't come in to see *me*."

La Raza Unida—Keeps on Keeping On

JIM HIGHTOWER

OCTOBER 29, 1976 — Texas' own home-grown political party, *La Raza Unida*, keeps hanging in there. The Legislature has tried to do away with it by rewriting the election rules, the current governor goes out of his way to assail the party and its leaders, and there are rifts within the party itself (particularly in Zavala County, *La Raza Unida*'s home base). Add to this the fact that the self-avowed poor people's party operates on a budget that wouldn't cover Calvin Guest's lunch tabs for a year.

But—despite the hopes, expectations, and best efforts of some people—the party refuses to fold its tents. *La Raza Unida* heads into its seventh year with determination, if not optimism. . . .

Where to from here? There has been a difference of opinion within the party over strategy; whether to campaign in statewide elections or to develop power in regional enclaves using that power to demonstrate the virtue of government by *La Raza* and expanding from there. The latter is a position long held by Jose Angel Gutierrez, the party's founder and now Zavala County judge. But it was the former position that prevailed at the state convention, as both Maria Elena Martinez and Daniel Busta-mente campaigned on the need to build party strength for statewide races in 1978.

Having chosen this path, the party must demonstrate in the '78 elections that it still has a credible hold on chicanos, as it did in 1974, when *La Raza Unida* received about 6 percent of the Texas vote. The party needs to do that well or better in 1978 if it is to lay claim to being a serious third party with long-term appeal to Texas chicanos.

Like any third party, *La Raza Unida* must hold its own the second time around, or it will begin to be considered a wasted vote by its own constituency, and it will find it increasingly hard to draw good candidates to its banner. Martinez and other *La Raza* leaders seem acutely aware of this, so they are pointing most of their resources and energy toward 1978. . . .

In particular, the party will be reaching out to urban chicanos. In his bid against Martinez to head the state executive committee, Bustamente stressed the necessity of this urban focus, and it appears to have taken hold within the party. *La Raza* faces a much different situation in the cities than it does in the rural counties, where chicanos are a majority of the population. *La Raza* is in no position in Houston, for example, to take over the city council, as it did in Crystal City. In addition, urban chicanos have not been shut out of participating in the Democratic party, as they were in rural South Texas, so there is less inclination to jump at the lure of a chicano party. Then there is the harsh reality that campaigning in cities costs more.

Nonetheless *La Raza* seems intent on broadening its urban appeal. Ms. Martinez points to *La Raza*-formed *Centros de Aztlan* in Laredo and Houston as examples of what the party can do to develop its urban base. These are service centers that assist urban chicanos with the sometimes unfathomable bureaucracies they encounter in seeking jobs, health services, immigration assistance, and the like. Martinez hopes that the party can operate Centros in other Texas cities. . . .

But the party's basic task in the next two years is political organizing. As both George Wallace and Eugene McCarthy have learned, it requires a herculean effort by third parties just to get into the game. There is some doubt, both inside *La Raza* and outside, that the party can muster the organizational strength to qualify for ballot position. Martinez and the state executive committee are laying siege on this problem early, launching a series of technical assistance workshops to train county and local party workers in the craft of ballot qualification. Their success in this effort will say a great deal about the party's future.

Unfortunately, jumping the legal hurdle will not be the last of *La Raza Unida*'s problems. For one thing, there presently is less *"unida"* in *La Raza* than is desirable for a struggling minority party, and the squabblers will have to reach some kind of accord before 1978 if the party is to mount a serious statewide effort.

Then there is the more serious matter of indictments against some *La Raza* party leaders. Ramsey Muniz, *La Raza Unida* standard bearer in 1974, is under indictment for marijuana conspiracy charges. In addition, Atty. Gen. John Hill and the Texas Rangers have had a sizable investigation task force planted in Crystal City for 10 months, and they allegedly have found what they came to find, for some Crystal City officials have been indicted on various charges of corruption. Whether these charges are true or not, the considerable publicity surrounding them does not enhance the image of *La Raza Unida*.

Gutierrez considers these indictments to be deliberate harassment by demagogic state officials ambitious for higher office. "Move the attorney general's office into any county in Texas for ten months and you've got to indict someone. Why just us? They're out to destroy the credibility of *La Raza Unida*," says Gutierrez.

In addition to Hill's Crystal City gambit, Gov. Dolph Briscoe has been whipping up on Crystal City, *La Raza Unida*, and Gutierrez, assailing them for "establishing a Little Cuba in Texas" through their effort to develop a community-owned farm. This amounts to a heavy dose of demagoguery, but again the impact of the publicity is to hang a hardcore radical tag on *La Raza*, making its organizing job that much more difficult.

If *La Raza Unida* can overcome these extraneous threats to its political germination, then it can face the regular political challenges of selecting candidates, raising money, and mounting a major statewide campaign — no small hill, even for a climber.

But *La Raza Unida* has been counted out before. As one of the delegates at the state convention told the *Dallas Morning News*, "people have been prophesying our demise ever since the party's inception and we're still around."

A Death in Dimmitt

P. C. JENNINGS

FEBRUARY 16, 1979 — The houses lining U.S. Highway 385 in Hereford have a solid, prosperous look. One-story brick homes that would fit nicely in the middle-class Dallas suburbs are set back on lawns divided by broad, direct driveways. Grain elevators tower over the center of town, testifying to Hereford's status as county seat of Deaf Smith County, the most productive agricultural county in Texas and hub of one of the richest agribusiness areas in the world. The people here are open and friendly, easy to talk to, proud of their heritage, their accomplishments and their way of life.

But behind their backyard lots, in some of which you can see ponies grazing, another impression of Hereford, not visible from the highway, awaits the visitor. Here you see the San Juan Mission barrio, a South Texas colonia improbably transplanted to this Panhandle community. Squalid shacks crowd the muddy streets. The air is thick with the stench of outdoor privies. The privately owned well that provides the residents' only water (at prices higher than city water commands) is polluted with raw sewage and has been condemned by state public health authorities. The Hereford city fathers have twice denied applications from the people who live here for annexation by the city, so the barrio receives not even the most basic municipal services. Although over half of Hereford's population is Mexican-American, city officials and the folks who put them in office are neither Mexican-American nor farmworkers, and they don't see why they should spend local tax money on the barrio's problems.

Twenty-one miles to the south on Highway 385 lies Dimmitt, county seat of Castro County, a smaller, somewhat less affluent version of Hereford. A drive out from the bank-like courthouse in the middle of town, past the packing sheds and the sugar refinery, almost to the edge of the surrounding fields, brings you to the Castro County labor camp — more precisely, the Castro County Agricultural Housing Authority — which consists of dormitory-style buildings enclosed by a six-foot-high, chain-link fence topped by strands of barbed wire. The barbed wire slants inward.

It was here on the morning of December 8 that Isidro and Rachel Aguinagas decided their infant son should be seen by a doctor. They took him to the public clinic in Dimmitt, where the child was found to be feverish, suffering from respiratory infection and dehydration and nearly dead. The doctor there told them to take the child at once to nearby Plains Memorial, a tax-supported public hospital, while he called ahead to have emergency care readied. The Aguinagases rushed to the hospital, but were turned away (so they later charged) by hospital administrator Jack Newsom, who told them through an interpreter that unless they could produce a $400 cash deposit the baby would not be admitted. Isidro Aguinagas's account of the incident: "The administrator asked me if I was working. I said I had found some work gathering corn. He said, 'If you are working, then you should have money.' I said, 'But I have not been able to work these few days because of the snow in the fields.' He said, 'No money, no nothing.'"

The Aguinagases then drove 45 miles to Tulia in adjoining Swisher County, but their son was denied admission at the county hospital there also, this time because they were not county residents. By now the child's condition had worsened, so they headed back toward Dimmitt with the intention of finding someone at the county courthouse who would help. But on the way, Isidro Aguinagas Jr. died.

The next day Father Raphael Chen, a Catholic priest who had been fighting the local establishment on behalf of the poor ever since he was assigned to the Amarillo diocese 17 years ago, got a call from one of his parishioners, who asked him to help arrange the immediate burial of an infant. Word of the circumstances surrounding the Aguinagas child's death had begun to circulate through the labor camp, and a sizable number of people attended the funeral. Deaths among the farmworkers here typically attract little notice, and Chen, surprised at the crowd, asked one of his parishioners for an explanation. Having heard the story of the previous day's events, he says, he paid the Aguinagas family a visit and asked them what their plans were. They told him they were leaving town after that afternoon. The priest paused for a moment and then said, "I have just buried your son. If that is how you want to leave things, fine." They asked him what would happen next. If they left, he replied, probably nothing. Then he asked them to think about the parents of the child that would die next time.

The Aguinagases decided to stay. Before the grand jury that convened to consider their complaint against Jack Newsom, they heard a doctor testify that the baby probably would have died anyway. Newsom claimed that the whole incident was based on a misunderstanding, on the parents' inability to speak English, and later announced that hospital policy has been "clarified" to insure that children under 12 would be admitted to the emergency room first and the question of payment would be taken up with the parents later. On December 20, while the grand jury deliberated, the *Hereford Brand*, a newspaper widely read in Dimmitt, ran a front-page story on the problem of uncollectable accounts at another area hospital.

Isidro and Rachel Aguinagas are now working again, getting up every morning before dawn, traveling as far as 130 miles to work in the fields. They return each night to the labor camp after dark. The expenses of the baby's funeral set them back, and now they are several weeks behind in their rent. But they are staying.

The mayor of Dimmitt has written a letter to the *Castro County News* complaining that the media has already found 5,000 people guilty of the baby's death, and he has a point. The gnarled rancher, the placid banker, the harried public official — these are decent, upstanding people who resent having to justify their ways to outsiders. The child's death, they insist, was due to "tragic circumstances," an "unfortunate misunderstanding," nothing more.

But the rationalizations wear thin when you hear from a lawyer at the local legal aid office, about the case of a woman brought into Plains Memorial for an emergency Caesarean section less than a year ago who was denied admission because it was Sunday and the money for her cash deposit was in the bank. How the money collected by frantic relatives and friends included rolls of coins which had to be unwrapped and counted before she was given treatment. Or Father Chen's story of the victims of a fatal car wreck arriving at the hospital, the bodies of the anglo teenagers in an ambulance, the bodies of the farmworkers in the back of a pickup. Or how school children who couldn't speak English were assigned to classrooms for the retarded. And eventually you hear enough to make you realize that the extraordinary thing about the Aguinagas family is not that they were ready to leave town the day of their son's funeral, but that they were willing to stay.

Bringing the Future Down to Earth

KAYE NORTHCOTT

DECEMBER 28, 1979 — The next 25 years. They ain't gonna be easy. The 25 beyond that I don't even want to think about.

Economically, Texas will be better off than most states, indeed, most nations, thanks to our natural resources and our increasing clout as the buckle on the Sunbelt. But we will be trying to cope simultaneously with unprecedented growth and the end of an era of plenty.

What New York is to the East Coast and Los Angeles/San Francisco is to the West Coast, Houston will be to the Third Coast. If the prediction by Lloyd's of London holds true, Houston will be the largest and most important city in the U.S. by the middle of the 21st century. For those of us who think that Houston is already suffering from terminal elephantiasis, this is not particularly heartening news. Growth will be a very mixed blessing.

Houston will continue to serve as the energy capital of the world, thanks to the concentration there of energy corporations, capital, and technology. The state's — as well as the country's — proven oil and gas reserves have been declining for a decade now, and oil is getting harder and harder to find. Industry experts generally concede that all of the fabulous shallow domestic fields already have been discovered. But there are still significant reserves to be drilled deeper in the earth in hard-to-reach, smaller pay zones. Oilman Michael Halbouty insists that there is as much oil and gas yet to be found in Texas as has already been discovered. But getting to it will be very costly.

Then, of course, there are the vast Mexican reserves, emphasized so tragically by the 200,000 barrel-a-day gusher now blackening the Gulf of Mexico. No matter how chary the Mexican nationalists may be of American involvement in the development of their reserves, they will have little choice but to make use of Texas equipment and technology. Pemex already has set up an office in Houston — its only office outside of Mexico — to hurry along orders of oil field equipment south of the border. Much of the Mexican oil will be refined along the Texas coast, and Texas will be its major customer for Mexican gas. For better or for worse, the Mexican oil discoveries will bind us even closer together.

Texas will probably decide that nuclear power is too costly to pursue any further than the plants already under construction. I would like to believe that the state will be turning to solar energy, but I fear we will be burning coal instead. Texas is sitting on enough low-grade near-surface lignite — about 12 billion tons — to meet most of the state's electricity generating needs for 30 to 60 years. The coal runs primarily in two bands, one long seam from Texarkana to Laredo and another more intermittent one parallel to and southeast of the first one. And underneath the shallow coal ranging between 200 and 500 feet below the earth's surface, is 100 billion tons of deep basin lignite, of which approximately 40 billion tons should be recoverable in the future. The tonnage of coal strip-mined in Texas increased tenfold during the 1970s, and, according to a 1979 Radian Corporation report, it will increase another tenfold by the end of the century. Approximately 900,000 acres of Texas are now under lignite lease, primarily to electric power and oil companies.

The best lignite — with the highest energy and lowest sulphur content — is concentrated in Northeast Texas, which also happens to have the abundant water supply necessary for power plant cooling ponds, dust control, and irrigation of reclaimed lands. The Tyler/Longview/Marshall corridor in Northeast Texas already is growing at a precipitous rate. Attracted by the area's abundant land, oil, timber, water, energy, and labor supplies, more new plants came last year to Longview, population 60,000 than to Houston, which is 25 times its size. A Texas A&M study has predicted that within the next 25 years industrialization along the lignite belt will rival the Ruhr Valley in Germany. Now there's an unappetizing prediction for you.

Because of its gentle terrain, Texas can more easily accommodate itself to strip mining than the hilly or mountainous states. Texas energy planners seem to believe that with proper safeguards strip-mined land could be reclaimed without severe alterations in the landscape. Unfortunately, the state has an abysmal track record on environmental protection. The state's strip mine regulations have been written to allow companies to put farm and timberland under the dragline without going to the expense of segregating the precious and fragile topsoil. Unless the regulations are tightened in the future, the mining process may render useless thousands of acres of productive farmland.

Beyond the hazards to the land, the burning of coal will pollute the air and cause acid rain, which has the potential for damaging crops and other vegetation. And if not carefully monitored, the mining process itself might contaminate our ground water supplies. The coal seams parallel the Carrizo-Wilcox aquifer, which will become increasingly precious to the state as West Texas begins to experience water shortages.

And what of the population during the next 25 years? Some Mexican-American politicians have already declared a demographic victory in Texas. They claim that by the year 2000 the minorities will become the majority and take political control of the Lone Star State. Certainly the minorities will amass greater political strength. We will start experiencing this power shift soon, since the 1980 census will provide data for political reapportionment of legislative and congressional seats in 1981. Since Texas is now under the aegis of the federal Voting Rights Act, incumbent politicians will not be able to get away with the sort of self-protective gerrymandering they have practiced in the past. The minorities and the urban areas will be the big winners in reapportionment.

But the demographic shift toward the minorities will not be as rapid as some have predicted. A few years ago researchers were estimating that by 1980 blacks and browns would be 40 percent of the Texas population. Willie Velasquez, head of the Southwest Voter Registration Education Project, the most potent Hispanic political project in the U.S. estimates that the minorities will be closer to 34 percent in 1980, up only 3 percent over 1970. This is due to the unanticipated influx of Yankees to the Sunbelt and the corresponding exodus of Mexican-American and undocumented workers to the industrial centers of the Midwest.

Meanwhile, over the next two or three decades, the median age of the state's population will jump to 35 years. The number of people aged 75 or older is growing at a rate two and a half times the rate of the population as a whole. This will place a great financial burden on the social security system and other retirement programs. Right now there are 4.6 workers paying into social security for every retired person. By the year 2000 that number will have shrunk to 3.5.

We will be living longer, but since almost no one survives into his eighth or ninth decade without developing chronic physical problems, we will be needing more and more health care. Since most of us no longer are cushioned by extended families, capable of caring for their elderly at home, we may reach a crisis in housing and nursing care for the aged. (If I had my druthers, I'd get myself adopted by a Mexican-American family, since they still care for their aged and will be on the political ascendancy as well.)

With the price of homes increasing twice as fast as family income, the tenant class will continue to grow. On the flip side of that coin, ownership of housing will become increasingly concentrated among the wealthiest 20 percent of the population, and a small but significant portion of our real estate will be owned by out-of-state and foreign investors who know little and care less about the quality of life in Texas.

The housing crunch is already upon us. A couple of days ago, a major homebuilder in Chicago announced that new homes are now out of reach of the middle-class family with an income of between $20,000 and $40,000 a year. He said that in the future he will be building homes and apartment buildings exclusively for the wealthy. He also warned the middle class not to expect to find desirable apartment units within their budget. Many in the middle class, who until recently luxuriated in the suburbs, will be settling instead for remodeling older homes or buying trailer houses.

Three years ago a Houston study predicted that by 1990 Harris County would have 700,000 blacks, 400,000 Mexican Americans, and two million whites within its borders. The minorities would make up 48 percent of the Houston population, the study said. These predictions may be skewed somewhat as white professionals return to inner-city neighborhoods in search of cheap houses to purchase and restore in close proximity to their downtown jobs. This "gentrification" of neighborhoods such as Clarksville in Austin, Munger Place in Dallas, and the Heights and the Binz in Houston is removing from the market some of the best rental property available to the minorities and the poor.

If the middle class is being squeezed by inflation, the poor are being crushed. A recent Harvard-MIT study indicates that a family of four earning $7,500 a year can't afford to pay anything for housing if life's other necessities are to be provided. Earlier this year, George Allen, justice of the peace for South Oak Cliff and South Dallas, the poorest and blackest sections of Big D, estimated with regret that he would make 12,000 evictions during 1979. Most of the evictees are people who simply can't afford the $175- and $200-a-month rentals that are charged even for the worst junker apartments in Dallas. Allen said he didn't have a clue as to where the evicted would go. Says Charlie Young of the East Dallas Tenants' Alliance, "They can't all return to the country. Three thousand family farms were shut down in Texas last year."

It's not just the plight of the Texas poor that we'll have to cope with during the next 25 years but the problems of the Mexican poor as well. There is literally no other border in the world like Texas's 1,200 miles of riverfront with Mexico. No other affluent country shares such a long and easily permeable border with a Third World country. There are currently 70 million people in Mexico, and this young, undereducated, and underemployed population is doubling every 20 years. For the sake of both Mexico's and Texas's future, we should hope that the Mexican government uses its newfound oil wealth to try to better the lot of the poor. Unfortunately, neither our government nor theirs has progressed beyond the trickle-down theory of wealth distribution. Both Texas and Mexico could be described in Ralph Yarborough's immortal words as "the happy hunting ground of predatory wealth."

The issues *The Texas Observer* confronted in its first 25 years were relatively simple. Government corruption? Throw the rascals out. Racism? Well, we'll just have to integrate. The Vietnam War? Bring it to a halt. The current issues — growing concentration of wealth, the devastation of the environment, the influx of illegal aliens, the impending water shortage, the urban problem, economic constrictions — are a lot more complex. More than ever before, Texas will need serious publications like the *Observer* with the foresight to look beyond short-term economic expediency to the linchpin questions of just exactly how we are going to blaze a civilized trail into the 21st century.

The Annual Gun Control Editorial

MOLLY IVINS

APRIL 25, 1980 — Hey-o sports fans, it's time again for the annual Gun Control Editorial! (Cheers, applause, whistles.) The old pink lady, that being the *Observer*, has been letting down the side in this regard in recent years, showing a tendency to let more than a twelvemonth show up between G. C. E.'s. But past and current editors are agreed that the great tradition should not be allowed to develop arteriosclerosis, so here we are again, back at the old stand, pushing our favorite commie plot — gun control.

Our favorite commie plot had the support of the late J. Edgar Hoover, has the support of the National Association of Chiefs of Police and for 60 years now, according to the public opinion polls, has had the support of over 70 percent of the American people. Experts on law enforcement, without any exceptions of which we know, believe that the single, most effective step we can take to curb crime in the U.S. of A. is gun control. So why, you may ask, has this simple, effective measure not been taken?

It is to this point that we address this year's Gun Control Editorial.

The answer, friends, is that a well-organized, highly effective, single-issue lobby group called the National Rifle Association terrifies politicians, thwarts the will of the vast majority and makes all our lives shorter and more dangerous by its stupid, stubborn, simple-minded refusal to consider even the most basic and logical forms of gun control. Do we dislike the NRA for doing this? Of course not. We admire the NRA, if we have any sense.

Stoutly and strongly does the NRA defend and protect the interests of its members, all of whom have minds riddled with boll weevils. (We are angry this year, and any NRA member who writes in threatening to shoot us for holding this opinion will have his letter turned over to the F.B. of I.)

So rank and so poisonous has the fear of the NRA's political clout become that it threatens not only cheap handguns, but also our hopes for a sane criminal justice system.

To wit, in the fall of 1978, the Carter administration did nominate for a high Justice Department post one Norval Morris, professor of law at the University of Chicago and a much respected authority on criminal justice, particularly the penal end thereof. Now Prof. Morris was not slated to have anything to do with gun laws. He was to have administered something called the Justice System Improvement Act: he is qualified, energetic and full of good ideas on the subject.

The Senate hearing to approve his nomination was slated for a Thursday. On the Monday before, the National Rifle Association noticed that Prof. Morris is co-author of a pamphlet entitled "The Honest Politician's Guide to Gun Control." It is a pithy work, chock-full of straight information. The NRA Xeroxed some pages of this booklet, distributed them to the members of the relevant committee and commenced to use its political muscle.

Sen. Jesse Helms, R-North Carolina, was prepared to die rather than vote for someone of whom the NRA disapproved; Sen. John McClure, R-Idaho, was no better: both were up for reelection. The Justice Department and the White House, showing all the courage of pusillanimous pissants, did nothing — within three days, Norval Morris was forced to withdraw his name from consideration for the post. The White House gracefully managed to show its relief.

The pernicious influence of the NRA did not begin there and does not end there; the lobby now challenges those nominated for judges' posts, should they favor gun control. To the best of our knowledge, they have not yet succeeded in knocking off a potentially good judge, but we place no great faith in the continuance of this happy state.

What do we do? The NRA has 1.6 million dues-paying members. In comparison, there are two lobby groups that favor gun control — the National Coalition to Ban Handguns and Handgun Control, Inc., with, respectively, 80,000 and 70,000 members.

We suggest to you that until the pro-gun control lobbies have the same political clout as the anti-lobbies, the NRA will continue to work its measly, miserable will on the rest of us. In other words, join, contribute, work. Don't just sit out there, favoring gun control and speaking up whenever Mr. Gallup comes by — dammit, do something.

Now, in a less heated vein, let us consider the latest record of carnage. The Texas Department of Public Safety informs us that in 1979, 124 people in the state died by means of firearms of an unspecified nature, 1,167 people were killed with handguns, 118 by rifle and 159 by shotgun. Police killed 44 felons, the DPS says, and another 38 were knocked off by private citizens. Further, 452 Texans met their Maker last year due to knives or other sharp instruments and another 78 bought it from blunt instruments.

What do we conclude from all this? As we have explained before, the *Observer* is not really anti-gun; it is merely pro-knife. We all want to make murder a more sporting proposition, right? Well, you have to catch a person before you can stab him, knives don't ricochet and people are seldom killed while cleaning their knives. Knives really have it all over guns. For that matter, long guns have it over handguns — it's hard to hide a rifle in your pocket while going in to stick up a Jiffy Mart.

Some people say to us, "What about cars? Sixty thousand people die on the highways every year, aren't you concerned about that?" Of course we are concerned about that! Great heavens, when did a bleeding heart liberal ever suffer from shortage of concern? We stay awake nights over highway deaths, don't you ever doubt it (55,55,55). But we are talking here about crime, brethren and sistren, crime.

We suggest to you that any politician who stands up to talk about crime, about law'n'order, about lenient judges should be shouted at without compunction unless he has come out in favor of gun control. Hypocrites!

One of the few sane rationalizations for handguns is that law-abiding citizens in high-crime areas need them for protection. We quote, out of many available sources on this misbegotten myth, Robert J. McGuire, police commissioner of New York City, April 2, this year. One fundamental point about the gun ethos in the city, he said, "is the uselessness of a gun in the hands of a shopkeeper or home dweller as an effective guard against crime and tragedy. Our department again and again finds that innocent bystanders and victims of holdups or burglaries are far more likely than criminals to suffer wounding or death in shootouts with bandits. Furthermore, the overwhelming majority of discharges of handguns owned by shopkeepers and home dwellers are accidental discharges, often resulting in death and injuries."

We are paying an unbearably high price for the false sense of security which being able to own guns gives to a few of us.

So far — it's early yet — this year's most prominent victim of our lack of gun laws is [former congressman and political activist] Allard Lowenstein, shot five times on March 14. Tomorrow and tomorrow and tomorrow we shall miss his incredible energy and his passionate sense of justice. The day before he died, Al Lowenstein called the people running the Kennedy campaign to ask them not to forget gun control, to please make some campaign ads about it. The *New York Times* said in an editorial, "Allard Lowenstein was a gallant crusader for a hundred causes, some lost, but none ignoble. . . . The only weapon he ever used was the sharp language of debate."

The man accused of killing Allard Lowenstein is so crazed he believes the FBI planted a receiver in one of his teeth. The man accused is demented, has a history of treatment in mental hospitals. He bought the weapon he is accused of using, a $120 Spanish-made handgun, legally, at a sporting goods store in Connecticut. He used his driver's license for an I.D.; that was all he needed. Had he been in Texas, he would not have needed even that.

There was no 24- or 48-hour hold period on the gun purchase, no chance to see if the man had a felony record or a history of mental disturbance, which could easily have been discovered.

Why is this too much to ask that the police be allowed to block the sale of guns to those who have records of felony or of mental disturbance? The vast majority of murders are impulse killings — why is it too much to ask that a person who wants a gun, who may well be in a drunken rage, be made to wait 24 hours? Of what practical or sporting use are handguns? Cannot a rattler be shot as well with a long gun? If there are some who enjoy firing handguns for sport, why should they object to having the things licensed, like those other killers, cars.

We know that most of you agree with us — the problem is that agreement is not enough. The NRA has been wonderfully successful at locating and mobilizing its constituency. We must go and do likewise. . . .

Consider What (You) Are Doing

BISHOP L.T. MATTHEISEN

AUGUST 28, 1981 — The announcement of the decision to produce and stockpile neutron warheads is the latest in the series of tragic anti-life decisions taken by our government.

The latest decision allegedly comes as a response to the possibility of a Soviet tank attack in Central Europe.

The [Reagan] Administration says the production and stockpiling of neutron bombs is a logical step in a process begun in 1978 under the [Carter] Administration.

Thus, both Democratic and Republican Administrations seem convinced that in accelerating the arms race, they are carrying out the wishes of the American people.

The matter is of immediate concern to us who live next door to Pantex [in Amarillo], the nation's final assembly point for nuclear weapons, including the neutron bomb.

It is clear now the military can — perhaps must — think in only one way; each enemy advance must be met with further advance on our part, no matter that the enemy must then, perforce, respond with a further advance of its own. No matter that we already have the capability of destroying each other many times over and that soon other nations of this imperiled planet will possess the same awesome power.

God's gifts may be used for evil or good, for war or peace. The God of Israel warned the people of ancient times that the military use of the horse is "a vain hope for safety. Despite its power, it cannot save." (Psalms 33:17)

Enough of this greater and greater destructive capability. Let us stop this madness. Let us turn our attention and our energy to the peaceful uses of nuclear energy; for the production of food, fiber, clothing, shelter, transportation.

We beg our Administration to stop accelerating the arms race. We beg our military to use common sense and moderation in our defense posture. We urge individuals involved in the production and stockpiling of nuclear bombs to consider what they are doing, to resign from such activities, and seek employment in peaceful pursuits. Let us educate ourselves on nuclear disarmament. Let us support those who are calling for an end to the arms race. Let us join men and women everywhere in prayer that peace may reign.

A Class Struggle

GEOFFREY RIPS

JUNE 1, 1984 — The long fight of Demetrio Rodriguez continues. Sixteen years after he first filed suit in federal court in an effort to force the state to provide equal education for his children, Rodriguez is once again a plaintiff in a lawsuit "to require the States to make permanent changes in the system of financing public school in the States in order to conform the State's financing system to the dictates of the State Constitution." . . .

"In the last twelve years," Rodriguez told a May 23 press conference in the Capitol, "we've had a promise of governors that they will address the problem of school finance in the legislature or in special sessions. We don't believe it will come in a special session. . . . We've been asked to give the legislature a chance by [Governor] Briscoe and by [Governor] Clements. . . . What is required is a restructuring of the school finance system, not a Band-Aid."

The choice confronting Governor Mark White and the legislature [in the summer of 1984] is the choice between a complete overhaul of the school finance system and a balm that will provide a few more dollars for poorer districts but will perpetuate inequities among school districts that will grow more pronounced with the years. According to the argument presented in the lawsuit in which Rodriguez is a plaintiff (*Edgewood I.S.D. v. Bynum*) the wealthiest school district in the state has over $12 million in property wealth per student while the Edgewood Independent School District in San Antonio, the second poorest, has $22,000 in property wealth per student. The plaintiffs, including eight Texas school districts, contend that the one million students in the state's poorest districts attend schools drawing on 16% of the state's property wealth while the one million students in the wealthiest districts go to schools that can draw on 64% of the property wealth of the state. The school taxpayer in a wealthy district would, then, be taxed at a far lower rate than the taxpayer in a property-poor district in order to come up with the same tax revenues.

But the wealthier districts, of course, do not tax at infinitesimal rates in order to provide the same local tax revenue as poorer districts. Instead, they tax at significantly lower rates than poor districts and come up with phenomenally higher revenues with which to operate. Iraan-Sheffield, the district with the second highest wealth per pupil ratio in the state, has 460 times the property wealth per student that Edgewood has. Its tax rate for maintenance and operation and building costs is one-twentieth that of Edgewood, yielding $5,633 in local enrichment money per pupil (ADA [based on average daily attendance]). Edgewood's tax effort, at twenty times the Iraan-Sheffield rate, yielded $41 per pupil in 1982-1983. Under the current state equalization formula, Edgewood received $1,601 in state money per student, compared to Iraan-Sheffield's $487 in state support. This provided Iraan-Sheffield with $6,120 per pupil and Edgewood with $1,642 per pupil. To compound the inequities, students from poorer districts in general require more funding for special education programs, such as bilingual or compensatory education.

"The state has a constitutional obligation to do its fair share to guarantee that students have a basic education, whether or not local citizens and [local] governments are doing their fair share," said Jim Shear, State Comptroller Bob Bullock's assistant director of research, assigned to the finance committee of the Select Committee on Public Education (SCOPE). Shear, with Brian Graham of the Comptroller's Office, is the principal architect of the financing plan presented by H. Ross Perot's select committee in its final recommendations on restructuring the education system in this state. The SCOPE plan calls for a radical reform of state education finance policies and will clash head-on with a plan being proposed by state Rep. Bill Haley, D-Center, which emphasizes teacher pay raises, includes some finance reform, and carries the imprimatur of State Education Commissioner Raymon Bynum. While the SCOPE plan has equalization and an actual cost-of-education index at its core — which move the state system a long way toward equalization regardless of additional tax revenue — the Haley plan would address equalization largely through greater expenditure of additional revenue.

As Jim Shear explains it, the SCOPE proposal is the result of a unique set of circumstances: the public demand for education reform, the state's financial condition (sans the budget surpluses available in past years), and the lawsuit filed in state district court. In addition, the legislature has mandated, with the passage of H.B. 246, a core curriculum, which every school district must provide by September 1984. . . .

The lawsuit, filed on behalf of the plaintiffs by the Mexican American Legal Defense and Educational Fund, asks for a declaratory judgment that the Texas school financing system violates the state constitution and the Texas Education Code and for a permanent injunction "to require defendants to design, implement, and maintain a constitutional system of public school finance which assures equal financial and educational opportunities in school districts without regard to their wealth. . . ."

By filing suit at this time, the plaintiffs indicated their lack of faith in the legislature's ability to resolve educational inequity and, at the same time, they increase the pressure on the legislature and White to change the school finance structure. H. Ross Perot has called it a suit "the state cannot win." The superintendent of the La Vega Independent School District in McLennan County is of the opinion that "the State has had ample time to do what needs to be done to have equity in this state. . . . [Because of the inequitable tax burden] we're going to lose the smaller school districts, and the poorer school districts will have real problems in getting accreditation."

Former state Sen. Joe Bernal of San Antonio said he doesn't think the legislature "can or is willing to make a change. The influence on the legislature from the upper two quartiles [in terms of property wealth] is greater than from the lower two." Bernal said that school finance reform is one of those socially significant reforms that, in Texas, requires the pressure of the courts. Only through the courts were such issues as the poll tax, one person-one vote, single member districts, permanent voter registration, and bilingual aid for some children forced upon the legislature. The education equalization suit, he said, will "put the pressure of the court on the legislature so the legislature can do what it's supposed to do."

The lawsuit lists Bynum, the State Board of Education, Governor

[Mark] White, Comptroller [Bob] Bullock, and the State of Texas as defendants. When Bullock was notified of the suit, he told the plaintiffs they had him on the wrong side and that he would join them if his equalization plan is not implemented in the special session.

. . . Education equalization cannot be compromised any longer. White's political future is staked on his ability to pass an education reform bill and a tax package to pay for the bill. . . .

And it's time the state heard from residents from the wealthier districts who favor equalization. It is assumed that these residents favor the status quo. But we all live in larger communities than a school district. We are all ill-served by education inequity. The plaintiffs in the lawsuit should not just be residents of poor districts with children in those schools. The citizens of this state should file suit against a system that prevents the state from realizing its full educational potential. They should join community organizations from school districts on the lower half of the property-wealth scale in their efforts to force legislators to produce an equitable plan for school finance. This is a civil rights issue. This is de facto segregation of educational opportunity. It is time to take a stand.

Who's Poisoning Texas?

MICHAEL KING

MAY 8, 1998 — Texas is Number One in air pollution.

Based on a report just released by state environmental groups — "Grandfathered Pollution: The Dirty Secret of Texas Industries" — Texas may also be Number One in officially pretending the problem doesn't exist. The report confirms that the state's most consistent responses to major industrial pollution have been to allow it and ignore it — and then claim not to know how bad it is. And unless outraged citizens can somehow force the state to do its job and require big polluters to clean up their operations, the current administration [of Governor George W. Bush] clearly intends to continue business as usual: allowing, and ignoring, the ongoing poisoning of Texas.

According to toxic release inventories maintained by the Environmental Protection Agency, in recent years Texas has led the nation in most categories of dangerous air pollutants. Considering only the national ozone standards — not even including the kind of concentrated industrial poisons commonly in the air along the Gulf Coast, in Dallas-Fort Worth or in El Paso — most Texans live in cities where the air is unhealthy to breathe and steadily getting worse.

Yet much of the state's industrial pollution — from Houston to Amarillo, Longview to El Paso — has been largely unregulated, and even *uncounted*, for nearly thirty years. Because of massive exemptions — free passes to pollute — written into the 1971 Texas Clean Air Act, major corporations have been allowed to continue pouring huge amounts of toxic smoke and chemicals into the atmosphere, much as they had done before the law was passed. Yet the Texas Natural Resource Conservation Commission, the state agency charged with defending the environment and public health against pollution, insists that, after more than twenty-seven years, it cannot even give a reasonable accounting of the actual amount of unregulated pollution. George W. Bush, with one eye on the Governor's mansion and the other on the White House, has announced that the best way to deal with the state's air pollution crisis is to ask those same corporations . . . to *volunteer* to reduce their toxic emissions. And the legislature shows every sign of going right along with the Governor.

Over the years, the TNRCC and its predecessor agencies have shown a heroic tolerance of environmental insults that ordinary citizens would quickly deem unacceptable. Perhaps less well known to the public is TNRCC's refusal even to account for the pollution it is charged with regulating. That dereliction was evident once again at the April 2 [1998] hearing of the House subcommittee on grandfathered pollution, when committee member John Hirschi asked Commissioner Marquez to estimate the current overall amount of "grandfathered" pollution. . . . Marquez told Hirschi that the agency was completing yet another industry survey, begun in November of last year, and therefore he "couldn't give a good estimate" until October of 1998. . . . That is the same answer — "Sorry, we just don't know" — the agency has been giving for years. . . .

So one citizen has done it for them.

Neil J. Carman, working from readily available public records in the TNRCC's Austin offices, has single-handedly managed to do what the agency, with its $395 million state budget and 2,800 employees insists cannot be done. Carmen, a tenacious, indefatigable researcher . . . is the principal author of "Grandfathered Air Pollution." The report . . . documents what citizens' groups have been saying for years . . . [that] grandfathered industrial pollution is much greater than the state's previous estimates; it is a huge part of the state's large and growing air pollution problem; and the grandfathered pollution exemption has allowed major industries across the state to avoid modern pollution controls and other requirements intended to protect the environment and public health. Moreover, the independent production of Carman's report, right under the agency's nose, confirms another long-standing charge against TNRCC: it is a captive regulatory agency, devoting much of its energy to defending or covering for the industrial polluters it is charged with regulating.

These are just a few of the principal findings of "Grandfathered Air Pollution":

- The grandfathered exemption allows more than 1,000 industrial plants across Texas — 43 percent of the state's approximately 2,500 active plants — to evade modern pollution controls and state permitting rules required of non-grandfathered facilities. . . .

- Of the 1,070 plants covered in the study, 916 are 99 to 100 percent grandfathered.

- The 1,070 heavily grandfathered plants analyzed emit as much nitrogen oxide — a key ingredient in noxious smog — as 18.4 million automobiles.

- Large plants and major industries . . . not small-volume sources . . . account for a major portion of the grandfathered emissions. The grandfathered emissions of just twelve companies emit 34 percent of the state's non-permitted air pollution. . . .

- Grandfathered industrial emissions are substantial contributors to the ozone smog pollution which determines urban "non-attainment areas" under E.P.A. guidelines. Specifically, in Houston-Galveston and Dallas-Fort Worth, *more than half* of the industrial pollution is grandfathered pollution migrating from *outside* the non-attainment zone.

. . . In the measured words of the report, Carman's findings mean that "billions of pounds of uncontrolled or poorly controlled air pollutants have been emitted by heavily or fully grandfathered plants in Texas since 1971," and much of the emissions continue unabated to this day. Without government action to require the grandfathered polluters to stop or radically decrease their emissions . . . the air in Texas cannot be cleaned up.

The grandfathered emissions calculations might seem only a technical argument, but these disputed estimates are at the center of a public debate over Texas air pollution that dates back three decades. When the state Clean Air Act became law . . . the grandfathered facilities were part of a deal made with industry, which promised that such facilities would be upgraded or replaced over time, and inevitably would become subject to the permitting process. Nearly thirty years later, that hasn't happened. Instead, companies with still-grandfathered facilities have maintained a significant economic advantage over their fully permitted competition, because it's often cheaper to operate without pollution controls, thereby passing the clean-up costs onto the public at large.

. . . The state's major environmental and public interest groups . . . have been loudly critical of the state's intention, proclaimed by Governor Bush, to address the pollution crisis in Texas by asking the grandfathered companies to "volunteer" to cut back on emissions. As of late April, the Governor and the TNRCC had announced that thirty-six Texas companies had joined the new CARE [Clean Air Responsibility] program. The companies promised emissions reductions, in total, of approximately 25,000 tons a year. When environmentalists pointed out that the promised (and as yet unconfirmed) reductions would do little to diminish air pollution, as they amounted to less than 2 percent of the *grandfathered* emissions alone, the program's supporters reacted angrily — not to the pollution, but to the criticism of the Governor's program.

. . . One refreshingly less-than-tactful witness against the voluntary program was Dean Cook, a member of the Pasadena local of the Oil, Chemical, and Atomic Workers union. He insisted that the pollution control program needed to be mandatory, and . . . asked the committee, "why should the polluters write the pollution laws?". . . "Voluntary compliance," Cook concluded, "is bogus."

. . . Terry O'Rourke, the Democratic candidate for Harris County judge, obviously agrees with Cook. The former assistant county attorney has made environmental issues central to his campaign, and he says he has found a ready audience among refinery workers and residents of the heavily polluted communities in East Harris County. "They used to say in the union movement," O'Rourke said, " 'Where there's smoke, there's jobs.' Now they say, 'Where there's smoke, there's cancer.'" . . . O'Rourke said the state is rapidly becoming irrelevant in the face of federal law, on the one hand, and public outrage, on the other. "Texas is number one in the nation in putting toxics in the air, and Harris County is number one in Texas. This 'volunteerism,' a sort of Kiwanis Club approach to public safety, is both obscene and absurd. . . . The fact that [Bush] has a Legislature that supports it is not going to be the surviving reality." He believes that the E.P.A. will eventually force Texas to reduce pollution, or local citizens will have to do so. To O'Rourke, the "overriding ethic" of industry and its supporters in the Legislature is, "We keep the air as dirty as we can get away with," when it should be, "How can we make it as clean as we can afford?" . . .

To Neil Carman, putting an end to the grandfathered pollution exemption would be only the first step in a program to get air pollution under control in Texas. "There's problems with standard exemptions, there's problems with the permitting process, there's problems with enforcement. But the thing about grandfathered pollution — as long as you don't have a formal permitting process, you cannot have an enforceable limit to emissions. . . . It's like they can go 125 [m.p.h.] on the interstate, and then when they get stopped, they tell the highway patrolman, 'Officer, I'm grandfathered.' As long as you don't kill somebody — with your car or your pollution — [the state's] not going to do anything about it." . . .

Killing Larry Robison

MICHAEL KING

OCTOBER 3, 1999 — Thus far in 1999, the state of Texas has executed sixteen people. That's a pace likely to exceed the twenty executions of last year, but short of the record thirty-seven in 1997. Another dozen executions are currently scheduled, through November, by the Texas Department of Criminal Justice. Since resuming in 1982, the executions occur so often now (a grand total of 180) they've become political background noise, failing to generate headlines unless the story carries some particular distinction in perpetrator or victim.

A few weeks ago, for example, Canadian citizen Stanley Faulder was executed, despite protests from the Canadian government and even Secretary of State Madeleine Albright that Faulder had never been accorded the consular rights due him under international law. The members of the Board of Pardons and Paroles and the Governor who appoints them were unmoved. When asked about the case, George W. Bush responded solemnly, "If you come to Texas, don't kill anybody," later voluntarily repeating that lesson after reading aloud to a group of schoolchildren. Neither the children nor the reporters in attendance asked the Governor if he therefore believed the state of Texas is exempt from the rule of law it imposes on its citizens — or whether foreign governments should henceforth feel free to ignore laws which would otherwise protect the rights of American citizens abroad.

The international issue was only one of several troubling in the Faulder case, including purchased testimony and evidence that Faulder perhaps suffered from mental illness or organic brain damage. And as recently reported in the political newsletter *Counterpunch*, during a youthful stint in a Canadian prison, Faulder, having asked for psychiatric help, was instead subjected to experimental drug treatment with doses of LSD, under research funded by the Canadian Defense Department and the U.S. Central Intelligence Agency. It is worth noting, of course, that even had Faulder's attorneys been able to prove mental illness, it might not have saved his life. Despite popular legend to the contrary, the number of capital defendants who make successful claims of insanity is virtually nil. And this year the Texas Legislature rejected an attempt to ban the execution of the mentally retarded, at least partly because of the resistance of the Governor.

Which brings us to the case of Larry Robison, scheduled to be executed August 17 for the brutal 1982 murder of Bruce Gardner, near Fort Worth. The evidence is abundant that Robison was completely insane at the time of Gardner's murder. He killed four more people the same night, beheading and mutilating his roommate in a manner he believed was being dictated by the voices in his head, the clocks in his room, the apocalyptic stories of the Old Testament. He readily confessed to the killings, and the four prosecutors developing the case were willing to accept a plea of insanity and permanent confinement to a mental institution. They were overruled by the Tarrant County prosecutor, and in court, the evidence of Robison's madness was ruled, for the most part, inadmissible — the jury in both his first and second trials heard almost none of it.

As Robison's family can easily document, the deafness of the state of Texas to Larry Robison's paranoid schizophrenia was nothing new. The Robisons spent the years preceding 1982 fighting for Larry's sanity, and have spent the years since fighting for his life. As a teenager he began acting strangely, hearing voices, believing he had secret paranormal mental powers. He joined the Army but was discharged after only a year — only much later was the family told that he was convinced he could control people and objects with his mind. It was easier for the Army to get rid of him than help him. Larry's condition continued to deteriorate, and for four years his parents attempted to get him medical treatment, to get him committed for mental care. At one point, Larry spent six months in jail because his parents could not find a hospital to admit him. Larry himself, in his more desperately lucid moments, begged them to help him. Again and again the Robisons were told,

"He's not on your insurance . . . he doesn't have his own . . . we can't commit him for more than thirty days . . . he's not your problem . . . and he's never been violent. Unless he does something violent, there's nothing we can do." On the bloody night of August 10, 1982, Larry Robison finally gave the state of Texas something to do. While in police custody, he tried to help the state along—two serious and almost successful attempts at suicide—but was revived from a coma to begin the death watch that will likely conclude this month.

Even after Larry's conviction, evidence of his insanity continued to accumulate. It was discovered that several of his relatives suffered from similar illnesses—confirming the diagnosis of schizophrenia, a congenital disease—although out of shame, family members had hidden the knowledge. His natural father had died of a brain tumor when Larry was two; a few years after his conviction, Larry's younger sister also became ill, and was diagnosed with schizophrenia. Her prospects are better, says her mother. It took seven years of fighting for treatment, but when mental health administrators tried to turn her away, Lois Robison would deliver a "three-minute version" of her son's story, and they eventually found a way to place her daughter in a residential program where she receives excellent care.

Lois Robison recites her son's harrowing story quietly, without hesitation, although with the execution date so near, her voice occasionally breaks. She and her husband, both teachers, have made a small crusade of defending their son's life, personally and through their work with Texas CURE, an organization devoted to better treatment for prison inmates. "Texas doesn't take care of its mentally ill," she says. "A lot of states don't, but most all of them in the nation take better care of them than Texas does. . . . They don't want to put out the money to do preventative treatment. They'd rather spend the money on executions." In Larry's case, that seems quite literally true. One can only imagine what the two million dollars spent on the average capital murder case—times 180—might have done for the mentally ill in Texas since 1982.

Larry Robison's case is certainly horrible, but is it exceptional? Only in degree. Based on her work with inmates' families, Lois Robison says, "We're not the only ones this has happened to. It's happened to I don't know how many people before." At this writing, in addition to Larry Robison, there are five Texas death row inmates scheduled to die in

August (some may be postponed). Of those five cases, three inmates exhibit evidence of severe mental illness and/or retardation.

Recently Lois Robison told a brief version of her son's story to a meeting of the Board of Pardons and Paroles. Some members seemed interested, she said, and two even thanked her for her testimony. "It should never have come to this," said Lois. "If we had been able to get him the treatment that we begged for, and he begged for, then these people wouldn't have died. It's basically down to mercy."

In a few days, the board members will be receiving Larry Robison's final petition for clemency, which they can recommend to Governor Bush. Larry's mother says she still has hope. Governor Bush has the authority to order one thirty-day stay of execution. The Board can urge the Governor to grant clemency. One can only hope that Lois Robison is right. Perhaps the Board and the Governor will choose compassion and reason over ideology and political expediency. Based on the record of the Board, this Governor, and the state of Texas, there is little reason to think so.

Color of Justice

NATE BLAKESLEE

JUNE 23, 2000 —

> Where the drug addicts at?
> Where the big houses?
> Where all the gold teeth?
> — Donnie Smith

> I got debts no honest man can pay.
> — Bruce Springsteen

When you think about crack cocaine, you think of burglaries, pawned televisions, and gang violence. You don't ordinarily think of shoveling shit. But that's what the drug life meant to Donnie Smith, who was, until an extraordinary and controversial drug sting [in 1999], part of the crack problem in the tiny Panhandle town of Tulia.

Smith worked at the Tulia Livestock Auction, or the "sale barn," as locals call the sprawling auction grounds just west of town. More than 100,000 head of cattle per year are sold at the year-round auction, located on a hot, windy stretch of Highway 86 about fifty miles south of Amarillo. The auction's weekly livestock sales provide another year's stake for Swisher County ranchers, and the related commerce the auction generates provides much of the cash that keeps the nearby town of Tulia, population 5,000, in business. The auction's steady need for manual labor also provided a ready source of cash for a handful of young black men in Tulia who smoked — and allegedly dealt — crack cocaine.

Thirty-year-old Donnie Smith was one of those men.

Swisher County attacked its crack problem with the sort of campaign that has become commonplace since Ronald Reagan declared war on drugs almost two decades ago. Using funds from a regional drug task force, the local sheriff hired an undercover agent, who began making buys in and around Tulia. Only a select few knew about the deep cover operation. But even those who did were not prepared for the results: over an eighteen-month period, in a town so small it doesn't even have a Dairy Queen, the agent allegedly made more than 100 controlled buys of illegal narcotics. Early on the morning of July 23, 1999 the arrests finally came. By the end of the week, it was evident that the forty-one suspects targeted by the sting had something in common. Thirty-five of the arrestees came from Tulia's tiny black community, which numbers no more than 350. Ten percent of the town's black population had been taken down by one undercover agent.

The local paper ran a photograph of young black men in their underwear and uncombed hair being led across the front lawn of the Swisher County Courthouse. An editorial in the *Tulia Sentinel* praised the sheriff and district attorney for rounding up the "scumbags" in town. The *Amarillo Globe-News* ran a laudatory interview with the undercover agent, Tom Coleman, an itinerant lawman from West Texas with no prior experience in undercover narcotics work. Coleman has since begun another undercover assignment for a drug task force in Southeast Texas. For his work in Tulia, the Department of Public Safety named him Outstanding Lawman of the Year.

Because of the disproportionate number of African-Americans targeted by the operation, the Amarillo chapter of the N.A.A.C.P. has gotten involved. But race is not the only troubling aspect of last summer's drug bust in Tulia. There was a notable absence of drugs — at least, in any appreciable quantity — in the Tulia drug underworld exposed by Agent Coleman, and the evidence presented didn't seem to fit the patterns of drug use in the community. And Coleman, upon whose sole testimony virtually all of the prosecutions were built, has a questionable past of his own.

Although the arrest warrants were served at dawn, surprising most of the defendants in their beds, no drugs, money, or weapons were seized in the roundup. Only a few of the alleged dealers were able to raise the money to bond themselves out of jail. Many lived in public housing or trailer homes. Of more than 100 cases filed, only one involved delivery of an amount larger than an "eight ball" (3.5 grams), about $200 worth of cocaine. Despite the small amounts involved, many cases were enhanced to first-degree felonies, punishable by life in prison, because the buys allegedly took place within 1,000 feet of a school or park.

If the "dealers" did not fit the usual profile, Tom Coleman's m.o. was no less unorthodox. Agent Coleman did not wear a wire during any of the alleged transactions. No video surveillance was done, and no second officer was available to corroborate his reports. Such measures, commonly employed by Department of Public Safety narcotics agents, were too dangerous for an agent operating in a small, tight-knit community, according to Sheriff Larry Stewart. In most cases, there were no witnesses at all, other than Coleman himself. Testifying in the first few trials, Coleman claimed to have recorded names, dates, and other pertinent facts about the buys by writing on his leg.

Then there is the evidence: the drugs Coleman allegedly bought in Tulia. Coleman made contact with a community of low-income crack smokers, primarily young black men like Donnie Smith. But strangely, almost every buy Coleman made was of powdered cocaine. Only a handful involved crack or marijuana. Such irregularities didn't seem to matter to the Swisher County juries that began handing down verdicts and sentences last winter. "Just mention drugs, and you can get a conviction in the Panhandle," one defense attorney later said.

The first two trials resulted in verdicts of ninety-nine and 434 years, respectively. Most amazing have been the sentences for defendants with no prior felony convictions, who would otherwise have been eligible for probation. Freddie Brookins, twenty-two, received twenty years for one count of delivering an eight ball. He had no prior record. Another defendant with no priors, twenty-three-year-old Kizzie Henry, got twenty-five years. The harsh sentences handed down early sent a message to the other defendants, who began to accept long sentences in plea bargains with District Attorney Terry McEachern. Fewer than ten defendants are still awaiting trial.

In recent months, defense attorneys have begun to raise questions about Coleman's background — relating to his employment history and the mysterious circumstances surrounding an indictment of his own, which came to light during the undercover operation. As cracks in

Coleman's credibility have begun to appear, District Attorney Terry McEachern's confidence in the cases apparently has begun to wane. Plea bargain offers have gotten progressively lower, and now a sort of stalemate seems to have set in with respect to the remaining cases. Meanwhile, the skepticism that was initially confined to the black community in this racially divided town has spread to the white community, where a few of Tulia's prominent white residents are beginning to ask questions about exactly what has been done in the name of justice in Swisher County.

Donnie Smith's creased face and wire-rim eyeglasses make him appear ten years older than his age. A short, slightly-built man, he speaks in a rural Panhandle accent, occasionally breaking up his sleepy cadence with bursts of street jargon. Although everyone in Tulia's tiny black community lost a friend or relative to the bust, Smith's family was hit hardest. "My little brother's in county jail and he hadn't went to court yet. My little sister got twenty-five years. My cousin got six years on a plea bargain. And my uncle got eighteen years. And all the people that got busted are friends of mine. Friends and relatives," Smith said earlier this month in an interview at Abilene's Middleton Transfer Facility prison unit. Donnie's mother, Mattie White, a correctional officer at a state prison near Tulia, claims that after the bust, the sheriff told her he had given the undercover agent a list of names to check out. Sheriff Stewart now denies that he pointed the agent in the direction of Tulia's black community. Stewart says he hired Coleman because of complaints about dealing to high school students, and that the operation happened to be steered toward the black community when Agent Coleman befriended an older black man, who served as Coleman's introduction to the drug community in Tulia.

Donnie Smith was Tulia High's Athlete of the Year when he graduated in 1989. It turned out to be the high point of his life. He married his high-school girlfriend and had two children. But the marriage ended badly, as did a brief stint at West Texas A&M University in Canyon. Smith also got into trouble with the law — a couple of fights led to misdemeanor charges. He found part-time work at the sale barn, a last resort for unemployed men in Tulia. He and his fellow laborers were not cowboys. They worked "in the shit," cracking open bales of hay for the cows to eat or running the livestock gate in the stifling, dusty barn on

Mondays, when buyers from across the Midwest came to bid on animals all day long. It wasn't glamorous, but it was steady work, and in Tulia there wasn't much else for someone like Smith to choose from. But the most important thing about the job from Smith's perspective — especially after he became addicted to cocaine — was that he could come in on a Saturday, work three days, and get paid in cash when the sale ended on Monday. It was the "sale barn" that provided Donnie Smith the money to buy crack cocaine. And it was a fellow employee, Eliga Kelly, who introduced Agent Tom Coleman to Donnie Smith.

Known to everyone in Tulia's tight-knit black community as "Man" Kelly, Eliga Kelly is an alcoholic who often worked weekends and Mondays at the auction to support his habit. Sometime in the summer of 1998, Kelly introduced Smith to a white stranger who called himself T. J. Dawson. Dawson, actually Agent Coleman, said he was working construction in the town of Happy, about fifteen miles away. Kelly told Smith he had known the man for years, though Coleman had only recently shown up in Tulia. Based on this assurance, Smith scored crack for Coleman on three or four occasions over the course of the summer. Although Smith was a regular crack smoker, he was not what most people would call a dealer. He took Coleman's money to his own supplier and used it to buy rocks for him — as well as for himself. According to Smith, the two smoked crack together in Coleman's truck on more than one occasion. Then, fed up with the drug life and wanting to become a better parent to his kids, who lived in Tulia with his ex-wife, Smith checked himself into rehab in Lubbock that winter and lost track of Coleman. When Smith finished the ninety-day program, he returned to Tulia, where he began working for a local farmer. He had been clean for six months when the police arrested him, along with dozens of others netted by Coleman, last July.

With no prior felony convictions, Smith was prepared to plea bargain. The small amounts he had delivered, combined with his status as a first-time felony offender, he figured, gave him a good shot at probation. Then he read the indictments. He was accused of delivering cocaine to Coleman on seven separate occasions. But only one delivery was alleged to be crack cocaine. The other deliveries were said to be powder, in amounts between one and four grams — making them second-degree felonies. The D.A. offered Smith forty-five years.

Smith knew something strange was going on. "I don't mess with powder, man. I don't shoot it and I don't smell it," he said. Unable to raise bail, Smith sat in jail in neighboring Hale County (the Swisher County lockup was filled by the sweep; some defendants had to be housed as far away as Levelland, 100 miles to the southwest) from July [1999] until February [2000], when he went to trial on the first count, a relatively minor charge of delivery of less than a gram of crack cocaine. On the stand he surprised everyone, including his own attorney, by admitting that he got crack for Coleman several times (although he denied making the specific delivery for which he stood accused). But he never delivered powder cocaine, he told the jury. Although Coleman asked for powder, Smith said, he didn't know where to get it because nobody he knew used powder. It simply never came up in his circle of friends. The jury convicted Smith and gave him the maximum sentence of two years. In light of the severe sentences already handed down in earlier felony trials, Smith's court-appointed attorney urged him to plead guilty to the powder charges even if he believed he had been falsely accused by Coleman. In a plea bargain with McEachern, Smith accepted an offer of twelve years.

Smith was not the only defendant in Tulia to have powder cocaine introduced as evidence against him. In fact, virtually everyone caught in the bust was charged with selling powder cocaine, in some instances up to a half-dozen counts. Tulia doesn't even have a fast food restaurant, much less a bar or nightclub. The per capita income is $11,000. Yet suddenly powdered cocaine, a drug normally associated with affluent users, seemed to be everywhere — at least everywhere in Tulia's hardscrabble black community. And while powder was everywhere, it only seemed to appear in small quantities — just enough to constitute a second-degree felony. Could there really be forty coke dealers in a rural Panhandle community? "Where the drug addicts at? Where the big houses? Where all the gold teeth?" Smith asked.

By all accounts, there was cocaine in Tulia. But much more cocaine passed through the town, by virtue of its location on Interstate 27, than ever landed there. Crack cocaine began to appear in the late 1980s, particularly in the black community. According to defendants interviewed for this story, there were no volume dealers in Tulia. The local drug scene was fueled by small amounts of drugs — usually a few hundred dollars' worth at a time — picked up in nearby Plainview or Amarillo. In a small town, word got around fast about who was holding what, and users looking to score would quickly arrive at the house with the drugs. "A good hour's run, and it's gone," one defendant said.

Yet by most indicators, Tulia never had a serious drug problem. In 1996, District Attorney McEachern told the *Tulia Sentinel* that he had prosecuted only about ten cases that year involving delivery or possession of illegal drugs in Swisher County. The county attorney reported handling about eighteen misdemeanor drug cases that same year, mostly for marijuana possession. And only eight of sixty-one referrals to juvenile probation that year were for drug abuse. Anecdotal evidence suggests that property crime — usually closely associated with a large addict population — was not a major problem in Tulia, where many residents still leave their doors unlocked. Polls of junior high and high school students in Tulia suggested some of the lowest rates of drug use in the region, much lower than statewide or national rates.

Yet some in the community saw a problem. A Tulia police officer told the *Tulia Sentinel* in 1996 that the department had compiled a list of "sixty known drug dealers" in town. In January of 1997, the Tulia school board adopted by a six-to-one margin a mandatory random drug testing program for all students involved in extracurricular activities. The one dissenting vote was Gary Gardner. One of Swisher County's most respected citizens, Gardner is an enigma in overalls. He lives in a rural village east of Tulia called Vigo Park, and he is the descendant of one of Tulia's oldest farming clans. He is a self-described redneck who likes to tell friends it took him twenty years to find a wife smart enough to marry. His vocabulary on race and ethnic issues has not changed since the 1950s. Yet he has emerged as one of the staunchest defendants of Tulia's disenfranchised and one of the most vocal critics of the 1999 drug bust that decimated Tulia's African-American community.

Gardner objected to the school drug testing policy because he felt it was unconstitutional, and would eventually result in a lawsuit. When he failed to convince the board of its folly, he fulfilled his own prophecy, refusing to allow his son to be tested and going to federal court to file a suit against the school district. Unable to find a lawyer to take the case, Gardner trained himself in the law, taking his eighteen-year-old son with him to the law library at Texas Tech University in Lubbock, and buying his own books from the law school bookstore. "The law's a simple deal," he says. "If you went to Bible school, can take a motor apart, and can read, you can be your own lawyer."

Once he locked horns with the school board, Gardner says, he began having trouble with all of Tulia's establishment, including local law enforcement. "In these small towns it's like Mexican judo," Gardner said. "Once you mess with one Mexican, 'ju' don't know how many of his cousins will come after you." Over the years, Gardner has been the meanest cousin of them all, intervening on behalf of several of his Hispanic employees who fell afoul of the law and were in danger of being railroaded by the legal system. "If you're black or Mexican in Tulia, and you get arrested, you plea out. You have to, because you can't afford a good lawyer," he said. Even if they could, a trial in Swisher County is simply not worth the risk, Gardner said: "Basically, in Swisher County, whatever Terry McEachern wants from a judge or a jury, he'll get."

When the big cocaine bust first went down, Gardner said he felt certain the defendants were all guilty. But as a former cop (he served briefly as a D.P.S. trooper in the late 1960s), he objected to the efforts by McEachern, Sheriff Stewart, and others to try the suspects in Tulia's two newspapers. He wrote letters to each of the forty-five defendants urging them to seek a change of venue. And he found that their responses were similar. "A bunch started writing me back with the same thing: 'I didn't sell the man that much stuff,'" he said. Gardner attended the first trial, that of Joe Moore. "That was a lynching," Gardner said of Moore's jury trial. But it was the testimony of Tom Coleman that really disturbed him. "He said a thing or two that stood my hair up on end," Gardner recalled.

Tom Coleman does not make a good witness. This is due in part to some of the same qualities that make him a good narc. A successful undercover agent must look like a hard-core drug user, the type of person who would buy drugs on the street from someone he does not know. Coleman fits the part. He is slightly built and short, with a pale, narrow face and a goatee. He wears his long, dirty-blond hair pulled back in a ragged pony-tail that extends down to his shoulders. When he appeared at an April hearing in Amarillo, called to revoke the probation of Tulia defendant Mandis Barrow, Coleman showed up wearing a dark sports coat over a dark shirt and dark tie, tight black jeans and cheap black loafers. He suffers from a form of astigmatism that causes his eyes to twitch, a condition he attempts to control on the witness stand by tilting his head slightly to one side, in a gesture that suggests he does not quite understand what he has just been asked. In testimony, he has a tendency to repeat questions before answering them, and to hedge every possible detail about his recollections. Given the opportunity, he offers long, rambling descriptions with plenty of irrelevant detail.

But there are other reasons why Coleman is not an ideal witness. After huge jury verdicts in a half-dozen trials, some cracks began to appear in his credibility. Tulia defendant Billy Wafer's probation-revocation hearing, held at the Hale County Courthouse in February, was the first major setback for the prosecution. Wafer had received ten years' probation in 1990 for a felony marijuana-possession conviction in Plainview. At the time of his arrest in Tulia, he had served nine and one-half years of the probated sentence, with no arrests or failed drug tests. Now he was facing up to twenty years in prison if his probation was revoked — a decision that rested solely on the testimony of Tom Coleman. In court Coleman testified that on January 18, 1999, he and Eliga Kelly had flagged down Wafer as they passed him on their way to Allsup's store on Highway 86. It was about 9:00 in the morning on a Monday. Coleman testified that he asked Billy to get him an eight ball, and to meet him at the sale barn with the drugs. According to Coleman, a woman showed up at the sale barn about an hour later with the cocaine.

But Wafer had a rock-solid alibi. At the time Coleman alleged he had met with Wafer to set up the buy, Wafer was at Seed Resources in Tulia, where he worked as warehouse foreman. Wafer provided time cards, and brought his boss in as a witness. His boss testified that there was no doubt in his mind that Wafer was at work, as scheduled, all morning long. Eliga Kelly was not called to testify (McEachern apparently thought that would not be necessary to win the case), leaving the case hinging on Coleman's word versus that of Wafer's boss, a respected member of the community. District Judge Edward Self declined to revoke Wafer's probation. (Wafer had already lost his job, however, having served thirty days in jail; he and his wife also lost a home loan they had negotiated just prior to the arrest.)

Could Coleman have simply gotten his dates and times wrong? According to Eliga Kelly, the transaction never occurred at all. Four days after Wafer's hearing, still angry from the blown case, McEachern appeared before Judge Self again, this time in Donnie White's trial, which had just gotten underway at the Swisher County courthouse. McEachern called Kelly, who had turned state's witness, to the stand. Though it was hardly germane to Donnie White's case, McEachern asked Kelly about the exchange with Wafer. Didn't he remember talking to Billy Wafer with Tom Coleman at the Allsup's, and how a woman had come to the sale barn later to deliver cocaine? "I remember talking to Billy," Kelly said, "but Billy told me to get out of his face." For reasons difficult to fathom, McEachern then went rapidly through the list of those arrested in the sting, asking Kelly if he had helped arrange drug deals with each of them. Again and again, Kelly testified that he had not.

In at least one case, Coleman seems to have been unclear on just who had supposedly sold him cocaine. Coleman alleged that Yul Bryant delivered an eight ball to him in May of 1999, shortly before the end of the undercover operation. When Bryant read the report on his case, he found that Coleman had described him as a tall black man with bushy hair. Bryant is five-foot-six and completely bald. From other details given in the report, Bryant was able to guess the identity of the man Coleman had described. Bryant contacted the man, one Randy Hicks, from jail and obtained an affidavit from Hicks, who selflessly confirmed that he was the man described in the report. Bryant sent that information to McEachern's office. According to Bryant's attorney, Kerry Piper, McEachern's investigator then called Coleman in, showed him pictures of Bryant and Hicks, and asked him to identify Bryant. Coleman pointed to the picture of Hicks, according to Piper. The case against Bryant (who was in Amarillo at the time of alleged buy) was quietly dismissed. The judge decided to revoke Bryant's parole anyway, for failure to report regularly to his parole officer, and he is serving four years in prison. Fortunately for the prosecution, as damaging to Coleman's credibility as these two cases are, neither were heard before a jury or published by any news outlet in the Panhandle.

With respect to botched identities and misremembered encounters, Coleman can perhaps make the argument that he was overwhelmed by the size of the operation he was running. But there is no doubt that Coleman lied on the stand on at least one occasion — in response to questions he was asked about his own criminal history. At Billy Wafer's hearing,

Wafer's attorney Brent Hamilton asked Coleman if he had faithfully completed his application for employment as a Swisher County law officer — specifically, whether he had listed previous arrests or charges filed against him. It should have been evident to Coleman that Hamilton was on to something, yet under oath and on the witness stand Coleman replied that he had never been arrested or charged for anything more serious than a traffic ticket "way back when I was a kid." In fact, shortly after the first Tulia trial ended, a defense attorney discovered that Coleman had been under indictment for a theft charge in Cochran County at the same time he was running the undercover operation in Tulia.

Until 1996, Coleman worked as a sheriff's deputy in Cochran County, his most recent law enforcement position. After he left the job, the county filed charges on Coleman for theft, allegedly for buying gas for his personal use on a county credit card. When Sheriff Stewart discovered the outstanding warrant in May of 1998, he had no choice but to "arrest" Coleman and collect bond from him in Tulia. Yet Coleman, already five months into the undercover operation at that point, was not fired. He was suspended temporarily until he got the problem "resolved." McEachern claimed he had no knowledge of the charge (though his sheriff certainly did) before the first three trials. When a defense attorney presented Judge Self with the new evidence concerning the prosecution's star witness, he sealed it. Efforts to introduce the evidence, along with other information about Coleman's past, to impeach his credibility have been unsuccessful. The theft charge was reported in a *Lubbock Avalanche-Journal* article in early May, however. Coleman has refused to answer questions about the charge. And when asked about Coleman's background, McEachern assured me that a thorough background check had been done. "Everyone in Cochran County had the highest recommendations for him," he said. "If you do a thorough enough exam on anybody you're going to find something. Who hasn't done something at one time in their life?"

It would not have taken a very thorough exam to determine that Tom Coleman was far less than a good candidate for the job Sheriff Stewart brought him to Tulia to do. According to records reviewed by the *Observer* and interviews with past associates of Coleman, each of his last two law enforcement assignments, as a deputy sheriff in Cochran County from 1994 to 1996, and as a deputy in Pecos County from

1989 to 1994, ended when Coleman abruptly left town, with no notice to his employer, leaving his patrol car parked at his house. In both cases, Coleman disappeared owing thousands of dollars in delinquent bills. His most recent employer, former Cochran County Sheriff Kenneth Burke, wrote a letter to the state agency that licenses peace officers, following Coleman's departure. "It is my opinion that an officer should uphold the law. Mr. Coleman should not be in law enforcement if he is going to do people the way he did this town," he wrote.

Because of strict rules governing the admissibility of evidence about an officer's history, Tulia juries have yet to hear the full story of Tom Coleman's law enforcement career. He grew up in Reeves County, the son of former Texas Ranger Joe Coleman. The senior Coleman, who died of a heart attack in 1991, was one of the most widely respected lawmen in West Texas. Tom left high school in the eleventh grade. He eventually received his G.E.D., at age twenty-seven, and shortly thereafter began work as a jailer in the city of Pecos. His first assignment as a peace officer was in tiny Iraan, in Pecos County.

In interviews with former co-workers and associates compiled for this story, as well as in documented interviews conducted by a court-appointed investigator during Coleman's 1994 divorce from Carol Barnett, an unflattering portrait of Coleman emerges. According to an officer (who requested anonymity) who served with Coleman in Pecos County for several years, Tom developed a reputation as unstable and untrustworthy. "He was a nut," the officer said. "He was very paranoid." Coleman was in the habit of carrying as many as three guns on his person at one time, according to the officer. On one occasion, according to Pecos County chief deputy Cliff Harris, Coleman accidentally shot out the windshield of his own patrol car with a shotgun, while he was seated in it.

Coleman was also a liar, according to his former Pecos County co-worker. "He was the type of person who would tell you anything, and would turn around — if you knew he wasn't telling the truth — and come back and correct it," he said. In an interview conducted during Coleman's divorce, a second former co-worker, Pecos County deputy Rick Kennedy, also described Tom as untruthful. "Tom can lie to you when the truth would sound better," he stated. Kennedy also described Coleman as a paranoid gun nut who could not go on a fishing trip without an assault rifle in the tent and on the boat. Nina McFadden, the wife of another of Coleman's former co-workers in Pecos County, also described Coleman as "paranoid" and a "compulsive liar," in a second interview conducted during the divorce. Both McFadden and another former associate in Pecos County, Bobby Harris (also interviewed during the divorce), alleged that Coleman warned them that his house was always booby-trapped when he was out-of-town.

According to Coleman's ex-wife, Carol Barnett, things began to go sour in Iraan shortly after their second child was born with albinism, which left her with very poor eyesight. Though Tom doted on his first child, a son, he shunned his infant daughter, and became more and more abusive toward Carol, physically and emotionally. The family was also deeply in debt, owing thousands of dollars to merchants and vendors, who readily extended credit to Coleman as a law officer. Finally, reeling from his father's death and fearing Carol would divorce him and take his son from him, he cracked, according to Barnett. He wrote a note to the sheriff blaming his troubles on his wife. Leaving his patrol car at his house, Coleman put his two-year-old son in the family car, pawned a gun for gas money, and drove to Sherman, where his mother had moved following his father's death.

Carol eventually recovered her son and, after a bitter, lengthy battle, won a divorce from Tom and custody of the children. According to Carol, after years of not paying child support, Coleman eventually gave up all parental rights to both children so that he would not have to pay. Carol filed a complaint against Tom for criminal non-support, in an effort to collect the back child support he owed. During the time Coleman was working in Tulia, according to a garnishment order from the attorney general's office, his paycheck was being garnished $200 per month for child support.

During the divorce, the Bureau of Alcohol, Tobacco and Firearms confiscated an illegal weapon from Coleman. The gun was an automatic assault rifle Coleman had acquired from his father's collection when he passed away. (Coleman has admitted to this incident in a hearing, though the judge ruled the information inadmissible.) According to Barnett, Coleman also inherited over 4,000 rounds of ammunition from his father, along with tear gas canisters and live World War II-era grenades, which he stored in a cupboard in the couple's bathroom.

After a brief stint as a jailer in Denton, Coleman's next law enforcement assignment was back in West Texas, as a deputy in Cochran County. That ended in 1996 when Coleman's live-in girlfriend, Carla Bowerman, took her child and fled to Illinois, according to Barnett, who was in contact with Bowerman at the time. Barnett said she urged Bowerman, in the interest of her own safety, to leave Coleman while he was away at work and to take a circuitous route to her destination. (Reached at her home in Illinois, Bowerman declined to be interviewed for this story.) According to a letter from Sheriff Burke, Coleman walked into the dispatcher's office in the middle of his shift and told her he was leaving. With no prior notice to the sheriff, and without even returning his patrol car to the station, Coleman simply left town. According to a written account by the dispatcher on duty, Coleman told her he had to go look for his wife (though he and Bowerman were never actually married). According to Barnett, Coleman followed Bowerman to her parents' hometown of Patoka, Illinois. He lived and worked in Illinois until he returned, alone, to Midland in 1997, where he was working as a welder when he applied for the assignment in Tulia.

The theft charge in Cochran County was filed a year after Coleman left town. According to records reviewed by the *Observer*, it stemmed from a co-worker observing Coleman using a county gas card to fill his personal vehicle. But what apparently spurred his former boss into action were Coleman's debts. According to documents reviewed by the *Observer*, the sheriff received half a dozen letters from the grocery store, the gas company, Coleman's mechanic, and others, all requesting assistance in collecting debts Coleman promised he would make good on but never repaid. An unusual deal was worked out: Coleman would pay back the money, over $6,700, as restitution, though the theft charge against him was for less than $100 worth of gas. In return, the charge would be dropped, and the vendors would not pursue civil charges against Coleman.

News of Coleman's history has filtered through the black community in Tulia. Some were not surprised. "Get a dirty man to do a dirty job," said Freddy Brookins Sr., whose son was sent to prison — like most of the defendants — based solely on Coleman's testimony. Brookins and others contend that white Tulia was ready to believe Coleman, however problematic the details of the operation, because fear and distrust of the black community underlies almost all public policy decisions in the town. Sometimes that sentiment is not too far beneath the surface. In a transcript of the debate over the school drug testing policy, white board member Sam Sadler described an after-school scene his wife witnessed: "[My son] has entered the sixth grade this year, and he is easily influenced. . . . The other evening when several bigger kids, some colored kids — not trying to pick on anybody — but they had him all huddled up in a huddle there. You know just really talking to him. . . . And you know you do your best at home and you try to explain, you tell and do everything you know how. . . . I think that's a pretty compelling interest [to drug test], to protect my son."

McEachern played on that fear in the first case brought to trial, that of Joe Moore. McEachern portrayed the sixty-seven-year-old Moore, a central figure in the black community, as a drug dealer who preyed especially on school kids. In the trial, Moore, who had two prior felony convictions (one for possession of cocaine in 1990) was sentenced to ninety-nine years, for two counts of delivering an eight ball of powdered cocaine to Coleman.

Though he was described by McEachern as one of the four major dealers, if not *the* major dealer in Tulia, Moore's dilapidated house in the heart of the black neighborhood does not suggest affluence. His yard is filled with junk he collected to sell for scrap. According to his longtime girlfriend, Thelma Mae Johnson, Moore had made a living for the last decade largely by raising hogs, which he fed with waste grain scavenged from grain elevators. On the day Johnson accompanied me to view the kingpin's estate, a Hispanic junk dealer and his son were towing off — on four flats — Moore's thirty-year-old International Harvester truck.

Moore, who agreed to be interviewed at the Middleton Unit near Abilene, claims he never dealt cocaine. He is a mountainous man with huge hands and shoulders so broad that two sets of cuffs had to be linked together when he was arrested. He speaks slowly, in a heavy country accent through missing teeth. As one of Tulia's longtime black residents, over the decades Moore's fortune has been a barometer for the rise and fall of black Tulia. Moore, or "Bootie-Wootie" as he is affectionately known in the black community, came to Tulia with his family in the 1950s. In his youth, he worked as a farm laborer with his family. Now stooped and limping, he was once legendary for his stamina as a hay loader and his ability to toss bales onto a truck one-handed. Most residents of the African-American community in Swisher County trace their roots to farm laborers who arrived a generation before Moore and lived in shacks on the white-owned farms where they worked. Entire families picked cotton or soybeans and grew their own vegetables. The second generation of black people moved off the farms to work at the town's many grain elevators or other ag-processing jobs. By the early seventies, most black men in Tulia worked at the Taylor-Ivins seed company. Black women, meanwhile, worked mainly at the Royal Park garment factory.

Moore made his living during that period — black Tulia's heyday — as a bootlegger. Like much of the Panhandle, Swisher County never legalized alcohol sales after prohibition. In practice, however, the county remains dry for blacks only. Whites drink legally at two unofficially segregated private clubs outside the city limits: the country club, where Tulia's more affluent citizens meet, and Johnny Nix's, which caters to farmers and cowboys. For blacks, there is bootlegging. For twenty years, Joe Moore and his brothers ran the only bar in Tulia, stocked with illegal beer purchased nineteen miles away in Nazareth, the nearest wet town. The juke joint, known as Funz-a-Poppin', was the worst-kept secret in town, according to Moore. It was located in an old converted hotel in "Niggertown," as Tulia's black west side was commonly called. Moore was bartender, bootlegger, and eventually caretaker for his three older brothers, each of whom died of cirrhosis. He became a central figure in Tulia's black community, where he was known as someone who could help out a single mother from time to time, or advise a neighbor having trouble with the sheriff.

Moore and his brothers were convicted of bootlegging in the early 1980s and fined, but the police never tried to shut down the bar, according to Moore. Instead, they put him on the "slow payment plan." Every month, Moore says, he reported to the sheriff's office and paid $200 in cash, all of which was proceeds from bootlegging. Moore cannot read or write. He says he received receipts for the money, but has no idea where it went, or what happened to the records after the bar was demolished in 1992.

Many of the buildings on Tulia's west side (now referred to as the "Sunset Addition"), including Moore's place, were pulled down in the early nineties to make room for a planned expansion of I-27 that never materialized. Thelma Mae Johnson, Moore's girlfriend of twenty years, said she and some friends later tried to organize a private social club in an empty storefront, so blacks would have a legal place to drink and socialize. The city quickly responded with an ordinance banning private drinking clubs within the city limits, and the idea died. Evening entertainment for blacks is confined mostly to house parties now, according to Billy Wafer, who moved to Tulia from Plainview because he felt it was a better place to raise his kids. "We get everybody over, drink, listen to music, talk real loud and tell lies, stuff like that," he said. Since the bust, though, things have been quiet in the black community. "Right now the atmosphere with the blacks is real scared," he said. "We don't know which way to turn without the law messing with us."

Losing Funz-a-Poppin' was a blow to a black community already in decline. The closing of Royal Park in 1979, followed by massive layoffs at Taylor-Ivins in 1985, devastated black Tulia. Families relocated to Plainview or Amarillo, to work in the beef-packing industry. Young people increasingly began to leave after high school and not return. Taylor-Ivins finally closed its Tulia facility in 1995, leaving the Wal-Mart Distribution Center in Plainview as the leading employer of blacks from Tulia. Women now largely work as maids or home-health care workers, or at the nursing home in Tulia. "There just aren't many places for them to work," County Judge Harold Keeter explained, referring to the predicament of the young blacks rounded up in the Tulia bust. Mattie White, who had three children arrested in the raid, including Donnie Smith, has a different take on the local economy. "There's plenty of kids my children's age working in the bank and in the department stores," she said. "But they're all white."

As the bust briefly made news around the state, Terry McEachern and Sheriff Larry Stewart have grown weary of fielding questions, particularly about the racial aspects of the sting. Yet several other questions remain unanswered about the operation. According to his own testimony, Coleman resolved his Cochran County theft charge by paying $6,700 in restitution sometime during the summer of 1998. Where Coleman got the money is unclear. His task force salary during that period, according to county records, was about $23,000 per year. After taxes, and the $200 per month garnished for back child support, he was taking home less than $1,500 per month. How did he come up with so much money in such a short period of time? Coleman testified in January that he received no outside income while he worked for the task force. By February, his story changed. His mother had given him several thousand dollars, he testified. By April, the scenario was that a friend of the family loaned money to his mother, who in turn gave the money to Coleman.

Several defense attorneys are working on another theory, one that may answer several questions about the operation. In at least one case, the head of the Amarillo D.P.S. narcotics lab testified that the powdered cocaine introduced into evidence by Coleman was unusually weak. In order to get a higher rate of return on their investment, dealers cut cocaine with a variety of relatively inexpensive substances, usually mild anesthetics. Wafer's attorney, Brent Hamilton, has requested that all of the cocaine obtained in over 100 buys be tested at once, to determine if a common source could be found (i.e. if they are all cut with the same amount of the same substance), and to see if the same knife or scissors was used to cut all of the baggies holding the drug. A common source would support a devastating theory: that Coleman himself bought a quantity of powder, perhaps in Amarillo, cut it very weak, and put it into evidence for buys he never actually made. He could then use the task force money from the buys he reported making to pay his restitution.

After leaving Hamilton's request pending for several months, Judge Self has agreed to allow five randomly selected samples to be tested. That test has yet to be done. In the meantime, according to Hamilton and other defense attorneys, since the testing plan was first proposed (and Coleman's credibility in general has been challenged), plea offers from the district attorney have gotten much more reasonable.

Coleman would not be the first West Texas narc to con his own handlers. In 1989, more than twenty-five indictments were dismissed in Sutton County when an undercover operation put together by the district attorney came to pieces. Sutton County Attorney David W. Wallace says he recalls having misgivings from the start. "I stayed as far away from it as I could. They hired a non-D.P.S. narcotics agent with a spotted history, or maybe they didn't check his history at all," Wallace said. "And he goes out and looks for people that are doing drugs. And based on his statements he is successful. But when the trials start coming around they find out maybe this guy isn't as honest and truthful as he holds himself out to be." After several cases had already gone to trial in Sutton County, the undercover agent, Lonnie Hood, was discovered to have planted evidence and falsified reports during an unrelated operation in Taylor County. As in Tulia, most of the Sutton County defendants had been in jail since the day they were arrested. Several had already been sent to prison. All were eventually released. In the aftermath, both the county and the district attorney's office were sued.

Roaming narcs-for-hire like Coleman have a poor reputation in the law-enforcement community, according to Amarillo defense attorney Jeff Blackburn. "They're at the bottom of the food chain. Other cops don't trust them." According to Coleman's ex-wife Barnett, Coleman applied to be a state trooper numerous times. "He's been riding on his daddy's shirttails for years, tryin' to be like his daddy," she said. Coleman was working as a welder in Midland when he heard about the job in Swisher County. After burning his bridges with his past two law enforcement employers, deep cover may have been his last chance to redeem himself as an officer. But Lawman of the Year? Those who know him aren't buying it. "Tom is very crooked," Carol Barnett said. "I would not be surprised a bit," that he fabricated buys. "He's the type of guy that would do something like that," one of Coleman's former coworkers in Pecos County agreed. "I guarantee you Tom Coleman didn't make no fifty buys."

Coleman declined to be interviewed for this story.

Approached outside of the courtroom in Amarillo, he would only say that his critics have it all wrong. "I got it all straight. I lived with them, I ate with them. I *was* them," he said.

Coleman was not one of them. Donnie Smith said he never even got close. "He was never at no parties, man," as Coleman had claimed in court. If he had been, "it would be like, 'He gots to go,'" Smith said. But he was also not a member of Tulia's white community. Why was a small community so ready to turn on its own, based solely on the word of a stranger? "The guilty verdicts don't have anything to do with the evidence," one defense lawyer said. "What they've done is they've rounded up all the people with bad reputations that they've had trouble with in the past. Then they use this guy and his testimony as a vehicle for the juries to run 'em out of town." It was not as if the defendants were unknown to the juries. The County Judge testified in Donnie Smith's case that he had known Smith for years and helped him get into rehab the first time he became addicted, out of fondness for the former football star. In fact, the list of defendants reads like a Who's Who of Tulia High sports heroes from years past. But that was then. "As long as you're in school, playin' sports, and winnin' for them, you're all right," Smith said. "Once you get out, if you don't move away, you in trouble. That's basically the way it is. And if you're a white or Spanish guy hangin' out with the blacks, you already in trouble."

That idea seemed to have particular resonance in the black community. All the whites arrested in the bust had ties to the black community (though none of them were paraded before the cameras on the morning of July 23). Ironically, it was one of those white suspects, William Cash Love, who made the only delivery in the entire operation of any substantial size: an ounce (28 grams) of crack cocaine. For that crime, along with several smaller deliveries, Love received a sentence of 434 years. The sentiment in the black community is that Love, a young white man who spent his entire life in the company of blacks, and who married a black woman (Mattie White's daughter Kizzie), was singled out to send a message about his lifestyle choice. "When we saw Cash, we didn't see white. We saw black," Billy Wafer explained. "They don't want 'em crossing over." The younger generation in Tulia is much less prejudiced, according to Wafer. "The young white kids are so intrigued by the slang, the talk, the way of life, how them young black kids walk the street all the time," he said. "That's what they're so fearful of, the influence on their kids, and that's the reason things are happening the way they are now."

The View from Outside: IBP Workers Protest Wages, Working Conditions in Amarillo

KAREN OLSSON

NOVEMBER 9, 2001 — The IBP beef processing plant in Amarillo, like meatpacking plants elsewhere, is separated into two sides: slaughter and processing, or *matanza* and *proceso*, as they are known to the Spanish-speaking workers who make up a majority of the IBP workforce. The function of each side corresponds to its name, and their joint purpose is to turn live cattle into hamburger, brisket, sausage, and other beef products. On the processing side, the task of boning chucks, in which meat is extricated from around the cow's neck vertebrae with a flexible knife, is one of the more difficult and highly paid jobs in the plant. Chuck boners, as a result, are among the more senior workers, and it was a group of chuck boners and other skilled workers who approached management in September with what they considered to be a serious problem in the way the plant was operating.

In beef processing plants, cattle carcasses move along on chains, past lines of specialized workers. At the September meeting, workers complained that many of the lines within the plant had been short-staffed for months, while the speed of the processing chain remained high — making IBP an even more dangerous place to work than it had been to begin with. (Meatpacking is the job with the highest reported injury rate in the country, with about a quarter of workers reporting injuries in 1999, and many more injuries go unreported.) Although IBP, now owned by Tyson Foods, is a giant company, wages at the plant — $9 to $11 per hour — weren't high enough, the workers said. Other meatpacking plants in the area were paying up to $2 an hour more, and IBP workers were threatening to apply for jobs elsewhere if the company didn't raise wages.

According to José Vazquez, a chuck boner who attended the meeting, the managers paid attention: "They said, 'Yeah, we agree with you. We're going to send this to corporate. Please don't quit.'"

Yet the following week, said Vazquez, "they came back with the answer: No. Not half a penny. They told us what they were going to tell us, and then they pushed us out the door. They had security and green hats [managers] there, saying either get off IBP property or be arrested. Then they blocked the hallway and pushed us out through the slaughter side." Roughly 50 people were forced outside, where Potter County sheriff's deputies were waiting with paddy wagons — though in the end, no one was arrested. Meanwhile, back inside the plant, word of what had happened quickly spread, and other workers abandoned their stations. "People just stood back from the table and let the meat go," said Martina Marcus. "I looked around and saw that people were not working. I saw some of my people, they were leaving, and I walked out with them." She made her way to the hallway, where six armed policemen and "every single green hat on the production floor" had formed a line to block the way to the telephones and the locker room.

By the end of the shift, hundreds of workers had walked out, and hundreds more, when they arrived for second shift, joined the protest outside rather than report for work. IBP declared their action an illegal strike, because it did not occur during contract renegotiation — the workers are represented by Teamsters union local 577 — and announced it would fire anyone who did not return to work by the end of that week. Nonetheless an estimated 500 to 600 people chose to stay outside.

Officials at IBP's South Dakota headquarters criticized the walkout and dismissed the workers' concerns. According to company spokesman Gary Mickelson, there is no staffing problem at the Amarillo plant. "They walked out over wages," he said. "After that, as we began to hire (new) people, their rhetoric changed in order to gain public sympathy." As for the staffing issue, said Mickelson, "Did they raise that with management before they walked out?" The requisite number of workers may change according to what product is being made by the plant, he added. "A lot of this is just a misunderstanding of our business."

In the weeks that followed, the workers who walked out, along with the smaller group who seem to have been locked out, found themselves saddled with two somewhat contradictory aims: to publicly criticize the working conditions they had endured on the job, which many did by rallying on the stretch of highway in front of the plant entrance, and to try, with the help of a group of local lawyers and a cadre of outside negotiators, to persuade the company to give them their jobs back. Those two goals correspond, in turn, to things that many workers would like to secure on a long-term basis: greater public awareness of the unsafe and abusive conditions in slaughter plants, and effective negotiating power within the company. Many say the Teamsters local, which did not play an active role in the recent negotiations, has long failed to provide the latter.

On October 26, IBP offered to take back most of the workers; whether they manage to improve the situation at the plant will most likely depend on whether they can change the union and retain outside support.

When I visited Amarillo one warm, windy day in late September, a couple hundred workers were stationed on the grassy roadside across the highway from the plant. Long rows of cars were parked there, tents and a tarp-roofed pavilion had been set up, and the protesters, almost all of them Hispanic, sat or stood around in clusters. The scene had the look of a strike from which the signs and placards had been removed — which is more or less what had happened. Shortly after the walkout, IBP obtained a court injunction which, among other things, ordered the protesters not to incite others to join them, and as a result they took down their signs. Activity centered around an orange and tan Silverado pickup, with American flags attached to the bed and a lone remaining sign — a tarp painted with the words "United As One" — draped over the side. In front of the truck was a microphone, hooked up to a Peavey guitar amp on the roof of the cab, and every so often someone stood in front of the truck and spoke to the crowd — making announcements, delivering encouragement, and leading the periodic cheers of "Sí se puede!"

Not long after I arrived, one of the speakers advised the protesters that there was a reporter present, and I was promptly surrounded by a dozen workers, one holding up a misaligned joint, another indicating fingers that no longer close to make a fist, a third and a fourth pointing to shoulders that have been operated on, all of them in turn describing the day-to-day difficulties of the meatpacking line. One woman said that she had been assigned to catch 16-pound bags of meat as they came off a conveyer belt, then throw them onto a table four feet away, and that she was repeatedly yelled at for not catching all the meat.

A man spoke of working with one other person on a knifing line designed to have four people; recently he had cut himself twice. "One day I told a manager we needed another worker, and he told me that I was crazy," he said.

"They tell you that you're crazy or that you're old," added another man. "I said that my arm hurt, and they told me I was old."

"They shouldn't have to use such bad language," said another. Several said they were frequently cursed at and referred to as wetbacks. The breaks keep getting shorter, others said, and sometimes management will stack all the breaks early in the shift, leaving workers to endure hours of repetitive, strenuous work without a pause. Women spoke of being asked to perform sexual favors in return for better work assignments. Plant workers requesting to go to the restroom are told to wait 40 minutes. "It's a mafia there inside," a man said, "a mafia of green hats, together with the union."

IBP built its Amarillo plant in 1974, not long after a bitter and violent 1969 strike by the Amalgamated Meatcutters' Union (which would later become part of the United Food and Commercial Workers) at IBP's Dakota City, Nebraska, plant. At the new Texas plant arrived a new union, the Teamsters, one not traditionally associated with meatpacking workers, though long associated with corruption and thuggish tactics. In Amarillo, many workers see the union as an extension of management. (Workers are not alone in that perception: In 1998, when I wrote a story about worker injuries at the plant, a former supervisor told me plainly, "We owned that union.")

Five years ago punch-room worker Juana Martinez asked to be appointed a shop steward—a union representative on the plant floor—"because I wanted to help the people." But her opportunities to do so were limited. Mostly she helped by translating for Spanish-speaking workers when they were being disciplined or fired, she says. She joined the union's safety committee, which met once a month, but "mostly they were talking about the balance of the bank account or things going on in Amarillo, not really about safety issues."

Union officials don't make much of a show of supporting the workers when reporters call. In 1998, when I contacted local president Jerry McCown to ask about injuries in the plant, including several recent amputations and a death, McCown (who has since retired) seemed unconcerned about the situation and described the company as "very safety-conscious." Right after the recent walkout, union president Rusty Stepp was quoted by the *Amarillo Globe-News* telling members to go back to work; otherwise he has remained in the background during the conflict. Workers say he chided them as they walked out and jested that he should have asked for a raise — for himself. According to one source present in negotiations between the company and worker advocates, the union officials at the meeting said close to nothing. "The way I see it, nobody wants that union," says Martinez. "They'd rather have a different one." Stepp earns $103,000 per year. He did not return phone calls for this story.

The troubles with the Amarillo union are not new ones for the Teamsters: Unrepresentative, undemocratic locals are one of the problems which the union's reformers have fought to address in recent years. According to an article in *Labor Notes*, the Amarillo IBP plant is one of three meatpacking plants in the country whose workers are represented by the Teamsters, and recently all three have seen strikes or walkouts attributable to problems with the union as well as with management. One of the other plants is also an IBP facility, in Pasco, Washington; there, after several years of struggle, workers aligned with Teamsters for a Democratic Union, a reform group, have taken control of the union.

In September Tony Perlstein, a Teamsters' organizer based in Pasco, took vacation time to visit Amarillo protesters and campaign for TDU candidates in the Teamsters' national election, which began in October. (Pasco union leader Maria Martinez is running on the reform slate.) What happened in Pasco, he says, "is the exact same thing [Amarillo workers] are going through — the speed of the line, the dangerous conditions, the bad pay, and a union incapable or unwilling to address those problems; it's the exact same. The company is the same, the conditions are the same." While the Pasco IBP plant is still by no means an ideal workplace, according to Perlstein, since electing new union leaders in 1998 workers have quadrupled the number of shop stewards, launched a safety campaign, and won a lawsuit forcing the company to pay millions in unpaid wages.

Could Amarillo workers follow Pasco's lead? Pasco's Maria Martinez paid a visit to the protesters in October, to campaign and to share her experience, and according to Juana Martinez her visit was well-received. But when it comes to organizing at the plant, the precedent is not exactly encouraging: Four years ago, with the assistance of local attorney Jeff Blackburn, a TDU official came to speak to a group of IBP workers. "We just got booed and spit on, because of the idea that they had to stay in the Teamsters union," Blackburn recalls. "The rank and file doesn't want to stay in the union." The following year, chuck boner Vazquez ran for president of the local and apparently lost — though he says he and other workers were not allowed to observe the vote tally. Last month's protest may have laid the foundation for a long-term push to reform the union, yet under the terms of the company's back-to-work agreement, it's likely that the company won't hire back some of the leaders who emerged during the walkout.

A certain degree of disorder seemed to prevail when I went to Amarillo, as a variety of advocates tried to help the protesters negotiate with the company. A group of local lawyers volunteered to represent the workers named in the injunction, but the lawyers deemed it unlikely that the protesters' jobs would be restored by legal means. Representatives of the Equal Employment Opportunity Commission and the Department of Justice's Community Relations Service had arrived for an audience with company officials, but initial talks yielded only a scheduling of further talks. Then on October 17, League of United Latin American Citizens (LULAC) President Rick Dovalina joined the government negotiators in a meeting with officials from the union, IBP, and Tyson Foods, which acquired IBP last year.

At press time, a back-to-work offer had been extended by the company, but not yet agreed upon. According to several sources, the company said it would hire back all but the 70 workers seen by them as responsible for inciting the walkout, while applications from the latter group would be entertained on a case-by-case basis. Although the plant may not seem like the kind of place anyone would be eager to return to, workers who'd walked out expressed a desire to go back. "I work in the worst job, but I love my job. I miss my job," says Juana Martinez. "We all love our jobs. The only thing that makes our jobs hard is the way they treat us."

Ronnie Dugger. Photo by Alan Pogue.

VII. CLOSING THOUGHT

IT'S ONLY RIGHT to let Ronnie Dugger have the last word. "Though the sheer buffeting of experience on his journey wore out any number of energetic young writers in the prime of youthful resiliency, Dugger has continued year after year to expose himself to the fissures and crevasses that define so much of the democratic landscape in Austin," historian Larry Goodwyn, a one-time *Observer* editor, wrote in 1974. "He is now a middle-aged I. F. Stone [legendary editor of the muck-raking *I. F. Stone Weekly*], which makes him a mere apprentice in that rather lonely and splendid craft of personal journalism that Stone best exemplifies. I, for one, anticipate that some 20 or 30 years hence, Dugger, in full iconoclastic maturity, might well resemble his illustrious and uniquely useful predecessor."

Char Miller

Journalism for Justice

RONNIE DUGGER

Fifty years ago when I was twenty-four we started putting out the *Texas Observer* every week. Since then one president has been killed in our state and we have produced three more, each one worse than the one before. Vietnam aside, in domestic policy there was a great deal to be said for Lyndon Johnson, including Medicare and civil rights; Bush I, Reagan's wavering shadow, did little but damage to the public good; Bush II stole the presidency and, in my considered judgment, has established himself already as the worst president in the history of the country. Throughout these fifty years the *Observer* has held its ground while we, the American people, have been losing ours. By the time the *Observer*'s actual fiftieth anniversary arrives, on December 13, 2004, our country may either have descended into first-strike war-making savagery for world domination in the bloodthirsty spirit of Stephen F. Austin's drive to exterminate the Indians, or we will have regained our footing for a bloodstained new start. Everything is at stake, and to try to say anything inspiring about these facts and this prospect would be folly. But as Gandhi insisted, one tries to do the right thing for the sake of doing the right thing, whether one will win or lose. We at the *Observer* have done our best, we are damn proud of what we have done, and we will continue working at journalism for justice as long as we are able and free.

When my thoughts range across my own part in bringing the *Observer* into being, I am proudest of our release of freedom of conscience into the socially myopic Texas culture. The way we set up and guaranteed the independence of the editors, subject to no orders from anyone and the only sanction the right of the owner or owners to fire them, has advanced open thinking here and is an invention of importance for the future of honest journalism and the freedom of the press.

I will give here some of my salient memories on how we got started and how we continued, but mine has been just one person's role. This "journal of free voices," now bimonthly, has persisted for half a century because of the hope, high-mindedness, cooperative work, and sacrifices of thousands of people, and it continues to exist because of the values, forbearance, and generosity of the fluid, tenacious community throughout Texas that its readers form and re-form year after year.

When we began, there was a silence in Texas about racism, poverty, and corporate power. As Ralph Yarborough never let us forget, we ranked dead last among the major states and next-to-last in the South in education, health care, and programs for the poor. We were as racist, segregated, and antiunion as the Deep South from which most of our Anglo pioneers had emerged. Mexican Americans were a hopeless underclass concentrated in South Texas. Women could vote and did the dog work in the political campaigns, but they were also ladies to be protected, above all from power. Gays and lesbians were as objectionable as communists. The daily newspapers were as reactionary and dishonest a cynical gang as the First Amendment ever took the rap for. An organized citizens' culture was as remote as Scandinavia. Gutsy bands of liberals in the legislature fought the oil companies and the big bankers, always losing, while the state's one political party, named Democratic, kept everything quiet, buttoned up, and rotten. We were Texas, a backwater, braggish and bigoted and brutal, slow and rich and poor. There was, though, a tradition of protest journalism that went back to the outbreak of populist papers in the late nineteenth century and William Brann's *Iconoclast* and that had narrowed at the time into the *Texas Spectator* and Paul Holcomb's *State Observer*.

When Paul tired out and decided to sell his weekly newsletter for five thousand dollars, a group of about 150 liberals, usually self-identified then as loyal Democrats who were pledged to support the then liberal Democratic presidential nominees, met in the Driskill Hotel and decided to buy it and turn it into their party organ in the state. I was known to some extent, having been a liberal editor of the student newspaper at the University of Texas in Austin and having written a column in a San

Antonio daily during a year's study abroad. One Saturday in October 1954 the Texas liberals called me down to the hotel, sat me down with a few of them around a table in the hotel restaurant, and asked if I wanted to be their editor.

I wanted no part of a newspaper controlled by a faction of a political party. At the same time my alienation from the national political culture, which by then had been thoroughly curdled by Joe McCarthy, was profound. I was planning on the ensuing Monday to drop down to Corpus Christi and go to work on a shrimp boat, jump ship in Mexico, work my way back up among the farm workers, and write a novel. Invited to speak to some of the liberals in the Driskill, I told them that I was a Democrat, but only as an independent, and I did not want to work on a party organ, but that if they would give me "exclusive control of the editorial content" I would take the job.

Expecting that they would decide to hell with that and I'd be off to Yucatan, I left, and they caucused and fumed. Later Bob Eckhardt told me that the soft-spoken Mark Adams, a New Dealer for whom the struggle was like unto a war, told the group, "If ever a rattlesnake rattled before it struck, Dugger did." In the late 1990s up in Washington State, before he died there, Mark, the *Observer*'s first printer, did not remember that he had said that, but I believe Eckhardt. Bob was a CIO lobbyist then, and later a legislator and congressman and the one Texan I have known who I believe should have been president. For his part he was skeptical about starting the paper because, as he knew from his association with the *Spectator*, the venture would cost large amounts of money that would therefore not be available for other progressive projects and candidates.

Undecided, they asked me to speak again to a larger gathering of their number. Overnight I wrote up a credo and a long list of totally neglected investigative stories that I would want the paper to do. To the larger group I repeated my terms, and they decided OK. We had a deal, and I turned in my tracks to do the newspaper. As the editor I would have exclusive control of all of the paper's editorial content. As the publisher they would have the absolute right to fire me anytime they wanted to. Unless and until I was fired I would run the paper.

About eight or nine of the supporters formed an editorial advisory committee. Activist Dell Sackett accompanied me on a trip around the state to drum up support for the project. By then I had begun to know many of the principals, including Mrs. R.D. Randolph, who was one of the five heirs to the huge Kirby lumbering operation in East Texas. Fed up with her life in the Junior League, two years earlier Mrs. Randolph had presented herself at Democratic presidential nominee Adlai Stevenson's headquarters in Houston, plunked down a thousand-dollar contribution, and asked what work she could do. Quickly she had become the no-nonsense chief organizer of the liberal Democrats in the precincts of Harris County.

For the next two months Dell and I barnstormed for the new paper. We were in Dallas at the home of George and Latane Lambert — this was where I first met labor organizer Fred Schmidt — when Bob Eckhardt telephoned me.

"Ronnie, I have something to tell you," he said.

"OK," I said.

"The editorial advisory committee has made a change in your editorial credo. Where you have, 'We will serve none but our own conscience,' they have made it, 'We will serve none but the newspaper's conscience.'"

The editorial advisory committee had voted to break our agreement. "Well, Bob," I said, "I have something I'd like you to tell them."

"What's that?"

"Tell them from me to go fuck themselves."

"Well now, Ronnie," Bob said, "I understand how you feel, but I have a suggestion."

"What's that?" I asked.

"Why don't you just not say anything now, and go ahead and put out your first issue with the statement as you have written it, and see what happens."

Doing that would not have occurred to me. This was the first of many dollops of wisdom Bob gave me through the years. I think I told him right there on the phone that I would do what he suggested, but in any case I decided within the hour that I would. In my first issue I did, nary a word of criticism did I ever hear from anyone, and half a century later the credo is still there.

In this way the editor's independence of the owners, subject only to their right to fire the editor, was established, and the *Observer* became a publication which by its structuring of editorial authority formally gives more range for the personal integrity of its editors than any publication I know of. When Willie Morris succeeded me as editor and Mrs. Randolph was the publisher, at my request she made the same deal with him that I had had, and when I became the publisher I explicitly made the same deal with every successive editor. The editors of the *Observer* are and have always been as free as they have the guts to be. Mrs. Randolph, stoking with Scotch her anger at me, fired me once (though she rescinded her decision later that night), and painfully enough when I was the publisher I fired three of the editors, but neither Mrs. Randolph nor I ever gave an editorial order to an editor, nor has the board that now runs the *Observer*.

It would be easy to gush over the fact that without certain wealthy angels the *Observer* would have had to close long ago, but it is not possible to overemphasize this fact's importance.

Many periodicals have tried to survive on our model of social seriousness, but most of them have failed financially (free papers with a liberal cut to them, but which stress entertainment, sex, and such, make it in cities here and there). *Observer* workers have accepted half-pay or less from the first. (Though I worked eight years for 120 of the 168 hours there are in a week, I started at $125 and ended up at $150; though the staff got health insurance, none of us got a pension.) Without substantial advertising you just can't produce, print, and distribute a good-enough serious regional publication to hold the readers and pay the bills. If you have wanted the freedom and ethical joy of working on the *Observer*, you've had to work for peanuts.

Even under those circumstances, Mrs. Randolph poured hundreds of thousands of dollars into the paper, and relatively large sums came, and repeatedly, from the enlightened oilman J.R. Parten of Madisonville, the passionately liberal banker Walter Hall of Dickinson, the old-world liberal Jesse Andrews of the Baker Botts law firm in Houston, and some others across the years. Mrs. Randolph's role as our major financial supporter into the 1970s, though, has been matched only by Bernard Rapoport of Waco, who succeeded her as the financial mainstay at the *Observer*, even as Molly Ivins succeeded to my role. These are the *Observer*'s share of the real-world major benefactors of high-minded enterprises who confound the beady-eyed ideologues who damn all the rich and stereotype them beyond the pale.

Whatever your opinions may be about how to organize the providing of life insurance, my first encounter with Barney Rapoport illuminates, by itself, the essential essence and spirit of the *Observer*. A year or two after we had started, people kept telling me there was this insurance man in Waco who would advertise with us. In my first and only attempt to sell an advertisement I drove up to Waco and called on the president of the American Income Life Insurance Company. He walked me across the street for lunch in a cafeteria.

After we sat down with our trays I said to him, "Mr. Rapoport, I'm here to sell you an ad if I can, but there's one thing I should tell you first."

"Fire away," or something like that, he said.

"As far as I can see," I said, "life insurance is basically a matter of likelihoods and actuarial tables. There's no need for competition and running up the cost of it with the overhead and profit of all these companies just to provide money when somebody dies. I think basic life insurance should be socialized."

"Well," Barney said, "I agree with you, so let's go on to the next subject." We did, and he has advertised with us ever since; he is now on our board.

While speaking of angels who really are angels, something else is important to think about, too. No one can count the thousands of people who have sent contributions to the *Observer* which, while relatively small ($35, $50, $15, $150), were real and sometimes painful sacrifices in their own financial situations. The goodness of people takes one form in their giving, and the amount of their goodness is independent of the amount of their giving. And the goodness of what citizens build together is the resulting community wherein they know and warm each other and are all equals.

My points of view, my opinions, unfolded in me as events unfolded in my life. I had been born into a devout, hard-working Catholic family in San Antonio, raised believing in good and bad. Our rented first floor of a house in the King William district at 302 Washington Street was across the street from the San Antonio River, beyond which the Mexicans lived on their vast West Side, acres and acres of poverty, misery, and the other kinds of violence. A loner, I read a lot, and while I was still in high school I was ethically impressed by the novels of Charles Dickens and by

Marx's labor theory of value. At UT I imbibed the values of the public good which prevailed in the Veblenian school of economics called institutionalism which was then dominant there, as singularly embodied in the teachings of Professors Robert Montgomery and Clarence Ayres.

The decisive ethical event of my youth occurred just across the border in Mexico while I was standing hanging onto a post in a third-class bus about to head south for the interior. My eyes fell upon a little boy who was standing on the street beside the front of the bus and staring upward at me. His clothes were ragged, his eyes locked on mine. I realized that to him I was a rich American, and I felt very deeply for him. The bus rattled off. After that, back in Austin listening as demagogues berated every attempt to favor the poor in legislation as socialist or communist and realizing that business bribery was the legislature's way of life, I understood that my state had been corrupted by the major corporations and that the daily newspapers, silent or abusive about almost everything that mattered, were a part of that corruption.

But I was innocent about power. Probably because the Catholics had convinced me to believe, by deductive implication, in the power of virtue, when I started putting out the *Observer* I thought that if you just showed people wrong they would make it right. For instance, I did a series on "The Slums of Texas." Surely, I half-thought, people are good, surely if you show them the slums across the tracks and in the shadow of the state Capitol they'll pass laws to make things right. But they did not. Loan sharks, I easily proved as a reporter, were charging the poor — what? — 1,500 percent a year. The legislature passed a law, all right — legalizing 360 percent. Fifty years later Texas still has the highest proportion of citizens, one in four, who have no health insurance. In a democracy that works, the truth should do it, but during my eight years' reporting on the *Observer* I had my first close encounter with the radical fact, still leering brutally at us all, that democracy the way we have and practice it does not produce sufficient justice.

Mark Adams was our first printer at his little printshop out West First Street, still setting type from the clacking keyboard of the old hot-lead Linotype machine. Often he and I adjourned across the street for coffee or lunch in a little café there. Senior to me in age, he gave his advice briefly and quietly from his great reservoir of reserve, then left me my head. He was later succeeded as our printer, with all our missed deadlines and late changes and dragged-out paying of our bills, by the activists and union printers Bill and Anne McAfee. Our first office was almost the whole left side of the first floor of the building that still stands at 504 West Twenty-Fourth Street, a block and a half from the northwest corner of the University of Texas Drag. For many years Jim Hightower, Kaye Northcott, Molly Ivins, et al. held forth in the treetops from the second floor of the building near downtown Austin at 600 West Seventh Street — there it was that Molly first deployed her rare gift for laughing at moral folly and Jim marshaled a brigade of college students to help us research the crimes of the corporations. Finally we settled, a few blocks on down one-way West Seventh, in the three-room office suite at 307.

During those first eight years, to me the *Observer* and Texas were the world, not to say the cosmos. At first I reported and wrote the paper by myself. I used ten or fifteen Texas dailies to keep up, was in and out of the legislature day and night, edited stories that began to come in, and every week or so hit the road in my green 1948 Chevrolet for reporting, 200 miles to Dallas, 500 to El Paso, 150 to Houston, 300 to the Valley. Every week the associate editor and I produced, made up, and proofread an issue. My wife Jean (now Mrs. Bob Sherrill), teaching school, accepting my recurring absences and taking charge in the raising of our two kids, bracing my principles when they needed bracing, for she was always to some degree ethically more radical than I, was a silent but crucial co-founder of the *Observer*. My profoundest memory is of being bent low at the printshop proofing the last page of the issue, finishing, and lifting myself up from it as the weight of the world ascended to wherever it spent the few hours we had before the cycle started again. Collectively we practiced the highest journalistic standards — seriousness of the subjects, fairness, and accuracy — which the *Observer* has now stood true to for fifty years. As we gained respect, Wick Fowler, a reporter and ally of the right-wing governor Allan Shivers, tried to compete us out of existence with a rival statehouse weekly, but it was his paper that had to fold.

A shy, shuffling fellow, Billy Lee Brammer, started dropping by the office after he got off work reporting for the *Austin American-Statesman* downtown. Just came in and sat around, watched, and we talked a little, as I clipped stacks of the dailies into the advancing night. Other than the fact that Billy Lee had studied English lit at North Texas State, I knew nothing about him. One night he offered to clip some of the papers — "Sure," I said, "thanks" — on the long, long workbench under the mantelpiece at 504. He quit downtown to become the first of my associate editors and turned in, for example, a rollicking exposé, available only in the little *Texas Observer*, of when the lobbyists treated the legislators to a wild weekend of feasting, gambling, and venery at the Kentucky Derby. He was so good that Senator Lyndon Johnson of Texas, although greeting our issues as they landed on his desk in Washington, I was told, with roars of rage, hired him away from us for his Washington staff. Later Billy Lee wrote the best novel by a Texan yet known to me, *The Gay Place*, in which the Johnson figure, in one scene, dispenses his wisdom from bed with young women on each side of him. Along in the late 1960s, the last time I saw Billy Lee before he died of an overdose, he emerged one morning from a bedroom on West Thirty-Second Street in Austin in his underwear, followed in a little while by two young women, in theirs.

Bob Bray was an entirely different cat, a reporter who just banged it out, a good fellow with a gap-toothed grin and a large, good family. He balanced his hard work for justice through journalism and sloshing down beer with me with time for fishing with his kids and teaming up with his long-suffering wife Nina calming them down when they were wild teenagers. After he left to become Senator Ralph Yarborough's press secretary in Washington he became for me the key relay in the marathon of events that created a 90-mile-long national seashore. I wrote an editorial in the *Observer* asking why not make the offshore Padre Island a national park; Bob, in his office in Washington, saw it, cut it out, and dropped it on Ralph's desk; the very next day, Bob told me in an excited phone call, Ralph had introduced the bill in the Senate to do it. Eventually it became law. Most of the rewards of reform journalism are elusive — reasoning from insults that you're scoring points, wondering if your work helped cause the public's mood to surge, seeing what your reporting should have caused become instead some sorry imposture. For Padre Island National Seashore I felt I had lofted an arrow that struck true. When I am on Padre I have a private pride and remember Bob.

When Larry Goodwyn was fifteen and I was fourteen, during World

War II, he and I were sports writers and pool sharks together at the *San Antonio Express-News*. Larry later turned up at the *Texas Observer* and at once turned our legislative coverage into analytical clarity. Larry knew, long before many of us did, that the crux of the systemic tragedy in Western economics is the strangling of small businesses and of economic competition itself by the major corporations. Reporting the legislature, he focused on the struggles between, on the one hand, the independent oilmen and small landholders and, on the other, the major oil companies. While we learned from Eckhardt's leadership in the Texas House, Eckhardt learned from Larry's reportage in the *Observer*. In due course Larry wrote *Democratic Promise*, the definitive history of American populism, and he continues to work, from Duke University, on the very American possibilities that were lost when the anti-federalists were crushed during the founding of the United States.

Willie Morris had caused such a ruckus kicking back at the censors of his editorials in the student newspaper at UT that he was a natural for the *Observer* from the first. Once, when he was my associate editor, Governor Preston Smith invited both of us down to the mansion, to find out, the governor said as I recall, "what you boys want." We talked to him about taxing oil and gas with severance taxes instead of poor people with sales taxes, and we thought he made some improvements along those lines in what he later proposed to the legislature.

We all drank a lot of beer together. Once Dan Strawn, our country farmer–oilman friend, photographed us at Scholz's, Willie shooting the finger in the Mississippi way and I, in the Texas. It was Willie and I who, with a carefully sequenced set of questions, drove the state's most prominent Baptist minister into pronouncing that no Catholic should ever be elected to any office at all; the UPI's report on that comment helped Kennedy, we believed, to neutralize that issue in 1960. But during Willie's watch our amiable liberal friend and pussymaster Rep. Charlie Wilson of East Texas led the legislature and its wobbly liberals into enacting the general sales tax. Willie went on to lead *Harper's* in a brilliant period against the Vietnam war, and Charlie went on in Congress to covertly engineer the funding of the Mujahedeen in Afghanistan.

Lyndon Johnson trapped all of us at the *Observer*, as he trapped everyone else and as history trapped him; there was a fatality to it all. I was snookered by his arrogance and bullying into opposing him frontally. After I had slammed him in editorials for making the rancid reactionary lieutenant governor Ben Ramsey the one Democratic national committeeman from Texas, Johnson invited me out to the ranch and told me that if I'd just stick with him we'd increase the *Observer*'s circulation tenfold. I spent the rest of the evening at dinner with him (and Ladybird and Mary Margaret Wiley) trying to explain journalism to him; he refused to admit that he understood me.

Johnson ruthlessly crushed, as best he could, the liberal movement that was rising behind the leadership of Yarborough and Mrs. Randolph in Texas in the 1950s because he could not control it and because predictably it would criticize him from his home state when he sold out on his way to the White House, as he knew that from time to time he would. My notions of how to make a better world were stunned into insensibility when, descending in an elevator in Chicago in 1960 during the Democratic National Convention, I learned that Kennedy had chosen Johnson to be his running mate. Since that killed the liberal movement in Texas outright, I was jarred with a compound sense of failure and of my insufficient understanding of life, and a year and a half later I quit as editor and embarked on the rest of the long life that I continue to live.

Another time I'll tell many stories, about Mrs. Randolph, Willie, Bob Sherrill, Lyman Jones, Greg Olds, Parten, Hall, Jim Presley and Henry B. Gonzalez, Elroy Bode, Molly, Kaye, Hightower, Rod Davis, Linda Rocawich, Geoff Rips, Frances Barton, Dan Strawn, Dave Denison, Lou Dubose, Barney Rapoport, Jim Cullen, Dubya and Harken Energy, David Anderson, David Armstrong, and more others than I can name, but I may not omit here Sarah Payne and Cliff Olofson.

Dell Sackett had become our first business manager; it was during an exchange with Dell about our McCarthyized political culture that I decided, damn the caution-mongers, we'd adopt the motto "an independent liberal newspaper." After a while the "devastating dames" in East Texas who were among the paper's founders, including Minnie Fisher Cunningham, Lillian Collier, and Mary Weinzerl, sent to us, to succeed Dell, a country schoolteacher from Trent, West Texas, Sarah Payne.

Of body Sarah was slender but strong. She had been a WAC in World War II. She spoke softly in a high voice. She kept the office and the records and managed the crises; she was always there; when nobody else was around she was the whole enterprise. When our hopes could not sustain her, her indignations did. State senator, later U.S. congressman, Henry B. Gonzalez of San Antonio used to come by to see her particularly and to go have Mexican food with her at Spanish Village on the upper Drag. As the work became too much for Sarah, Cliff Olofson appeared, I don't know why or from where, to work with her. I think her hair was not white when she came, but it was when, leaving work alone on a winter evening, she slipped on the ice on the front steps and broke her hip. Confined from then on to bed, she withered and died. One cold and windy day on the West Texas plains Ralph Yarborough was one among us at her funeral.

I do not know that Cliff had any work interest in his AIDS-foreshortened life except the *Observer*. His and my bond was very close. Rather than speaking of his idealism and his loyalties he embodied them in his work day after day. He toiled over the business manager's tedious, detailed, repetitive tasks day and night, weekends, whatever was needed. No chore was too menial; his pride was in what we were doing together. When we'd run out of money he'd stop paying his own salary first, give up his room or apartment, and sleep nights on the floor underneath his worktable. Once we realized, too late, that he had been paying a lot of *Observer* bills with his own credit card. Sarah Payne, and after her Cliff Olofson, guaranteed and validated what the rest of us were doing. If they believed in us we could believe in us.

The *Observer* is instructive about human endeavors in several basic ways. It originated in a group's desire to mount and control a journalistic challenge to dominating power, but they accepted my will to express my own honesty, and the direction, not the exact content, became the accepted expression of the group's desire. Co-workers have appeared as if by materialization out of the morning dew. From newspapers, from universities, from public schools, from small businesses, from remote East Texas farms, from law offices, they have come forth: "Can I help?" They saw what we were doing and they gave their hearts freely as one gives love freely. This is the substance that has become incomparably more than the beginnings; this is the rising of human nature in Texas to the possibilities of high-mindedness and fellow feeling, the rising that is the *Observer* community. Every volunteer, every pro bono lawyer, every tipster in cowed East Texas or shut-down Dallas, every scribbler in some godforsaken little town, every reporter sneaking hours in a newspaper office, every friend or lover putting staffers up for the night, every county attorney warning of danger, every contributor of money, every contributor of ideas, every contributor of ideals, and every reporter and clerk and editor and telephonist who has dropped out of the ranks and helped — they are why the *Observer* is here after fifty years, they, they, *they*, each and every one, give us in Texas not only conscience and decency persisting but hope for human nature.

We all knew from the first that we were taking on the Establishment, the powers that be; we all understand what we have been doing all these years. We are part of a specific line of tradition in Texas, Sam Houston, the populists, Jim Hogg, Brann, Jimmy Allred, Minnie Fisher Cunningham, Bob Montgomery, Maury Maverick, Ralph Yarborough, Bob Eckhardt, Frankie Randolph, Jim Hightower, Molly Ivins, a tradition that in turn is part of the never-ending revolt of people everywhere against embedded privilege and power. I know the muddles, the waste and loss we have had, but damn, this is a good way to live! We live and work strong, respected among people we respect, and in the darkest times more strength comes flowing into our beings from further kinships felt, with the sixth-century-B.C. inventor of democracy in Greece, with Spartacus, with Jesus, with John Stuart Mill, with Franklin and Paine and Jefferson, with Charles Dickens, with Thoreau, Whitman, Susan B. Anthony, with Norman Thomas, Walter Reuther, Eleanor Roosevelt, with Gandhi, Camus, Orwell, with Martin Luther King. From our shining college town in our backward American state we have sounded out, forged, constructed, and maintained a haven for free conscience that has earned a permanent place in the human record. Long live, long live, the *Texas Observer*.

Contributors

RODOLFO F. ACUÑA is a professor of Chicano studies at California State University at Northridge and the author of *Occupied America: A History of Chicanos.*

MICHAEL VANNOY ADAMS received an M.A. in American Civilization from the University of Texas at Austin, a D.Phil. in American Studies from the University of Sussex in England, and a certificate in psychoanalysis from the C. G. Jung Institute of New York, where he now lives and practices.

FRANCES BARTON was a member of the *Texas Observer* staff in the 1980s.

ROY BEDICHEK was a naturalist, educator, writer, and the longtime director of the University of Texas's Interscholastic League. Among Bedichek's best-known works is *Adventures with a Texas Naturalist.*

JAKE BERNSTEIN is coeditor of the *Texas Observer.*

NATE BLAKESLEE is a former editor of the *Texas Observer* who received the magazine's only nomination for a National Magazine Award for his groundbreaking coverage of the Tulia drug bust.

ELROY BODE is known for his El Paso perspective and for crafting some of the finest portraits of the Texas Hill Country. Among his books are *This Favored Place: The Texas Hill Country* and *Home and Other Moments.*

BILL BRAMMER is a former editor of the *Texas Observer*. He wrote for *Time* before becoming a journalism professor at Southern Methodist University and writer-in-residence at Bowling Green State University. His experiences as press aide for then senator Lyndon Johnson in the 1950s helped shape his 1961 award-winning novel, *The Gay Place*.

ROBERT BRYCE, a longtime staff writer for the *Austin Chronicle*, has published work in the *New York Times, Talk, U.S. News & World Report, Salon,* and *Mother Jones*.

GARY CARTWRIGHT, a finalist for a National Magazine Award, contributes to *Harper's, Life, Esquire,* and other publications. The author of several books and movie scripts, he is currently a senior editor at *Texas Monthly*.

JO CLIFTON worked as a journalist for the *El Paso Times*, the *Austin American-Statesman*, and the *Texas Observer* before becoming an assistant attorney general and a municipal court judge in Austin. She is now the editor of *In Fact Daily*, a Web-based newsletter of Austin city hall affairs.

ROD DAVIS was editor of the *Texas Observer* in 1980–81. He is the author of the novel *Corina's Way* and an investigative report, *American Voudou: Journey into a Hidden World*. His work has appeared in *Best American Travel Writing 2002* and numerous other publications.

DAVE DENISON, a former *Texas Observer* editor and Nieman Fellow at Harvard, has edited the *Arlington (Massachusetts) Advocate* and *CommonWealth Magazine* and was books editor at the *American Prospect*. He is currently a freelance writer.

J. FRANK DOBIE was a prolific folklorist who taught at the University of Texas and devoted himself to the Texas Folklore Society, becoming Texas's leading cultural spokesperson. His work *Coronado's Children* won the Literary Guild Award, and President Lyndon Johnson honored Dobie with the Medal of Freedom, the nation's highest civil award, days before he died in 1964.

LOU DUBOSE edited the *Texas Observer* for eleven years before becoming political editor at the *Austin Chronicle*. He coauthored, with Molly Ivins, the best-selling *Bushwacked: Life in George W. Bush's America* and *Shrub: The Short but Happy Political Life of George W. Bush*.

RONNIE DUGGER is the founding editor and longtime owner-publisher of the *Texas Observer*. He has written hundreds of articles for publications such as the *New Yorker*, *Harper's*, the *Nation*, and *Atlantic Monthly* and has written several books, including biographies of Lyndon Johnson and Ronald Reagan. He is also the founder of the Alliance for Democracy.

BOB ECKHARDT, a prominent labor lawyer and politician who fought for progressive causes, was a longtime supporter of the *Texas Observer*. In his seven-term tenure in the U.S. House of Representatives, Eckhardt sponsored the Toxic Substances Control Act, which enabled the Superfund program, and the War Powers Act.

LARS EIGHNER, a short-story writer, parlayed his experiences as a homeless person into his critically acclaimed memoir, *Travels with Lizbeth*.

GLEN L. EVANS is known as the dean of Texas paleontology and the father of geoarchaeology and is author of *Wildness at Risk*.

JOHN HENRY FAULK, author and humorist, began his fight for First Amendment rights when he was blacklisted from radio in the 1950s. Faulk won his case and went on to a successful career as an activist and broadcaster.

RUPERTO GARCIA, a staffer at the *Texas Observer*, was executive director of the Mexican American Legislative Caucus in the 1980s.

DAGOBERTO GILB is the author of *The Magic of Blood*, *The Last Known Residence of Mickey Acuña*, *Woodcuts of Women*, and most recently *Gritos*, a collection of essays, many of which first appeared in the *Texas Observer*. A longtime resident of El Paso, he now lives in Austin.

LAWRENCE GOODWYN is a former editor of the *Texas Observer* who teaches history at Duke University, where he is professor emeritus. He is the author of the landmark history of the Populist movement, *Democratic Promise*, and *Texas Oil, American Dreams*.

CARLOS GUERRA, a columnist for the *San Antonio Express-News*, has led numerous civil rights battles in South Texas. He is one of the founders of the Mexican American Youth Organization and the Raza Unida Party.

BILL HELMER, who received his bachelor's and master's degrees from the University of Texas, was on the staff of the National Commission on

Violence in 1968–69 and was a senior editor at *Playboy* from 1969 to the 1990s. He is the author of *John Dillinger: The Untold Story, Baby Face Nelson*, and *The Saint Valentine's Day Massacre*.

DAVE HICKEY, a recipient of the MacArthur Award, is a widely published writer of fiction and cultural criticism. A former gallery owner, *Village Voice* contributing editor, and *Art in America* executive editor, Hickey is a professor of art criticism and theory at the University of Nevada, Las Vegas.

JIM HIGHTOWER is a former editor of the *Texas Observer* who has dedicated his life to the cause of progressive populism. He cofounded the Agribusiness Accountability Project and served as the Texas agriculture commissioner in the 1980s. Hightower is known for his fiery radio commentaries and his nationally published column. He is the author of *Thieves in High Places: They've Stolen Our Country and It's Time to Take It Back* and *There's Nothing in the Middle of the Road but Yellow Stripes and Dead Armadillos*.

PAUL HOLCOMB was editor and publisher of the *State Observer*, one of the *Texas Observer*'s forerunners, and contributed to the first issue of the *Texas Observer*.

JOE HOLLEY, a former *Texas Observer* editor, is the *San Antonio Express-News* Insight editor and a regular contributor to *Texas Monthly, Columbia Journalism Review*, and the *New York Times*. As editorial page editor at the *San Diego Tribune,* he won the Pulitzer Prize.

SARAH T. HUGHES was a representative in the Texas House in the 1930s and was Texas's first female district judge and first female federal judge, and her name was placed in nomination for vice president of the United States at the 1950 Democratic convention. Judge Hughes, who heard *Roe v. Wade*, swore in Lyndon Johnson following the assassination of President Kennedy.

MOLLY IVINS, a three-time Pulitzer Prize finalist and recipient of numerous journalism awards, has served as coeditor of the *Texas Observer* and as the Rocky Mountain bureau chief of the *New York Times*. Ivins is the best-selling coauthor, with Lou Dubose, of *Bushwacked: Life in*

George W. Bush's America and *Shrub: The Short Happy Life of George W. Bush.* Her nationally syndicated column appears in over two hundred newspapers.

P. C. JENNINGS is a freelance writer living in Houston and is currently writing a history of that city.

LARRY L. KING is the prolific author of Emmy Award–winning documentaries as well as screenplays, short stories, and thirteen books, including *The Best Little Whorehouse in Texas.* A former Nieman Fellow at Harvard, King has taught at Duke and Princeton Universities.

MICHAEL KING is a former editor of the *Texas Observer* who has received three Association of Alternative Newspaper awards. He is currently the news editor at the *Austin Chronicle.*

MICKEY LELAND, a spokesperson against hunger, was a member of the Texas legislature in the 1970s and 1980s. He served as chairman of the Democratic National Committee's Black Caucus and was instrumental in securing relief for refugees in Sudan and Ethiopia.

ARCHBISHOP ROBERT E. LUCEY was widely known for his social activism championing San Antonio's poor.

LARRY McMURTRY is the author of the Pulitzer Prize–winning novel *Lonesome Dove* and numerous other novels and essays. He is the owner of Booked Up, a used bookstore in Archer City, Texas.

BISHOP L. T. MATTHEISEN is a retired priest who served the Amarillo community for many years.

MAURY MAVERICK JR., a zealous protector of First Amendment rights, won fame in the 1950s for battling Joe McCarthy, and later during the Vietnam War for defending conscientious objectors. Maverick had a column in the *San Antonio Express-News* that ran for over twenty years and was honored by the American Bar Association for his exemplary pro bono activism.

WILLIE MORRIS, a Rhodes scholar, won praise for his bold editorship of the *Daily Texan*, the *Texas Observer*, and *Harper's Magazine*. He wrote numerous books, including *North Toward Home* and *My Dog Skip.*

AMADO MURO (Chester Seltzer) adopted his pen name from his wife's maiden name, and it earned him acclaim as a young Mexican American writer even though he was neither young nor Mexican American.

DEBBIE NATHAN is a Texas native who has lived in Houston, El Paso, and San Antonio. She is the author of *Women and Other Aliens: Essays from the U.S.-Mexico Border* and coauthor, with Michael Snedeker, of *Satan's Silence: Ritual Abuse and the Making of a Modern American Witch Hunt.* She currently lives and works in New York City.

KAYE NORTHCOTT, like Willie Morris and Ronnie Dugger, was politicized by her experience as editor of the *Daily Texan.* After editing the *Texas Observer* from 1968 to 1976, she was a reporter and editor at the *Fort Worth Star-Telegram.* She currently edits *Texas Co-op Power.*

GREG OLDS was born in Kansas, grew up in Oklahoma, and moved to Texas in 1950. He received his journalism degree from the University of Texas at Austin in 1958. After working on weekly newspapers and small dailies, he joined the *Texas Observer* in 1966 and served as an associate editor and later as editor.

KAREN OLSSON began work as an intern at the *Texas Observer* in 1996 and later became an editor. She left in 2002 but continues to write for the magazine. Her work has appeared in *Texas Monthly* and *Mother Jones*, and her first novel, *Waterloo*, was published in 2004.

AMÉRICO PAREDES, an acclaimed Mexican American folklorist, organized the Folklore Archives at the University of Texas at Austin and was a founder of the university's Mexican American studies program. He is perhaps best known for his 1958 book about the legend of Gregorio Cortez, *With a Pistol in His Hand: A Border Ballad and Its Hero.*

BILL PORTERFIELD, who wrote for the *Dallas Times Herald*, is a noted Texas writer whose works include *Loose Herd of Texans* and *Texas Rhapsody: Memories of a Native Son.*

FRAN BURTON PRESLEY wrote a series of deft sketches of her home region of east Texas for the *Texas Observer* in the 1960s.

BUCK RAMSEY wrote cowboy poetry that defines the modern genre. His work has been featured at the Smithsonian and the Gene Autry Western

Heritage Museum, and his recordings of traditional cowboy music have been honored by the National Endowment for the Arts and the National Cowboy Hall of Fame.

GEOFFREY RIPS, a former editor and publisher of the *Texas Observer* and a member of the Texas Democracy Foundation Board, is the author of the 1981 classic *The Campaign Against the Underground Press*.

A. R. "BABE" SCHWARTZ served for twenty-five years in the Texas legislature, where he was among a small clutch of progressive reformers. He is a lobbyist in Austin.

BOB SHERRILL, an early editor of the *Observer* and longtime investigative reporter, is author of *The Accidental President*, *Why They Call It Politics*, among other books.

THOMAS SUTHERLAND was an English professor at the University of Texas at Arlington. As executive secretary of the Texas Good Neighbor Commission, he helped to desegregate the Texas public schools on behalf of Mexican American children.

JAMES STANLEY WALKER is an architect and the recipient of the Texas Society of Architects Award for Excellence in Reporting on Architecture.

RALPH YARBOROUGH, the "People's Senator," served in the U.S. Senate from 1957 to 1970 and was the only southern senator to vote for the 1964 Civil Rights Act. He sponsored legislation on education and mental health, and his environmental initiatives led to the creation of Padre Island National Seashore, Guadalupe Mountains National Park, and Big Thicket National Preserve.